# ARTHUR RIMBAUD

RIMBAUD IN PARIS IN 1871
*a drawing by Cazals*

# ARTHUR RIMBAUD

by
ENID STARKIE

A NEW DIRECTIONS BOOK

First published as New Directions Paperbook NDP254 in 1968
Manufactured in the United States of America
New Directions Books are published for James Laughlin
by the New Directions Publishing Corporation,
333 Sixth Avenue, New York 10014.

SECOND PRINTING

*For*

MAURICE BOWRA

in admiration and friendship
to whom the study of Poetry
in England owes so much

# CONTENTS

# CONTENTS
## PART THREE

# ILLUSTRATIONS

# INTRODUCTION

ALL those who study Rimbaud soon reach a gulf of mystery which their imagination and intuition seem unable to bridge. There are three major problems to solve. Firstly—can a correct picture of the poet be painted from the incalculable contradictions and complexities with which the critic is faced, a picture which will make him recognizable as a human-being and not merely a collection of abstractions loosely strung together? Secondly— when was *Illuminations* composed? Before or after *Une Saison en Enfer* or partly before and partly afterwards? Each position has its passionate adherents, and the dating of this work is the most burning Rimbaud problem today. And thirdly—can a satisfactory explanation be given for his abandonment of literature at the height of his power, when he was twenty—or thereabouts? Formerly the most widely held opinion was that this had happened when he was nineteen, but, since then, it has been considered possible that he may have written for a couple of years more. However, some modern critics have returned to the first point of view.

Although Rimbaud ceased to write at an age when others are only beginning, he remains, nevertheless, one of the greatest French poets in the last years of the nineteenth century, and he occupies as well a significant place in French colonial history. He who, in the days of his belief in art, had dreamt of becoming a seer, an angel, the equal God, became, when he ceased to write, first a vagabond and ultimately—after toying with the idea of taking holy orders—a tough trader on the Somali coast and in Ethiopia, perhaps implicated in the slave traffic and certainly in the illicit gun trade. Although he was capable of the completest forms of asceticism, he could, at the same time, indulge in the fullest debauch.

It is difficult to reconcile all these contradictions and to fuse them into a coherent whole. The French citic, Jean Cassou, is of the opinion that to attempt such a work of fusion is profitless. Yet, if the different elements are given without any connecting link, something essential is lost. The real 'I' of a person is something more than a physical unity, a tying together of a collection of unrelated qualities. There must be some common factor to all these contradictions. There must be one thread which outlines the psychological patters. This vital thread is the interesting one to discover, but very difficult to find.

The mystery of Rimbaud's silence from his early twenties seems to defy interpretation. Some critics claim that he deliberately decided to write no more; that he consciously said farewell to literature when he wrote *Une Saison en Enfer*. Nevertheless, attractive though this explanation is—artistically—the facts do not seem to bear it out. Some, on the other hand, claim that when he became a man, he had nothing further to say; that poetry had been for him, what it is with many adolescents, merely the upheaval in his nature caused by puberty. This does not, however, explain his agony of mind in *Une Saison en Enfer*, where he reviews his past errors and decides that the kind of art which he has hitherto practised, is a sin and a delusion; it does not explain his suffering at his renunciation.

Nor is the sterility, which yet another critic has found and which he attributes to sexual impotence, a satisfactory solution. Rimbaud ceased to write at the height of his powers, and no flagging works have ever been found. Neither have any of the psychoanalytical studies been helpful. Analysts are more eager to file the case neatly, in a well-defined and well-known category, than to observe it disinterestedly. They have a 'ready-reckoner' for most problems, and their analyses of the works of writers seem more often ingenious and clever rather than true. The validity of the psychoanalytical approach to works of art is doubtful. It cannot reveal much that is illuminating for literature. The same things are said—indeed must be said—about inferior works as about works of genius. Psychoanalysis is unable to estimate quality since it has no point of contact with literary excellence.

Yet these logical and ingenious psychoanalyses of a writer's work are often tempting to produce and, with such a method—given a little imagination and subtlety—few poems would escape the accusation of being the outcome of a Freudian complex. The seemingly innocent nursery-rhyme, *Three Blind Mice*, for instance, could be proved, if a similar method were applied to it, to be a sorry example of sexual obsession. The most superficial examination makes it abundantly clear that it was written by an adolescent whose virginity has become irksome to him and who, by reason of his religious training—or some other inhibition—which has held chastity before him as an ideal, can find escape only in this covert manner. He identifies himself with the three mice, in a subconscious blasphemy against the Holy Trinity—three persons in one—in an attempt to humiliate a religion which has imposed on him this burdensome ideal of chastity. The mice are blind because instinct is blind and does not realize what it is following. He runs after the farmer's wife who symbolizes Woman in general; Eternal Woman bigger and stronger than he; Natural Woman, the nearest to Mother Earth, a farmer's wife. But he is timid and full of fears and consciousness of guilt; there is the castration obsession. She cuts off his tail with the carving knife—*penis* is the Latin for *tail*—since punishment inevitably follows sin—or so the religious teaching has it—and it is only just that the part through which he has sinned should be the part through which he suffers.

But the ideal and intelligent psycho-analytical study of Rimbaud might prove helpful and fruitful provided the analyst were a genuine and intelligent observer and researcher who did not start from preconceived notions and try to force the poet into a ready-made, factory-made mould. The analyst usually starts from the wrong end; he knows—or thinks he knows—certain facts of the poet's character and nature and then compels the writings to prove his contention, instead of using the writings to reveal the poet's inner personality. One critic has explained all the poems through his view that Rimbaud had a 'mother-fixation'; while another has interpreted everything through the light of homosexuality. Such rigid interpretations give a wrong emphasis to many of the poems. At one time poetry was for Rimbaud the means of discovering the unknown, and he thought that by breaking down the barriers of logical and intellectual control he would become a sensitive instrument to receive impressions from the beyond. But in removing deliberate control he wrote—without knowing it—of what was hidden from his conscious mind. He released experiences, and symbols to express them, from his subconscious mind of which he himself was ignorant, and these images were conditioned not only by his dreams and aspirations, but also by his inhibitions and his obsessions. The most constant of his obsessions, and the one which brought him most unhappiness, seems to have been his inhibition in front of women. All the poems which express the emotion of love—except those of his early youth—reflect distress and uncertainty. Although his relationship with Verlaine brought him, for a time, happiness and a sense of release, and coincided with his period of greatest creative activity, it left him, even in its early stages, with a sense of guilt and dissatisfaction. He remained to the end *une âme veuve*.

The central thesis of this study of Rimbaud is that, at the height of his greatest creative activity, he believed that like Faust, he had acquired supernatural powers through the agency of magic, that he imagined, like him, he had become the equal of God and eventually that his sin of pride and arrogance had been as great, as deserving of condemnation. Yet the study of Magic was not sinful in itself since, in the mind of the serious student, it did not consist in the work of a witch or sorcerer—the brewing of foul charms. Magic was the art of the Magi, it was the fount of all wisdom, the first of all the great arts. Magic was a science which came from the Magi, the wise men of the East, a science of nature by which man could eventually possess a certain relative omnipotence and could therefore act in a supernatural manner. But there were two kinds of magic—black and white; and two kinds of magicians—Joseph and Moses the good; Merlin and Julian the Apostate the bad. Rimbaud came eventually to the conclusion that he had been a Merlin and had practised sinful magic, that in so doing he had run the risk of damning himself and had brought himself to the borders of madness. At the time of his belief in his new art he thought that poetry was the greatest element of magic, that it was the means of penetrating into the unknown and of becoming identified with God. Later, when he came to believe that, like Lucifer, he had sinned through pride, he saw that poetry was not a means of discovery, that it had been for him, what it was for everyone else, a vehicle for self-expression and that his visions were not 'illuminations' but merely 'hallucinations'. *Une Saison en Enfer* sets forth the agony of this discovery, his *mea culpa*, and indicates what is to be his new view of the world and of the poet's function. He tried to find satisfaction in the material world of everyday reality, in the world of men. But, after visions of God and Eternity, the material world of cities and democracy proved disappointing. He came to believe that poetry was only one form of expression—and not the highest—of the evolution of mankind. He finally turned his thoughts to languages and science, and to the most abstract and objective form of expression —to mathematics. Eventually he cast even these aside, trying to find the full expression of everything in action. Had not his master Michelet said that the modern hero was to be the man of action?

There seems to lie Rimbaud's ultimate tragedy, the deliberate and mistaken turning away from his own mode of expression, poetry, for, as far as we can judge, the only moment of real happiness and satisfaction which he ever enjoyed in his life was during the period of his creative activity, when he believed in art and in himself. But he seems to have been more concerned with his poetry as an expression of his philosophical ideas than with it as an art. He was a religious nature looking for spiritual certainty and his philosophical theories engrossed him. Although he was a magnificent artist—and a study of the few manuscripts we have proves this—although he could calculate to a nicety his artistic effects, he considered poetry always as a means to an end, and the end was an intellectual and a spiritual one. There are many examples of poets who abandon poetry in search for similar philosophical conceptions, who squander their magnificent poetic gifts, or else sink into madness.

A poet's philosophy is not generally the concern of the literary critic. It is of small importance what philosophy a poet holds. Good philosophy does not make good poetry nor weak philosophy mar it. Yet Rimbaud's poetry cannot be understood at all unless his philosophy is understood, for it was his special brand of philosophy which inspired him to write his special kind of poetry, and which made him eventually abandon it when he believed that there were other and better ways of attaining his goal.

It is fashionable today to draw parallels between Rimbaud and authors whom he could not have known, to compare him with writers such as Dostoieffsky, Marx, Nietzsche, Kierkegaard and many others. This study does not attempt to draw such parallels, not because they are not an interesting and fruitful study in themselves, but because they do not get one any nearer to an understanding of Rimbaud himself. But this study does endeavour to show him moving against the background of his time, against the literary and social conventions of his own age, amongst those with whom he came into contact, to show their effect on him and his on them. It endeavours to discover what influences helped to form his personality and talents. The expression 'sources' is deliberately avoided since the discovery of a writer's alleged sources is a form of criticism much overdone today. It is however always psychologically interesting to notice what writers have attracted an author, and why he goes for inspiration to certain material rather than to another. I have always thought that if one could discover everything which Rimbaud read, much of what is obscure in his writings would become clear—at least intellectually if not artistically. The bulk of his work was written before he was nineteen and his experience was largely through books. It is not claimed that this will explain the magic of a poem, any more than it would explain a vision. Baudelaire used to say that the best criticism of a work of art would be another work of art. It is, moreover, impossible to set down the processes of pure art as a formula, but it is interesting to inspect the colours on the palette of a great painter, even if these cannot explain the masterpiece; interesting to examine the crucible of a poet's mind to see the rough ingredients which the flame of genius fuses into a rare metal—perhaps the *philosopher's stone*—produced by artistic alchemy. It is interesting to see what unexpected material becomes a great poem—a trivial vaudeville by Scribe; odd scraps from books of magic or alchemy; passages from fellow-poets. Ignorance of these ingredients does not diminish the pleasure in the poems —the greatness lies elsewhere—but knowledge of them teaches us something concerning the poet's mind. I have tried in each of Rimbaud's periods, to show what were his intellectual pre-occupations.

This is the third complete work that I have produced on Rimbaud—as well as two others dealing with his Abyssinian career—one in English and one in French. In the second version of the book I was able to correct certain errors in the first, due to insufficient and faulty material, and to throw further light on the little-known period of his life, between 1874 and 1879. But the most important difference between that and the earlier book was the belief that Rimbaud had absorbed large quantities of the lore of magic and alchemy, and that this had an influence not only on his philosophy and aesthetic doctrine, but also on his style and imagery. In this further book, I have not changed my opinion about this, but I feel that I was inclined earlier to exaggerate what he might owe to specific writers, such as Ballanche, in the formulation of his theories, and I now believe that he could have obtained similar material from any illuminist writer, and from the popular sources of occult philosophy.

The most important development between this and my previous book is that the major part of the manuscript of *Illuminations* is now accessible, and I have been able to consult it. A thorough study of that vital text is now at last possible, and I have completely revised what I earlier wrote about it. Although, in general, I have not altered my earlier view concerning its date, I have discussed the conflicting theories about this work, which have appeared since my last book was published. Some of the most interesting studies of Rimbaud's writings have appeared during the past twelve years.

There has also been produced, since my previous book went to press, a very good and reliable edition of all Rimbaud's writings, including his correspondence—the first of its kind—which appeared in 1946. All this has made possible a far more thorough study of the poet than hitherto.

There are new views and considerations interspersed through this book, but the original and unpublished documents are the same as those which served for the first and second versions—some indeed are now no longer unpublished: the seventy-eight volumes of diplomatic correspondence from the Foreign Office records—these are the basis of the account of the Abyssinian period; the unpublished documents from the Doucet Collection in the Bibliothèque Sainte-Geneviève in Paris—I was not permitted to copy the papers but only to take notes from them. They contain an interesting document from the pen of Delahaye—Rimbaud's closest school friend—entitled *Verlaine et Rimbaud*, some of which material, but not the whole of it, he used for his *Souvenirs Familiers*. There are, as well, letters from him to Verlaine and to Germaine Nouveau dealing with Rimbaud. These letters exist, unfortunately, only in fragments, as the text is on the reverse side of drawings which alone were intended to be preserved. Nevertheless, scrappy though they are, they help to a better understanding of Rimbaud in that mysterious period of his vagabondage from 1875 to 1879, when he was, in the words of Verlaine, 'l'homme aux semelles de vent'.

I was granted the inestimable privilege by my friend Henri Matarasso, bibliophile and passionate lover of Rimbaud, of consulting and using all the papers of the Rimbaud family which came into his possession in 1938. He acquired them from the widow of Paterne Berrichon, whose first wife was Rimbaud's youngest sister Isabelle. Paterne Berrichon, when he started on his biography of the brother-in-law whom he had never known, approached all those who, even remotely, had had any connection with him. When one examines these papers, one realizes how thoroughly he carried out his work, and how far afield he went in his investigations. In his own biography he was not able to use all that he had accumulated, for he did not know enough to see the relevance of the information; and also he used only what would help him to paint the picture which the family wished posterity to see; he used nothing which would tarnish that fair image. But he destroyed nothing, and the material is there for others to use: full letters from people long since dead, who had known Rimbaud in France, in Aden, on the Somali coast, and in Abyssinia. It is difficult to describe the emotion felt on opening the suit-case full of papers half a century old, the cheap suit-case which had accompanied Rimbaud on his adventurous journeys, on the Red Sea coast and into the uplands of Ethiopia. There are letters from Delahaye; from Bardey, his employer at Harar; letters to Rimbaud himself from his clients and partners in Abyssinia and on the Somali coast; the accounts of his commercial transactions. The bulk of these documents deal with the last ten years of his life. I found amongst them further and conclusive proof that he was, in some measure, implicated in the traffic of slaves. The report in the Foreign Office records, which I had previously discovered, merely stated that he had accompanied caravans conveying slaves to the coast—this was normal as these caravans were the only ones seriously guarded. I now found proof that he himself had tried to purchase slaves. The letter is from Ilg, King Menelek's Swiss engineer, refusing his assistance to obtain slaves in the interior. 'As for slaves' wrote Ilg on 20 August 1890, 'I can't undertake to obtain them for you. I've never bought slaves and I don't want to begin. Even for myself I wouldn't do it.' It is very likely, however, that Rimbaud found someone else less squeamish than Ilg to oblige him. Amongst the documents are also all the family papers. Isabelle's notes for Paterne Berrichon, when he was writing his biography of her brother, and it can be seen that all the alterations, omissions and embellishments were her responsibility and not his—although he has always been blamed for them. There are also Madame Rimbaud's letters to her daughter, and these bring one to a clearer understanding of that dour, almost inhuman woman, who was, nevertheless, capable of showing nobility and generosity; and on whom the critics have usually been so hard. Most pathetic of all is the private journal of Vitalie, Rimbaud's elder sister, who died at the age of seventeen, which tells of the journey which she and her mother made to London, early in the summer of 1874, to visit her brother who had fallen ill. From this journal can be seen that there was talent to spare in the family, and that it was not Arthur alone who cherished the ambition of becoming a writer. In a mild, romantic and girlish way, little Vitalie had a gift for writing—she was only fifteen when her journal opens— and obviously she saw herself already in the role of a budding author.

Most of these documents have now been published in the *Oeuvres Complètes* of Rimbaud in the *Bibliothèque de la Pléiade*, edited by Jules Mouquet and Rolland de Renéville. This is the edition always referred to throughout this book.

I would like to thank Monsieur Julien Cain, *Administrateur* of the Bibliothèque Nationale in Paris, for his kind help in obtaining for me access to various manuscripts; and Monsieur Pierre Bérès for allowing me to consult the manuscripts of *Illuminations* in his possession. I would also like particularly to thank my friend Henri Matarasso for his further kindness to me, in granting me permission to reproduce the portrait of Rimbaud in his possession, painted by the minor Belgian painter, Jef Rosman, as the poet lay in bed after being wounded by Verlaine in Brussels in July 1873. It was discovered by chance in 1947. Its chief interest lies in the fact that only one other authentic portrait of Rimbaud is known, *Le Coin de Table* by Fantin Latour, painted in January 1872. Jef Rosman was not a great artist, but his portrait gives a true likeness of Rimbaud at this tragic moment of his life. It has been described—and the circumstances of its discovery—in *Un Nouveau Portrait de Rimbaud* by H. Matarasso, in *Le Mercure de France*, on 1st September 1947.

ENID STARKIE

OXFORD
*September* 1960.

# PART I

## CHAPTER I

## THE PARENTS

O N the borders of Belgium, in the north of France, stretching along the banks of the Meuse, were once upon a time two twin towns called Charleville and Mézières, separated only by a small stretch of open country. With the passing of time, however, each town shot out its suburbs across the dividing no-man's-land and now they form one single entity, the modern city of Charleville-Mézières. But before the Franco-Prussian War they were two very distinct provincial towns each jealous of its own character and independence. Mézières was the older, an ancient citadel town, a prefecture, nestling in the shade of its tall grey walls that Bayard had defended. Proudly it raised aloft, above its roofs, the spire of its medieval church and openly expressed contempt for its younger sister and rival, Charleville, only a couple of centuries old and not ashamed of being a town of careful business people, whose chief preoccupations were material and prosaic. Yet Charleville has, in many ways, more charm for us to-day than Mézières. It was built in the days when town planning was the fashion and architects realized the beauty of large open spaces flanked by buildings nobly and harmoniously planned. The Place Ducale, in the centre of the town, built on the model of the Place des Vosges in Paris, is perfect of its kind. It was Duke Charles of Nevers, the founder of the city, who planned and paid for it, and it is a fitting tribute to his memory. His statue rises in the centre of the cobbled square, and round it crowd the carts on market day, and the caravans in the season of the yearly circus. This is the heart of the town and from it radiate the chief arteries. There is the Rue du Palais, called after the old ducal palace, which, in 1870, ended ingloriously in the Rue de Flandre, a sordid and slummy street. There is next the Rue de la République, leading through the Rue Thiers—formerly the Rue Napoléon, where

23

Rimbaud was born—to the Cours d'Orléans, now infelicitously renamed the Cours Aristide Briand, one of the best streets of the town, looking like a Paris boulevard with its flowering chestnut-trees. On the third side of the square is the Rue du Petit Bois, which used to end in a lovely wooded park unfortunately now turned into a vulgar sports stadium. On the fourth side La Rue du Moulin leads to an old mill on the banks of the Meuse, a tall building of similar style to the houses in the Place Ducale, and built at the same time, in 1606.

When a traveller comes to Charleville from the busy and noisy capital, he immediately feels the charm of the town and a sense of peace descends on him from the quiet, noble buildings, but this may be because he is not obliged to spend his days among them. Arthur Rimbaud was born in Charleville and did not come to it from outside. The past had no glamour for him, neither had historical buildings, and the peace of the Place Ducale merely irritated him. He felt stifled in the bourgeois atmosphere of the town, in its conservative and stupid content, and he was unable to appreciate the subtle charm of its faded pastel shades. It is a town for those who, having lived strenuously, feel that they have now earned peace; for those who want nothing more from life than a glass of beer in the quiet square in the evening, or a mild game of dominoes that will not over-tax brains that have grown sluggish, and who are satisfied to enjoy, as chief excitement, the military band on Sundays in the shady station square. It is a town for those whose lives have become so uneventful that they have nothing left to hide, since in Charleville everyone knows everyone else and the business of each is the business of all. Looking up at the houses as one passes through the streets, one notices that all the windows have their curtains pulled a trifle awry, and from behind these crooked curtains peep prying and inquisitive eyes.

Yet even for Arthur Rimbaud Charleville held some compensation, for it lies on the banks of the Meuse. The river flows from the east, skirting Mézières, and slips past Charleville, as if it had no wish to tarry, away to the north to the woods, the hills and the valleys which appear so often in Rimbaud's work and were the scenes of his many wanderings. It is gentle swelling plateau country, with soft billowing woods and here and there a twisted northern pine adds a rougher note. There, amongst the lush grass on the banks of the river, over which a light mist seems to hang day and night, Rimbaud, whenever he could escape his mother's vigilance, lay and dreamed, filling his mind with the images that were to become the substance of his later poems.

As the Meuse slips past Charleville it divides in two; the larger portion flows away past Mount Olympus, the other along by the Place du Saint-Sépulcre, now called Place de l'Agriculture. Here, in the backwater, the river is peaceful and scarcely seems to move. In Rimbaud's day tanners used to anchor a little raft in midstream, from which they used to hang their hides to soak in the river. A little boat was always moored to the quay by a heavy iron chain, to take the tanners backwards and forwards to their raft. In this little boat Arthur Rimbaud used to play as he waited for the morning school bell to ring, and dream that he was far away at sea.

The Place du Saint-Sépulcre is a big square open on one side, at the river's edge. In this square stand the Public Library and, in Rimbaud's day, the Collège de Charleville where he was educated. With the Place du Saint-Sépulcre Charleville ends, a low wall separates it from the river and on the other bank there were only hills and woods.

In this quiet little provincial town Arthur Rimbaud lived the first sixteen years of his restless, adventurous life. His father was not from the district, not even a northerner, he was a Bourguignon of Provençal extraction, who, in his own way, led as adventurous a life as his son. From a simple recruit he rose to the rank of captain and he spent the greater part of his army years in foreign service.[1] He was a man of middle height, fair-haired and blue-eyed like his son, with the same high intellectual forehead, the same slightly tip-tilted nose and the same faintly sensual mouth. When he was eighteen, in 1832, he enlisted and, as he was very intelligent and passably well educated, he was soon promoted. He became a sergeant-major and, after nine years of service, an officer. As a lieutenant he went to Algeria, and there, with the natural taste and facility for languages which his younger son inherited, he quickly mastered Arabic; this led him to high administrative posts in the Algerian political service, a rare occurrence for an officer who had risen from the ranks, especially in those days. He was eventually appointed to the important political service post at Sebdou.[2]

This was the heroic period of French occupation of Algeria, in the early days, when the armies led by Bugeaud, Cavaignac and Bedaud struggled strenuously against the Sultan of Morocco and against the various tribes that were always in revolt. Lieutenant Rimbaud was with the troops in Algeria at the moment of Bugeaud's victory at Isly in 1844, when the French army, a mere 10,000 men, conquered the Moroccan troops, 45,000 strong.[3] It was the following year that he was appointed to the political service, and in 1847 he was made 'chef du bureau arabe' at Sebdou, which post he held until he left Algeria in 1850.

During his first year of office the revolt of Sidi-Brahim occurred which Bugeaud felt obliged to repress with very severe measures. This naturally led to great hardships for the native population and made the task of those entrusted with the administration extremely difficult, but it is said that Lieutenant Rimbaud acquitted himself of his duties with exemplary wisdom and justice. Sebdou was an important post; it had direst influence on the policy of Moroco, for it was from there that the movements of the Emir could be watched. Lieutenant Rimbaud's chief duties consisted in sending, every fortnight, a report on the political situation, all the news of his district and all the rumours. He was, moreover, responsible for law and order in his district and for the collecting of taxes and dues. It was a post of extreme responsibility and confidence.

It has always been assumed that it was from his father that Arthur must have inherited the restlessness and instability of his temperament, yet the facts disclosed by Godchot bear a totally different interpretation. On the contrary, the father seems to have been a fine soldier, a trustworthy officer, and a conscientious and valuable administrator. His humanitarian treatment of the natives whom he governed, which is clearly revealed in his reports, seems to have been far in advance of his time.[4] As 'chef du bureau arabe' he showed, as Godchot proves, an aptitude for administra-

tion rarely found in officers who have risen from the ranks and
who have enjoyed no educational advantages. His career is one
of which any son might feel proud. He was decorated with the
Crimean medal and the military medal of Sardinia, and in 1854
he was made a 'Chevalier de la Légion d'Honneur.' He moreover left the plan of several literary works.[5] *Correspondance
Militaire*, *Eloquence Militaire*, and *Livre de Guerre*. In the *Eloquence
Militaire* it appears that he drew an interesting comparison between classical orators and those of modern times, while the *Livre
de Guerre* was to deal with his campaigns in Algeria, in Crimea and
in Italy. He also translated the Koran into French and it was with
the aid of this that his son later studied Arabic.

The new republican government of 1848 brought about a
change in the administration of Algeria; the Chasseurs d'Orléans,
Lieutenant Rimbaud's regiment, was recalled, and he left Algeria
in 1850. Two years later he was promoted to the rank of captain
and he was sent with his new regiment to Mézières.

It was in Charleville, one Sunday afternoon, while strolling in
the square and listening to the band, that he casually made the
acquaintance of Marie Catherine Félicité Vitalie Cuif.

We do not know why his choice fell on her, for she was neither
young nor beautiful; it was she, perhaps, who decided that he
was to be her husband, for at no moment of her life had Vitalie
Cuif lacked courage or determination. He was sentimental and
lonely, and perhaps it was her large dowry that finally clinched the
matter. She is said to have brought him £1,200 in ready money
and to have had expectations of another £1,800. The Cuif family
were a solidly established Ardennais family of good yeoman stock.
The father, Jean-Nicolas Cuif, owned a farm at Roche which
he had hitherto worked with the help of a son and his daughter,
but there was another son as well.

Before the publication of Godchot's investigations into the
family history, nothing whatsoever had been known of the two
Cuif brothers since Madame Rimbaud, profoundly ashamed of
their manner of living, had always kept their existence dark. Now
Godchot's investigations suggest that it was from his mother's
family and not from his father, that Arthur Rimbaud inherited

the instability of his character and his bohemian ways. The elder of his uncles, Jean-Charles-Felix Cuif, was a wild fellow nicknamed the African on account of his adventures in Algeria. He disappeared when he was only seventeen, to escape arrest for theft, reappearing later, a couple of years after his sister's marriage to Captain Rimbaud; but he came back a sick man and died the following year at the age of thirty. It is, however, the other brother whose career is more significant. Charles-Auguste Cuif was five years younger than his sister and during his brother's absence had lived at home with his father and sister helping them to work the farm. It is alleged that it was to escape from Vitalie's severe discipline that he married at the early age of twenty-two. His action was, however, unnecessarily precipitate, for before the year was out she herself married and left home. To enable her to marry an officer her father gave her a large dowry, and to compensate his son for the future loss of heritage, ceded to him the farm at Roche, intending henceforth to live with his daughter at Charleville. It was then unknown whether the elder brother was still alive. Charles Cuif then moved with his wife into the farm, but he was a lazy spendthrift who was already a confirmed drunkard, and he soon went through the money that had been intended to run the farm. Next he began to ill-treat his wife so that she left him and returned to her own people. Now, with nothing further to restrain him, Charles completely neglected the farm, allowing it to go to rack and ruin, so that it was bankrupt when Jean-Felix turned up from Algeria. Jean-Felix insisted on being given his part of the paternal wealth, and since Charles was willing to sell out his share for a sum of ready money, the elder brother was now given possession of the entire farm, but he only enjoyed it for one short year. When he died Vitalie seized hold of it and refused to pay her young brother his fair share of his brother's inheritance, but Charles was by now too much befuddled by drink to realize exactly was what happening. When his ready money was spent he became an out-and-out tramp, a disgrace to the countryside. His sister now pretended that he was no relative of hers, and whenever he came to the farm she would ask him for his papers, and often had him hunted away from her door like a beggar.

Sometimes she would give him small sums of money to persuade him to keep away from the district. Nevertheless, in spite of the hard life he led, Charles seems to have prospered in health, for he outlived all his nephews and nieces and died at the ripe age of ninety-four. Right to the end he kept his violence and did not even then compromise. On his deathbed, in a home run by a religious order, he refused the ministrations of a priest and the last sacraments, but asked instead for a litre of red wine. The nuns, who were genuinely fond of him in spite of his blasphemous opinions, granted his request. With his ebbing strength he seized the bottle and drained it to the last dregs, then lay back on his pillows and quietly died.

When the family history is known it is easier to sympathize with Madame Rimbaud's severity towards her children. She hoped, by careful training and ceaseless watchfulness, to prevent her sons from following the same evil paths as her own brothers. Rimbaud's school friend Delahaye once said to Godchot: 'I must admit that even if Arthur had had a mother as gentle as the Virgin Mary, he would nevertheless have gone off on adventures, for he was a born gipsy.'[6]

Vitalie Rimbaud was a hard and severe woman, though she was capable of nobility and grandeur, and, at times, even of sympathy. She believed that strictness of training was essential to the young, especially to boys, and that it was criminal to spare the rod. She was a tall, thin woman with the large knotted hands of a peasant, and she was proud and energetic in her bearing. Her hair was of a dark chestnut colour, always smoothly brushed to her head with no artificial waves or curls to soften its hard line round her brows, and her eyes had the same level honest gaze as those of her son, Arthur. Her nose was straight and somewhat pointed, her mouth was a thin, hard line and her voice had a biting, rasping quality. In religion she was bigoted, in morality prudish, and she was obstinate almost to the pitch of insanity. She would admit of no reply or contradiction or appeal, and she moved inflexibly on towards the accomplishment of what she considered her duty. She was fond of her children, though she would not have thought it right to allow them to know this, and she was proud of them as well, especially of her younger son, the prodigy of the town, of whom she expected so much. She would not have been human had she calmly accepted to see him throw away all hope of a brilliant future to become a hooligan, a vagabond and a tramp like her own good-for-nothing brother Charles. Yet beneath her hard exterior she hid a warm and passionate heart which eventually burned itself out since she would allow none of its warmth to escape. Arthur Rimbaud, with his morbid integrity of mind, his obstinacy, his unwillingness to make any concessions, his horror of revealing his gentler feelings, was more like his mother than he would have cared to admit.

Captain Rimbaud married Vitalie Cuif in February 1853 and the following November Jean-Nicolas-Frederick was born and Jean-Nicolas-Arthur the next year on 20 October 1854. It was impossible for the mother, with two young children, to follow her husband from garrison town to garrison town and she therefore remained with her father in Charleville. After the two sons three daughters were born; the eldest died in infancy, the other two were Vitalie and Isabelle.

Arthur was born in the busy thoroughfare that runs into the Place Ducale, a street of rich shops, crowded on market day with the overflow of carts from the square. The only account we have of his birth is the grandiloquent description by Paterne Berrichon, in terms similar to those used by Rabelais to describe the birth of Gargantua. From this account it would seem that Arthur was a prodigy from the very instant he issued from his mother's womb. After the nurse had washed him, she laid him down on a cushion while she left the room to fetch the swaddling clothes. When she returned, however, she found, to her amazement, that the infant no longer lay where she had deposited him, that he had rolled on to the floor and was crawling to the door, to begin already his life of wandering.[7]

It is very probable that it is Rimbaud himself who was the source of this legend and that it is from his friends that Paterne Berrichon obtained the information, In his 'magician' phase Rimbaud identified himself with Merlin and there is, in Quinet's

*Merlin l'Enchanteur*, a fantastic account of the birth of the magician. The day after his birth his mother, who was holding him, was weeping bitterly—her child had been fathered by Satan himself—when the baby spoke to her and begged her not to cry any more. Amazed and terrified she dropped the infant on the floor. He got up unhurt and, stepping out of his swaddling clothes, walked up and down before her reading from an open book words of comfort and encouragement.[8]

Life did not run smoothly in the Rimbaud family. The Captain was good-tempered, easygoing and generous; all he asked was a cheerful atmosphere round him and happy faces, but he soon found it difficult to keep his gaiety at close quarters with his wife. In everything she was the exact opposite to him. She was stingy in money affairs where he was lavish, bigoted in her religious views where he was free-thinking, rigid in her morality whereas he was somewhat lax, and, moreover, she was completely lacking in a sense of humour. It is said that she treated him with the same severity which she meeted out to her children, that she tried to eradicate what she considered failings in him and to counteract his levity.

The wrangling between husband and wife grew in intensity and bitterness with the passing years and there is no doubt that the memory of the discord between his parents left a lasting mark on Arthur's sensitive nature. He used to tell his closest friend Delahaye that his earliest recollection was of a quarrel between his father and his mother, in which each in turn had seized a silver bowl, one of their few treasures, and had flung it on the floor with an echoing noise that had resounded all through the flat and had terrified the children.[9]

Old Cuif died in 1858, after the birth of the fourth child, when Arthur was four. He had, in a certain measure, managed to keep the peace between his daughter and her husband, but now that he was gone their married life became unendurable. After the birth of Isabelle, when Arthur was six, they separated and never met again. Little is known of Captain Rimbaud's later life. He retired from the army in 1864 and lived quietly in Dijon until he died in 1878, fortified by the rites of the Roman Catholic Church.

He played no further part in his children's life, he had no share in their training or upbringing, and he never saw them again.

Thus, from the age of six, Arthur was handed over entirely to his mother's charge and care, to a woman made anxious by financial worries and bitter by her husband's abandonment. With their grandfather now dead the children experienced little warmth and love and there was no one to whom the boys could go for advice and sympathy. This early loneliness and lack of affection warped Arthur's personality, making him feel different from other boys, solitary and set aside.

It was not an easy matter for the mother to bring up four children on a small income, with no one to help her and advise her, but she consecrated herself to the task with all the jealous and passionate devotion of which she was capable, hoping to make of her children her own work of art. And so, that they should come under no other influence than hers in what the Jesuits consider the most vital years of a human being's life, they had no other teacher than herself until they were seven years old. Yet her exaggerated severity did not eradicate the grievous faults which she saw, with terror, spring up; it merely drove them underground to appear elsewhere with renewed vigour.

CHAPTER II

## THE EARLY YEARS

AFTER Captain Rimbaud left his wife she moved from the Rue Napoléon to an old street leading off it, called the Rue Bourbon. With her income reduced she was now obliged to tighten the purse-strings, and the Rue Bourbon had not the distinction of the Rue Napoléon with its rich shops; it was somewhat sordid and slummy, inhabited only by the poorest working people. There was in the life of the street a warm and homely familiarity that was distasteful to the morbidly reserved and dignified Madame Rimbaud. Mothers talked to one another from their doorsteps,

RIMBAUD AT THE TIME OF HIS FIRST
COMMUNION
*Photograph lent by Mr. H. Matarasso*

DELAHAYE

IZAMBARD

shouted to one another from their windows across the street, and, when they were in need of anything, came to borrow it from their neighbours without any false shame. At all times in her life Vitalie Rimbaud had kept the doors of her home barred against all but a very few—indeed she was never known to associate on intimate terms with anyone—and now she lived, for over two years in the Rue Bourbon, treading her way, in splendid and proud isolation, through the mire of the street, never sinking into it and scarcely soiling her feet. But to her children, to Arthur in particular, the life around them was a constant source of interest and delight, offering more possibilities of adventure than the life in their previous respectable quarters. Secretly, when his mother's back was turned, he used to slink off to fraternize with the children of the poor whose life he envied since it seemed to him more full of colour and excitement than his own.

> Pitié! Ces enfants seuls étaient ses familiers
> Qui, chétifs, fronts nus, œil déteignant sur la joue,
> Cachant de maigres doigts jaunes et noirs de boue
> Sous des habits puant la foire et tout vieillots,
> Conversaient avec la douceur des idiots!
> Et si, l'ayant surpris à des pitiés immondes,
> Sa mère s'effrayait; les tendresses profondes
> De l'enfant se jetaient sur cet étonnement.
> C'était bon. Elle avait le bleu regard,—qui ment![1]

But Madame Rimbaud discovered the illicit adventures of her sons and she began to be anxious lest her children should become like the children of the poor, adopt their rough manners and their coarse way of speaking. She had other ambitions for her sons and they must not be allowed to turn into mere working men. She thought that she would not be fulfilling her duties as a mother if she permitted the present state of affairs to continue and she determined to move at whatever sacrifice. Perhaps she had managed to put money by during the exile in the Rue Bourbon, perhaps the farm at Roche was bringing in more. In 1862, when Arthur was nearly eight, they left the slummy street and moved to one of the best quarters of the town, the Cours d'Orléans, with its elegant little *hôtels*, a wide boulevard lovely in the spring with its flowering chestnut-trees, lovelier still in the autumn when they had turned a deep gold, and fresh even in the middle of summer.

Hitherto the boys had had no other teacher but their mother, but now they were to start school, for they were almost nine and eight respectively, and they must begin to learn Latin and Greek which their mother did not know. They were sent to the little Pension Rossat and the first literary work of Arthur's which has come down to us was produced in his early days at school. It is a composition worthy of quotation since it reveals an amazing power of description and observation, an unusual facility in the use of language, for a child of about nine. This is the opening paragraph of an essay of many pages whose length alone—about 700 words—is an achievement for so young a boy.

Le soleil était encore chaud; cependant il n'éclairait presque plus la terre; comme un flambeau placé devant les [illegible] ne les éclaire plus que par une faible lueur, ainsi le soleil, flambeau terrestre, s'éteignait en laissant échapper de son corps de feu une dernière et faible lueur, cependaut laissant encore voir les feuilles vertes des arbres, les petites fleurs qui se flétrissaient, et le sommet gigantesque des pins, des peupliers et des chênes séculaires. Le vent refraîchissant, c'est-à-dire une brise fraîche, agitait les feuilles des arbres avec un bruissement à peu près semblable à celui que faisait les eaux argentées du ruisseau qui coulait à mes pieds. Les fougères courbaient leur front vert devant le vent. Je m'endormis, non sans m'être abreuvé de l'eau du ruisseau. Je rêvai que j'étais né à Reims, l'an 1503, etc. [2]

To say that this passage shows the influence of French romantic prose does not make it any the less remarkable when the age of the writer is taken into consideration.

Madame Rimbaud was anxious that her boys should not waste the education so expensively provided for them; they were to become learned men and rise in the social scale. She herself supervised their homework, continuing to train them with the same austere severity and the same lack of warmth and affection. Sometimes she would send them both supperless to bed because they had been unable to recite, without a slip, the hundreds of lines of Latin verses she had set them to learn from memory, as a punishment for some trivial offence—and also to improve their facility in the language. At this time Arthur disliked school work and moreover resented his mother's slaps and ear-tweaking as an affront to his human dignity. In the essay previously quoted he gave his views on the study of languages; these show clearly the precocious intellectual forcing to which he was subjected at so early an age and which may, partly, explain his later hatred of all learning.

J'aimais peu l'étude, c'est-à-dire d'apprendre à lire et compter; mais si c'était pour arranger une maison, cultiver un jardin, faire des commissions, à la bonne heure!—Je me plaisais à cela. Pourquoi—me disais-je—apprendre du grec, du latin? Je ne le sais! Enfin on n'a pas besoin de cela. Que m'importe à moi que je sois reçu? A quoi cela sert-il d'être reçu? A rien, n'est-ce pas? Si pourtant; on dit qu'on n'a une place que lorsqu'on est reçu. Moi je ne veux pas de place; je serai rentier. Quand même on en voudrait une, pourquoi apprendre le latin? Personne ne parle cette langue. Quelquefois j'en vois, du latin, sur les journaux; mais, dieu merci, je ne serai pas journaliste. Pourquoi apprendre de l'histoire et de la géographie? On a, il est vrai, besoin de savoir que Paris est en France; mais on ne demande pas à quel degré de latitude. De l'histoire, apprendre la vie de Chinaldon, de Nabopolassar, de Darius, de Cyrus, et d'Alexandre et de leurs autres compères remarquables par leurs noms diaboliques est un supplice. Que m'importe à moi qu'Alexandre ait été célèbre? Que m'importe? Que sait-on si les latins ont existé? C'est, peut-être, leur latin, quelque langue forgée; et quand même ils auraient existé, qu'ils me laissent rentier et conservent leur langue pour eux. Quel mal leur ai-je fait, pour qu'ils me flanquent au supplice? Passons au grec. Cette sale langue n'est parlée par personne au monde! Ah! saperlipotte de saperlipopette! sapristi! moi je serai rentier. Il ne fait pas bon de s'user les culottes sur les bancs, saperlipopettouille! Pour être décrotteur, gagner la place de décrotteur, il faut passer un examen; les places qui vous sont accordées sont d'être ou décrotteur, ou porcher ou bouvier. Dieu merci, je n'en veux pas, moi, saperlipouille. Avec ça des soufflets vous sont accordés pour récompense. On vous appelle animal ce qui n'est pas vrai. Ah! Saperpouillotte. (La suite prochainement.) ARTHUR. [3]

But hardest of all for a boy of Arthur's temperament was the constant supervision to which the children were subjected; they were never allowed to leave their mother's sight for fear they might fall into some unexpected evil ways. Until the boys were sixteen and fifteen respectively, she used to wait for them every day at the school gate to walk home with them, for only in this manner could she be sure that they did not loiter on the road with undesirable acquaintances.[4] When Arthur wished for peace and solitude for reflection he was obliged to lock himself in the lavatory, and he spent there many hours.

L'été
Surtout, vaincu, stupide, il était entêté
A se renfermer dans la fraîcheur des latrines:
Il pensait là, tranquille et livrant ses narines.[5]

Of all the dreary days in the dreary week, Sunday was the dreariest of all and Arthur longed to be like the neglected children of the poor whom he had once seen in the Rue Bourbon, to escape this boredom and ennui.

Il craignait les blafards dimanches de décembre,
Où, pommadé, sur un guéridon d'acajou,
Il lisait une Bible à la tranche vert-chou . . .
Il n'aimait pas Dieu, mais les hommes, qu'au soir fauve,
Noirs, en blouse, il voyait rentrer dans le faubourg.[6]

Delahaye describes wittily the sight of the Rimbaud family setting off each Sunday morning for High Mass, and the people standing on the pavement to watch this strange procession pass.[7] First came the two little girls, hand in hand, with their clean white cotton gloves and their black buttoned boots; next came the two boys, in their black jackets and home-made slate-blue trousers, with their round white collars and their funny little black bowler hats, each carrying, clasped in his hand, a bright blue cotton umbrella. Finally, the procession ended with Madame Rimbaud, walking alone, in her stately dignity, as rigid as a sergeant-major, dressed in unrelieved black from top to toe.

It seems that the mother had bought cheaply at a sale an immense roll of the slate-blue material and that the boys, all the years they were at school, never appeared in any other trousers but those cut by their mother, with her own hands, out of the never-ending length of light blue serge.

Since the children remained obedient and outwardly well-behaved the mother thought that all was well, and closing the book, she would turn away with an easy heart. She did not, however, realize what revolt lay smouldering in the little boy who looked up at her out of such innocent blue eyes.

> Et la Mère, fermant le livre du devoir,
> S'en allait satisfaite et très fière, sans voir,
> Dans les yeux bleus et sous le front plein d'éminences,
> L'âme de son enfant livrée aux répugnances. [8]

Arthur's greatest pleasure, as a child, seems to have been reading; like any ordinary little boy his favourite books were fairy tales and stories of adventure, the novels of Fenimore Cooper and Gustave Aimard. [9] It was in his reading that he lived most intensely, a fantastic life of his own, in which the events and happenings round him became transfigured and transformed, became fused with the scenes which had no reality except in his imagination. Later the memories of his childhood came back to him, not in clear and ordinary recollections, but as memories of a strange and bewildering world and he could never say then whether what he remembered had in fact happened or whether it was merely a figment of his imagination. This makes any study of the poems built on the memories of childhood so complex, and the interpretation of them so difficult.

Although Rimbaud had never seen the sea, it was chiefly of the sea that he dreamed as a child and it symbolized for him everything that was most beautiful and free. He used to lie in his room on lengths of linen cloth which his mother had bought for household purposes, pretending that they were sails and that he was far away on the ocean.

> Il lisait son roman sans cesse médité,
> Plein de lourds ciels ocreux et de forêts noyées,
> De fleurs de chair aux bois sidérals déployées,
> Vertige, écroulements, déroutes et pitié!
> —Tandis que se faisait la rumeur du quartier,
> En bas,—seul, et couché sur des pièces de toile
> Écrue, et pressentant violemment la voile. [10]

The place of all others where he loved most to be was in the tanners' little boat which was moored to the quay near school. He used to insist on his brother's leaving the house early in the morning with him, so that they could have time to sit in the boat and wait for the school bell to ring. Sometimes Arthur would stand up in the boat and sway it from side to side, as if it were being buffeted by a violent storm and he would then cry to his brother to look at the immense waves beating against the stern of the vessel. Sometimes, on the contrary, he would merely lie prone, not allowing Frederick to make the slightest movement, lest he ruffle the peaceful waters, and then he would gaze down into the depths, seeing in the weeds beneath him tropical vegetation and strange ocean monsters. But inevitably the school bell rang and he was obliged, reluctantly, to tear himself away from his dreaming.

When Frederick was twelve and Arthur a year younger the boys were sent to the Collège de Charleville and they were both placed in the same form, but the younger boy soon outstripped his elder brother. This was the year of his First Communion and he was, at the time, deeply religious. All the affection and warmth of his heart that found no outlet at home he lavished on Jesus Christ who, by dying to save him, had shown him more love than he had ever received from his mother. Arthur then devoted to his religious practices all the passionate fervour he was later to devote to any interest that seized his fancy, but the passion burned itself out as quickly. At the time of his First Communion he was possessed by a burning faith, a passionate piety, that made him eager and ready to become a martyr. One day he attacked a group of boys bigger than himself whom he had seen playing with the holy water in the font outside the church, and splashing one another with it; but they set on him all at once and trounced him soundly, calling him 'sale cagot', a dirty hypocrite.

It was that same year, when he was twelve, that the school authorities began to notice him as a pupil of promise. He astonished his form master, one day, by producing a résumé of ancient history, an account of Egypt, Syria and Babylon which was said to show a power of exposition and a maturity of mind remarkable in so young a child. The master showed it proudly to the Principal of the college, saying: 'Mark my words, this is the beginning of an infant prodigy in the scholastic world!'[11] Now Arthur Rimbaud, the professional prize-winner of the school, was beginning to appear, and some of his unspent passion and ardour went to the acquiring of knowledge so that this passion soon possessed him to the exclusion of almost everything else.[12]

As soon as he reached the third class his mother began to plan a brilliant scholastic future for him. She had by now abandoned all hope of making anything of Frederick in the intellectual field, for he was lazy and slow and no amount of threats or punishments could induce him to learn anything. He accepted everything with tearful or stoic resignation, using his share of the family obstinacy and intelligence in obstruction, until he finally achieved his aim, to be left in peace to wallow in his ignorance, and to allow his younger brother to outstrip him. Now Madame Rimbaud overcame her innate dislike of spending money and engaged the services of Arthur's form master, M. Lhéritier, for private lessons for her younger son so that he could leave all the other boys far behind him.

This M. Lhéritier, a dark little man with a deep resonant voice, was quick-tempered and ready to boil over at the slightest provocation; he was, however, very kind and was passionately devoted to literature, provided it was strictly in accordance with the rules of Boileau.[13] His quick temper and his faculty of passing swiftly from a state of great indignation to one of extreme gaiety made him popular with the boys; popular also were his innocent little jokes and his childish tricks to amuse his class; only with Arthur did these fall flat. Arthur disconcerted him and he did not know how to take him; he could see that although the boy always smiled politely at his efforts to enliven the class, he was not really amused. He never succeeded in gaining his confidence and, moreover, he mistrusted his timid reserve which was in fact the result of shyness. His influence was, nevertheless, beneficial to Rimbaud, for he inculcated in him a love of Greek and Latin and of the best French classical literature. He was the first person to encourage the boy to write original verse in both French and Latin. With the help of Lhéritier's private lessons Arthur finished the school year with brilliant success.[14]

Then the family made the final move of Rimbaud's childhood; this time they settled on the Quai de la Madeleine, now Quai du Moulinet, on the Meuse, not far from the Place du Saint-Sépulcre. The flat looked out on the beautiful seventeenth-century mill, and Arthur, from his window, could now gaze on the ever-changing face of the river and the woods on the opposite bank.

He had by now entered on his teens and was becoming someone of importance at school. It does not seem, judging from the accounts of whose who knew him as a boy, that he was unhappy or unpopular amongst his school-fellows, at all events during his last three years, for we know of several close friends of his and of two inseparable and devoted companions, Delahaye and Labarrière.[15] It is true that in their early days at school the Rimbaud brothers had not been popular; they were considered to look more peculiar than boys should ever look, in their absurd clothes which they were, moreover, always terrified of tearing or soiling. They were considered soft because they were always neat and tidy and because their mother would never allow them to join in any out-of-school intimacy or games. For a long time they were considered prim and stand-offish.[16] Then Labarrière began to talk with Arthur and to make friends with him, telling the other boys that he was very different from what he had seemed at first, that, in fact, he was very interesting. Labarrière's opinion carried great weight in the school and once he had passed the Rimbaud brothers they were accepted without question by all the other boys as well.[17]

Very soon Delahaye, Labarrière and Arthur Rimbaud became the closest friends; they did everything together and called themselves the Three Musketeers. They encouraged one another to deeds of daring, lent each other books and helped each other with their school preparation. Labarrière had, however, at the time, a far higher opinion of the intelligence of Delahaye than of that of Rimbaud whom he considered primarily a hard-working 'swot', and his ultimate fame as a writer came to him as a great surprise.[18]

There is no evidence that Arthur Rimbaud was, while at school, in any way undisciplined or troublesome. He was, outwardly, at least, the good boy and the model pupil. 'Il suait d'obéissance' he was later to say of himself.[19] He was an extremely hard-working little boy who puzzled his masters by his exemplary conduct and frightened his school-fellows by his unfailing omniscience. Yet the boys did not dislike him and they relied on him for help, knowing his kindness and friendliness would never fail them. It is said that while the master was writing on the board, his back turned to the class, Rimbaud would, in a few moments, produce a set of Latin verses for each boy in the form. The title was the same, the one set for the exercise, but the verses, in each case, would be different, so that the master should not guess that they were all from the same hand. Arthur obviously enjoyed being the best boy in the school and being pointed out to others as a prodigy of learning. In this school glory he found compensation for the humiliations he was obliged to endure at home, for the cuffs and slaps that were meted out to him, for the ignominious punishment of being sent supperless to bed. Many of the teachers thought him conceited, or imagined that he could not fail to be so, and they tried to discover flaws and blemishes in his work which they could censure, but in vain. His lessons were always well learnt and his exercises without mistakes, and they were obliged, unwillingly, to allow him to outstrip the boys of his own age.[20] The Principal of the college once spoke warmly of him to one of the masters who only answered in a surly voice, 'Yes! he's intelligent all right, but he'll end badly.' Another day the same teacher said: 'There is something about his eyes and his smile that I don't quite like. I tell you he'll end badly.' He never knew whether Arthur was making fun of him or not, and he had the uncomfortable feeling that the boy must be up to some mischief, but he could never catch him at any misdemeanour. He felt that he was being continually observed by those clear blue eyes fixed on him in so critical a gaze from the front row of the form. There was nothing, however, that any master could do, for he was the most brilliant pupil in the school.[21]

Even at this early age Rimbaud was not slow in putting himself forward and in bringing himself to the notice of those in high places. Without telling anyone and without asking anyone's advice, when he was only thirteen, he sent a poem of sixty Latin hexameters to the Prince Imperial on 8 May 1868, to congratulate him on the occasion of his First Communion. The Prince's tutor wrote to the Principal of the school, in the name of his royal pupil, and asked that the author of the verses should be publicly thanked for his kind attention.

At this time also Rimbaud was beginning to take an interest in modern literature and to cherish the ambition of becoming himself a poet since, under Lhéritier's encouragement, he had begun to write original verse.

Here once again he acted consistently in accordance with his character at this time, as a model pupil would, for it was the poetry upheld by authority that he admired, the staid and well-established Parnassian school. It was on the model of these conservative masters of poetry that he himself tried his hand at verse and indeed succeeded in publishing a poem in *La Revue pour Tous* in January 1870 when he was only fifteen. The poem, *Les Étrennes des Orphelins*, is a remarkable production for a boy of that age, even though it may not possess any permanent value. It is a poem that François Coppée might have written, and it may well have been inspired by his *Reliquaire* published in 1866. It also bears resemblance to *Les Pauvres Gens* of Victor Hugo reprinted in *La Revue pour Tous* on 5 September 1869; and to *La Maison de ma Mère* by Marceline Desbordes-Valmore, published in the 6 November issue of the same year. Madame Rimbaud subscribed to the periodical and Arthur must have known the poems.

Rimbaud's chief intellectual characteristics at this age, were a remarkably good memory, an amazing power of clever imitation, and a great facility for expressing himself. These qualities are first seen in his Latin verses which reveal, if nothing else, a range of reading and a faculty for assimilation of vocabulary and turns of phrase uncommon in a schoolboy.[23] Indeed, one of these poems, written just after his fourteenth birthday, and thus a year before *Les Étrennes des Orphelins*, is very striking and prophetic. It is an amplification, not a translation, of five lines from *Ode IV, Book III* of Horace. In three hours, under examination conditions, he wrote fifty-nine Latin hexameters. It opens with a description of the spring countryside which anticipates the young poet's French nature poetry. In this he declares that, in the midst of the beauty around him, he is able to forget the boredom of school and the dreary lessons of his teachers. Eventually he lies, half asleep on the banks of a river, and a flight of doves descends from the heavens towards him, bearing garlands of bay leaves. The birds fly around his head and crown him. Then they bear him aloft to their mountain fastness and lay him down. They fly away only to return this time with a laurel wreath which they bind around his head. Then the heavens open and he sees Apollo flying above clouds of gold who, with a celestial flame, inscribes on his brow, 'Tu Vates eris' —the Latin 'Vates' means both seer and poet. His limbs are suddenly suffused with warmth. The doves then change their shape and appear as Muses who lift him in their arms, thrice uttering the prophecy, 'Thou shalt be a seer and a poet!' and thrice crowning him with laurel.

Up to now Rimbaud had shown himself to be nothing more than a good pupil; he had not thought independently for himself and it had not occurred to him to question the intellectual and spiritual food that was set before him. He seems to have desired nothing more than to do what he was told and to win praise and approbation from those who taught him. His whole horizon was bounded by school, since in school alone was he truly happy. At home, on the contrary, nothing ever won him praise, neither good reports, nor prizes; nothing ever brought softness to his mother's eyes; no success seemed to give her pleasure, or at least no pleasure that she showed to her children.

We do not know what fire of rebellion smouldered within Arthur Rimbaud, nor what went on behind his placid blue eyes with their rare and occasional blaze. Certainly, as long as he was at school, there was no visible and outward sign of revolt, and this explains his mother's surprise and bewilderment when, a year later, he broke loose; she could not then understand how it came about that he, who had, hitherto, been so good, so obedient, so sensible, should behave in so undisciplined and so wild a manner. Now she congratulated herself on having so brilliant a son, a son who was so '*raisonnable*' and who offered so few problems.

In 1870 the great event of Rimbaud's early youth occurred, the coming of George Izambard as a master to the Collège de Charleville. His was the first important influence in his life.

<br>

CHAPTER III

## LES LAURIERS SONT COUPÉS

IZAMBARD was a young man not many years older than his pupils, since he was only twenty-one when he came to the Collège de Charleville in January 1870. His interest in literature was not solely theoretic and scholastic for he was himself a poet of some promise and he did not intend to remain permanently in the teaching profession. He was thus calculated to understand Rimbaud who needed literary encouragement and sympathy. The other masters encouraged his aptitude for learning, Lhéritier alone had thought of cultivating his imagination and his talent for writing, but he had not understood or liked the boy. For the rest of the teaching staff he was only the valuable race-horse who must be carefully trained for the July Examination Stakes and they made use of his brains but were somewhat afraid of them.

George Izambard himself had spent a lonely and solitary youth, though he had always been treated with affection and kindness. But he had been entirely brought up, away from other children, by three elderly maiden ladies, the Gindre sisters, distant connections of his parents. His father was a commercial traveller who had lost his wife during a severe cholera epidemic shortly after the birth of George. One of the Gindre ladies had been staying with the mother at the time of her death, and she took the four motherless children home to her sisters, to remove them, for a time, from the house of death. The three elder children eventually returned to their father, when he was able, once more, to make a home for them, but the baby was considered too small to be moved, and he remained for the time being with the Gindre ladies. His father, however, seems permanently to have omitted to fetch him, and he was eventually adopted by the three sisters whom he came to consider as his only relations. They lived in the town of Douai, in the north of France, and there he spent his childhood and school days. He passed his *baccalauréat* at the age of fifteen and after continuing his studies at the University of Paris, obtained his *licence* when he was eighteen. He then began his career as a teacher and was finally nominated as form-master to the highest class at the Collège de Charleville when he was only twenty-one. He had started his studies in Paris when he was little older than Arthur Rimbaud was now, and there had become imbued with strong republican and radical views. During the last years of the Second Empire Paris was swarming with potential rebels and in all the student cafés on the left bank of the Seine were to be found young men talking rank treason. Like all advanced young men of his day, Izambard was violently opposed to the government of Napoleon III.

On his arrival at the college his colleagues, naturally, told him of the brilliant boy of the school, young Arthur Rimbaud, who, in the public examinations of the previous summer, although then only fourteen, had carried off the First Prize from much older competitors, and of whom so much was expected. He was said to be the ablest scholar the school had ever seen. Yet everything that Izambard heard of him did not predispose him in his favour, and he contemplated without much warmth the prospect of such a pupil. By temperament he was not given to admiring the good boys of the school, intellectual spongers and cringers he considered them, who tried to ingratiate themselves with their masters and who wished to be approved and highly thought of by those in authority. Climbers in school life, climbers in university life and climbers in the life of affairs were anathema to him.

His first impression of Arthur Rimbaud was, however, one of complete surprise.[1] The first day he entered his classroom he saw, seated amongst a herd of rough youths, a small boy of angelic countenance who looked up at him out of widely staring, ingenuous blue eyes; his hair was plastered neatly to his head with water and his hands with their unbitten and well-cared-for nails were folded on the desk before him. This boy, so small and boyish for his fifteen years, could not be the monster of erudition he had been led to expect. The general impression he gave was that of a good little boy, rather frail in health, very nervous and shy, since he blushed whenever suddenly addressed. As far as could be discovered he did not seem to have any desire to break loose from discipline, to discover or to experience anything on his own; he seemed to have no longing for adventure. Only once did Izambard see him misbehave in school.[2] One day, in class, when the boys were occupied in writing an exercise in Latin verse, Izambard heard a voice cry from the back of the room, 'Sir! Sir! Rimbaud is cheating, he has just slipped a note to his neighbour.'

It is probable that Arthur, following his usual practice, was trying to help one of his slower friends. Izambard seized what he thought was the note, but discovered that it was only a harmless piece of paper, and he held it out to the class to exonerate Rimbaud. Then Rimbaud, half rising in his seat, with great dignity, flung his dictionary at the head of his accuser, and sat down again with disdainful and stoic resignation. That was the only occasion when he was known to have been guilty of a violent action in school.

Soon Izambard began to know the shy little boy outside school hours and found in him an unexpectedly interesting companion. Arthur used to wait for him at the college gates, like any sentimental schoolgirl waiting for an adored mistress, to walk home with him, grateful to be permitted to carry his books. Now that he had turned fifteen his mother no longer called for him at school and he was free to come and go as he liked. He was glad to talk to a sympathetic spirit of poetry and especially of his own literary dreams. It was a new world that Izambard now opened up to him, a world where literature was part and substance of one's daily life, and was not merely the lifeless matter that is found in books. Outside the school Izambard treated his pupil as an equal, an intellectual equal, and he discussed literary problems

with him, without any condescension, as he would have with one
of his own contemporaries; he was indeed conscious that he himself was gaining much from these conversations. Arthur, who was
silent at home, silent even amongst his own friends, used now to
talk freely. He was unused to being treated as a grown-up whose
opinions were worthy of attention; he was used to clouts and
slaps and to being constantly reminded that he was only a child
who could hold no views of his own. He blossomed quickly
under this treatment, became ready to believe that there was
something in him worthy of interest, and that his previous good-
boy efforts were not sufficient, nor all that could be expected of
him. As a result he gave to Izambard a grateful and deep affection, the kind of affection he was never to give to another human
being, unless it be, in his last years at Harar, to his Abyssinian
servant boy, Djami. Izambard describes the extreme delicacy of
all Rimbaud's dealings with him, how he never took an unfair
advantage of his friendship and never put him in an awkward
or uncomfortable position.

As a result of the lack of warmth and affection at home, Rimbaud had been, from his earliest years, of a solitary disposition;
his sisters were too young for companionship and his brother too
loutish. His mental development was so far in advance of that of
boys of his own age that for real intimacy he needed friends many
years older than himself. And so, even at school, he remained
solitary in the midst of the friends who liked him; these were
friends with whom he played, but he could not have confided in
them, they could not have shared his inner life. He had never been
capable, and was never to be capable, of the warm, animal intimacy of the young, their instinctive and physical intimacy, like
that of kittens rolling together in a basket. There was much in
him that could be hurt and he needed to protect his spiritual
privacy from invasion. Yet he longed for a sympathetic and close
friend to inhabit that inner kingdom with him, an older and
understanding friend to whom he could show its beauties and
treasures. There is no doubt that Izambard helped the blossoming
of Rimbaud's nature and had a beneficial action on him. The sad
thing was that this influence was not more prolonged and that

events so soon separated them. He encouraged Rimbaud in independence yet kept his rebellious spirit within bounds and prevented him, as long as his influence lasted, from taking irretrievable steps that he would afterwards regret. As long as Rimbaud was in touch with him he remained less bitter, able to think of others as well as of himself, and able to discipline himself.

Rimbaud soon confided to Izambard the difficulties he had in obtaining books and the ruses to which he was obliged to resort to procure them. He used frequently to borrow them from bookstalls as he passed, stopping to browse among the set-out volumes, and more often than not he would be afraid to return them later for fear of discovery. Hearing this Izambard lent him books of his own, later made him free of his library and guided his reading into new channels. Under his new master's guidance he read more widely in Greek and Latin literature than many a university student, and in French a whole new world was opened up to him. Hitherto he had only studied the Golden Age of the seventeenth century, so poor in lyric poetry, now from Izambard's library he read the Pleiade and Villon and also the writers who had been rebels in their own time and in opposition to authority and tradition. Rabelais, Montesquieu, Voltaire, Rousseau and Helvétius.[3] He was able also to indulge his passion for Parnassian poetry which, hitherto, he had known chiefly from extracts published in reviews. Izambard shared his interest in these poets and possessed a fine library of their works.

Madame Rimbaud did not, however, approve of the friendship between master and pupil, for she did not think that Izambard was having a good influence on her son, who was now becoming restive under home discipline. She thought also that he was depraving the boy, when she discovered him one day poring over *Les Misérables* of Victor Hugo, and she wrote to Izambard to protest.[4]

Monsieur [she wrote], I am extremely grateful to you for all that you are doing for Arthur. You give him advice and help him with extra teaching outside school hours. All these are attentions which we have no reason to expect. But there is one thing that I cannot approve of and that is, for instance, the reading of the book you lent him the other day (les misérables, V. hugot.) [sic] You must realize, even better than I, that great care is needed in the choice of books that are put in the hands of children. And so I am forced to believe that Arthur must have got hold of the book without your knowledge. It would certainly be dangerous to allow him to continue such reading.

I have the honour, monsieur, to present you with my respects.

V. RIMBAUD.

On hearing of the matter the Principal of the college advised Izambard to call on the outraged mother to see what his powers of persuasion could achieve. Madame Rimbaud had once before complained to him that one of Arthur's school-fellows had lent him Musset's *Confession d'un Enfant du Siècle* which she considered liable to undermine all moral principles and she maintained that the school authorities were guilty of a grave dereliction of duty in allowing such a thing to happen.

Izambard, however, achieved nothing by his interview. The boy's ears had already been boxed for his share of the offence, and the mother was adamant about refusing permission for future reading. But Izambard did not consider himself bound by her prohibition and did not cease lending his pupil books that interested him; the only difference was that these were now read in the master's lodgings instead of at home. This veiled support against his mother's autocratic rule sowed in Arthur's mind the seeds of the conviction that rebellion might be successfully attempted, that home tyranny need not necessarily be permanent, and, moreover, that if one were prepared to accept all consequences, however unpleasant, one's parents had no means in their power of coercing one. We do not know to what extent Izambard encouraged this spirit of revolt in Arthur. His mother certainly believed that he was responsible for the rebellion of her son and for his ultimate break away from all discipline.

It was during the last year of Rimbaud's school days, when he was fifteen, that we have the first large batch of poems from his pen. It began with the poem previously mentioned, published in January, 1870, in *La Revue pour Tous*.[5] There can be no doubt that it was due to Izambard's encouragement that he afterwards produced the large number of poems that were composed before the end of the scholastic year. There is *Sensation* in March, *Le Forgeron* and *Credo in Unam* in April, *Ophélie* in May, *Le Bal des Pendus* in June, *Les Morts de Valmy*, *Le Châtiment de Tartuffe* and *Vénus Anadyomène* in July, while in August, before the next literary period begins, we have *Ce qui retient Nina*, *A la Musique* and *Comédie en Trois Baisers*. The larger proportion of these poems can be proved to be derivative, but the first of them, *Sensation*, seems to be original in inspiration and to have arisen from personal experience.

> Par les soirs bleus d'été, j'irai dans les sentiers,
> Picoté par les blés, fouler l'herbe menue;
> Rêveur, j'en sentirai la fraîcheur à mes pieds,
> Je laisserai le vent baigner ma tête nue.
>
> Je ne parlerai pas, je ne penserai rien:
> Mais l'amour infini me montera dans l'âme,
> Et j'irai loin, bien loin, comme un bohémien,
> Par la Nature,—heureux comme avec une femme.[6]

*Le Forgeron*, written the following month, although it shows an astonishing facility for a boy of fifteen, reveals less individual promise. It is reminiscent of Chateaubriand, Michelet and Hugo; indeed it would not seem out of place in *La Légende des Siècles* or *Les Châtiments*, nor would it disgrace them. It is here that we see Rimbaud, for the first time, flaunting the red Phrygian cap and the poem has a freedom of language and an inspiriting sway of eloquence which Hugo's revolutionary poetry does not surpass.

The next poem *Credo in Unam*, now called *Soleil et Chair*, was written only a few days later and Rimbaud sent it to Banville. The letter which accompanies the poem is revealing since it shows the young poet's anxiety to conciliate the *Parnasse* and to be as highly considered by the academic writers of his day as he was by the school authorities.

Cher Maître [he wrote],[8] We are now in the month of love and I am almost seventeen.* It is the season of hopes and dreams as they say

---

\* He was in point of fact only 15 years and 8 months.

and I, a child touched by the finger of the Muse—please forgive this if it is a platitude—have begun to give expression to my beliefs, my hopes and my feelings. All this is the substance of poetry, this I call Spring. And if I send you these few verses, through Lemerre, the good publisher, it is because I love all poets, all good *Parnassians*, since the poet, *par excellence* is a *Parnassian* in love with ideal beauty; it is because I admire in you, oh! very naïvely, a descendant of Ronsard and a brother of our poets of 1830, a real *Romantic*, a real poet.

That is all! All this is very foolish I fear. But so be it! In two years time, in a year perhaps, I shall be in Paris. *Anch'io*, gentlemen of the press, and I shall be a *Parnassian* too. I swear, cher Maître, that I shall always worship the two goddesses, the Muse and Liberty. Do not frown too much as you read these verses. You would make me mad with joy and hope if you could only find a little place for *Credo in Unam* amongst the *Parnassians*.* The poem would be the *Credo* of the poets. Oh! mad ambition!

ARTHUR RIMBAUD.

On the copy of the poem itself he wrote, 'If only these verses could find a place in the *Parnasse Contemporain!* Are they not the belief by which poets live? I am unknown, but what matter? All poets are brothers. These lines express faith, love and hope. That is all! Cher Maître, do come to my help! Raise me up a little. I am young! Hold out your hand to me!'

Banville answered Rimbaud's letter and kept it, as well as the poem, carefully filed amongst his papers, but he did not find a place for it in the *Parnasse Contemporain*. Yet it is a magnificent piece of writing, better than many poems included in the collection. It is a pantheistic *Credo* of 164 lines. In most parts it is not to be differentiated from the work of Banville or Leconte de Lisle, but it stands the comparison proudly. Rimbaud succeeded, with astonishing certainty of touch, in adopting and making his own the technique and the methods of composition of the masters of his day, and in so doing he learned his trade. In subject matter the poem was probably inspired by *Le Satyre* of Victor Hugo and by *L'Exil des Dieux* of Banville; critics have also alleged

* Banville was a member of the selection committee for the *Parnasse Contemporain*, a periodic collection of selected poems by the poets of the movement.

that it owes much to Lucretius; while in form it is pure Leconte de Lisle or Banville. The first verse, however, contains a passage that could only come from the pen of Rimbaud himself, that is already stamped with the hall-mark of his own particular genius. It reveals the personal and sensual attitude to nature which is the striking characteristic of his mature poetry.

> Le Soleil, le foyer de tendresse et de vie,
> Verse l'amour brûlant à la terre ravie.
> Et, quand on est couché sur la vallée, on sent
> Que la terre est nubile et déborde de sang,
> Que son immense sein, soulevé par une âme,
> Est d'amour comme Dieu, de chair comme la femme,
> Et qu'il renferme, gros de sève et de rayons,
> Le grand fourmillement de tous les embryons. [9]

*Ophélie*, written in June, is a poem of some charm similar in inspiration to Millais's picture of the same name. This work has a quality which is reminiscent of English poetry, although Rimbaud, at the time, knew neither English nor English literature; it is written in the style of pre-Raphaelite poetry which was to become popular in the 'eighties. It is a mode unfashionable to-day; this should not, however, make us insensitive to the grace and harmony of the lines, and to the astonishing talent and mastery which they reveal in a schoolboy of fifteen.

> Sur l'onde calme et noire où dorment les étoiles,
> La blanche Ophélia flotte comme un grand lys,
> Flotte très lentement, couchée en ses longs voiles.
> —On entend dans les bois lointains des hallalis.
>
> Voici plus de mille ans que la triste Ophélie
> Passe, fantôme blanc, sur le long fleuve noir;
> Voici plus de mille ans que sa douce folie
> Murmure sa romance à la brise du soir.
>
> Le vent baise ses seins et déploie en corolle
> Ses grands voiles bercés mollement par les eaux;
> Les saules frissonnants pleurent sur son épaule,
> Sur son grand front rêveur s'inclinent les roseaux.

Les nénuphars froissés soupirent autour d'elle.
Elle éveille parfois, dans un aune qui dort,
Quelque nid, d'où s'échappe un petit frisson d'aile:
—Un chant mystérieux tombe des astres d'or.

                                            etc., etc.[10]

No mention need be made of *Le Bal des Pendus*, written in the same month, since it is pure Banville.

In the meantime the school year was drawing to its close, bringing near the time for the examinations. Both master and pupil were increasing their efforts, so that when July finally arrived, Rimbaud was more than ready. The candidates were invited, that year, by the Academy, to compose in Latin Verse an original address by Sancho Panza to his ass, and it is said that the examiners themselves were amazed by the quality of Rimbaud's achievement. Once more, in the Concours Académique he carried off the First Prize from older competitors, and in the school examinations swept the board, winning all the first prizes in his form, except two.[11]

The news of Rimbaud's success in the Concours Académique reached the college at the same time as the news of the outbreak of the Franco-Prussian War and fell flat in comparison with the national excitement. In a paper called *Le Pays*, a journalist by the name of Paul de Cassagnac, in a grandiloquent article, summoned France to answer the call and to come forward to save 'la Patrie en danger,' just as in 1792 all parties had forgotten their different political opinions and had gone forth to rescue France from the clutches of the common enemy. These noble sentiments, however, had been preceded by a purely dynastical exhortation written in the following terms. 'This war is, at the moment, urgently needed in the interests of France and of her dynasty. The government of Napoleon III owes it to the government of Napoleon IV to remove from its paths all the stones which might make it stumble during its first steps.'[12] These sentiments outraged radicals and republicans like Izambard, who had little use for the government of the Second Empire. It was probably under the inspiration of such views that Rimbaud wrote the rousing sonnet, *Les Morts de Valmy*, which he presented to his master at the first class of 18 July 1870.

In the same month, in the midst of war reports and his grief at the imminent departure of his friend and master, Rimbaud wrote his first cynical and somewhat obscene poems, though the obscenity is only of the schoolboy variety, *Le Châtiment de Tartuffe* and the coarser *Vénus Anadyomène*, 'belle, hideusement, d'un ulcère à l'anus'.

Later it will become apparent that whenever Rimbaud was subjected to any unusual strain this showed itself outwardly in the coarseness of his speech or writing. Izambard used to say that after a dispute with his mother Arthur would become scatological in his conversation, but never otherwise; it may be believed that these two poems were the result of some such clash which must have been particularly unendurable to him since he knew that the only remedy he had against solitude and misunderstanding was so soon now to be reft away from him.

The prize-giving at the Collège de Charleville was fixed for 6 August. The boys had been asked to give the money intended for their prizes to the war effort but Rimbaud had refused as he did not approve of the government—he was a republican.

Izambard did not remain in Charleville for the ceremony. As soon as his classes were over he returned home to Douai since, with the unsettled state of the country, it was uncertain what the future might have in store for him. 'What on earth shall I do when M. Izambard is gone?' said Rimbaud to a friend of his master, Deverrière. 'One thing is absolutely certain and that is that I'll not be able to endure this life for a whole year. I'll run away. I know how to write. I'll become a journalist in Paris!'

'And do you think it is as easy as all that?' asked the older man, who was cherishing the same ambition, but with the caution of his maturer years. 'How will you be able to fight your way alone?'

'Well! then I'll fall by the wayside!' answered the boy desperately. 'I'll die of hunger on a heap of stones, but I'll run away!'

'I absolutely forbid you to do any such thing!' broke in Izambard who had been listening to the conversation, 'be patient for one year more. Don't run your head against a stone wall! All the prizes you'll receive in a few days' time will soften your mother towards you. Stay and finish your course. Pass your *baccalauréat*.'

On 24 July Rimbaud accompanied Izambard and Deverrière to the station and stood disconsolately on the platform as the train swept them away from him. He was sunk in grief, the first passionate grief of his life.

A fortnight later the prize-giving was held and on that hot August afternoon, Arthur Rimbaud surrounded by his proud family walked among the admiring citizens of his native town, weighed down under the burden of many gilt-edged, red-bound volumes and the shiny, varnished pasteboard laurel wreaths which the French authorities bestow so lavishly on prize-winners, while his Academy medal hung from his button-hole. But the glory and the fame tasted bitter to him, and in the midst of success he was conscious only of failure. The one person who had illuminated his life with radiance, who had filled it with sweetness and had given a deeper significance to knowledge, was gone and was never likely to return. Arthur Rimbaud now found his achievement meaningless and despised the honours that were being showered on him. He was not yet sixteen, nevertheless this August afternoon marked the end of his school-days, for when the autumn came he had become another person and had broken entirely with his old life.

His mother, however, walked proudly at his side, unconscious of what the future was to bring. Though her rugged features wore an impassive look she exulted inwardly, and built golden palaces in the air for her child to inhabit. There were many possibilities open to this wonderful son of hers. There was the possibility of academic distinction, or the promise of fame as a writer. Whatever he chose to undertake success was already assured, for had he not shown that he could beat all comers, that he was capable of hard work, and that he was eminently teachable.

Judging from outward signs alone, his mother was not wrong in feeling secure. There was nothing yet to show that he was going to break away from all restraint. Even his poetry was satisfactory and gave no hint of what his real talent was to be. It was conventional and conservative, following as it did the approved models. It was good, remarkably good for a boy of fifteen, but it showed more power of clever imitation than genuine originality. He had read much, understood much and assimilated much. He did not, at this time, dream of any other future than that of a successful writer enjoying full approval; he did not see himself as a misunderstood genius, and would not have considered this an eventuality to be desired. He accepted the given hierarchy of literary values; his poetry had no positive faults, it showed remarkable achievement, but there was nothing in it to give promise that he was to become one of the most daringly original writers France has ever possessed.

CHAPTER IV

## FIRST FLIGHT

THE summer holidays of 1870 were dreary holidays for the Rimbaud children. They had hoped to spend the time in the country, but they could not leave Charleville on account of the war, for they were not far from the battle zone and it was uncertain whether they might have to evacuate their house.

With nothing to do Arthur became bored and restless, and heavy depression settled on him. In these conditions relations between his mother and himself became even more strained than usual, and there was nothing now to take his mind off his loneliness. He had no friends with whom to spend the time, there were no new books in the bookstalls amongst which to browse, for the war prevented supplies coming from Paris. He had, luckily, still the use of Izambard's library. Before the master departed from Charleville he left the key of his flat with his landlord so that Rimbaud could go there to read whenever he felt inclined. It was a quiet little flat among the trees in the Cours d'Orléans, a cool and pleasant refuge during the stifling August weather. Rimbaud, being a voracious reader, had finished all the books

56

before the end of the month and there was nothing further for him to do.

You are indeed lucky to be no longer in Charleville [he wrote pathetically to Izambard,[1] at the same time proud to be able to despise his own town]. My native town takes the first prize for imbecility among all other provincial towns. Because it is near Mézières, because it sees a few hundred soldiers strutting up and down the streets, the whole benighted population shouts and gesticulates in a smugly swashbucklerish manner, much more so than the besieged in Metz or Strasbourg. It's terrific all these retired grocers who stick on a uniform! It's marvellous the amount of side that notaries, tax-collectors and other pot-bellied bourgeoisie put on, who parade their patriotism, rifle on shoulder, at the gates of Mézières. My country rises up, I for my part prefer to see it seated. Don't stir your feet, that's my motto. I am out of my element, sick, furious, stupid and utterly discomposed. I had hoped for sunbaths, long walks, rest, travel, adventures and all sorts of gipsy wanderings. I had particularly hoped for books and papers. The post brings absolutely nothing to the bookstalls, Paris doesn't care a rap about us. Not a single new book! It's death! I am reduced, in the matter of papers, to the honourable *Courrier des Ardennes*—proprietor, director and sole editor, A. Pouillard. This rag typifies the aspirations, the wishes and the opinions of the population, and so you can imagine what it's like. It's foul! One is an exile in one's own country. Luckily I've got your room—you remember you gave me permission to use it —I carried off half your books. What can I say? I have read all your books, all. Three days ago I was reduced to *Les Épreuves* (Sully Prudhomme) and to *Les Glaneuses* (Paul Démeny). And then that was all! I've nothing left now! Your library, my last plank, has given out. . . . I enclose some verses of mine. Read them one morning in the sun, as I wrote them. You are no longer for me a teacher—at least I hope not.

Good-bye and send me a letter of twenty-five pages, very quickly, *poste restante*.

A. RIMBAUD.

PS.—Very soon I shall give you some startling news of the kind of life I'm going to lead after the summer holidays.

Perhaps the poem enclosed was the delightful *Comédie en Trois Baisers*, published under the title, *Première Ivresse* in *La Charge* on 13 August. In feeling it would correspond with his description.[2]

—Elle était fort déshabillée,
Et de grands arbres indiscrets
Aux vitres jetaient leur feuillée
Malinement, tout près, tout près.

Assise sur ma grande chaise,
Mi-nue, elle joignait les mains,
Sur le plancher frissonnaient d'aise
Ses petits pieds si fins, si fins.

—Je regardai, couleur de cire,
Un petit rayon buissonnier
Papillonner dans son sourire
Et sur son sein,—mouche au rosier.

—Je baisai ses fines chevilles.
Elle eut un doux rire brutal,
Qui s'égrenait en claires trilles,
Un joli rire de cristal.

Les petits pieds sous la chemise
Se sauvèrent: "Veux-tu-finir!"
—La première audace permise,
Le rire feignait de punir.

—Pauvrets palpitants sous ma lèvre,
Je baisai doucement ses yeux;
Elle jeta sa tête mièvre
En arrière: "Oh! c'est encor mieux! . . ."

"Monsieur, j'ai deux mots à te dire . . ."
—Je lui jetai le reste au sein,
Dans un baiser, qui la fit rire
D'un bon rire qui voulait bien. . . .

—Elle était fort déshabillée,
Et de grands arbres indiscrets
Aux vitres jetaient leur feuillée
Malinement, tout près, tout près.

Or it might have been the equally happy and charming poem,
*Ce qui retient Nina,* written on 15 August 1870, in which a romantic

young man describes to his lady-love the delights of a day spent in the open, and all that the prosaic damsel can say in reply to his rapture is: 'Et mon bureau?'

The other poem written in August, *A la Musique*, expresses Rimbaud's growing irritation against bourgeois platitude and convention, his disgust with their smug and happy content. It is a good example of his ironic and satiric vein.

His restlessness reached its climax when Frederick, only a bare year older than he, a hefty lad not yet seventeen, ran off to the war and even managed to be enrolled as a volunteer. One day, seeing a regiment pass in the streets, without more ado he followed it to the station, and climbed into the train with the soldiers. They, amused at the daring and the cheeky spirit of the young fellow, enlisted him as an auxiliary, and with them he went through the seige of Metz, not returning home until November.[3] 'If Frederick has managed to run away from home,' said Arthur to himself, 'why not I as well?' He then laid his plans for escape. On 28 August, three days after he wrote to Izambard, he was walking with his mother and the two little sisters in the meadows on the banks of the Meuse. Suddenly he left them saying that he wished to go home to fetch a book to read. It was not, however, home that he went, but to the station, and boarded the first train leaving for Paris. For many months his dream had been to reach the capital, the centre of literary life, yet in the working out of his plan of escape it can be seen how childish and puerile he still was as a consequence of his mother's training, in spite of his fifteen years and his great scholastic achievements. Other boys, intellectually less mature than he, would have possessed more sense of reality and would have laid their plans more efficiently.

He boarded the train without a penny in his pockets and set off thus for Paris. It is alleged that he first sold his prizes for twenty francs, but this story does not ring true. He had little time to effect the sale of the books, and he arrived in Paris without a ticket and without the wherewithal to pay for one. He was then arrested and taken to the police station.

It is easy to picture the wretched mother's anxiety and distress when she arrived home and found that her son had not reached the house, and, like every mother in similar circumstances, she imagined all manner of hideous possibilities. She thought that the Germans might have taken him a prisoner, for they were at that time rapidly advancing towards Charleville. All through the night, writes Paterne Berrichon, she wandered through the streets of Charleville and Mézières, in a state of indescribable anguish, looking for her son. She made the round of the cafés and knocked at the doors of those who might know of his whereabouts. No one, however, had seen him. The following day the French army suffered a serious defeat at Beaumont, the German troops made a further advance, and her anxiety was thereby increased. She had received no news of Arthur yet and was to receive none for over a week. Nothing was heard of him until his spirit was broken and all his courage had ebbed away.

On 5 September he wrote to Izambard telling him that he had been arrested on his arrival in Paris for travelling without a ticket and without the means for paying for one on the journey. Since he had no papers in his possession and would give no name and address, he was taken to the prison of Mazas. After a week of prison régime, when the time for his trial drew near, the tough fugitive vanished, leaving in his place a terrified little boy, a child who had never, even for a day, left his mother's side, and had never before done anything on his own initiative. He wrote in great distress to Izambard, his closest friend and the one person on whom he could rely, and begged him for help.

Cher Monsieur [he wrote],[4] What you advised me not to do I did. I left home and came to Paris. I played that prank on 29 August. I was arrested as I left the train for not having a sou in my pocket and for owing the railway company thirteen francs. I was taken to the police station and to-day I am awaiting my trial at Mazas. Oh! I hope in you as in a mother! You have always been a brother to me. I beg you most earnestly for the help you offered. I have written to my mother, to the *Procureur Impérial*, and to the chief of the police at Charleville. If you do not receive any news for me on Wednesday morning, before the train that leaves Douai for Paris, do, I entreat you, take that train and come and fetch me, giving warning by letter or going to the public prosecutor begging him to let me off, answering for me and paying my debt. Do all you can, *as soon as you receive this letter*, write I command you, to my poor mother to comfort her, write also to me. Do everything you can. I love you as a brother, and I'll love you as a father.

YOUR POOR RIMBAUD.

P.S. And if you come to Mazas, you'll take me back with you to Douai, won't you?

By the same post Izambard also received a letter from the governor of the prison asking him to come to Paris and to remove the boy. Izambard did all that he was requested, except go to Paris. He wrote to explain matters to the *Procureur Impérial*, he sent money and begged the governor to dispatch Rimbaud to Charleville, or, if that was not possible on account of the war, to send him to Douai. A few days later Rimbaud arrived at Douai, somewhat humiliated and shamefaced, but happy nevertheless, to have got out of his scrape so easily. He gave a lurid and highly coloured account of his adventures, his arrest, his cross-examination, the disinfecting of his clothes on his arrival at the prison, and the terror he had felt when he had been locked into his cell. Now that everything was over he enjoyed recounting his experiences and found therein outlet for his descriptive talent. It is said that the poem, *Les Chercheuses de Poux*, composed in Paris the following year, refers to the ministrations of Izambard's 'aunts', when they cleaned his hair of the lice acquired in prison. This suggestion has more verisimilitude than the usual one, that the 'chercheuses' are Madame de Banville and Madame Georges Hugo.[5] In any case, Izambard later referred to one of his 'aunts' as 'la chercheuse de poux'.

Now that Rimbaud was found, the most urgent matter was to get in touch with his mother, but this was not easy on account of the war. Letters from Douai to Charleville could not be sent direct, they had to make a detour through Belgium. And so it happened that Arthur was obliged to remain for three weeks at Douai with Izambard's 'aunts'. Izambard had, however, insisted that he should write to his mother himself, in a contrite and humble frame of mind, while he himself wrote as well, begging for merciful treatment for the culprit, in view of the severe lesson he had already received. Then Rimbaud, having written his *mea culpa*, proceeded to enjoy to the full his first holiday away from home and the unwonted affectionate treatment of the Gindre sisters.

With the defeat of the French army at Sedan and the capture of Napoleon III, the war changed in character. It ceased being a mere dynastic struggle and became a national concern. With the result that many republicans like Izambard were suddenly seized with patriotic fervour and enlisted. Izambard's ardour affected Rimbaud, so that he too volunteered for service, but was turned down on account of his age. Izambard not being immediately able to leave for the front—he was untrained and there was, moreover, a shortage of arms—temporarily joined the Garde Nationale and obtained permission for Rimbaud to be enrolled in the company as well. And so it came about that Rimbaud was for three weeks a member of the Garde Nationale, and, shouldering his broomstick, he drilled with the others. He was deeply grieved that there were no arms available for them, and his concern was to manage to obtain a rifle before he returned home. He drew up, in the name of his fellow members of the Garde, a petition to protest against the iniquity of the lack of arms for those prepared and willing to defend their country in its hour of danger.[6] His letter was intended also as a vote of censure on the Mayor of Douai who, as a supporter of the Imperial régime, had laid the blame for the lack of arms to the score of the new *Gouvernement de la Défense Nationale*, whereas, in Rimbaud's opinion blame should solely have been attributed to the local councillors. The letter is surprising, coming from a boy of fifteen.

[We the undersigned members of the National Guard of Douai, [he wrote], desire to protest against the letter of the Mayor of Douai on the agenda for the meeting of 18 September 1870. In answer to the numerous complaints of the National Guard who are unarmed, the Mayor draws attention to the orders given by the Minister for War. In this letter he seems to accuse the Minister of want of forethought and alacrity. Without wishing to set ourselves up in the position of defenders of a cause already won, we have the right to draw the attention of the public to the fact that the shortage of arms at the present moment must be attributed solely to the lack of forethought and alacrity of the government which has just fallen, from the consequences of whose evil administration we are still suffering. We must appreciate the motives which urge the *Gouvernement de la Défense Nationale* to keep the few remaining arms for the army on active service; these forces must certainly be armed before us. Does this mean that no arms will be issued to three-quarters of the National Guard, determined, nevertheless, to defend themselves if they are attacked? Certainly not! They do not intend to remain useless and arms must be found for them. It is the duty of the municipal councillors, elected by them, to procure these arms for them. The Mayor, in such cases, should himself take the initiative, as he has already done in many other communes of France. In his commune he should set in motion all possible measures for the purchase and distribution of arms. Next Sunday the municipal elections are to be held and we shall vote only for those who have shown by their actions that they have our real interests at heart.

The letter was to be signed and circulated, but Rimbaud, being only fifteen, was unfortunately neither of an age to vote nor to remain away from home without his mother's consent. The document bears only one signature, that of its originator. Before it had time to be circulated Madame Rimbaud's answer arrived for Izambard, and it was so violent and abusive in its tone that Arthur swore that nothing on earth would induce him to return home. Izambard lost his temper with his pupil; the boy was insolent to him in reply; there was a general commotion which was eventually pacified by the three old aunts.

The result was that Rimbaud finally agreed to go home. Izambard then wrote once more to Madame Rimbaud to explain to her the nervous state in which her son was and begged again for leniency for him. He offered to send him home in company with Deverrière to make sure that he did not take to his heels again once he had the money for his fare in his pocket; Deverrière was, in a few days' time, to go on business to Charleville. Before Izambard's letter had been able to reach her, she wrote again.

Sir [she wrote], I am very anxious and do not at all understand the prolonged absence of Arthur. He must have understood, from my letter of the 17th, that he was not to remain another day at Douai. The police are now taking steps to discover his whereabouts and I fear that before you receive this he may have been arrested once more. In that case he need not attempt to come home for I swear that I shall not receive him. It is impossible to understand the madness of this child, he who is usually so good and quiet. How could such a wild idea have entered his head? Who could have suggested it to him? But no! I must not believe that! One is not fair when one is unhappy! Please be good enough to advance ten francs to the wretched boy, send him away and tell him that he must come home immediately. I have just come out of the Post Office where they have refused to issue a postal order as the line is closed between here and Douai. What am I to do? I am in great distress. May God not punish as it deserves the wilfulness of this child.

I have the honour to present you with my respects.

V. RIMBAUD.

On receiving this letter Izambard decided that he himself would deliver the boy home. He would, in any case, be obliged, in the near future, to return to Charleville to arrange for the removal of his furniture and books.

Nothing, however, could raise Rimbaud's spirits during the long and tedious journey from Douai to Charleville. Terrified at the prospect of the reception that was awaiting him at home, he sat huddled up in the corner of the carriage and did not open his lips.

When the prodigal was handed over to his mother she forthwith seized him by the ear and bundled him into the house, then she turned on Izambard with such violent abuse that he was glad to escape as soon as possible, but sorry to be obliged to leave the unfortunate culprit to so rough a fate.

After dispatching his business Izambard left Charleville for some days. He found, however, on his return, in the first week in October, a letter from Madame Rimbaud begging him to come to her aid once more as she was at her wits' ends with anxiety. Arthur had run away again and she had no idea of where

'Ma Bohème' *by Valentine Hugo*

VERLAINE AT THE TIME OF HIS MEETING
WITH RIMBAUD

he could have gone. Izambard, though loath to have any dealings with her after his previous reception, agreed, nevertheless, to make an attempt to discover the whereabouts of the fugitive. All Rimbaud's friends were known to him—they were his pupils—and he decided to begin his investigations with them. He went first to Fumay where Léon Billuart lived and found that he had at least started on the right track. Arthur had in fact spent a night with him and had left saying that he was going to Des Essarts at Charleroi whose father was editor of the local paper, and that he hoped with him to obtain journalistic work.

When Izambard reached Charleroi, Des Essarts informed him that Rimbaud had indeed arrived some days previously, in a state of exhaustion through fatigue and hunger, hoping to be invited to stay the night. Unfortunately, Des Essarts' parents took a dislike to Rimbaud from the first moment. They found it hard to believe that a boy who was allowed to tramp the countryside in war-time at his own free will, and who looked, moreover, a complete vagabond, could be a school-fellow of their son. Rimbaud, realizing that he was not being a success, proceeded, in his nervousness, to make himself even more disliked. When the coarseness of his conversation brought a blush to the little sister's cheeks, when he dared to call prominent men of the day, 'that scoundrel so-and-so, and that turn-coat so-and-so,' then M. Des Essarts thought that it was time to end the visit and he requested his son's guest to depart.

After leaving the house, still without having had a meal, Rimbaud tramped on foot towards Brussels. In a letter to Belluart he said that he had for sole supper that evening the delicious, savoury smells floating up from basement windows of the houses that he passed in Charleroi, where the roasts and the stews were being prepared for the tables of the rich. With this aroma still lingering in his nostrils he went and nibbled, by moonlight, the bar of chocolate his friend had given him for the journey.[8]

Izambard had now reached a dead end for he knew of no acquaintances of his pupil outside France. To his amazement, however, he discovered, on reaching a friend's house in Brussels, whose name he had once casually mentioned in Arthur's hearing, that the boy had arrived a few days before, seemingly half-starved, with his clothes hanging on him in rags and his shoes falling to pieces. In Izambard's name he begged for a night's shelter, saying that his family had sent him on a trip round Belgium for the sake of his education, but that he had unfortunately spent all his money. He was given a change of clothes and a small sum of money and he had departed, next morning, without revealing his destination.

On reaching Douai the following day Izambard found him sitting in the parlour in the midst of the aunts, quietly copying out his poems, with the neat writing and scrupulous care of the model pupil. He was clean and tidy and looked so supremely happy that Izambard had not the heart to scold him as he deserved, especially as the aunts were obviously pleased to have him to look after and to spoil. They said that he arrived three days before and that when they opened the door to his ring, he said shyly: 'You see I've come back!' Their hearts had been touched by this proof of affection and simple trust.

The poems which he was copying out with such diligence and care were those he had written on his tramp through France and Belgium. Soon he exhausted the paper which the 'aunts' gave him and when they suggested, economically, that he should write on both sides of the sheets he answered, very shocked, 'But poets never write on both sides of the paper!' These poems can be called the poems of his first manner, the first poems of individual and personal expression, and they show a marked advance on those written before the close of the school year, even though he had not yet completely emancipated himself from established literary influences.

In spite of hunger and hardship, these two weeks of liberty, of untrammelled wandering seemed to have been the happiest that Rimbaud had ever spent, the happiest perhaps in his whole life. There is no bitterness or coarseness to be found in the poems which resulted from them; there is only the expression of celestial happiness, of joy in freedom, and of delight in mere living. The poem that best expresses his state of rapture is *Ma Bohême*.

Je m'en allais, les poings dans mes poches crevées.
Mon paletot aussi devenait idéal;
J'allais sous le ciel, Muse! et j'étais ton féal;
Oh! là là! que d'amours splendides j'ai rêvées!

Mon unique culotte avait un large trou.
—Petit-Poucet rêveur, j'égrenais dans ma course
Des rimes. Mon auberge était à la Grande-Ourse.
—Mes étoiles au ciel avaient un doux frou-frou.

Et je les écoutais, assis au bord des routes,
Ces bons soirs de septembre où je sentais des gouttes
De rosée à mon front, comme un vin de vigueur;

Où, rimant au milieu des ombres fantastiques,
Comme des lyres, je tirais les élastiques
De mes souliers blessés, un pied prés de mon cœur![9]

The poems which he was copying are of varied inspiration. There are first poems in the style of the Flemish school of painting, similar to the poems to be written after 1880, by the leaders of the Belgian Renaissance. *Les Effarés, La Maline, Au Cabaret Vert* and *Le Buffet*. There are poems inspired by the political situation: *Le Mal, Rages de César, L'Éclatante Victoire de Saarbroucke*, and *Le Dormeur du Val*. In *Les Effarés* and *Le Dormeur du Val* we find that quality of compassion which is a feature of Rimbaud's personality and work. The sleeper in the second poem is a soldier lying dead under the trees in the valley, whom Rimbaud must have seen on his wanderings. There is also *Ma Bohême* quoted above and the delightfully musical little poem, *Rêvé pour l'Hiver*.

L'hiver, nous irons dans un petit wagon rose
    Avec des coussins bleus.
Nous serons bien. Un nid de baisers fous repose
    Dans chaque coin moelleux.

Tu fermeras l'œil, pour ne point voir, par la glace
    Grimacer les ombres des soirs,
Ces monstruosités hargneuses, populace
    De démons noirs et de loups noirs.

Puis tu te sentiras la joue égratignée . . .
Un petit baiser, comme une folle araignée,
　　Te courra par le cou.

Et tu me diras: 'Cherche!' en inclinant la tête,
—Et nous prendrons du temps à trouver cette bête
　—Qui voyage beaucoup.[10]

The poems of this period show a happy innocence and a purity that he never again recaptured.

In the midst of this idyllic scene—Rimbaud copying out his poems, surrounded by the three admiring old aunts sitting by with their knitting—Izambard sounded the knell of the return home. 'We don't want to turn you out,' he said, 'but before the law we have no right to keep you, for you are a minor.' Rimbaud immediately understood, and that he was placing his friend and master in an awkward position. He became submissive at once and answered quietly, 'I realize all that very well, I knew it. You say what I'm to do and I'll do it.' Izambard's first task was to inform Madame Rimbaud that her son was found. This time she would, however, send no money for his return, but insisted that he was to be brought home through the offices of the police. Izambard went to interview the sergeant at the police station and extracted from him the promise that the boy would be kindly treated on the journey to Charleville. Then he went home to fetch the vagabond. He found him standing, pale but resigned, waiting for him in the hall with his pathetic little bundle under his arm. When he saw that his master had come and that it was really time to go, he said good bye to the aunts and promised them faithfully that he would be good. They had grown very fond of him and did not like to see him leave, for they had not found him difficult or troublesome, on the contrary; with kindness and affection, he became once more the good little boy he had been in the past who asked for nothing but love and understanding.

On the way to the police station Izambard, out of his deep affection, spoke to him seriously of his concern for his future, of the fame that could await him, if he did not spoil his chances, of all that he hoped from him. As he spoke he could not keep the emotion from appearing in his voice and it seemed to him that Arthur understood and was touched. But he could never know with Rimbaud, for the boy was always tongue-tied and awkward whenever he was stirred to feeling.

Then Izambard handed him over to the care of the police sergeant and that was the last time he ever saw him.

Shortly after he reached home Rimbaud wrote to him.[11]

Monsieur, for you alone this. I came back to Charleville the day after I left you. My mother received me and I am here completely idle. It seems that she won't put me to school as a boarder until January 1871.

Well! I've kept my promise. But I'm dying and deliquescing in the dullness, in the drabness and in the foulness around me. You see I still persist in loving liberty and a lot of things like that. All very pitiable isn't it? I was going to run away to-day, and I could have run away. I had new clothes and I would have sold my watch and then long live liberty! But I stayed, I stayed. And yet I long to run away, many, many times. Here goes! With my hat, my coat, and my hands in my pockets, I'm off! But I'll stay, damn it, I'll stay! I didn't promise as much as that, but I'll do that to deserve your affection. You said that to me and I'm going to deserve it. The gratitude I feel for you I can no more express it to-day than I could the other day. But I'm going to prove it to you. If it were only a question of doing something for you, I would die to do it. I give you my word of honour. I have a lot of things to say.

Your "heartless",
A. RIMBAUD.

## CHAPTER V

# CŒUR SUPPLICIÉ

HAD the Collège de Charleville been able to open that autumn term Arthur Rimbaud might have given up his bohemian ways and have settled down to regular work. The war, however, was being continued by the *Gouvernement de la Défense Nationale* and most of the teachers of the school were either at the front or else acting as special constables. The greater part of the pupils, moreover, came from the district now occupied by the Prussians and they and their parents were too busily engaged in serving their conquerors to have any time or thought for mere education. It was therefore considered unnecessary to open the school for the boys who came from Charleville and Mézières, especially as fresh accommodation would have had to be found for them, since their own building had been temporarily commandeered as a hospital.

For Arthur Rimbaud this life of enforced idleness, with no fixed occupation, was disastrous. All might have been well had he been able, as he wished, to enlist as a soldier, but he still looked far younger than his sixteen years and he was always turned down. In company with Delahaye he spent his days in long country rambles, in interminable discussions on literature and especially on politics.[1] That year the autumn lingered on, as if loath to bring on the fighting troops the rigours of winter, and the weather remained warm and mellow. In the morning, as soon as breakfast was over, the two boys used to make their way to the wood of Saint-Julien, the Bois de Boulogne of Mézières. Then they crossed the fortifications which had been added, one after the other, since the time of Bayard, and eventually reached the little park called Le Bois d'Amour; here they had complete solitude for their discussions. The park began by a gravelled path running between two high stone walls; then came a hawthorn hedge and the famous avenue of lime-trees, their favourite resort. This was Le Grand Jardin, which before the Revolution had been part of a private property. In this little garden, far from prying eyes, they would lie and smoke in the warm autumn sunlight.[2] It was here, and at this time, that Rimbaud was fast gathering the impressions that were to become later the substance of *Illuminations*. It is clear that the sensations which he experienced during these months meant much to him and that he saw in them great significance. It is as if in the midst of the war and destruction around him, he felt with a new intensity the extraordinary beauty of the countryside which he had come to take for granted.

Later, when the weather finally grew too cold for sitting out of doors, they discovered in the gardens opposite the Bois d'Amour a little tool-shed. It was sheltered from the prevailing wind and there, in comparative comfort, they sat for hours smoking and talking like old-age pensioners. Sometimes they ran short of tobacco, for Rimbaud had no pocket money and was obliged to rely on the generosity of Delahaye whose supply was not always sufficient for more than the smallest smoke. But when they had no tobacco they contented themselves with puffing at their empty pipes. They used to bring books with them and Rimbaud would read aloud to his friend, commenting on the texts he chose. He had a talent for elocution—every year he had gained a prize at school for declamation—and Delahaye was always moved to hear him read. It was almost always poetry that he chose. He had not yet outgrown his admiration for the *Parnasse*, though he had added to his heroes the new poet Verlaine. He knew *Les Poèmes Saturniens* and *Les Fêtes Galantes*, but the war had prevented the publication of *La Bonne Chanson*. In him Rimbaud admired the freedom of his prosody and his technical innovations. Verlaine, even as early as *Les Poèmes Saturniens*, had allowed himself more technical liberty than any other nineteenth-century poet, except Sainte-Beuve. Before ever meeting him Rimbaud had learnt much from him of the craft of poetry.

It was, however, not only literature that the two young friends discussed, but politics and the urgent need for revolution and change. The new government was the object of wide-spread and violent criticism. In Charleville it was popular with no party. It was abused by those who regretted the fallen Empire and by the advanced republicans who thought it reactionary. At this time there sprang up everywhere the usual flourishing crop of rumours of profiteering and swindling on a fantastically large scale, which has always been a characteristic feature of French political life. Schneider alone was alleged to have defrauded the country to the tune of £400,000 for armaments. As usual everyone in power was said to be a traitor to his country and *vendu* to the enemy. All this anger, however, boiled away in the steam of conversation, and no steps were ever taken to replace those who gave satisfaction to no one.

Even boys of Rimbaud's age were affected by the general spirit of revolt symptomatic of the dissatisfaction which was suddenly to burst out, not many months later, in the *Commune*. He was developing a hatred of all government, of all authority, and this flame was fanned into activity by his growing resentment of his mother's severe discipline. He would willingly then have welcomed all forms of destruction, so long as Charleville and the life he knew could be swept away to ruin. He was able even to view without too great distress the cutting down of the beautiful trees in his beloved Bois d'Amour to stem the Prussian advance. Trees that had proudly stood for centuries were slaughtered and laid low in a moment. One day, when he and Delahaye reached their favourite haunt, they found the two lime-trees which they had most loved lying like two stricken giants, cut away from their roots. Rimbaud loved the Bois d'Amour as he would have loved a woman and he gazed sadly down at the fallen trees; then a fierce look came suddenly into his eyes as he clenched his fist and cried, 'There are some destructions that are necessary. There are other trees that have stood for hundreds of years that must also be cut down; other shades whose pleasures we must forgo. On the root of society itself must the axe now be laid. Every valley shall be filled, every mountain shall be brought low; the crooked shall be made straight and the rough shall be made smooth. Opulence will be razed to the ground and individual pride will be cut down. Bitter envy and stupid admiration will be supplanted.'[3] Even in his conversation Rimbaud adopted the Biblical language, which was later a feature of *Illuminations* and *Une Saison en Enfer*.

In spite of all efforts, however, the Prussians drew near to Charleville and Mézières. Mézières, where Delayahe lived, was bombarded on 20 December and the town caught fire. That day Madame Rimbaud locked all her brood into the flat, allowing none of them to venture forth in the streets for fear that she might lose one of them; ever since Arthur's escapades she was in constant anxiety about them. Delahaye and Rimbaud were now separated and Rimbaud suffered an agony of suspense on his friend's behalf, since no news had come, except a vague rumour that his house had been burnt to the ground and that the whole family had perished in the flames. As soon as he could elude his mother's vigilant eye, he escaped to Mézières to look amongst the ruins of the house for some trace of his lost friend. There, as he was searching among the heaps of débris, a neighbour informed him that the whole family had been saved and were being given hospitality by relations in the country. Rimbaud's only concern was now to reach Delahaye and to bring him some books to occupy his time. In spite of the danger he made his way to the farm that was sheltering the family, bringing with him as an offering his most recent discovery, Baudelaire's translation of Poe's works and *Le Petit Chose* of Daudet. He hid the emotion and anxiety he had felt on his friend's behalf beneath an expression of gruff and hearty cheerfulness and would not allow him to express his gratitude for the attentions he had received. It was ever thus with Rimbaud. In him, as in his mother, emotion rarely expressed itself in outward manifestations, and he was always embarrassed when others sought to thank him or to show their appreciation.

Next the Prussians came and occupied Charleville and Mézières, and Rimbaud and Delahaye walked amongst them with a sneer of contempt on their faces. The end, however, was near; and the siege of Paris was drawing to its close. It had lasted 135 days and the winter, though late in coming, had been the severest known for many years. The people of Paris were tired of the siege, tired of the *Gouvernement de la Défense Nationale*, and there was already the smell of revolution in the air. The National Guard, which was to be one of the most troublesome elements of the *Commune*, sat about in the taverns drinking heavily. Wine there still was in plenty and it replaced the lack of food, but it did not improve tempers or quiet unrest. On 6 January the first red poster appeared on a wall in Paris. Rumours of an armistice with Germany percolated into the city; there was a riot on 22 January, but this was the last protest against surrender. The armistice was signed on 27 January and the following day the unpopular *Gouvernement de la Défense Nationale* resigned to make way for the National Assembly to be elected at Bordeaux. Then, to the horror and amazement of republican Paris, all the provinces, except for a few of the larger towns, voted solidly extreme right wing and royalist. Thiers and Bismarck now began to discuss the terms of peace, and the preliminaries started at Versailles on 19 February. When the terms became known Paris was disgusted at what it called the treachery of the new government and there were rumours that the capital was going to give trouble. The National Guard refused to give up their arms and there were scuffles in the streets of Paris. The theft of arms from the arsenals became a common occurrence and the theft of old-fashioned weapons from the armouries even commoner. Terrified by the thought of the coming disorder, and longing for escape from the stifling atmosphere of the siege, all the bourgeois families who could afford to do so left Paris to visit relatives in the provinces. It is said that 100,000 people left the capital at that moment, but this loss was counterbalanced by the influx of young hot-heads from the provinces or the men with advanced views who saw in Paris the only chance of resisting the forces of reaction. There swarmed also into the city the hordes of disgusted demobilized soldiers, half-starved and ragged, the rogues and adventurers of every nationality who are always able, like carrion crows, to smell out a sick or dying body. These vultures of every revolution gathered round to see what they could pick up for themselves in the general confusion, to see what they could find, of profit or adventure, in the agony of their unfortunate country. There flocked into Paris, Irishmen, Italians, Poles and Arabs, all on the pretext of helping France to retain her liberty, but all adding to the general confusion and to her ultimate suffering and loss.

The National Guard now began to give trouble and to organize the revolt. On 29 January they attempted to set up a military dictatorship at the Hôtel de Ville, but the authorities discovered the plot through their spies, and the leaders were arrested and condemned to imprisonment. Nevertheless, in spite of all efforts the National Guard was becoming more powerful, especially the battalions from the working districts, since the bourgeois battalions were spontaneously disbanding. A committee was formed, the Central Committee of the Federate Battalions of the National

Guard, whose authority soon began to make itself felt in Paris and to baffle the police. From the very start the ideas of the International Socialists had a strong influence on this committee, which took on itself the duty of advising the citizen-electors in such a way that 'the working man, the producer, is equally called upon to represent the nation.'⁴ The committee was to be a kind of soviet which eventually would become all-powerful in the government of the country.

News of the activities of the National Guard reached the provinces and it was then that Rimbaud decided to go once more to Paris, this time to help in his country's fight for liberty. He had been, the previous year when at Douai, a member of the National Guard and he probably now hoped to be taken on immediately as a Guard in Paris. His desire to leave Charleville was increased by the fact that, the school having reopened, his mother was expecting him to resume his studies. On 15 February classes began again in a disused theatre which the authorities had rented since the hospital had not yet vacated the college building. Two of the three Musketeers, Delahaye and Lebarrière, anxious about their future careers, returned dutifully and obediently to school, and Madame Rimbaud expected her son to do likewise. But he was scornful of the action of his friends, declaring categorically that he would not return to school, that there were other and more important things to do at this crisis in the affairs of France, and that in any case he felt no aptitude for the stage. This was a reference to the building in which the school was now functioning.⁵ He sold his watch and on 25 February he left for Paris. The money thus obtained was sufficient only to pay his railway fare and he arrived in the capital penniless. He had somewhere got hold of the name and address of André Gill, the famous caricaturist, and with his habitual coolness, due to a complete lack of knowledge and experience of worldly matters, he arrived unknown and unannounced at the artist's studio. Gill was not then at home but the door of his room was, as always, unlocked. Rimbaud entered and, being tired after his journey, he lay down on the divan and was soon fast asleep. It was thus that Gill found him on returning later. When he pushed open his door, he stopped on the threshold and looked with amazement at the huddled, untidy figure asleep on his couch. His first thought was that it must be a burglar—yet why should any thief enter a poor artist's unlocked studio—then looking again he saw that it was only a child. He shook the sleeping boy to awaken him and said, 'Who are you and what are you doing here?' Rimbaud sat up bewildered at having been suddenly roused and answered, rubbing his eyes, that he was Arthur Rimbaud from Charleville, a poet who had come to Paris to make his living. Gill was touched by his extreme youth and his appearance of a lost child. He was kind-hearted and he gave him ten francs, all the money he had in his possession that day, but told him that there was nothing in Paris for a poet during these troubled times and advised him to go home to his mother. Rimbaud[6] pocketed the ten francs but he did not return to Charleville, he wandered about Paris in search of work, looking for someone to help and advise him on how to live and how to come to his country's aid. He tried to get into touch with the revolutionary leader Vermersch, who was at that time living in Baudelaire's old flat in the Ile-Saint-Louis and trying to emulate his poetry, but evidently he did not manage to meet him.[7] In the letter he wrote on his return to Charleville he does not mention having come into contact with anyone of importance, or having done anything significant; he talks only of the new and exciting books he saw in the bookstalls; it is a long list he gives, but he seems only to have been able to read one, through lack of funds to purchase them, *Le Fer Rouge ou Les Nouveaux Châtiments* of Glatigny. For a fortnight he remained in Paris and we do not know how he filled his time, except that he endured great poverty and hardship. It seems that he knocked about the streets of the city with no one to help him. It was a bad time to be in Paris, all those who had money had left and there was no food to spare. Rimbaud ate the scraps of food that he picked up at night out of the dustbins, the crusts of bread that he found in the streets, or he begged from those who went by. At night since he had no fixed abode, he slept under bridges, in the doorways of houses, in the barges moored along the banks of the river. Later he wrote in *Une Saison en Enfer*,

Ah! les haillons pourris, le pain trempé de pluie, l'ivresse, les mille amours qui m'ont crucifié! . . . Je me revois, la peau rongée par la boue et la peste, des vers pleins les cheveux et les aisselles et encore de plus gros vers dans le cœur, étendu parmi les inconnus sans âge, sans sentiment. J'aurais pu y mourir. . . . L'affreuse évocation! J'exècre la misère.[8]

He was in Paris when the peace preliminaries were drawn up on 26 February, when Thiers was forced by Bismarck into a position in which a clash with Paris was inevitable. The terms were more severe than Thiers had anticipated. The cession of Alsace-Lorraine and the indemnity of five milliards were bad enough but the insistence on the occupation of Paris by the Prussian troops was considered the final insult not to be forgiven. The Central Committee of the National Guard published in the leading papers on 25 February a resolution carried at their meeting the day before. 'At the first sign of the Prussian entry into Paris, every Guard pledges himself to assemble at once in arms at the usual rallying place and to march thence against the enemy invader.'[9]

On the 26th, while Thiers was signing the treaty at Versailles, 40,000 men and women marched at midnight up the Champs-Elysées. But it was only a false alarm which led to nothing. The Bureau of the Central Committee, however, was influenced by the wiser councils of the International and the Syndicates. It advised against resistance, which would simply be to invite the sacking of the town by foreign soldiers. The Prussians, they pointed out, would, if attacked, merely do the work of French reactionaries by 'drowning the claims of social reform in a sea of blood.'[10] In spite of continued enthusiasm, the Bureau had enforced its decision on the Central Committee as a whole, and on the 28th it, together with the International and the Syndicates, published a black-bordered poster forbidding the resistance and ordering instead a complete boycott of the invaders. So great was its authority that when the Prussians entered Paris, on 1 March, and rode down the Champs-Elysées, they were assailed only by the gibes of guttersnipes. A silent and mournful crowd glowered at them. Not a shop or a café was open; no one spoke to them. They were isolated as if they had been lepers. And when they departed, on 3 March, a great bonfire was kindled at the Arc de Triomphe to purify the soil fouled by the invader's tread.

The Central Committee was now a definitely revolutionary federalist organization completely controlling the city.[11] It was then that Thiers planned to disarm the National Guard in Paris and this was the beginning of the trouble that broke out in the *Commune*. The National Guard was preparing Paris to resist the tyranny of the new government. Things were beginning to look exciting in the capital and then, for some unexplained reason, Rimbaud departed and returned to Charleville. It is impossible to understand what it was that persuaded him to leave the capital just then when the fight, which he had come to see and to help, was reaching its critical stage. It is said by some critics that he returned to Paris later during the *Commune*, but it is difficult to see how this can be true. The elections took place on 26 March and the *Commune* was installed in the Hôtel de Ville on the 28th. There then existed in France two governments, the Bordeaux elected government, now sitting at Versailles, and the *Commune* in Paris. The second siege of Paris, that by the Versailles, began on 2 April. We know from a letter[12] that Rimbaud was at Charleville, at all events, from 10 March until 17 April, and after 13 May. It is naturally possible for him to have visited the capital between 17 April and 13 May; it would have been difficult to enter Paris after the siege had begun, but not totally impossible. Delahaye states categorically that Rimbaud visited Paris during the Commune, that he went there in April, joined the insurgent army and remained there until the town was taken by the Versaillais.[13] The last part of this statement is manifestly incorrect since the Versaillais entered Paris only on 22 May and Rimbaud was already back in Charleville on 13 May. Delahaye might possibly be mistaken only in the dates, although correct in the fact itself. It is, however, also possible that he may have confused Rimbaud's visit during the troubled time before the *Commune* with a visit during the *Commune* itself, for he wrote his book half a century after the events related. Rimbaud mentions nowhere a visit to Paris during the *Commune* although in a letter he talks of the earlier one. And, moreover, in a letter to Izambard of 13 May he writes, 'This is what keeps me back when wild rage urges me on towards the battle in Paris where so many workers are now dying, at the very moment that I am writing to you.' He was referring to his new literary theories and the words do not read as if they had been written by someone who had just returned, as it is alleged Rimbaud returned, in a state of complete disillusionment with the rebellion.[14] In the following letter he writes: 'If you do not answer you will be hateful, for in a week perhaps I shall be in Paris.'[15] Neither do these words seem to have been written by a young man who has come back, less than a week before, disgusted with the *Commune*.

If Rimbaud was indeed in Paris for the *Commune* the events must have made little impression on him, and he can, in any case, have spent little more than a week in the capital. The extreme dates for his visit are from 17 April until 13 May, and six days would have to be allowed, each way, for the journey on foot to and from Paris. It is not very likely that he started on 17 April, the very day he wrote to Démeny, and it is even less likely that he would write his first *Lettre du Voyant* the very day of his return from Paris, in a state of extreme exhaustion and disillusionment. It would seem, moreover, impossible that fighting in the insurgent ranks, he would have had the peace of mind required to elaborate the complicated literary doctrine which we find, enunciated in the letters of 13 and 15 May.

Delahaye always said, and others have repeated it after him, though the grounds for holding the opinion have never been stated, that *Cœur Supplicié* which Rimbaud enclosed in his letter to Izambard on 13 May, was written after he returned from the *Commune* and that it is the account of the treatment to which he had been subjected at the barracks of the Rue de Babylone, when he is said to have been assaulted by the soldiers. There is, however, nothing in the poem to preclude its referring to his earlier visit, at the end of February. At that time he wandered about the city, in the direst poverty, picking up a night's shelter wherever he could find it, and he may have spent some nights in barracks with the soldiers, or the National Guard. What is certain is that the poem is the outcome of some very bitter and painful experience which left an indelible mark on him, and whether this experience took place in March or in May, before or during the *Commune*, is really immaterial. It may be believed that it was this incident which made him return to Charleville, at the beginning of March, when everything in Paris was calculated to keep him. It is probable that some startling experience shocked and terrified him, driving him home for refuge. All through his life, much as he disliked home. Rimbaud always returned there for shelter, when conditions outside became more than he could endure. One realizes immediately that a world of experience separates *Cœur Supplicié* from all his earlier work. It is the first poem that expresses profound feeling, a deep wound in his nature, a crack small as yet running through his whole fibre, which will gradually widen until the complete break will be seen in *Une Saison en Enfer*.

Up to now Rimbaud had remained, in spite of his intellectual maturity, a child in experience, who had been carefully sheltered from the ugly side of life. It is true that like all imaginative children he had thought much about love and passion, but only in a literary manner. It is quite obvious from the poems he had written before April 1871 that he had as yet had no sexual experience and singularly little sexual curiosity; even his imagination had remained innocent and child-like. The only person ever to have stirred his emotions was Izambard and his affection for his master was shy, unexpressed and probably not fully realized by himself. At sixteen, when he went to Paris, he still looked like a girl, with his small stature, his fresh complexion and his reddish-gold wavy hair. It is probable that he then received his first initiation into sex and in so brutal and unexpected a manner that he was startled and outraged, and that his whole nature recoiled from it with fascinated disgust. But though this experience brought him shock and revulsion so great that he fled from Paris to hide his wound at home, there was more in it than mere recoil. It was not solely an unpleasant experience which had disgusted him and against which he could stiffen himself; it was one that did not leave him indifferent, nor his senses untouched. It was a sudden and blinding revelation of what sex really was, of what it could do to him, and it showed him how false had been all his imagined emotions. He returned to Charleville a changed being, shattered and enlightened by the experience through which he had gone, and he was never the same again.

This experience was probably the most significant event in Rimbaud's early life, and had he been personally psycho-analysed —not merely his work—psychologists would have seen in it the turning point of his development, and would have traced to it the source of much of his later maladjustment and distress. It is only after this experience that we find in him a disgust of life, an inability to accept it as it is, coupled with a desire to escape from reality—either into the past of his childhood, when he had been innocent and pure; or into the beyond where there was neither vice nor sin; or else into a world of his own creating, where there was nothing but beauty. He was fully conscious, himself, of the great change that had taken place in him, and that his earlier poems were false, based as they were on derivative experience. In a letter to Démeny which accompanies a second version of *Cœur Supplicié, Cœur de Pitre*, he wrote:[16] 'You must burn, for I wish it and I think that you will respect my wish as that of a dead man, burn all the poems which I was foolish enough to give you on my visits to Douai!'

*Cœur Supplicié* is the outcome of Rimbaud's experience and this first title expresses the sense of the poem more truly than does the name he ultimately gave it, *Cœur Volé*. It was the first version he sent to Izambard with the words: 'Ca ne veut pas rien dire! This does *not* mean nothing!'[17] These words indicate that the poem meant much to him and he was afraid that his master might not take it seriously. Earlier in the same letter he said: 'I implore you not to score it too much with your pencil or with your mind.'

*Cœur Supplicié**

Mon triste cœur bave à la poupe . . .
Mon cœur couvert de caporal.†
Ils y lancent des jets de soupe.
Mon triste cœur bave à la poupe . . .

* Certain variants of the first version are here kept.    † Caporal = shag.

Sous les quolibets de la troupe
Qui lance un rire général,
Mon triste cœur bave à la poupe,
Mon cœur couvert de caporal.

Ithyphalliques★ et pioupiesques†
Leurs insultes l'ont dépravé;
A la vesprée ils font des fresques
Ithyphalliques et pioupiesques
O flots abracadabrantesques,‡
Prenez mon cœur qu'il soit lavé;
Ithyphalliques et pioupiesques
Leurs insultes l'ont dépravé!

Quand ils auront tari leurs chiques,§
Comment agir ô cœur volé?
Ce seront des refrains bachiques
Quand ils auront tari leurs chiques;
J'aurai des sursauts stomachiques
Si mon triste cœur est ravalé!
Quand ils auront tari leurs chiques,
Comment agir, ô cœur volé?

Izambard did not, however, realize what had been happening
to his pupil; he did not understand the poem, nor how much it
had meant to him. He thought it was, merely, as he said, a hoax
in the worst of taste, and he considered the verses disgusting. He
did not wish to take up the disapproving school-teacher attitude,
but determined, nevertheless, to give his pupil a lesson in a practical manner. In acting thus he saw himself as being very broad-
minded and tolerant, very much one of the boys themselves. He
answered with a parody of Rimbaud's poem, not without skill
and cleverness, but showing complete insensitiveness to what
his pupil was suffering at the moment, and a total lack of comprehension of the poem.[18] 'You see,' he wrote in the letter which
accompanied his effort, obviously very proud of his achievement,[19]
'to be absurd is within the scope of everyone.'

★ Ithyphallus = phallus in erection.　　† Pioupiou = common soldier.
‡ Abracadabra = a cabalistic word supposed to cure certain ills.
§ Chique = quid of tobacco.

It is probable that Rimbaud was bitterly hurt at the lack of understanding on the part of the friend in whom he had always trusted and who had never failed, hitherto, to give him sympathy. Now, at this extreme crisis of his life, he only gave him gibes and mockery. What is certain is that after this Rimbaud shut himself away from Izambard and made him no more confidences. There is only one further letter to his former friend, a cool and practical letter with no evidence of warmth or affection, no sign of intimacy and trust. Later it was to Démeny, and not to Izambard, that he wrote for help and advice when he was planning a subsequent visit to Paris, when he wished to go no longer as a beggar, but with prospects of finding employment that would permit him to live. In the last letter he wrote to Izambard he made no mention of the large batch of poems which he had just completed. The close friendship which had been the deepest emotion of Rimbaud's boyhood was now at an end.

CHAPTER VI

LE VOYOU

RIMBAUD returned home on 10 March in a state of psychological turmoil and distress and this manifested itself outwardly in the unruliness of his behaviour. Never had he been more impossible to deal with, never more argumentative or insolent in his manner. He was determined to do all he could to scandalize everyone and to bring his family's name into disrepute. He refused to wash any more and he allowed his hair to grow until it hung in dirty, untidy ringlets over his shoulders; he used to wander up and down the chief streets of Charleville in the most crowded hour of the evening, the time of the 'apéritif,' in his dirty clothes, with his unkempt hair, his hands in his pockets, smoking a short pipe and, what was considered most outrageous of all, smoking it with its funnel pointing downwards. One day a wit, thinking to shame him, handed him threepence and told him to go and have his hair cut. Rimbaud, however, bowing with mock gratitude, accepted the coins and went, beneath the nose of the donor, into the nearest tobacconist to buy some more shag. Next, when the *Commune* started, he walked up and down in front of the chief shops of the town, crying to their owners: 'Beware! Your hour is at hand! Order is vanquished!'

The following month, on 12 April, the Collège de Charleville finally opened its doors in its own building.[1] Madame Rimbaud begged her son to return to his studies with his friends, since life was becoming normal in the provinces, and again he refused to have anything more to do with scholastic learning. He managed, however, to obtain some menial post on a local newspaper, *Le Progrès des Ardennes*,[2] and with this he was able, for a time, to appease the wrath of *La Bouche d'Ombre*—his disrespectful name for his mother, after the ponderous metaphysical poem by Victor Hugo, on account of the weighty and religious nature of her frequent utterances. The paper was, however, suspended five days after his appointment, and he was once more without employment.

While the other boys were at their lessons he used to loiter, in his filthy clothes, his battered hat sitting perched on the top of his thick long hair, and his pipe in his mouth, in front of the open windows of the school, looking in, with a sneer of contempt on his face, at the scholars bending over their books. He used to dawdle as long as he could, on his way to the library next door.[3] His daily presence was a constant source of annoyance to both masters and pupils and the Principal considered that he was being a pernicious influence on the boys and giving the school a bad name, but there was nothing that anyone could do for he was transgressing no law. The authorities, moreover, thought with regret of all the prizes which Rimbaud had carried off the previous summer and how, this year, there was no other scholar to win similar laurels for the college. They sighed as they recalled the hopes that they had once built on young Arthur Rimbaud.

Rimbaud was, however, enjoying at the time a spurious popularity and he had many acquaintances who were only too ready to encourage him in his unruliness. He hung about the cafés for the larger part of the day, waiting to find someone kind enough to offer him a drink or a fill of tobacco, and he paid for these with the biting irony and ready wit which he had latterly developed and which his hearers always found entertaining. When it was a question of being cynical or obscene he was able to forget his paralysing diffidence and shyness; he was tongue-tied only when he talked of what really moved him. The provincial café-loungers enjoyed hearing his blasphemous utterances against Church and priests; they appreciated particularly the contrast between the obscenity of his language and the childishness and innocence of his face. They were always prepared to pay for his drinks for they knew that he was in better form and more unguarded in his speech when he was oiled with a pint of beer or a glass of brandy. Writing to Izambard he boasted: 'I am cynically living on others and digging up any old fool of a school friend that I can find. Everything dirty and ugly that I can think of, in words and actions, I dish it up for them and they pay me "en bocks et en filles".' Most critics have misunderstood these last words and have interpreted them as meaning that Rimbaud was now consorting with prostitutes. The word *fille* does not, however, only mean *prostitute*, it is also a measure of brandy.[4] It is far more probable that he was paid by his friends for his lewd stories, as they all sat together in a café, with drinks than with money for prostitution.

Rimbaud was now trying to break away from all restrictions, mental, physical and moral and he used to claim to have no principles. Louis Pierquin, who had been at school with him, relates how, one evening at the Café Dutherme, Rimbaud made a violent attack against those whom he called 'les gêneurs' in life, those who stood in the way of others more able and less scrupulous than they. 'One must clear away all that rubbish,' he cried fiercely, 'at whatever cost! I would not hesitate, myself, to resort to murder and I would take the acutest delight in watching the agony of my victims.'

Fot a quarter of an hour he did not cease fulminating against the greater part of the human race who, he asserted, ought to be exterminated by slow torture and he spoke with every appearance of the deepest conviction.

This was Rimbaud's most violent and scatological period and his conversation and his poems show the obscene visions in which he wallowed. Delahaye relates[5] that he would invent lewd stories about himself, attributing to himself monstrous and repulsive actions and he used then to be overjoyed when people sitting near him in a café would get up and leave the table. There was a story he particularly enjoyed telling and each time he told it with added details, how he delighted in enticing bitches to his home whom he found wandering without their owners in the streets, and of his practices with them.

Yet all this only tends to prove his pitiable state of inner turmoil; all this violence and obscenity seemed to have its roots in the utter desolation within him, in a deep-seated wound. It was as if the shock he had just received in Paris had opened up an abscess that had been forming for many months, as if this shock had suddenly brought him face to face with himself for the first time. For almost a year now, ever since he left school the previous summer at the age of fifteen, he had been living under acute nervous strain. He had seen the crash of the Empire and war at home; his native town had been bombarded and he had gone in fear for the safety of one of his closest friends; he had lost the company of the only person in whom he had perfect confidence and trust. All stability had departed from his life, all discipline had been relaxed; he had run away from home, had lived in Paris in the most abject poverty and he had encountered the most searing experience of his life. All this was sufficient to upset the equilibrium of a more strongly balanced youth than Rimbaud.

The core of his being was purity and innocence with a yearning for absolute perfection; his sensitiveness was now wounded by the ugliness he had encountered and he revolted against it. Suddenly he felt that he could not endure life any longer, the inherent conditions of it seemed to him insufferable and he hit out against them. He never recovered from this shock and his difficulty remained henceforth his inability to accept life as it was. Life for ever afterwards seemed to him an outrage. The only relief he found in his utter desolation, lost in the midst of all these human beings whom he loathed and despised, was the relief of complete

86

disgust. Since he was unable with his reason to justify his revolt, his unconscious refusal of life, he took his own kind of revenge in wallowing, as it were, to the shame of all those who knew him in the filthiest part of the road. His abandonment of personal cleanliness was only a further symptom of his unhappy state of mind. The poem he wrote at this time, *Les Sœurs de Charité*, expresses vividly his distress.

> Le jeune homme dont l'œil est brillant, la peau brune,
> Le beau corps de vingt ans qui devrait aller nu
> Et qu'eût, le front cerclé de cuivre, sous la lune,
> Adoré, dans la Perse, un Génie inconnu,
>
> Impétueux avec des douceurs virginales
> Et noires, fier de ses premiers entêtements,
> Pareil aux jeunes mers, pleurs de nuits estivales
> Qui se retournent sur des lits de diamants;
>
> Le jeune homme, devant les laideurs de ce monde,
> Tressaille dans son cœur, largement irrité,
> Et, plein d'une blessure éternelle et profonde,
> Se prend à désirer sa sœur de charité.

But nothing can bring him comfort and peace, neither women nor love, nor yet study, nor even the beauties of nature. Literature and justice and all other powers are of no avail; all that he can hope is the final and terrible embrace of death.

> Qu'il croie aux vastes fins, Rêves ou Promenades
> Immenses, à travers les nuits de Vérité,
> Et t'appelle en son âme et ses membres malades,
> O Mort mystérieuse, ô sœur de charité. [6]

In the most brutal manner and without previous preparation, Rimbaud had been faced with the problem of sex and he had been shocked, stunned and obsessed by it. Hitherto he had only thought about love; it was an emotion that flowed and emanated from him, but did not yet need a vessel to receive it. There is great innocence in his early love poetry. He imagined that his love would ultimately be directed towards some woman, like those

of whom he read in the poets he admired—Banville or Leconte
de Lisle—a woman with the sexlessness of a Greek statue. But no
girl had ever looked at him or taken him seriously. He was too
shy, and looked too much of a child, with his rosy cheeks, his
curly hair, and his cracked, uncertain voice of an adolescent. But
now his senses were awakened and his body left curious and
hungry for satisfaction. He made one pathetic effort to gain
experience, but he set about it clumsily and failed. Pierquin
relates,[7] that in May 1871, Rimbaud wrote to him to describe
an assignation he had made with a girl older than himself, the
daughter of a magistrate. He had asked her to meet him in the
square at Charleville, but she did not come alone; she was accompanied by her maid, and he said that he had remained as dumb and
as terrified as 'seventy-six thousand new-born puppies'. The girl
had been cruel and heartless; she had made fun of him, of his
childish appearance, his shyness and his shabby clothes.

There is another girl mentioned but we do not even know her
name, and the evidence of her existence is of the flimsiest. Delahaye relates that Rimbaud went to Paris in February 1871 accompanied by this young girl, and that it is of her that he wrote in
Sonnet des Voyelles. If indeed this girl did exist and went to Paris
with him, their relationship must have remained purely platonic
for, on their arrival in the capital, she is said to have left him and
to have returned home.

Pierquin further relates how, one evening, as he sat with Rimbaud in the Café Dutherme at Charleville, he said to him, to make
conversation, 'Well! and how are your love-affairs progressing?
Have you heard from the girl?' He said that Rimbaud suddenly
looked at him, with a look of great sadness and suffering, and
answered: 'Do please shut up!' Then he laid his head down on
his arms on the table and wept. At nine o'clock he got up and
said, 'Come, let's go!' At the edge of the forest, about a mile
from the town, he shook his friend's hand and, without saying
another word, went off alone through the woods. He was four
or five days without seeing Pierquin again. Pierquin thought that
Rimbaud was still thinking of the girl from the Paris episode,
but it may well have been the other. Rimbaud's pride was always

like an open wound, he had no armour against humiliation, and now, embittered by his experience with a woman, he turned against the whole sex with disgust, and vowed that he despised them all. 'Oh! mes petites amoureuses, que je vous hais!' he wrote in a poem.[8] Most of his poems at this time express a disgusted obsession with women, a morbid horror of all that is woman.

All that is a woman's physical life seemed an insult and an outrage to man. In *Les Sœurs de Charité* he wrote:[9]

> Mais, ô Femme, monceau d'entrailles, pitié douce,
> Tu n'es jamais la *Sœur* de charité, jamais,
> Ni regard noir, ni ventre où dort une ombre rousse,
> Ni doigts légers, ni seins splendidement formés.
>
> Aveugle irréveillée aux immenses prunelles,
> Tout notre embrassement n'est qu'une question:
> C'est toi qui pends à nous, porteuse de mamelles,
> Nous te berçons, charmante et grave Passion.
>
> Tes haines, tes torpeurs fixes, tes défaillances,
> Et les brutalités souffertes autrefois,
> Tu nous rends tout, ô Nuit pourtant sans malveillances,
> Comme un excès de sang épanché tous les mois.

Had he here been able to find natural experience, his later life may well have been vastly different. With the conviction of his permanent failure with women—later he wrote 'l'orgie et la camaraderie des femmes m'étaient interdites'[10]—his thoughts may have turned to other forms of love and to the obsession of his Paris experience. Now we can find expressed in his writings, for the first time, the problem of sin, the struggle between the angel and the devil, which is so striking a characteristic of his mature work, a strife he was never able to resolve in himself. There is the clash between desire and his early principles, between his longing for complete independence and expression and the restrictions of external discipline and conventional morality. Rimbaud was not yet able to go his own way and merely ignore the forces that were trying to oppress him; he felt that he must

first break them. And since the Church was the greatest obstacle
to his desire to be a law unto himself, to make his own morality,
it was the Church that he most violently attacked, the Church
that keeps its flocks in ignorance in order to keep it permanently
in subjection.

> L'enfant se doit surtout à la maison, famille
> Des soins naïfs, des bons travaux abrutissants.[11]

He had read in Proudhon, 'Dieu c'est le mal!' and this phrase
echoed and re-echoed through his fevered brain at this critical
moment of his intellectual development. This was the time, when
he used to scribble on the seats in the park at Charleville, 'Merde
à Dieu!' Later he imagined, in his great arrogance and pride,
that he himself would be able to cut down the tree of good and
evil, to atrophy its roots and thus wipe out the conflict which has
existed, since the coming of Christianity. But at the moment, he
was only lost and his state of revolt mingled with uncertainty,
his struggles with himself, are well expressed in the poem *Les
Premières Communions*. It is also clear from this poem how much
in his revolt is due to sexual causes. The distress of adolescence, of
youth, has rarely been better rendered. This poem has usually
been regarded as Rimbaud's most revolting piece of blasphemy,
but it is perhaps the finest and most powerful poem of this period.
It describes the state of mind of a little girl on the eve of her
First Communion and the way in which chaste, religious thoughts
mingle, in her imagination, with unchaste preoccupations, how
her awakening sexual desire finds an outlet in her love for Christ
her Saviour.

> Des curiosités vaguement impudiques
> Épouvantent le rêve aux chastes bleuités,
> Qui s'est surpris autour des célestes tuniques,
> Du linge dont Jésus voile ses nudités.
>
> Elle veut, elle veut, pourtant, l'âme en détresse,
> Le front dans l'oreiller creusé par les cris sourds,
> Prolonger les éclairs suprêmes de tendresse,
> Et bave . . .—L'ombre emplit les maisons et les cours.

Et l'enfant ne peut plus. Elle s'agite, cambre
Les reins et d'une main ouvre le rideau bleu
Pour amener un peu de fraîcheur de la chambre
Sous le drap, vers son ventre et sa poitrine en feu.

A son réveil,—minuit—la fenêtre était blanche
Devant le sommeil bleu des rideaux illunés;
La vision la prit des candeurs du dimanche
Elle avait rêvé rouge. Elle saigna du nez.

Then, not being able to sleep again, she went down into the yard
outside, where the air was fresh and the stars were shining brightly
in the dark sky.

Elle passa sa nuit sainte dans des latrines,
Vers la chandelle, aux trous du toit coulait l'air blanc,
Et quelque vigne folle aux noirceurs purpurines,
En deça d'une cour voisine, s'écroulant,

La lucarne faisait un cœur de lueur vive
Dans la cour où les cieux bas plaquaient d'ors vermeils
Les vitres; les pavés puant l'eau de lessive
Soufraient l'ombre des murs bondés de noirs sommeils.

Rimbaud next imagines that she is old, looking back on the night
before her First Communion and he makes her then cry:

J'étais bien jeune, et Christ a souillé mes haleines;
Il me bonda jusqu'à la gorge de dégoûts!
Tu baisais mes cheveux profonds comme les laines,
Et je me laissais faire . . . ah! va, c'est bon pour vous,

Hommes! qui songez peu que la plus amoureuse
Est, sous sa conscience aux ignobles terreurs,
La plus prostituée et la plus douloureuse
Et que tous nos élans vers vous sont des erreurs!

Car ma Communion première est bien passée.
Tes baisers, je ne puis jamais les avoir sus:
Et mon cœur et ma chair par ta chair embrassée
Fourmillent du baiser putride de Jésus.

91

And the poem ends with the revolt of the poet against Christ who has permitted all this deception and useless suffering.

> Christ! ô Christ, éternel voleur des énergies,
> Dieu qui pour deux mille ans vouas à ta pâleur,
> Cloués au sol, de honte et de céphalalgies,
> Ou renversés, les fronts des femmes de douleur.

Now, at this time, he missed the sympathetic friendship of Izambard which he had enjoyed the previous year, for his solitude and loneliness were more than he could bear. Izambard's place at the school had been taken by a refugee from Lorraine, called Edouard Chanal. He was a big man with a shaggy fair beard and kindly blue eyes and his face expressed the serenity that comes from extreme simplicity of nature. He had a great love of literature and thought that the pursuit of beauty purified man's lower instincts and strengthened his will. His taste was sure, but not conventional and hide-bound, and his methods of teaching were, for his age, enlightened. He did not, as did all his colleagues, make his pupils study a text or comment on it. His aim was to inculcate in them a love of literature and of beauty, and so he read to them, in his beautifully modulated voice, his favourite fifteenth- and sixteenth-century poets which were not prescribed for the examinations. There was much in Chanal that would have appealed to Rimbaud who admired simplicity and directness above all other qualities, and the pity was that they did not meet when the boy was so much in need of a friend whom he could both admire and trust. Delahaye was for ever singing the praises of the new master, little realizing that he was rousing his friend's envy and regret. Then, one day, Rimbaud, as he was walking in Le Petit Bois, suddenly came on Chanal sitting alone on a seat and he was much tempted to accost him. He thought that the master might be able to help him in his perplexity and distress of mind. But when he tried to speak he felt his tongue cleave to the roof of his mouth and his usual shyness overcame him; he walked backwards and forwards in front of the seat where Chanal sat, trying to screw up his courage, but he did not dare address him. Perhaps if Chanal had looked up at him boldness might have come to him, but the master was occupied with his own thoughts and went on smoking his pipe, looking into the far distance, unaware of the shy youth standing before him. Then Rimbaud, discouraged, abandoned the effort and walked away without saying a word.[13]

Yet Rimbaud, at this time, was not totally idle. He spent long hours in the public library reading philosophy, magic and occult literature. He was gradually evolving his theory of poetry and of the function of the poet. He was also reading all the subversive literature he could discover, all the satanic literature he could lay hands on, all works conventionally held to be immoral. It was then that he began to discover the writings of Baudelaire. At first it was the realism of Baudelaire that attracted him, his anticlericalism and what he imagined was his love of satanism. It is said that the librarian at the public library did not approve of the nature of his reading, deeming it unsuitable for a boy of sixteen, and refused to allow some of the books to be delivered to him. It was to satirize him that Rimbaud wrote the mordant and bitterly ironical poem, *Les Assis*, one of his most original poems, in imagery and vocabulary, which is unique in French literature.

The literary period which runs from Rimbaud's return from Paris in the middle of March 1871 until the autumn of the same year, was one of great activity. In the earlier months he composed the large batch of obscene and violent poems which were engendered by the perturbed state of mind in which he came back from Paris. In April and May we have *Les Assis*, *Cœur Supplicié*, *Paris se Repeuple*, *Chant de Guerre Parisien*, *Mes Petites Amoureuses*, *Les Accroupissements*, *Les Poètes de Sept Ans*, and *Oraison du Soir*. In June he wrote *Les Pauvres à l'Eglise* and *Les Sœurs de Charité*, in July, *Les Premières Communions* and *Ce qu'on dit au Poète à propos de Fleurs*, and in September *Le Bateau Ivre*. It is probable that to this period belongs *Un Cœur sous une Soutane*, though it is not absolutely certain that it is by Rimbaud, but in style and in conception it is similar to the poems written at this time. If indeed it is from his pen, which is very probable, it must have been written during this period. It sets forth a state of distress similar to that expressed later in *Les Déserts de l'Amour*.

It is interesting to notice in the poems of this literary period the change that has come over the realism of Rimbaud since the days, not so very far distant, when he wrote *Les Etrennes des Orphelins* and even later *Les Effarés*. Then it was the sentimental realism of Coppée that he practised, now he favours the stark and brutal realism of Baudelaire. *Les Pauvres à l'Eglise* is a picture that Baudelaire might have painted. It describes the poor parked in church, like cattle in their wooden pens, their breath steaming into the cold air. Happy and humble, like beaten dogs, they are glad to escape for a moment from the cold outside, glad to sit there heavily, thinking nothing; the women are glad to escape from their drunken husbands and to rest after the six days of toil which God has imposed on them as a penance for a sin committed by others in the dawn of time. There they sit with unseeing eyes, not uttering even a prayer.

> Dehors, le froid, la faim, et puis l'homme en ribote.
> C'est bon. Encore une heure; après, les maux sans nom.

And the poem ends on a note that recalls *Le Reniement de Saint-Pierre* of Baudelaire.

> Et tous, bavant la foi mendiante et stupide,
> Récitent la complainte infinie à Jésus
> Qui rêve en haut, jauni par le vitrail livide,
> Loin des maigres mauvais et des méchants pansus,
>
> Loin des senteurs de viande et d'étoffes moisies,
> Farce prostrée et sombre aux gestes repoussants;
> —Et l'oraison fleurit d'expressions choisies,
> Et les mysticités prennent des tons pressants.
>
> Quand, des nefs où périt le soleil, plis de soie
> Banals, sourires verts, les Dames des quartiers
> Distingués,—ô Jésus!—les malades du foie
> Font baiser leurs longs doigts jaunes aux bénitiers.

*Paris se repeuple*, a description of the riff-raff that Rimbaud saw streaming into Paris when the siege by the Germans was raised, although it may owe something to *Le Sacre de Paris* of Leconte de

Lisle, owes more to Baudelaire's description of Paris as a prostitute whom, in spite of her vice and her weakness, he cannot fail to love.

The poems of this period prove that Rimbaud has finally emancipated himself from the influence of the *Parnasse* which hitherto has been the strongest inspiration of his poetry.

While he was pouring out in these poems his accumulated bitterness, a vital change was taking place within him and he was maturing his *Théorie du Voyant*. Although this doctrine was roughly set forth in the letters of 13 May and 15 May, before some of the poems described above were finished, he did not in them put into practice his new theory of poetry.[14] Poetry, according to his doctrine, was to be more than mere iconoclasm, more than the mere destruction of accepted values; it had its positive beliefs, its spiritual function. These poems were the result of the state of mind and spirit which made it necessary for him to find new values; they were the outcome of his spiritual irritation, the final clearing away of the abscess and the draining of the pus. They were the work of preparation, the breaking down of all the old barriers of decency, of discipline, of conventional morality, so that the new work could rise on new foundations. Everything had to go before the new theory could work and then, when all the past had been cleared away, Rimbaud wrote no more obscene or blasphemous poetry. Poetry was then the means of exploring the infinite; it was spiritual and mystical.

## CHAPTER VII

## LE VOYANT

WHILE the superficial regions of Rimbaud's mind were occupied with blasphemy and obscenity, while his outward life was as depraved as his humble circumstances permitted, in the core of his being he was looking for some escape from the world that revolted him, he was searching for an ideal in which to lose himself and which would make him forget the reality whose conditions he was incapable of accepting. He was looking for something that would seize hold of him and lift him out of himself, something that would suddenly illuminate everything and give significance to the squalor with which he was surrounded, something that would even make clear its necessity and extract gold from the mud. Baudelaire had said, addressing Paris as it lay stretched before him, with its hovels and its brothels, its prostitutes and its pimps, with its misery and its vice:

> Car j'ai de chaque chose extrait la quintessence;
> Tu m'as donné ta boue et j'en ai fait de l'or.[1]

Rimbaud could not accept the possibility that the squalor he saw around him and which made his gorge rise with disgust, should be no more than squalor, that it should have no further significance and use. From his earliest infancy he had thirsted after God and had thought that he had found him. Then he had turned against Him, had hated Him because He had become identified for him with authority and tyranny, with the restrictions that hindered his own natural development. He had then delighted to mock the image which he had previously adored and to spit on it, but he had gained no satisfaction from trampling his idol underfoot; his thirst for the absolute remained unquenched. He needed something else, something that would give him back the sensation of absolute truth, absolute perfection and absolute bliss. The cry that had burst from Baudelaire in his agony, 'N'importe où, pourvu que ce soit hors de ce monde,' now echoed in the depths of Rimbaud's desolation. He felt that he must find some means of coming to terms with himself, he must abandon his natural inclinations and desires or else discover some justification for them. He was not satisfied to be a self-indulgent sinner, a sinner through weakness who later lamented his fall from grace. The complete liberty of mind which seemed to him the supreme good, the revolt against accepted facts, against the very conditions of existence, now led him to search for a super-realism. He tried to escape from his daily existence by the discovery of a world whose reality he only dimly perceived, in which he would no longer be bound down by the ordinary appearance of things. Poetry was to be no longer the expression of himself, nor the reflection of the sordid world around him, it was no longer to be an end in itself; it was to be the means of exploring the beyond and a vehicle for penetrating therein. Literature was to be closely allied to a prophetic sense and to mysticism, the most sure means of taking possession of *l'ineffable*. The poet was to become, as it were, a medium, the unconscious instrument of some power speaking through his lips. He was to be able to soar beyond visible reality, to explore the secret reality beyond this world and to reflect it, to become the shadow of the eternal mind. Occupied with these new visions Rimbaud neglected and even seemed to forget politics, or thought it necessary to sacrifice them. This is *l'idée* that kept him at Charleville whilst rage, nevertheless, urged him on towards the battle in Paris where so many workers were dying.[2]

Rimbaud now came under a new and important influence, that of Charles Bretagne, whose acquaintance he made as he knocked about the cafés of Charleville in search of free drinks and free smokes. He was a strange and original character, this Charles Bretagne, a customs official who was at the same time an amateur fiddler and draughtsman of no little skill and, who besides, dabbled in magic and the occult. He was a sturdy and stocky, middle-aged Fleming, with a jovial, loud voice and still louder laughter. This laughter, rumbling up from his capacious chest like a volcano in eruption, made the most innocent remark of his seem fraught with a delightfully witty and pornographic meaning. With his square face and full beard he liked to imagine that he resembled Henry VIII, but in reality he bore a closer resemblance to the good-humoured bourgeois which smile down at us from the Flemish pictures by Ruben and Jordaens. He enjoyed the good things of this life, wine, women, his pipe and literature, and he stinted himself in none of them. He was a strange contrast to the other bourgeois citizens of Charleville and particularly to his fellow *fonctionnaires* who sat in the square on Sundays listening to the band, and whom Rimbaud has satirized in his poem, *A la Musique*. He was notorious and infamous for his blasphemous opinions and for being the fiercest and most voracious 'mangeur de curés'. He was one of the few people at this time who encouraged Rimbaud intelligently, not merely urging him along his career of vice. In his opinion the life of the body was important, but the satisfying of the senses was not to be taken as meaning a neglect of the life of the mind. He treated Rimbaud as an equal, indeed enjoyed his company; he laughed at his cynical jokes and irony, encouraged him in them and made him feel a very daring and intelligent fellow. He fully realized his financial state and with him Rimbaud was always certain of a free drink and a fill of tobacco. In the evenings with Bretagne and similar old cronies, he sat, hour after hour, at the Café Dutherme, drinking beer and laughing heartily at the obscene jokes that were always made if Bretagne happened to be present. This was the kind of life that he had always been told was the primrose path that led to eternal destruction, but now it seemed to him supremely good, to develop his faculties, to enable him to forget his paralysing shyness and to express himself without false shame. He, who had always been tongue-tied in company, could now, after a glass of beer, express himself fluently in speech as he had never expressed himself before and amuse others who were glad of his company. He became known as a wit whose acid irony spared no one. The theory now sprang up in his mind that alleged vice may be, after all, a valuable instrument for breaking up the chains that bind the human spirit to the material world, and Bretagne encouraged him in this belief. In the Middle Ages, says Delahaye, Bretagne would probably have been a demono-logist or an alchemist, and it is very likely that he would have been burnt at the stake as a sorcerer. He believed in magic, in the occult, in telepathy, and he made a study of them. It was he who gave Rimbaud an interest in these subjects and lent him books out of his own library, or borrowed them from others for him. It would be impossible to overestimate the importance of his influence on Rimbaud during this period, and it was with him that Rimbaud spent the larger part of his time, either at the Café Dutherme or else at his flat. He used to play to Rimbaud on his fiddle or else amuse him by showing him his latest caricatures of the Church dignitaries of Charleville; he would listen to his poems, criticize them, praise them or blame them, but his remarks always showed appreciative understanding, albeit his own taste favoured the obscene poems or those that blasphemed against God and the Church. He was to Rimbaud not merely an encouraging elder friend, but a genuine admirer who believed in his ultimate possibilities. And, as he had a large acquaintance amongst literary men, he set to work to get Rimbaud known amongst them.[3] Soon his influence began to supplant entirely that of Izambard. Indeed, the letter which Rimbaud wrote to his former master on 13 May is somewhat ironic and contemptuous in tone; it seems to mock him for having gone back to his teaching so easily, when fighting was still continuing. 'Well! So you are a teacher once more!' he wrote. 'One owes a duty to society, you say. You belong to the teaching body and so you are running along in the right rut.' He could not resist the temptation of trying to shock his master by describing the kind of parasitic life he himself was leading, cadging drinks from others and paying for them in lewd stories. The letter reveals a faint irritation and a desire to wound. 'At bottom you consider only subjective poetry in your theory of art. Your obstinate resolve to return to the scholastic feeding trough—please forgive me—proves that. But you will end in smug self-satisfaction, having achieved nothing because you will not really have wanted to achieve anything. Not to mention that your subjective poetry will always remain hideously mawkish and insipid. One day, I hope, and may others hope the same thing, I shall see objective poetry taken into account in your poetic theory.'

Under the influence of Bretagne Rimbaud now began to read on new lines. It was no longer merely literature that he studied, but occult philosophy, magic and the Cabala, and he devoured these books with the same avidity that he had previously devoted to his other studies. It is not possible to discover precisely what it was that he read, since he himself does not mention the books. We know that he could buy no books since he had not the means to do so, but he borrowed extensively from the public library and from Bretagne, who also procured him books from other sources. It is therefore insufficient to consult the books which exist in the public library at Charleville and to imagine that this is the full extent of his reading.

It has been suggested by a critic, in an ingenious study, that Rimbaud drew the substance of his *Théorie du Voyant* from Indian philosophy and this work sets out to prove that Rimbaud is yet another Eastern philosopher whose doctrine is closely allied to Buddhism.[4] It is true that Rimbaud talks frequently and glibly about the East as being the centre of all wisdom and of the world having lost its soul by moving westwards. There is, however, no evidence in his writings that he knew more about the East than was common property amongst ordinary literary people, more than could have been gleamed from magazine articles. Rimbaud was sixteen at this time, he knew no other languages but French, Latin and some Greek; he had no money to purchase books, he was dependent on a provincial municipal library and on what he could borrow and it is very unlikely that he could have got hold of rare or esoteric books. His attitude to learning was that of his years, that of a student who imagines that he has mastered a subject because he has read about it in secondary authorities, and it is hard to believe that he can have had any knowledge of Indian religious thought except what he could have learnt from French, nineteenth-century literature. On examination his knowledge of Eastern philosophy proves vague, superficial, and no more extensive than the material contained in Lamartine's *Cours Familier de Littérature*, in which a large section is devoted to the literature and philosophy of the East. In any case the East was one of the chief sources of poetic inspiration amongst Parnassian poets. Burnouf's history of Buddhism, the translation of the *Rig Véda*, the *Ramayana*, the *Bhagavata Gita* and *Bhagavata Purana* led the poets to a different conception of reality and made them consider the world as little more than a beautiful dream and an illusion. Rimbaud could have gained some knowledge of Eastern philosophy from a reading of the Parnassian poets who had been his literary masters.

On the other hand the claim of certain critics that he made a profound study of occult and illuminist philosophy would seem to be better-founded. Nevertheless a study of occult and illuminist philosophic texts shows that here also his knowledge was not profound, that it consisted largely in the reading of certain nineteenth-century authors and—as far as his literary doctrine at this stage was concerned—in the partial adoption of their ideas. The beliefs from the occult doctrine which attracted him, and of which he made use, were those he could have picked up from contemporary writers, or else verbally, from Charles Bretagne. Romantic and post-Romantic religious thought, moreover, owes more to occult philosophy than has hitherto been imagined. The occult sources of pre-Romantic literature have been exhaustively investigated by Viatte,[5] but since he stops short at 1820 the work still remains to be completed for the later writers. In *Hugo et les Illuminés de son Temps* he has also studied Victor Hugo from this point of view and Denis Saurat has shown in *La Religion de Victor Hugo* how much that poet's philosophy is based on the Cabala. This method could with advantage be applied to other writers. Even materialistic and realistic Balzac reveals, in works such as *Séraphita* and *Louis Lambert*, to what extent some of the substance of occult philosophy has permeated nineteenth-century writers. Indeed Gérard de Nerval can only be understood with a knowledge of alchemy. Viatte's work proves the prevalence of illuminist doctrine in eighteenth-century France, how it radiated from its chief centres in Bordeaux and Lyons and how this influence continued among the early Romantic writers such as Joseph de Maistre, Ballanche, Senancour and Charles Nodier. There occurred about 1820 a second wave of Swedenborgianism when Moet made the first complete French translation of the Swedish philosopher's works. This subsided but interest was again revived after 1840 by Le Boys des Guay's translation, and it was during this period that Baudelaire came under the influence of his ideas. But there were other illuminists of more popular appeal than Swedenborg. There were Père Enfantin, Pierre Leroux, Hoené Wronski, Esquiros and Eliphas Lévi—to mention some of the best known. It is evident that Rimbaud, in making use of occult theories, did not need to have delved very deeply into philosophy; it was only necessary for him to have read certain writers of his own time.

It is interesting, both for a study of Rimbaud and of the nineteenth century in general, to realize the prevalence of occult theories which were, amongst certain writers, the same common coin that Freudian and Marxian theory is to-day amongst many who have never read a line from these two thinkers. Baudelaire was much interested in the writings of Lavater, Swedenborg and Joseph de Maistre—not to mention minor writers such as Hoené Wronski—and it can be said that his religious and æsthetic views were largely formed by this study.

Thus it can be seen that Rimbaud could, from the reading of Baudelaire alone, have absorbed much occult thought, at all events in its æsthetic application. Indeed it will be seen that the writings of Baudelaire are largely responsible for the substance of *La Théorie du Voyant* as formulated by Rimbaud, and that he intended to continue from where his predecessor had stopped. There is, however, one great difference between the two poets. Baudelaire through everything remained essentially Catholic and he grafted occult theories on to his fundamental and native Catholicism. Whereas Rimbaud wished to return to the days before the advent of Christianity, to the days when the dilemma of right and wrong did not exist. He discovered, however—and that was part of his tragedy—that one is—as he says—a slave of one's baptism; one cannot efface it; one cannot return to the days when there was no consciousness of sin; one cannot extirpate entirely the tree of knowledge, for its roots have spread their ramifications through one's whole being. Baudelaire accepted the doctrine of original sin and used occult philosophy to endeavour to explain the nature of God and Eternity. Rimbaud would accept nothing. In his arrogance and pride he wished to alter everything himself, to make his own way alone into eternity, to force his way into the presence of the Eternal, and not—as Baudelaire thought essential—to win that promotion through long and patient endeavour. To achieve this he was eventually prepared to use magic—which is in fact a form of religion relying on drugs and suggestion rather than on personal effort—to gain the vision of God. Later, as he progressed in his part of *voyant*, he came to rely more and more on the theory and symbolism of magic and alchemy—though, even at this time, it is doubtful whether he ever had recourse to obscure works. It is very unlikely that he read all the books—in Latin and in French—which Godchot gives as existing in the Municipal Library at Charleville.[6] One can find no evidence of his having borrowed from them. The ordinary books to be found on the shelves of anyone interested in magic—as Bretagne was—would be sufficient for an understanding of his ideas—of his *Théorie du Voyant* at all events. Franck's *Histoire de la Kabbale* of 1843, but most especially the works of Eliphas Lévi which had a popular vogue during the last years of the Second Empire: *Dogme et Rituel de la Haute Magie* of 1856, *L'Histoire de la Magie* of 1860 and *Les Clefs des Grands Mystères* of 1861. To these should be added the works of Baudelaire. There is nothing in Rimbaud's theory of poetry which is not to be found somewhere in these writings.

Those who wish to make of Rimbaud the heir of all the ages will consider it a sacrilege to say that the sources of his thought go no further back than half a century. It must, however, be remembered how few months—no more than weeks—he used for the building of his literary theory. It cannot have been more than two months, from the beginning of March until the second week of May, since he was in Paris at the end of February until 10 March, and there is no evidence that before the end of the Franco-Prussian War he was interested in the occult or in any doctrine of poetry.

On the other hand, those who wish to believe that he spun his theories from his inner consciousness alone, will consider that it is diminishing his originality to show the sources of his raw material, to show whence he may have borrowed his ideas. But the power of invention seems rarely to accompany great literary genius; it is the minor writers who conceive the brilliant ideas which they drop carelessly by the wayside for greater writers to pick up. All great writers have robbed the hives of diligent bees and, paradoxically, genius might be said to be the faculty for clever theft.

It is natural that Rimbaud should have gone to literature rather than to life for his material. He was not yet seventeen, his most intense form of living had been, on the whole, through books, and the world of literature had been to him a kinder world than the material world. He possessed a unique power of assimilation and his imagination and memory were a rich storehouse of literary and philosophical ideas. From the wealth which he had consciously and unconsciously borrowed elsewhere, he created something which was his alone.

CHAPTER VIII

# THE CABALA

THE Cabala is the basis of all illuminist and occult philosophy. It is an ensemble of Hebrew traditions concerning the interpretation of the Old Testament, said to have been first given to Adam, then communicated orally to later initiates, and occasionally written down. The Cabala is sometimes called High Magic, and its origins are uncertain. It is not known whether it arose in Alexandria, or whether it was only of medieval invention. What is certain is that in western Europe it always sprang into prominence at moments when the power of the Church was in a weakened condition—during the Renaissance, at the end of the eighteenth century and with Positivism in France after 1830. In these periods of religious doubt and uncertainty the inherent need for mysticism expressed itself in this manner. Franck, who has written the most exhaustive study of the Cabala, is of the opinion that it owes nothing to Platonic philosophy since Plato was unknown in Palestine at the time he claims that the Cabala arose. Neither is it, according to him, an outcome of the school of Alexandria because he believes it to be of earlier date and because the Jews professed aversion and contempt for Greek civilization at the very moment when they were considering the Cabala of divine revelation. In his opinion the tradition was established long before the birth of Christ. But the resemblances it undoubtedly possessed with the beliefs of certain Persian sects lead one to believe that the Cabala probably owes much to Zoroaster and to the religion of the Chaldeans, amongst whom the Jews were exiled for seventy years; it is known that Zoroaster taught in the capital of Babylon during the time of the Jews. The teaching of Zoroaster later spread to India during the years 549–539 B.C. and this fact would explain the similarities that undoubtedly exist between the Cabala and certain Indian beliefs.[1]

The Calaba is thus the core and centre of all occult and illuminist doctrine and its influence is seen in the works of writers like Pico della Mirandola, Reuchlin, Paracelsus, Boehme, Robert Fludd, Swedenborg and Pasqualis, to mention some of the more important exponents. Freemasonry is the biggest European cabalistic association.

Cabalists all recognize religion as the most profound need of humanity and speculation on the nature of God as man's highest function.

Rimbaud did not accept or use the full creed or all the dogmas of the Cabala and there is no evidence that he closely studied even the popular texts, or that he was interested in the different aspects which the doctrine took among the various sects. A full understanding of the intricacies of the Cabala would have been beyond his years and beyond his somewhat journalistic attitude to learning, but from the popular books mentioned in the previous chapter he gathered certain general ideas and principles which were valuable and fruitful to him.

The chief claim of the Cabala, and of all illuminist doctrines, was to the possession of powers to unfold the secrets and mysteries of creation and particularly to reveal and explain the divine nature of God. In cabalistic doctrine God was the supreme melody of which man was only the harmony, that is to say merely one note of the divine chord but blending perfectly with the melody and enriching it,[2] God, the Ancient of the Ancients, was One, at the same time known and unknown, distinct and separate from all things and at the same time united with them. Everything harmonized with Him and He, in His turn, harmonized with all things. He had at the same time form and no form, but in assuming shape He gave existence to all things that now exist. The

Ancient of the Ancients, the unknown of the unknown, was a lighthouse standing high above the world and man could only know of its existence through the light that fell on him from above and shone before his eyes with so much brightness and abundance. What is called here below His Holy Name is nothing more than this blinding radiance.[3] Eventually when the highest life is reached, in that Holy of Holies, all souls unite with the Supreme Soul and each completes the other. There everything becomes perfect unity, perfect harmony; all that has hitherto been scattered and divided over the face of the world, becomes one. Then the creature will not be distinguishable from its creator; the self-same thought will vivify it, the same sun lend it its brightness. Then the human soul in complete harmony with God will rule the whole universe and what it orders God will perform.[4]

The sun has always been chosen as the emblem of this unity and consequently also the emblem of perfect love. But the sun itself cannot be apprehended, only the light and the heat that come therefrom. Occultists of all times have seen in the sun the symbol of the universal energy of our system. Swedenborg says that if God appears in the heavens as the sun it is because he is the Divine Love by which all spiritual things exist, in the same way as it is by means of the sun that all natural things thrive. Divine love shines down on us like the warmth and light of the sun.[5] Rimbaud in his writings shows particular affection for images of the sun and in *Vagabonds*, talking of the part he had meant to play in his relationship with Verlaine, he writes: 'J'avais en effet, en toute sincérité d'esprit, pris l'engagement de le rendre à son état primitif de fils du soleil.'

When man has reached the state of becoming a son of light, either through his own efforts or through the short cut of the exercise of magic powers, he finds his natural ability increased tenfold and he becomes, sometimes, an independent creator like God. For man is a link in the chain that binds God with the rest of creation, the biggest and most important link. He stands on the frontier that separates the two worlds. He is the medium of exaltation of the lower regions of creation and the path by which God's influence permeates its inmost depths. He unites in himself the essence of the three natural kingdoms of the world and he is free, free as the rest of creation is not, free in thought, free in flight, the symbol of God Himself.[6]

Lévi calls on the poets of the future to arise and to rewrite the divine comedy, not according to the dreams of man, but according to the laws and mathematics of God.[7] The poet of the future, however, will be able to achieve this aim only by becoming a *voyant*, by allowing himself to harmonize completely with the laws of eternal power and strength. If he can achieve this he will become assimilated to the eternal creative power of the universe; he will himself become a creator like God.[8] He will have radically changed his whole being, and by reason of this change will be able to see things invisible to others. If man can learn to develop all his inherent and latent powers there is nothing that he will not be able to apprehend. For the knowledge of everything is in man in the same way as it is in God, only a heavy veil of darkness hides it from his view and prevents his seeing these things and understanding them. Rimbaud writes in *Une Saison en Enfer*: 'Enfin, ô bonheur, ô raison, j'écartai du ciel l'azur, qui est du noir, et je vécus, étincelle d'or de la lumière *nature*.' If man can slough off human egoism and human personality and learn to use his faculties, then he can illuminate the darkness with light and seize possession of the treasures of the universe. Nothing will be able to withstand the power of his will when he will have learnt to move it in harmony with the force of Divine Love. He will become an illuminist and the term *illuminist* means one who enjoys and possesses light. By continued effort at self-culture and the eradication of human egoism the soul becomes worthy of receiving this light, of becoming the conductor of this radiance. In the olden days the philosophers claimed that they themselves discovered the truths which they taught; but they were mistaken, for it was God who chose them as the instrument of transmission of his thought.

When the *voyant* has become translated into light and has placed his own frail will into direct communication with the eternal will, he will be able to direct that will like the point of an arrow, and to send peace or turmoil into the souls of other men, and he will be able to communicate, from a distance, with other *voyants*.[9]

Finally he will be able to hear the furthermost voices, he will become the universal and single voice himself, the great creator, exempt from everything, from ordinary blame and condemnation. Whatever sin he commits, whatever evil action he performs, he will be beyond all censure, for God says, 'I am the universal soul and in me are good and evil correcting one another, neutralizing one another. Whoever knows this does not sin, for he is universal.'[10] Evil and sin are only the occasion and the beginning of good.[11] Rimbaud wrote in *Une Saison en Enfer*, 'Moi! moi qui me suis dit mage ou ange, dispensé de toute morale.'

It must, however, not be imagined that this state of illumination brings personal happiness, and this is important for an understanding of Rimbaud. The penalty paid for this initiation is suffering. 'To work means to suffer,' wrotes Lévi,[12] thinking probably of the origin of the French word, which comes from the Latin, meaning torture. 'Each great grief endured, each suffering undergone is an accomplished progress. Those who suffer much live more than those who do not know how to suffer.' And again he says: 'Woe betide the man who is unable and unwilling to suffer!'[13] Rimbaud wrote, at the moment when he was deliberately depraving himself by 'le dérèglement de tous les sens,' that the suffering the poet endured was stupendous, 'Ineffable torture où il a besoin de toute la force surhumaine, où il devient entre tous le grand malade, le grand criminel, le grand maudit—le suprême savant.'[14]

These sufferings are, however, worth the price that is paid for them since he who is initiated and who knows how to command his faculties is King of all nature. He can reign in heaven by faith and on earth by Science; he can command suffering and death.[15] He is above all affliction, above all fears, he can neither be overcome by disasters nor vanquished by his enemies. He can see God face to face without dying and converse freely with him. He disposes of the health and lives of others, he can bring them, at his own will, suffering or death. He knows the reason of the past, the present and the future, the secret of the resurrection of the dead and the keys of immortality are in his hands.[16] There are no limits to his power for he has become one with God. He is now a creator in his right whose powers extend to the whole universe; he can reach the birds in the air, the fishes in the water and the wild animals in the forests.[17] This final state of initiation will only be achieved when man shall have learnt to know himself thoroughly to have developed all his inherent qualities and to have cultivated each his own special talents and characteristics.[18] The first duty of man, according to Lévi, is to understand himself and what is taking place in him, to perceive the significance of what he is experiencing. When a great genius prophesies he is only in reality remembering a sensation he has experienced, for the future is in the past, the past is in the future, and everything is in him.[19]

Eventually art will be as accurate as science, and philosophy will be as inevitably and as immutably stated as mathematics. *Real* ideas, that is to say those identical with the Eternal Being, are the scientific formula of reality and they will furnish exact proportions and equations as strict as those of numbers. Error will no longer be possible except through indolence and ignorance, for real knowledge cannot make a mistake. Religion will then have nothing to fear from progress, for it will itself take the direction and point the way.[20] Æsthetics will be a science and will no longer be subordinated to the taste of the moment and to its caprice. Beauty is only the radiance of truth and it should be possible to submit to unerring calculations this light whose source will be known and determined with exact precision. Poetry then will no longer be evil and poets will cease being the dangerous enchanters that Plato wished to banish for his Republic. They will be the musicians of reason and the mathematicians of harmony.[21]

But to reach this happy state humanity will have to adopt a new and altered conception of the *ego* and banish the individualistic philosophy which has prevailed since the coming of Christianity, and it is this conception, according to Lévi, which is at the root of the poetic failure of the West. This theory is one of the central and most important tenets of Rimbaud's æsthetic doctrine. It is the old conception of God, which is fast dying, which has produced the civilization which is dying too, and we can hope, says Lévi,[22] one day to see the God of our barbarous fathers become the devil of our more enlightened children. The poets, with their newer and truer conception, will be the angels —messengers—of the men to come. It seems probable that when Rimbaud uses the word *angel* he uses it with the similar meaning of 'messenger'. Real poets are emissaries from God and those who do not heed them will not be blessed by Heaven.[23] Then everything which hitherto has been faulty will be reborn immortal and perfect. Everything which all previous art had only dimly sketched will be united and will form the perfect image of the Eternal.[24] The sublime mission of poetry will be to substitute gods for men, the causes for the effects, eternal conceptions for the fleeting visions which have always passed for thought on earth.

But to express these eternal and permanent truths the poets of the future must not remain content with the languages of the present which are mere dialects not understood beyond their local place of origin. Saint-Martin, the occult philosopher, the pupil of Martinez Pasqualis, conceived the idea of a Golden Age in the future, whose symbol was to be one single language accessible to all. In the writings of all occult philosophers great stress is laid on the importance of words in themselves, through their sound, their very essence, independently of their logical meaning. It is important to realize this when studying Rimbaud's poetry and his adoption of this principle is reponsible for much of his alleged obscurity. For occult thinkers there is a mysterious symbolism contained in the word itself, often in the separate letters of the word, and a secret meaning in each number. The whole meaning of the Cabala is contained in what the masters call the thirty-two paths and the fifty doors. The thirty-two paths are thirty-two ideas attached to the ten numbers and the twenty letters of the Hebrew alphabet. Number one meant supreme power, two supreme wisdom, three intuitive intelligence, four kindness, five justice, six beauty, seven victory, eight eternity, nine fecundity and ten reality. In the same way each letter of the alphabet had a definite meaning. The first letter meant father, the second mother, the third nature, the fourth authority, the fifth religion and so on through the twenty different letters.

It comes as a surprise to find a dignified place allotted to women in occult theory and it is probably from Lévi's *Histoire de la Magie* and from his *Émancipation de la Femme* that Rimbaud borrowed the idea expressed in his *Lettre du Voyant* of the part that woman was to play in the poetry of the future, for it is the only time that he speaks of women with idealism. 'The word became man,' writes Lévi,[25] 'but it will only be when it becomes woman that the world will be really saved. It is the maternal genius of religion that will teach man the sublime beauty of the spirit of charity, then reason will become reconciled with faith because it will comprehend and explain the sweet rapture of self-abnegation.' And again he says, 'Woman is the queen of harmony and that is why she must be at the head of the regenerating movement of the future. Woman is higher in the scale of love than man and when love comes to the fore then woman will be the queen of the universe.'[26]

These, briefly stated, are the ideas from occult philosophy which attracted Rimbaud and from which he drew some of the material for his poetic doctrine. It must not, however, be imagined that this is the whole of the Cabala, or that it is the whole of Rimbaud's poetics; but a close study of his æsthetic theory will reveal how large a part these theories play in his conception of poetry.

CHAPTER IX

# BAUDELAIRE

THE greatest literary influence that Rimbaud experienced at this time was certainly that of Baudelaire, not only in his actual poetry, but in his æsthetic theories and in his attitude to life. Baudelaire was one of the first poets whose art becomes a complete picture of life in all its complexities, in which the highest mingles with the lowest, aspirations with failures; it is flesh and spirit, dream and nightmare all at once. This characteristic of his work made a strong appeal to Rimbaud.

Baudelaire's mature work is primarily an expression of his search for spiritual values and spiritual reality. His æsthetic doctrine is closely linked with his spiritual convictions and we cannot understand the one without realizing the other. Poetry and criticism are two facets of his artistic nature, two aspects of the same experience. He considered all artistic creation in the light of spiritual activity, an attempt to make concrete a transcendental experience. One expression of this experience was the crystallization—unconscious almost—in the poem; the other—conscious— was a meditation on the nature of the experience and a discourse on the form in which it took shape. He believed, to speak in Swedenborgian language, that all things in the material world were a correspondence of things in the spiritual world, that they were only the imperfect images of heavenly beauty. The hidden and mysterious relation that binds the objects in the material world to those in the spirit world is what we call *correspondences*. And it is not possible for us to see the objects in the spirit world except indirectly through their symbols. These symbols are the language of nature, a hieroglyphic language spread out before us unread, or else only imperfectly read. Swedenborg thought that the great thinkers were those who could see beyond the shell into the heart of things, who could decipher the mysterious hieroglyphics. And so all true art necessarily becomes the expression of aspiration towards perfect beauty, but it can only be the symbol of this beauty, its imperfect image, whose value will solely depend on the degree of spiritual development of the poet, on his power of divination. Baudelaire was convinced that only artists who had reached a high state of spirituality would be successful in discovering images, metaphors and analogies for the adequate rendering of their vision. He believed that genius lay not in the power of invention, but in the faculty of reception. The artist can be no more than a translator, or a *déchiffreur*.

Rimbaud was fully aware, as few poets of his age were, of the significance of this aspect of Baudelaire's art. 'Mais inspecter l'invisible et entendre l'inouï étant autre chose que de reprendre l'aspect des choses mortes. Baudelaire est le premier voyant, roi des poètes, un vrai Dieu.'[1] Later, imagining that he was following

Baudelaire, he did all in his power to increase artificially his power of reception.

The theory of *correspondances* was with Baudelaire not merely a spiritual doctrine; it was closely linked as well with his conception of the unity of all art. All art—whether it be music, painting or poetry—seeks to enter into contact with eternal beauty which it dimly perceives through the natural objects which hide it from view, and each art renders this vision in its own idiom, in its own language, although the experience is identical in each case. A musician will say that colours and perfumes reach his inner consciousness in the form of sound, since physicists assert that hearing is only inward seeing and for the musician that inward seeing, that musical seeing, is more perfect than the other. Indeed the musician will not be fully conscious of the significance of what he has seen until he has translated it into his own idiom, the language of sound. Baudelaire dreamed of a complete fusion of all the arts, one total and perfect expression of beauty appealing to all the senses at once. Rimbaud, in his conception of art, went, theoretically at all events, further than Baudelaire, though in actual *transposition d'art* he did not succeed in reaching what Baudelaire was able to achieve. Baudelaire tried to approximate chiefly to music in his poetry, not simply to copy the harmonious sound of sweet music, but to reach the same power of suggestion and of evoking a state of mind. Critics have often spoken of the music of Rimbaud's poetry and have, in this, compared him to Baudelaire. Yet the musical quality of Rimbaud's verse is of an entirely different quality to that of Baudelaire, of a different realm one might say. The critics who compare the two poets seem to consider music as being merely something that caresses pleasingly, without rough jarring, the organ of hearing. But music is more than a sequence of pleasant sounds and the music of Baudelaire's poetry does not solely consist in verbal harmony. When he wrote: 'La poésie touche à la musique par une prosodie dont les racines plongent plus avant dans l'âme humaine que ne l'indique aucune théorie classique,'[2] he did not mean that poetry should content itself with copying the sweet sounds of music, that it should become what, conversely, some music is, programme music, like the famous *Battle of Prague* so popular with our grandmothers. He meant that a poem should have the power of evoking in the reader, by whatever means it chose to use, whether by harmonious or inharmonious lines, the sensation which music had aroused in the poet; that it should have the evocative and suggestive power which music possesses to a greater degree than any of the other arts. He believed that music possessed the power of magic, the faculty of creating psychological 'états d'âme'.

The musical quality of poetry, in the deepest meaning of the expression, can therefore not be measured by a mathematical formula of beautiful or harmonious sounds, of a combination of vowels and consonants. There are many beautifully harmonious lines—especially in the poems of Victor Hugo—that are, nevertheless, not deeply musical, that have none of the evocative power of music, and their melody fades away when the last syllable is read, as suddenly as a note on the paino becomes mute when the sustaining pedal is released. The musical quality of poetry is more closely linked with imagination and psychological associations than it is with mere sound. Rimbaud's poems prove that he undoubtedly possessed a sure ear for sonorous effects, both delicate and sublime, and his lines are melodious without being musically evocative; but he never gave evidence that the hearing of great music meant anything to him, or that he was sensible to its suggestive and evocative power, though he was later to consider its possibilities as an abstract language independent of logical meaning. He does not seem to have been conscious of music as an art, nor indeed of any other art but poetry. It is doubtful whether he can ever have heard any other music but the brass band blaring in the square at Charleville on Sundays, or the amateur performance of Charles Bretagne. Had he been asked to state what music meant to him he would probably have replied that it was the song of the birds in the early morning, the cool murmur of the streams in the Ardennes forests during the noonday heat, and the sighing of the wind through the trees at evening. This would not have been an adequate answer for a musician, nor would it have satisfied Baudelaire.

Baudelaire had laid great stress on the value of dreams, on the importance of a faculty for dreaming in creative artists, and he experimented with various methods for inducing or increasing that faculty in himself. 'To dream magnificently,' he said, 'is not a gift granted to all men. The power of dreaming is a divine and mysterious power. It is through dreaming that man communicates with the dark dream by which he is surrounded.'[3] Rimbaud, in order to have frequent communication with the dark dream around him, resorted to drugs and alcohol, and hoped by these means to reach a permanent state of magnificent dreaming. The dreams and vision which Baudelaire had described in *Les Paradis Artificiels* seemed to him to be the true substance of poetry. He knew from his own experience how even a small quantity of alcohol had the power of loosening his tongue, of making him forget himself and his inhibitions, of making him write more freely, and he wondered what heights he might be able to scale if he had access to stronger means. He was carried away by Baudelaire's lyric description of hashish intoxication.

Le haschisch s'étend alors sur toute la vie comme un vernis magique; il la colore en solennité et en éclaire toute la profondeur. Paysages dentelés, horizons fuyants, perspectives de villes blanchies par la lividité cadavéreuse de l'orage, ou illuminées par les ardeurs concentrées des soleils couchants,—profondeurs de l'espace, allégorie de la profondeur du temps,—la danse, le geste ou la déclamation des comédiens si vous vous êtes jetés dans un théâtre,—la première phrase venue, si vos yeux tombent sur un livre,—tout enfin, l'universalité des êtres se dresse devant vous avec une gloire nouvelle et non soupçonnée jusqu'alors. La grammaire, l'aride grammaire elle-même, devient quelque chose comme une sorcellerie évocatoire; les mots resusscitent revêtus de chair et d'os; le substantif, dans sa majesté substantielle, l'adjectif, vêtement transparent qui l'habille et le colore comme un glacis, et le verbe, ange de mouvement, qui donne le branle à la phrase. La musique, autre langue chère aux paresseux ou aux esprits profonds qui cherchent le délassement dans la variété du travail, vous parle de vous même et vous raconte le poème de votre vie; elle s'incorpore à vous, et vous vous fondez en elle. Elle parle votre passion, non pas d'une manière vague et indéfinie comme elle fait dans vos soirées nonchalantes, mais d'une manière circonstanciée, positive, chaque mouvement du rhythme marquant un mouvement connu de votre âme, chaque note se transformant en mot, et le poème entier entre dans votre cerveau comme un dictionnaire doué de vie.[4]

It was small wonder that Rimbaud thought this state of intoxication worthy of achievement, since all his senses would then be more acute and more capable of receiving sensations. His eyes would be able to see into infinity, his ears to perceive sounds that were normally inaudible. Even the following stage was precious, that of hallucination, when external objects gradually and successively assume weird and strange shapes; when sounds turn into colours, when colours seem to continue in music and music itself becomes a series of numbers. A voice finally cries to the drug addict—alas! it is his own voice. Baudelaire hastens to add, though Rimbaud did not heed the aside—and this voice says to him: 'Tu as maintenant le droit de te considérer comme supérieur à tous les hommes; nul ne connaît et ne pourrait comprendre tout ce que tu penses et tout ce que tu sens; ils seraient incapables d'apprécier la bienveillance qu'ils t'inspirent. Tu es un roi que les passants méconnaissent, et qui vit dans la solitude de sa conviction.'[5] Rimbaud noticed particularly the reply. 'Toutes ces choses ont été créées *pour moi, pour moi, pour moi!* Pour moi l'humanité a travaillé, a été martyrisée, immolée,— pour servir de pâture à mon implacable appétit d'émotion, de connaissance et de beauté. Personne ne s'étonnera qu'une pensée finale, suprême, jaillisse du cerveau du rêveur. *Je suis devenu Dieu!*'

This passage transported Rimbaud as it was to transport many a later writer who understood no more than Rimbaud did the real meaning of the words, nor the significance of the conclusions. Baudelaire, who worshipped truth, however unpalatable. was incapable of accepting the Artificial Paradises, or the backstairs entrance into Heaven through a gratuity pressed into the hand of the keeper of the heavenly gate. He might play with these things and experiment with them, but he would never be mistaken as to their true nature and their intrinsic value. It is in the moral conclusion that Baudelaire's real meaning is to be found and it is he himself who calls it the moral. For him, although he tried it himself and enjoyed the experience, the taking of drugs was fundamentally an immoral act, as immoral as suicide. Indeed he considered it a slow and certain moral suicide. 'En effet il est défendu à l'homme, sous peine de déchéance et de mort intellectuelle, de déranger les conditions primordiales de son existence et de rompre l'équilibre de ses facultés avec les milieux où elles sont destinées à se mouvoir, de déranger son destin pour y substituer une fatalité d'un genre nouveau. . . . Tout homme qui n'accepte pas les conditions de la vie vend son âme.'[6]

That is where Rimbaud differed from Baudelaire; he would not accept the conditions of human life, but intended to alter them himself. Baudelaire warned his readers to beware of the visions they received under the influence of drugs, telling them that these visions were, when one was fully awake, not as beautiful as they had seemed when decked out in the tinsel trappings of intoxication. For himself he had once wondered whether he could obtain from drugs spiritual gain and whether he could make of them, as it were, a kind of thinking machine, a useful instrument for composition. If this were possible then sacrifice of dignity, honour and free will would not be too heavy a price to pay. He came, however, to the conclusion that the sacrifice would be in vain, since drugs can only reveal to man what is already in himself.

Rimbaud was prepared to sacrifice himself for the sake of the experiment, for the sake of discovery, for had not Baudelaire declared that the role of the artist demanded of him the completest form of self-abnegation? With his habitual lack of moderation, he was ready to die and to sacrifice all he possessed in the interest of the moment. He was prepared to go farther than Baudelaire would have gone. Baudelaire, as a Christian, was not prepared to sacrifice his soul, though this might happen through his inherent weakness. He would never willingly have sacrificed his human personality, his human integrity, his ultimate salvation. To Rimbaud this undue value placed on individual human personality and on the human soul and its salvation was nothing more than the remains of outworn and out-of-date egoism. With a martyr's passion and self-abnegation he was prepared to sacrifice them and to keep nothing for himself of his physical or his spiritual being. He wished to go on from where Baudelaire had stopped short, at whatever the cost to himself, and to penetrate into eternity.

> Plonger au fond du gouffre, Enfer ou Ciel, qu'importe?
> Au fond de l'Inconnu pour trouver du *nouveau*.[7]

## CHAPTER X

# THE ÆSTHETIC DOCTRINE

AT the moment when Rimbaud conceived his æsthetic doctrine he was merely a young man of promise who had not yet written any work that was fully and completely his own. Even his most original poems still showed some traces of the influence of the writers he had admired. It is after the doctrine has taken shape that we find him tearing himself away from all influences— literary and personal—from Izambard, from Delahaye, from Bretagne, from everyone and everything in order to discover what was in himself, and to become truly himself. From that moment—alas for his popularity with his contemporaries—he ceased entirely to be assimilative. Had be been plunged into the literary life of Paris at the earlier stage of his development, it is conceivable that he might have been a success. But the pride and arrogance which are the most striking characteristics of his new phase made him impatient of any outside influence and restriction, intolerant of the old fossils of the literary world who still clung to the principles of the Parnassian School which he himself had already cast away on the rubbish dump, and who had not even yet reached a full understanding and appreciation of Baudelaire, now dead four years. When he met them he spared none of them his contempt.

In his *Lettres du Voyant* Rimbaud has thrown out the ideas as they occurred to him, in confusion, without arranging them according to a plan, and his doctrine loses thereby strength and driving power, since the theory does not stand out clearly or with force. The doctrine is unfolded in two letters written in 1871, the first to Izambard of 13 May, and the second to Paul Démeny of 15 May. In these letters he has merely jotted down the points as they occurred to him and they do not make a compact whole. The two letters form the rough draft, the notes, as it were, for his *Art Poétique*. Critics usually state that the second letter is the completed version of the rough draft send to Izambard two days previously. Yet on close examination, this does not seem to be the case. The second letter is undoubtedly fuller than the first, of greater scope, but it is every bit as formless. It is probable that further points of interest had occurred to Rimbaud since the writing of the first letter and that he had added them to his material, without yet thinking of composing a plan. The second letter gives the impression of having been as hurriedly written as the first.

From the Cabala, the books of magic and the works of occult writers, Rimbaud obtained the material for his doctrine, and in Baudelaire he found a model of what a *voyant* should be. He imagined that it was freedom from moral inhibition and prejudice and addiction to drugs and alcohol that had made of Baudelaire what he was, that these had helped him to burst asunder the fetters that normally bind the human spirit. He knew that this had brought Baudelaire great suffering but he was prepared to accept for himself the same suffering, if he could thereby become a great poet. He did not know—Baudelaire's letters to his mother had not yet been published—his horror of his weakness and his struggles to eradicate in himself his vices.

To make Rimbaud's doctrine stand out more clearly, the scattered ideas have been here arranged according to a plan, for it is certain that had he been composing on *Art Poétique* he would himself have put order into these notions.

To clear the ground for his own conception, Rimbaud reviews the poetry of the world since the beginning of all time, and, like the occult thinkers, comes to the conclusion that it was amongst the Greeks alone that true poetry was to be found. 'Toute poésie aboutit à la poésie grecque,' for it is they alone who understood on what principles poetic composition should rest. He had read

Plato and would have known the following passage from *Ion*.[1]

All great poets, said Socrates, epic as well as lyric, compose their beautiful poems not by art, but because they are inspired and possessed. And as Corybantian revellers when they dance are not in their right mind, so lyric poets are not in their right mind when they are composing their beautiful strains; but when falling under the power of music and metre they are inspired and possessed; like Bacchic maidens who draw milk and honey from the rivers when they are under the influence of Dionysius but not when they are in their right mind. And the soul of the lyric poet is the same, as they themselves say; for they tell us that they bring songs from honeyed fountains, culling them out of the gardens and dells of the Muses; they, like the bees, winging their way from flower to flower. And this is true. For the poet is a light and winged and holy thing, and there is no invention in him until he has been inspired and is out of his senses, and the mind is no longer in him; when he has not attained to this state, he is powerless and is unable to utter his oracles.

After the Greeks, according to Rimbaud, poetry became solely an amusement and a pastime. Poets were mere writers, civil servants, *fonctionnaires*, little more than scribblers. From the time of the Greeks until the Romantic movement only literary men and versifiers were to be found, but no real poets. Poetry was no better than rimed prose, a society game, an *avachissement* of innumerable generations of fools, since poetry died with the advent of Christianity. Only Racine was great—potentially great at least—but he was cramped by the narrowness and the rigidity of his literary form. With the Romantic Movement, however, this lamentable state of affairs began to alter and these later poets possessed vision without realizing it themselves. Hitherto, says Rimbaud, the Romantic poets have only been imperfectly studied from their most important aspect. And who indeed could have studied them? Not the critics, hidebound as they were by outworn literary conventions; nor the writers themselves, by reason of the very nature of their inspiration. How could they comprehend the full significance of what they were singing since 'the song is rarely the work, that is to say the thought sung and understood by the singer'?[2] And thus the Romantic poets were *voyants* without fully realizing it themselves. 'La culture de leurs âmes s'est commencée aux accidents. Locomotives abandonnées mais brûlantes, que prennent quelque temps les rails.'[3] Lamartine was a *voyant* but he was stifled by his archaic literary form; Hugo was too pigheaded, but nevertheless he *saw* certain things in his later works. And then Alfred de Musset, what can be said of him? Rimbaud pours on him the same contempt expressed by Baudelaire and shows the same scorn of French taste because it could call him a great poet. 'Musset, tenfold loathsome to a suffering generation like ours, carried away by visions of higher things which his angelic sloth only insults. Oh! these mawkish *Comédies et Proverbes*! Oh! the *Nuits*! Oh! *Rolla*! Oh! *Namouna*! It is all so hideously French, that is to say loathsome to the highest pitch. Oh! Musset! Charming his love, isn't it? That painting on enamel, what solid poetry! French poetry will long continue to be enjoyed—but only in France. Every grocer's assistant is capable of reeling off a Rollaesque apostrophic poem; every budding priest has five hundred lines buried in the secrecy of his diary. At fifteen these outbursts of passion awaken the lusts of adolescents; at eighteen, at seventeen even, every schoolboy who has the chance acts like Rolla and writes like Rolla; some may still even die of it. Musset was able to achieve nothing! There were visions behind the veil that hid them, but he only closed his eyes. Let the fine corpse remain dead! Henceforth we shall not even bother to awaken him with our curses!'

Then Rimbaud reaches Baudelaire. 'But to inspect the invisible and hear things unheard being entirely different from gathering up again the spirit of dead things. Baudelaire is the first *voyant*, King of poets, a real God! Unfortunately he lived in too artistic a *milieu* and his literary form, so often praised, is trivial. Unknown discoveries demand new literary forms.'

The only way, Rimbaud maintains, of becoming a real poet is to become a *voyant*, a ravisher of the celestial fire.[4] The poet must become a seer whose mind can penetrate into infinity, beyond the veil of reality which hides it from our view.[5] It is, however, impossible for the poet to become a seer unless he abandons the old conception of what is human and individual personality.[6] 'If all the old fools,' writes Rimbaud, 'had not stuck to the false conception of the *ego* we should not now have to sweep away these millions of skeletons which, since time immemorial, have accumulated the product of their one-eyed intellects, at the same time priding themselves on being their originators.'[7] In occult theory primordial thinking is an autonomous activity whose object the thinker is. The outworn conception of the personal writer producing his own work is totally false. The writer is merely the vehicle for the voice of the Eternal, he himself is of no account for he is merely the unconscious expression of someone speaking through him. 'It is wrong to say *Je pense*, one should say *on me pense*.'[8] The poet cannot know why it is precisely he who has been chosen; he has had no say in the matter and it has occurred without his volition. In the same way, Rimbaud adds, the brass has made no effort to be made into a trumpet and the wood has had no choice in being fashioned into a fiddle.[9] 'Je est un autre,' Rimbaud repeats several times. One swing of the bow and the song comes into being; the fiddle, however, has done nothing and yet the music bursts from it. Thus it is with the poet, another being plays on him, creating the harmony while, unconsciously and automatically, he produces the strains that are put in him. Then he listens, spellbound, to the melody he has unknowingly created. 'I am present at the birth of my thought, I look at it and I listen!'[10] Yet he no more than the rest of us knows whence it comes nor what it really is.

The poet can, nevertheless, of his own accord make an effort to become a suitable wood for the celestial fiddle. To achieve this end he must break down entirely everything that builds up human personality, all that distinguishes it, all the egoism that forms it. He must break it up, just as the soil is broken up by the plough, he must uproot from it all the weeds of habit and prejudice, for only in a soil thus prepared will the seeds of the invisible world grow and flourish. All means that will bring about this state of oblivion of self will be good; drugs, alcohol; everything that can lift the human soul out of its mortal shell and plunge it into eternity. Everything is good that breaks down the control of reason: everything is precious that can succeed in freeing the faculties from their normal inhibitions. What harm if the means are poisonous, what harm if they inevitably produce mental instability? They are the fertilizers that prepare the soil, the manure, and from that poisonous and decaying matter the sweetest flowers will spring. Therefore, says Rimbaud, the poet must deprave himself and degrade himself in order to break down all the normal restraints, all the dykes that have been built up round the human personality by discipline and training. 'Le poète se fait *voyant* par un long, immense et raisonné *dérèglement* de tous les sens.' He must experience all forms of love and madness so that he may keep only their quintessence. From Baudelaire he learned the value of dreams induced by such methods, but here he parts company with his predecessor. Baudelaire always kept, in the midst of his worst aberrations, a sense of sin; Rimbaud, however, would not feel that for him debauch was vice; he was certain that he himself was above the reach of sin. Later, looking back on the errors of this time, he said: 'Moi! Moi, qui me suis dit mage ou ange, dispensé de toute morale, je suis rendu au sol.'[11]

For Rimbaud, however, this incursion into a life of vice was to prove no pleasure of self-indulgence; it was, on the contrary, a descent into Hell. Debauchery was to bring him nothing but torture, and it needed, on his part, great courage to continue. He was, however, all through his life to prove capable of the most extreme physical and intellectual self-mortification, to be prepared to mutilate himself when he thought it necessary. This suffering was, moreover, an essential part of his doctrine. 'The suffering is tremendous,' he wrote, 'it is the most exquisite torture and the poet will need all his faith, all his superhuman strength, for he becomes "le grand malade, le grand criminel, le grand maudit et le suprême savant".'[12] That is Rimbaud's aim all through his artistic life, to become 'le suprême savant'. It is interesting also to note that Verlaine, when writing of certain poets —amongst them Rimbaud—calls them 'les poètes maudits'.

This idea of suffering was not engendered by the well-known gloom of the 'day after the night before'; it was a conception he borrowed from Baudelaire. Had not Baudelaire spoken of 'la fertilisante douleur' and 'l'indispensable douleur'. Lévi too had written in a similar strain in *Les Clefs des Grands Mystères*. What harm if the individual poet suffers and is lost? What harm if he falls by the wayside? Says Rimbaud 'Qu'il crève dans son bondissement par les choses inouïes et innombrables.' Other poets will come after him, take the torch from his fallen hand, and go on from 'les horizons où l'autre s'est affaissé.'[13]

Mankind, said Rimbaud, was thirsting for this new poet to arise. 'We are asking the poet for something new—ideas and form—Every old fool imagines that he has satisfied this demand. But it is not that at all!'[14] The poet's chief duty is not only to penetrate into the beyond, but also to gather up the ideas which the Universal Mind throws off in every age. Hitherto man has collected only a few of these notions, unconsciously. His duty is, consciously, to 'define the sum of unknown which is present in our time.'[15] In doing this he will inevitably outstrip his own age; he will lead the world in its triumphal march of progress; he will be a 'multiplicateur de progrès'.[16] Even in this world he will participate in the future life. Here Rimbaud follows, very closely, cabalistic doctrine. In company with many illuminists, he believed that all means were justified—whether magical or natural—to force one's way into the presence of the Eternal.

The final apotheosis of the poet would be reached only when he had acquired full knowledge of himself, of all his faculties and how best to use them; when he had fully developed his inherent powers and qualities. Only when he had fully cultivated his soul would he reach infinity.[17]

When the poet has reached this holy of holies he must not rest content, in selfish and beatific contemplation; he must make his visions known to others.[18] He has charge of humanity, of all the lower creatures, and his duty is also to free woman so that she too can participate in the work of discovery. Woman, in Rimbaud's opinion, would be the great poet of the future.[19] 'These poets will exist when the age-long slavery of woman shall have ended, when she will be able to live by and for herself; then man —hitherto abominable—having given her her freedom, she will be a poet too. Woman will discover the unknown. Will her world be different from ours? She will discover things that will be strange and unfathomable; repulsive and delicate. We shall take them from her and we shall understand them.'

These visions from another world will, however, be impossible to render in the ordinary outworn language, at the poet's disposal and therefore a new language must be discovered which will be capable of expressing *l'ineffable*, a new language not bound by logic, nor by grammar or syntax. 'A language must be found!' cries Rimbaud, 'and moreover, every word being an idea the time for a universal language will come.' This was also the view of Ballanche the occult philosopher.[20] In Ballanche's conception language was not merely a vehicle for expressing concrete ideas, or for communicating with other men. Language was, he said, gifted from its very beginning with a sort of superhuman intuition. Our modern use of language can give us no conception of the value put on the word itself amongst primitive people, for the word originally was able to give the full image of the object named. It had a kind of 'illumination' of its own of which the dead signs which we use to-day can give us no idea. The earliest hymns were composed solely of nouns and adjectives, there were no verbs, for these were not necessary. This was, in a certain measure the aim that Rimbaud was to seek to achieve in his poetry, to simplify language, omitting what was not strictly essential, and to give back to individual words the full meaning they had once possessed. Hence his poetry is often difficult to understand and the meaning sometimes escapes us, for we have lost the faculty of feeling words in this manner. Amongst occult thinkers great stress was laid upon the importance of each individual word, since they held the belief that the word and the total idea were so completely fused that in a language properly used no explanatory clauses or words were necessary for the single word, perfectly chosen would alone give a clear conception of the idea which the author wished to convey. Rimbaud prided himself on having invented such a new language. 'I prided myself on having invented a new poetic language accessible, one day, to all the senses at once, but for the moment I kept for myself the translation. At first it was only experimental. I expressed silence,

darkness; I noted the inexpressible'.[21] Although Rimbaud failed
in his attempt—he himself acknowledges this failure—his experiment proved that poetry cannot be defined as being either the
subject or the form of the composition; poetry is a state of mind or
soul—'un état d'âme' the Symbolists were to call it later—and
this state of mind or soul will find its own inevitable expression.
The new language was to be, in Rimbaud's words: 'de l'âme
pour l'âme, résumant tout, parfums, sons et couleurs.'[22] We shall
see an attempt to put this into practice in *Sonnet des Voyelles*.

The literature which Rimbaud now wished to see established
was no longer to be dependent on the vagaries of changing taste
and fashion; it would be destined to remain stable for ever, since
it would be based on permanent and unchanging values, the laws
of which would be as immutable as those of mathematics. 'Toujours pleins du *Nombre* et de l'*Harmonie* les poèmes seront faits
pour rester. Au fond ce serait un peu la poésie grecque.'[23] Ideas,
in the platonic sense, were to be the ultimate subject-matter for
all art, permanent and unchanging ideas, not transient, personal
emotions.

It is possible that Rimbaud may have read an article on Scho-
penhauer which appeared in *La Revue des Deux Mondes*, on 15
March 1870, one of the first articles to be published in French on
the philosopher who was to exercise so deep an influence on the
Symbolist movement.[24]

It is possible to say [wrote Schopenhauer] that ideas alone are the
object of all art. It is in fact ideas which architecture and music, sculp-
ture and painting, and finally poetry, seek to express through the
different means which characterize their different arts. Art, like philosophy, with which it has much in common, with which it is intimately connected, exists solely in the disinterested contemplation of
things, and the faculty of putting them before others in that aspect is
the essence of genius. In achieving this man is freed from the shackling
bonds of vulgar reality, carried away from the torrent of petty interests
and trivial thoughts.

Rimbaud believed that no poet capable of fulfilling this function
had yet arisen because man 'was not yet fully awake, not yet
given over completely to the fulness of the great dream. Author,

creator, poet! That man has not yet existed. The day however must come, when humanity, after having stifled for two thousand years its poetic and creative powers, will, in one tremendous upheaval, free itself from its bonds of spiritual slavery. Rimbaud's secret hope was that he might himself be the great poet and liberator. He was nevertheless conscious that at the moment he had not yet fully worked out his system of poetics. In conversation with Delahaye he used to let fall unfinished sentences that his friend only dimly comprehended and these half-formulated opinions show how confused he still was concerning what he really thought, and how much he was still groping after his ideal.[25] 'At the moment I have only a glimpse of the ends and the means' he used to say. 'New sensations, stronger feelings to communicate through words! I see, I feel, but I cannot yet formulate it all, nor express it as I would wish to express it. I must feel and see more. When one has reached full knowledge of a new and richer language and proficiency in its use, then youth is probably over, and the sensitive faculties, sensibilities, have become sluggish. They must be roused! Drugs, perfumes! The poisons taken by the Sibylle!'

The poetic doctrine had come to him too quickly, in so few weeks, and he had not yet had time to test it thoroughly, nor to experiment with his tool. He had, moreover, not yet had the opportunity of trying all the means which he considered necessary to produce the receptive state of the *voyant*; he was far from having achieved his aim of 'le dérèglement de tous les sens'. How indeed could he, in a little provincial town, he who could not even afford to stamp his letters, obtain the rarest and most expensive of drugs, and how could he experiment in all forms of debauch and depravity? His mother's plan was to keep him entirely without money, hoping thereby to make him return all the sooner to a reasonable view of life and of his future. On the grounds of his lack of opportunity to put into practice his full doctrine of poetry, it is reasonable to consider the poems mentioned in a previous chapter, even though some of them were finished actually after formulating his theory, as belonging to the earlier literary phase, and as not fulfilling the conditions of the *Théorie du Voyant*. There are reasonable grounds also for placing even *Le Bateau Ivre* in the same category, in seeing in it the last poem of his youth, the greatest poem of that period—if not indeed of his whole literary career. The *voyant* poems begin later, after he reached Paris, and probably included *La Chasse Spirituelle*, alleged by Verlaine to have been his greatest work. It has, unfortunately, not come down to us since the manuscript was irretrievably lost when Verlaine left his wife.

CHAPTER XI

## LE BATEAU IVRE

THE gestation and formulation of his poetic doctrine was a powerful goad to Rimbaud's creative faculty, and it was during the months from April to June that he composed all the obscene and blasphemous poems mentioned in an earlier chapter. In July he also wrote one of the ablest and wittiest—if not the most attractive—of his poems. *Ce qu'on dit au Poète à propos de Fleurs*. It is a poem of astonishing originality in vocabulary and images, and it bears some resemblance in tone to *Les Assis* which was written in April, though it is more comic and less bitter. In the letter to Banville with which he enclosed the poem, we can see how much the youth has grown in literary confidence and independence since the previous year when he last wrote to his literary master. Then he had written humbly, as a dutiful follower of the *Parnasse*; he was the same good boy that he had been at school, anxious to please and ready to assimilate everything which his elders were prepared to give him. Now, on the contrary, there is a certain insolence in his attitude and style, a certain condescension—the same insolence and condescension which we see in the letter he wrote to Izambard on 13 May. He is after all a *voyant* and so why should he defer to anyone, however celebrated? He signs himself *Alcide Bava*—*Bava* because it is a word which he greatly affected during this period,* and *Alcide* because this is one

* Baver = to dribble.

of the names of Hercules who accomplished the great labour of cleaning out the Augean stables, just as Rimbaud intended to clean out the Augean stables of literature.[1]

Monsieur et cher Maître! [he wrote][2] You will remember having received from the provinces, in June, 1870, a hundred or a hundred and fifty hexameters from me under the title *Credo in Unam*. You were kind enough then to answer. It is the same fool who sends you the verses here enclosed, signed Alcide Bava.—Pardon!—I am eighteen now.* I shall always love the poetry of Banville. Last year I was only seventeen. Have I improved?

Alcide Bava
ARTHUR RIMBAUD.

There is a cool impudence on Rimbaud's part—which is probably not unintentional—in sending Banville a poem which makes fun of the Parnassian attitude to flowers. It is cut flowers that Banville especially favours; he is a florist rather than a horticulturist.[3] No poet has ever put so many flowers in his shop window, so many camelias, such a profusion of violets, and especially lilies—never has poetry enjoyed so many lilies. Rimbaud, in his poem, has the effrontery to laugh at the lilies, roses and violets on the heights of Parnassus. The lilies he calls 'ces clystères d'extase', and the violets 'le crachats sucrés des nymphes noires.'

It is in the poems of this period, from April until his departure for Paris in September, that we find Rimbaud's daring experiment in vocabulary, in his use of words never hitherto used in poetry—trivial words, scientific words, obscene words, and colloquial expressions. It is the language of this period which influenced the poets of the succeeding generation such as Laforgue, and, through them, reached the modern poets of almost every country. Verlaine did not appreciate verbal eccentricity and linguistic tricks and when Rimbaud came under his influence, he abandoned this form of originality. *Illuminations*, his most advanced work in conception and in technique, in the use of imagery, grammar and syntax, shows few or none of these verbal eccentricities.

* He was, in fact, only 16 years and 9 months.

With his new-found confidence Rimbaud now felt that it was time for him to try his luck once more in Paris, in the centre of culture, where he would be appreciated and understood. He did not want, this time, to endure the same sordid conditions as on his previous visits; he wished to be self-supporting, to find some employment which would permit him to earn his living and, at the same time, give him leisure for writing. He then approached Démeny, Izambard's friend, for advice. His letter shows how young and unformed he still was; it is the letter of a child trying to appear grown-up and practical; it shows, moreover, how uncertain he was of himself and of what he was capable of doing in Paris. There is pathos in this helplessness of the youth not yet seventeen who had already composed masterpieces of French poetry.

Monsieur [he wrote][4] you force me to make my request all over again! So be it! Here is the whole of my lament. I'm trying to express it calmly but my practice in calmness is very limited. It's now more than a year since I gave up ordinary life for what you know. I'm imprisoned in this indescribable Ardennais country, seeing no one, absorbed in an obstinate and mysterious work, squalid and absurd, answering only with silence crude questions and vulgar abuse, and showing myself full of dignity, but I've at last driven my mother to take horrible decisions, my mother who is as inflexible as "soixante-treize administrations à casquette de plomb'. She wants to force me to work for ever in Charleville. 'You must have a job by such and such a date,' she says, 'or you'll not be kept any longer!' I refused that sort of life, without giving my reasons—it would have been lamentable to do so. Up to to-day I've been able to put off the final reckoning. She's even reached the pitch of wanting me to run away. Then, with my lack of experience, and without a livelihood, I'd soon end up in a reformatory, and no one would ever hear of me again. That's the gag of disgust which is being rammed down my throat. But it's all very simple. I'm asking for nothing except information. I'm prepared to work, but in freedom, in Paris which I love. Imagine I'm a tramp arriving in Paris without means of support, what should I do? You said to me once that whoever is prepared to work for a shilling a day can go to such and such a place, do such and such a thing, and live in such and such a way. Then I begged you to tell me what kind of work wouldn't take up too much of my time because meditation needs enormous stretches of free time. If I'm to go to Paris I must be able to be financially independent. Don't you think this is sincere and honest? It seems to me strange that I should have to insist on this. The following plan occurred to me, the only one which seemed to me practical and reasonable, and I'll give it to you in another form. I'm full of willingness. I'm doing my best to speak as intelligibly as a miserable man can . . . And so, not knowing what you might answer, I'll cut short these long explanations. I'm prepared to trust your experience and your kindness, which indeed I blessed when I received your book. Would it displease you to receive some specimens of my own verse?

We do not know how Démeny answered—if at all—but it was not through his agency, or his advice, that Rimbaud finally went to Paris.

At last, when no help came, Bretagne said to him one day, 'Why don't you write to Paul Verlaine?' And he gave him a letter of introduction.[5] Rimbaud was overjoyed for Verlaine was for him Baudelaire's successor as a *voyant*. He wrote off immediately, enclosing some of his poems which he and Delahaye transcribed in their best copper-plate handwriting. Verlaine was absent from Paris when the letter arrived, but he found it on his return and he answered immediately, praising the poems but making certain reservations about the vocabulary and imagery which Rimbaud used. He did not care for the coarseness of certain expressions, nor for the triviality of some of the slang. He held out to Rimbaud the possibility of being able to invite him to come to Paris, but added that he would like first to consult some of the well-known writers of the day. Then he showed the poems to Philippe Burty, Charles Cros and Léon Valade. Like him they were astounded by the originality of Rimbaud's poetic talent. Encouraged by this praise, Verlaine decided to summon Rimbaud to Paris. 'Venez, chère, grande âme' he wrote,[6] 'on vous appelle, on vous attend.' With his usual generosity and kindness of heart, he did not merely content himself with summoning the young poet from the provinces, but sent him the money for his railway ticket and also an invitation to stay with him and his wife. In his second letter, Rimbaud had said to him:

I plan to write a long poem, but I can't work in Charleville. I'm prevented from coming to Paris as I'm without money. My mother is a widow, and very pious. She only gives me ten centimes every Sunday to pay for my seat in church.

In a burst of enthusiasm and hope Rimbaud did, in fact, compose his long poem before he left for Paris, the longest poem he was ever to write, *Le Bateau Ivre*.

Rimbaud wrote *Le Bateau Ivre* without ever having seen the sea. It possesses the same astonishing verbal virtuosity which is found in *Ce qu'on dit au Poète à propos de Fleurs*, the same originality in the invention of words to suit his purpose, the same daring in the choice of images and metaphors, but the poem is not ironical; it is inspired by a deep emotional and spiritual experience. It is also an anthology of separate lines of astonishing evocative magic which linger in the mind, like isolated jewels, independent of their context. Such lines as 'Les flots qu'on appelle rouleurs éternels de victimes' or 'Et j'ai vu quelquefois ce que l'homme a cru voir.' Or again:

> Pareils à des acteurs de drames très antiques,
> Les flots roulant au loin leurs frissons de volets.

And 'Baisers montant aux yeux des mers avec lenteur', or 'Je regrette l'Europe aux anciens parapets'. There are many others.

The poem is the fulfilment of the earlier vision in *Les Poètes de Sept Ans*,[8] when, lying on lengths of linen cloth, pretending they were sails, he imagined that he was far away at sea, in the freedom for which he longed, In those days, however, he knew well that it was only a dream, but now, with Verlaine's invitation, there was the hope that it would be realized and that he would finally reach the complete liberty for which he had craved since his earliest childhood.

As is usual with Rimbaud, the starting-point of *Le Bateau Ivre* is in his reading and a score of works could here be cited as 'sources' of the poem. Two works which seem particularly to have affected his imagination in its composition are two books which were very popular with the young at the end of the Second Empire: Figuier's *Ocean World* and *The Sea* by Michelet—we know that he read avidly both these authors. The former existed in a special edition for prize-giving, bound in red or in blue, and profusely illustrated. It is quite possible that Rimbaud had been awarded it amongst the large number of prizes which he won in 1869 or 1870.

Both Figuier and Michelet describe in vivid and picturesque language the fabulous monsters of the deep—the flying fishes, the sea-horses and the various forms of marine life which look, in the sea, like magical flowers. The astonishing phenomenon of the phosphorus impressed the imagination of both writers. Figuier describes his vessel as ploughing its way through a fiery mass composed of organic bodies swimming in the sea at various depths, the colour of which, in respose, was of an opal yellow mixed with green, but on the slightest movement they assume a luminous brilliance passing through shades of the deepest red, orange and green, and azure blue. The ship, as it plunges through the waves, seems to be advancing in a sea of bright flame, which is thrown off by the vessel like lightning.

This vast field of sea is formed of myriads of phosphorescent creatures which float and play on the surface of the waters like glittering particles of living fire which pursue and catch up with each other. Michelet describes the immense tract of phosphorus like a milky sea, the soft white light of which grows by degrees more animated and changes to the colour of burning sulphur, in which luminous creatures revolve on their own axis or roll along like balls of fire—first opaline yellow, then shaded with green, next breaking into a glow of red and orange, finally ending in a sombre blue. Meanwhile, on the horizon, flinging out underneath the waves streamers of many colours and of infinite length, the transparent bodies pass slowly through the sea, like actors in a silent comedy. This description recalls Rimbaud's 'arcs-en-ciel tendus comme des brides sous l'horizon des mers,' and his waves with their 'figements violets pareils à des acteurs de drames très antiques' and 'l'éveil jaune et bleu des phosphores chanteurs'.

Michelet describes the effect of a storm at sea in which the atmosphere becomes thick and dark like an immense funnel at the bottom of which lies the ship, as if in the depths of a volcanic crater. Up above is the opening with the glimpse of light and it is as if the ship was being slowly sucked up towards this opening until it is suspended in mid air, between sky and sea. Rimbaud too describes the 'cieux ultramarins aux ardents entonnoirs'.

One can imagine Rimbaud, as a boy, poring over these lovely books with their beautiful pictures which winged his fancy to further visions. But these were not the only books that he remembered as he wrote *Le Bateau Ivre*. Many other works went also to the composition of the poem—Jules Verne's *Twenty Thousand Leagues under the Sea*, Hugo's *Toilers of the Deep*, Poe's *Gordon Pym*, *The Descent into the Maelstrom*. Many other works could probably also be cited. Yet, if all the bits and snippets could be unravelled, they would not explain *Le Bateau Ivre*. The greatness is Rimbaud's alone.

The initial point of departure is certainly *Le Voyage* of Baudelaire and Rimbaud wished to continue from where Baudelaire had stopped. *Le Voyage* had kept to the regions of this world, to the contemplation of 'le spectacle ennuyeux de l'immortel péché'. Wherever Baudelaire had gone, as he wandered over the face of the world, he had only met the same things, the selfsame things in different colours.

> Amer savoir, celui qu'on tire du voyage!
> Le monde, monotone et petit, aujourd'hui,
> Hier, demain, toujours, nous fait voir notre image:
> Une oasis d'horreur dans un désert d'ennui!

Only at the very end of the poem did he conceive of flight beyond the boundaries of this world. On the last journey, whence there is no return, he will set sail on the sea of darkness, with a heart full of yearning, hoping that on this last journey he may reach a land where he will find something that will bring peace and satisfaction to his heart and ease the longing which the world has never been able to assuage.

> O Mort, vieux capitaine, il est temps! Levons l'ancre!
> Ce pays nous ennuie, ô Mort! Appareillons!
> Si le ciel et la mer sont noirs comme de l'encre,
> Nos cœurs que tu connais sont remplis de rayons!

Verse-nous ton poison pour qu'il nous réconforte!
Nous voulons, tant ce feu nous brûle le cerveau,
Plonger au fond du gouffre, Enfer ou Ciel, qu'importe?
Au fond de l'Inconnu pour trouver du *nouveau*!

Rimbaud would not be tied down nor shackled by the *ennui* of this world nor its limitations. Disgust he knew and understood, and revolt, but never *ennui*. He was a *voyant* and he would sail immediately in his mad boat—for it was his right—into the very kingdom of the future. It was here and now he would scale the heights of Heaven and plumb the depths of Hell; here and now, in this life, he would see everything, hear everything, experience everything; he would not wait to slough off human shape. He would see the invisible and express the inexpressible. 'J'ai vu quelquefois ce que l'homme a cru voir.' He was impatient to escape and to wash himself clean from the defiling filth of this world.

Plus douce qu'aux enfants la chair des pommes sures,
L'eau verte pénétra ma coque de sapin
Et des taches de vins bleus et des vomissures
Me lava, dispersant gouvernail et grappin.

Et dès lors, je me suis baigné dans le Poème
De la Mer, infusé d'astres et lactescent,
Dévorant les azurs verts; où, flottaison blême
Et ravie, un noyé pensif parfois descend;

Où, teignant tout-à-coup les bleuités, délires
Et rhythmes lents sous les rutilements du jour,
Plus fortes que l'alcool, plus vastes que nos lyres,
Fermentent les rousseurs amères de l'amour!

Thus the *bateau ivre* drifted away without guidance, with all its crew massacred save the poet alone—here he was as solitary as he was to remain all though his life—and the mad adventure began. For months it drifted at the mercy and will of the waves as they beat against the rocks; it floated in amongst islands that no man had ever seen and the poet saw rainbows stretched, like giant reins, beneath the sea, holding back a team of watery sea-horses. The waves were luminous with the phosphorus lights and the foam burst into flower, while the ocean's slow heave rippled and shimmered with light like the opening and closing slats of venetian blinds.

> J'ai vu le soleil bas, taché d'horreurs mystiques,
> Illuminant de longs figements violets,
> Pareils à des acteurs de drames très antiques,
> Les flots roulant au loin leurs frissons de volets!
>
> J'ai rêvé la nuit verte aux neiges éblouies,
> Baisers montant aux yeux des mers avec lenteurs,
> La circulation des sèves inouïes
> Et l'éveil jaune et bleu des phosphores chanteurs.
>
> J'ai suivi, des mois pleins, pareille aux vacheries
> Hystériques, la houle à l'assaut des récifs,
> Sans songer que les pieds lumineux des Maries
> Pussent forcer le muffle aux Océans poussifs.

This last verse is a characteristic example of the manner in which Rimbaud's creative imagination works, how images from several sources converge and fuse to form a single vision. In *The Descent into the Maelstrom* Poe likens the sound of the rising storm to a stampeding herd of wild buffaloes. This vision of the buffaloes —the 'vacheries hystériques'—brings to Rimbaud's mind the thought of the Camargue where the fighting bulls are bred. In the Camargue, on an island at the mouth of the Rhône, is the little town of Les Saintes-Maries-de-la-Mer, where, according to tradition, the three Maries—Marie Jacobé, Marie-Salomé and Marie-Madeleine—with their black servant Sara, Lazarus and Saint Maximin landed after being buffeted by the waves and suffering a fate similar to that of Rimbaud's *bateau ivre*. It is of them he probably thought when he said that the Maries had been able to 'forcer le muffle aux Océans poussifs'.

The feast of 'Trois Maries'—25 May—is celebrated by an important bull fight, while their black servant Sara is the patron saint of gipsies and they come there in pilgrimage from the four quarters of the globe.

At last Rimbaud's *bateau ivre*, like Michelet's ship, felt as if it were being drawn upwards and away from the world, suspended between heaven and earth, by the 'ardent entonnoir' of the sky. Then, just at the end, when he was about to burst into Eternity, the water suddenly dropped, the funnel of the sky vanished, he was hurled down to the world of reality again—this was a favourite device with Baudelaire—and the poem ends unconsciously prophetic of the poet's destiny, showing the vanity of all his dreams.

> Mais, vrai, j'ai trop pleuré! Les aubes sont navrantes.
> Toute lune est atroce et tout soleil amer:
> L'âcre amour m'a gonflé de torpeurs enivrantes.
> O que ma quille éclate! O que j'aille à la mer!

If he must come back to earth, if he must content himself with the waters of this world, then all he asks for are the waters of his childhood and his mind goes back to the early days when he had sailed on the Meuse a frail paper boat, the only craft he then possessed to bear his dreams away into infinity.

> Si je désire une eau d'Europe, c'est la flache
> Noire et froide où vers le crépuscule embaumé
> Un enfant accroupi, plein de tristesses, lâche
> Un bateau frêle comme un papillon de mai.

He knew that his wild journey was over and he must content himself with everyday reality.

> Je ne puis plus, baigné de vos langueurs, ô lames,
> Enlever leur sillage aux porteurs de cotons,
> Ni traverser l'orgueil des drapeaux et des flammes,
> Ni nager sous les yeux horribles des pontons.

In this poem Rimbaud reached one of the highest peaks of his art, and produced also one of the great masterpieces of French poetry.

At this time Delahaye tells us in *Souvenirs Familiers*, Rimbaud was trying to publish his compositions in the paper called *Le Nord-Est* which was founded on 1 July 1871 by the radical party. It was edited by Henri Perrin who, for a short time after Izambard's departure, had succeeded him as teacher at the Collège de

Charleville. Rimbaud submitted burlesque poems but Perrin, who was not gifted with much sense of humour, did not like to feel that he was being made fun of and refused to consider them.

No contribution appeared in the *Nord-Est* under Rimbaud's name, but Jules Mouquet was convinced that the satirical article entitled *Lettre du Baron de Petdechèvre* and signed 'Jean Marcel' was from his pen, and in the Introduction to the edition which he published in 1949, he makes a very good case for this attribution. It is dated 9 September 1871 and it was published on 16 September. It is written in the same vein of bitter irony and satire as in Rimbaud's poems, *Les Assis* and *Paris se repeuple*, and his prose work, *Un Cœur sous une Soutane*, and it is hard to believe that there could be anyone else in Charleville at that time capable of writing in this style. There are many passages characteristic of Rimbaud's brand of humour.

Il faut que nous nous reposions maintenant; nous l'avons bien gagné, ce repos qu'on veut nous mesurer parcimonieusement. Nous avons réorganisé une armée, bombardé Paris, écrasé l'insurrection, fusillé les insurgés, jugé leurs chefs, établi le pouvoir constituant, berné la République, préparé un ministère monarchiste et fait quelques lois qu'on refera tôt ou tard—Ce n'était pas pour faire des lois que nous étions venus à Versailles! On est homme, Anatole, avant d'être législateur. On n'a pas fait ses foins, on veut faire au moins ses vendanges.[9]

The humour and the craftsmanship of the whole article are worthy of a writer far older than Rimbaud, who was still only sixteen.

By the time it appeared Rimbaud, however, was on his way to Paris—or already there. He was overjoyed at Verlaine's invitation and thought that he was now started on his career of fame in the capital, where he would live at close quarters with the greatest poet of the day. Yet in the moment of his triumphal departure nervousness suddenly overcame him. How would he be received over there in Paris, would they be disappointed when they saw him? Delahaye did his best to encourage his friend, but he remained frightened. He knew that his clothes were shabby, for his mother refused to buy him any that year. He was uncertain of how to behave in society and he knew that timidity always swept over him at the moment when he most wanted to speak freely and to impress his hearers. He knew well that he would remain awkward and tongue-tied when he would be expected to shine and to express his opinions.

Rimbaud's departure for Paris is an important milestone in his literary career and it is necessary to realize the state of mind in which he left Charleville—a state of great mental exaltation and maturity coupled with complete inexperience and abysmal ignorance of the world. In spite of all his theories he was far from having practised the 'dérèglement de tous les sens'. He had no money for drugs—indeed these would, in any case, have been difficult to obtain in a town like Charleville—and the only drinks he had ever enjoyed were those he had managed to scrounge from friends and acquaintances. As far as his connection with prostitutes is concerned, no evidence is forthcoming but the misinterpreted line from the letter to Izambard. It is highly probable that, when he went to Paris in September 1871, he had had no experience of sex beyond the incident expressed in *Cœur Supplicié* which had awakened his curiosity, leaving him obsessed and unsatisfied, and which had inspired the blasphemous and obscene poems of the period now ending.

# PART II

## CHAPTER I

## THE VERLAINES

AT the time when Rimbaud went to Paris in the autumn of 1871, Verlaine was living with his wife's parents in the Rue Nicolet in Montmartre. He had lost his Civil Service appointment on account of his suspected sympathy with the Commune; but it is probable that his dismissal, or rather non-reappointment, by the new régime, was in part due to his inefficiency and to his intemperate habits. During the disturbed period of the war and the revolution he had slipped back into his bachelor way of life and taken once more to drink. It had been to remove him from the temptations of such associations that his mother had married him to Mathilde Mauté de Fleurville. Now that he was earning nothing his own private income, added to the marriage portion of his young wife, was no longer sufficient to keep them in bourgeois comfort, especially since Mathilde was expecting a baby. The young couple therefore went to live with the Mauté de Fleurville, who owned a small *hôtel* and garden in a quiet street in Montmartre.

Mathilde Verlaine was glad to return once more to what she still regarded as her home, for she much preferred the leisured ease of her parents' house to her more bohemian life with her husband. With naïve pride she expatiates in her memoirs on the splendour of the house, the two large reception rooms and the dining-room on the ground floor, all opening on to the trim garden, her parents' rooms on the first floor and that of her half-brother Charles, while the second floor was given over to the 'jeune ménage'. The house contained as well a library and a guest-room.[1]

The Mauté de Fleurville came of respectable moneyed bourgeois stock who had no legitimate claim to nobility. They had amassed a fortune, probably in business, though this is nowhere stated, and, as was frequently the case in the Second Empire, had then added the 'particule' to their name to give it the appearance of the nobility which they considered fitting to their fortune. As a young man M. Mauté de Fleurville had taken his degree in law at the University of Paris, but he never practised his profession, and his daughter was deeply offended when Lepelletier once described the father-in-law of his friend Verlaine as a former 'notaire'. Her father, she proudly declared,[2] never earned any money in his life, 'il n'a jamais rien fait que vivre selon ses goûts'. After the war and the Commune, he lived in ease, and respectability with his wife and family in their comfortable home in Montmartre.

Madame Mauté de Fleurville prided herself on her acquaintance with art and on her association with those who produced it. Her son by her first marriage, Charles de Sivry, was a composer of light music who enjoyed some fame in his own day, and she herself was a well-known music teacher. At this time, in 1871, young Claude Debussy was her pupil. She was proud to think that her son-in-law, Paul Verlaine, was highly spoken of in the best literary circles of the day as a poet with a future, for she had heard him praised by well-established Parnassian poets and Academicians—she was a believer in those to whom honours had been awarded. She had been pleased to give her only daughter to so eminent a man of letters and had been willing to overlook the lapses of which she had been informed, considering them to be merely the inevitable wild oats of a young Parisian, such as could, with firmness, be eradicated after marriage. She liked to think of herself as a patron of the arts, as an encourager and discoverer of unknown and young talent. She listened with great interest when Paul Verlaine spoke of the bright new star which was rising on the distant provincial horizon of literature. She thought that here was her chance of staking out her claim before anyone else heard of this young poet, and in imagination she already saw herself pointing out to future admiring audiences the famous poet, Arthur Rimbaud, whom she had rescued from great poverty and obscurity, and who had made his début from her house. He was said by her son-in-law to show promise of surpassing even Victor Hugo. It was she who suggested that Paul should invite his young friend to stay at her house, but little did she know what a monster she was introducing into the family nest. She was told that he was young and she expected to see a youth with the Botticelli angel face of Alfred de Musset as a young man. The Romantic movement had given the general public very definite ideas of what the appearance of a poet should be. Well known were the pictures of Chateaubriand looking out to sea with dreaming eyes and wind-swept locks curling round his noble brow. Well known too were the God-like grace of the young Lamartine and the austere distinction of de Vigny. But most beloved of all was Alfred de Musset's picture in his Renaissance page costume.

Madame Mauté de Fleurville did not hope that a contemporary poet could rival these gods of her youth, but she expected him at least to seem *distingué*. Even if he could not look, like Hérédia, a Spanish grandee, he could at least look a respectable schoolmaster like Mallarmé. It would never have entered her head that anyone of note could look as Rimbaud had looked the first time she set eyes on him; she could never have believed that anyone who looked like that could ever come to any good. She had only seen such men lounging on the seats in the boulevards, especially since the war, when the police had become so lax. No one like that had certainly ever entered her house.

Rimbaud's visit was a disaster from the very beginning. Verlaine and Charles Cros had gone to the station to meet him, but through some mistake they had missed him. To a country-bred lad like Rimbaud the walk meant nothing, and finding no one to meet him he set off on foot for Montmartre and arrived alone, hot and dusty, to the consternation of Madame Mauté de Fleurville and her daughter. Mathilde never forgot the amazement both she and her mother had felt when the country youth was shown into the drawing-room where they were sitting waiting for him to arrive with Verlaine, and wondering what he would be like. Now they saw a coarse young peasant, with rough hands and a face red from exposure to wind and sun. He was at this time just beginning to shoot up and his old clothes of the previous year were by now too small; the sleeves did not cover his knobbly wrists and the trousers, the famous slate-blue trousers, did not reach the coarse blue cotton socks hand-knitted by his mother. He was, moreover, extremely dirty and untidy; his hair was standing on end as if it had never been brushed, and what looked like a dirty string slung round his collar, served as a tie. Worst of all he had arrived without any kind of luggage whatsoever, no toothbrush, no hairbrush, no change of linen.[3]

Rimbaud had always possessed an uncanny, animal-like sensitivity to atmosphere and now he was quick to feel the impression that he was making. He sensed immediately, beneath the mannered politeness of mother and daughter, the hostility and the disapproval. In such cases he always became surly and silent, hiding his emotion beneath insolence. The two women were trying to entertain him, or, more correctly, trying, under great difficulties, to fulfil what they considered the social obligations of gentlefolk —they cared little whether their guest was entertained or not— when Verlaine and Cros arrived back from the station.

Verlaine too could not disguise the astonishment he felt on seeing a mere boy sitting in the drawing-room, when he had expected to find a man of over twenty, someone nearer his own age. Suddenly he saw a leggy boy with wild hair and the awkward movements of a growing youth who has not yet learnt what to do with his unwieldy limbs, and who cannot control his cracked voice. But above the scraggy and clumsy body of an adolescent not yet fully grown he saw a child's face, round-cheeked and rosy, with the purest and most piercing blue eyes he had ever encountered. He insists on the good looks of Rimbaud at this time and describes his extreme beauty of face at the age of sixteen. It appears to have been only prejudice and antipathy which made Mathilde Verlaine and so many others describe him as coarse and ugly.

The first dinner was a complete fiasco. Madame Verlaine and Madame Mauté de Fleurville paralysed Rimbaud with their bright, meaningless conversation, and he was, moreover, unused to the company of women. They darted endless and pointless questions at him concerning his journey and his future plans; and from the height of Parisian condescension, asked for his opinion of French provincial life. Rimbaud's views on this subject would in any case not have been mentionable in polite society. Charles de Sivry's brittle Parisian chatter also irritated him and soon he made no further attempt to hide his contempt of his hosts. In more propitious circumstances he would have found Charles Cros sympathetic but he was now ill at ease and bewildered, and he was still further discomfited when Cros fired questions at him concerning his æsthetic principles and his literary doctrine, and when he openly analysed his work. Rimbaud was tired and in a state of confusion, and he never was at the best of times a fluent conversationalist; now he lapsed into gloomy silence and remained tongue-tied, answering only in monosyllables the questions good-naturedly put to him. He gave the impression of surliness and ill-temper, but in truth he was more deeply sunk in misery and distress, more profoundly disappointed, than he had ever been in his life.

Looking back on the evening later, Verlaine could never remember more than one remark which Rimbaud had made, and this had no bearing on literature. There was present in the room during the meal a little dog, Madame Mauté de Fleurville's most treasured possession, a pampered and spoilt little darling but good-humoured and well-behaved, and it ran from one person to another begging for scraps of food, soliciting affection and caresses. Rimbaud, whom its antics soon began to irritate, looked down at the pretty creature and said in tones of the deepest contempt: 'Les chiens, ce sont des libéraux!'

As the meal progressed Rimbaud became more awkward and insolent. Before dinner was over and coffee served, to the horror of the ladies, he drew his filthy pipe from his pocket, crossed his legs and, leaning his elbows on the table just as if he were in a low pub, moodily puffed his evil-smelling tobacco smoke over the dinner-table.

The evening which was to stretch out indefinitely with stimulating literary conversation, ended early. Madame Mauté de Fleurville, alleging that Rimbaud must be feeling tired after his journey, and would not wish to remain up chatting, gave the signal for withdrawal not long after the meal had ended.

Rimbaud's visit never recovered from the failure of the first evening, and he made no further efforts to ingratiate himself with his hostess; in fact he did all he could to outrage her feelings by his expressions of opinion and by his conduct. He was determined that if she thought badly of him she should have ample grounds for this view. One day Verlaine on returning home found his friend smoking and sunning himself as he lay stretched in the October sun on the gravelled path that led to the house. He could be seen by every passer-by and the inhabitants of that respectable neighbourhood stood staring in at him in great amazement. There ensued much talk in the district about Madame Mauté de Fleurville's strange guest and all agreed that it was indeed curious that she should permit her son-in-law to consort with such a wild hooligan. And the gossip spread and developed through all the *loges de concierge* of the quarter.

Madame Mauté de Fleurville was firmly of the opinion that Arthur Rimbaud was depraving her son-in-law, leading him into debauch and inciting him to open rebellion. In this she was unjust, for Verlaine had, to a certain extent, escaped from the meshes of conjugal discipline before the coming of Rimbaud to Paris. He was after all ten years older than his young friend; he had knocked about the Latin Quarter since his adolescence; as a youth he was alleged to have practised sodomy and he was already a confirmed drunkard by the time of his marriage with Mathilde Mauté de Fleurville. At first, carried away by the new delights of married life with a wife only just seventeen, he had settled down temporarily under the stern discipline of his father-in-law. But conjugal respectability had begun to pall before he met Rimbaud, especially latterly, when the delicate health of his pregnant wife deprived his sensual nature of the physical joys which, hitherto, had made his bondage bearable. It would be nearer the truth to say that it was he who helped Rimbaud to reach the 'dérèglement de tous les sens' which was the latter's aim. There is no doubt that Rimbaud was an apt pupil who encouraged his elder and, driving him on to further deeds of daring, incited him against home discipline. Verlaine now knew that he had support for his most outrageous conduct and that he would no longer have to face alone the disapproval of his stern mother-in-law, that it was Rimbaud indeed who now received the brunt of disapprobation.

On 30 October 1871 George Verlaine was born and for three whole days after that everything went well. Verlaine was all that a proud young father should be. He returned every day for dinner and spent the evening with his wife. Then, on the fourth day, his good resolutions broke down under the strain of his model behaviour. He remained out until two o'clock in the morning and returned home in a state of advanced intoxication. Alcohol, and especially absinthe, was always poison to him; he came back in a nasty frame of mind and threatened all those whom he encountered. He went straight to his wife's room and when she begged him to retire to his he refused. The monthly nurse began to grow frightened and threatened to summon the parents for help, but Mathilde did not wish them to be called. Next, in spite of all remonstrances, he lay down on his wife's bed, fully dressed as he was, with his boots still on his feet and his hat on his head; he lay with his head to the foot of the bed and placed his muddy feet on the pillow close to Mathilde's face, and in this manner soon fell into a drunken sleep. Next morning, when Madame Mauté de Fleurville came to see her daughter, she was horrified at the sight of her son-in-law still lying there fast asleep and fully dressed, and Mathilde adds that her mother, in spite of her usual kindness, was indignant.[6]

In the meantime, however, old Mauté de Fleurville returned home from his shooting party in the country and the strong man immediately put down his foot, with all the pother that always arises when the masculine head of the house takes action. In violent terms he demanded what the women of the house had been about in permitting such conduct to continue and said that he would not endure the presence of this interloper in his house one moment longer. He informed his son-in-law that he must, forthwith, find another abode for his undesirable friend.

When Rimbaud had departed, Mathilde entered the guest-room to have it set to rights and she found, to her amazement and revulsion, little insects crawling over the pillow, which she had never seen before, but her mother, apparently more experienced, informed her that these were lice. She told her husband what she had found, hoping to disgust him with his friend but, Paul only burst out laughing in her face and said that Rimbaud liked to keep such parasites in his hair to have them handy to throw on the priests whom he passed in the streets. [7]

Rimbaud, however, had not waited to be turned out by Mauté de Fleurville, or for Verlaine to find him other lodgings. He fled, of his own accord, without telling anyone where he was going—this was easy since he had no possessions except the clothes on his back. But Verlaine felt responsible for him and his kind heart was troubled to think of his young friend alone and friendless in Paris without any means of subsistence, and he looked for him everywhere that he could think of, but did not succeed in finding him. It was only some weeks later that he met him by chance in the street and he was then startled by the change in him. His appearance of bucolic health had completely vanished and he was pale and hollow-cheeked, in rags and covered with vermin. Since he had left Montmartre he had tried to obtain work, but in vain; he had done any odd job that he could pick up in order not to starve; amongst other things he had peddled rings for keys in the streets. [8] He had lived in the same state of destitution which he had known during his previous visit. Moved to tears by the sight of his poverty, Verlaine gave him a square meal and then brought him to Charles Cros and André Gill, who were to look after him until some permanent arrangement could be made. [9] Verlaine next approached Théodore de Banville, whose kindness and generosity to unknown and struggling artists was proverbial. Banville remembered the name of the young poet who had written to him on two occasions from Charleville and he rented for him an unfurnished attic in the house in which he himself lived, in the Rue de Buci, off the Boulevard Saint-Germain; this his mother furnished with the things most urgently needed. Ever since his earliest years, Madame de Banville had carefully tended her only son, encouraging and fostering his poetic talent, and priding herself that in so doing she was a better and more understanding mother than the mother of his unfortunate friend,

Charles Baudelaire. Théodore was now close on fifty, one of the best considered poets of the day, and she still looked after him with the same jealous and sympathetic care. Thinking of his early years, her heart was touched at the sight of the young poet from the provinces, a mere child, who had come far from his own mother's care, without a penny in his pocket, to fight his way in the heartless town of Paris.

She and her son provided him with a roof over his head, but it was Charles Cros who fed him—as is learnt from the unpublished letter to Pradelle, in the Bérès documents, dated 6 November 1871. Eventually several men of letters subscribed the sum of three francs a day for his current expenses. On this he would not certainly grow rich or self-indulgent, but he would, at least, not starve.

Rimbaud did not, however, remain long in the rue de Buci. It is alleged that the neighbours complained to Banville of his guest's conduct, and that as a result of this he was requested to leave the house. It is said that when he first went to his new room in his verminous, filthy clothes, he could not bear the thought of defiling so fresh and clean a lodging. He then undressed and, to the horror of the people living on the opposite side of the street, stood naked at the open window to fling the bundle of dirty clothes into the thoroughfare below.

It is here, we are told, that he wrote *Les Chercheuses de Poux*, inspired by an event of the previous year. In spite of the subject-matter, the extreme loveliness of the lines has an evocative power which suggests a poem by Baudelaire:

> Quand le front de l'enfant, plein de rouges tourmentes,
> Implore l'essaim blanc des rêves indistincts,
> Il vient près de son lit deux grandes soeurs charmantes
> Avec de frêles doigts aux ongles argentins.
>
> Elles assoient l'enfant auprès d'une croisée
> Grande ouverte où l'air bleu baigne un fouillis de fleurs
> Et dans ses lourds cheveux où tombe la rosée,
> Promènent leurs doigts fins, terribles et charmeurs.

Il écoute chanter leurs haleines craintives
Qui fleurent de longs miels végétaux et rosés
Et qu'interrompt parfois un sifflement, salives
Reprises sur la lèvre ou désirs de baisers.

Il entend leurs cils noirs battant sous les silences
Parfumés; et leurs doigts électriques et doux
Font crépiter, parmi ses grises indolences,
Sous leurs ongles royaux la mort des petits poux.

Voilà que monte en lui le vin de la Paresse,
Soupir d'harmonica qui pourrait délirer;
L'enfant se sent, selon la lenteur des caresses,
Sourdre et mourir sans cesse un désir de pleurer.

After leaving the Rue de Buci, Rimbaud camped for a time with the composer Cabaner, sleeping on his sofa. Cabaner used to live in the Hôtel des Etrangers, in the Rue Racine near the Odéon, and he was the vaguest and most absent-minded of creatures who never knew or minded how many people made use of his room for a night's shelter. He thought of nothing beyond his art and he had only been very dimly conscious of the siege of Paris by the Prussians. When the second siege started, that by the Versaillais, he said: 'What! are the Germans at it again?' Then, noticing amazement and disgust on the faces of those who were listening to him, he quickly corrected himself, saying: 'Goodness! It has lasted so long that I thought it must be some other country by now.'[10]

He was a man of emaciated, almost diaphanous appearance, whose face seemed to consist solely in a soft, flowing beard and a pair of large, dreamy eyes. Verlaine used to call him 'Jesus Christ after three years of absinthe'.[11]

It was when Rimbaud was camping with Cabaner that Delahaye saw him for the first time since his departure from Charleville. He found him in the dirty little lounge of the hotel surrounded by a crowd of men of letters, and he was lying, apparently asleep, on the sofa, unconscious of all who were around him. Suddenly he stretched himself, sat up rubbing his eyes and made a grimace of disgust. He was just coming round from a hashish trance which had proved most disappointing. He had lain down expecting to enjoy the loveliest of visions but all he had seen was a series of black and white moons chasing one another, at various speeds, across the sky. This must have been his first experience of drugs; it was November 1871.

Then Delahaye looked again at his school friend and saw how much he had altered during the two months he had spent in Paris. He had shot up more than a foot; he was no longer a boy, but a tall and lanky youth, and he was most distressingly thin. He looked filthy and sordid, draped as he was in an old second-hand overcoat, several sizes too large for him, which hung in tatters from his thin shoulders, and with this he wore a battered old grey felt hat. Delahaye, who was at heart a respectable bourgeois, was shocked at the appearance of his friend.

Next, when he had exhausted Cabaner's hospitality, Rimbaud slept for some weeks in the studios of those willing to grant him the charity of a night's shelter. Finally, however, Verlaine rented for him a room in a little street off the Boulevard Montparnasse, the Rue Campagne-Première, then, as now, a street of artists' studios. This was in January 1872 and Rimbaud occupied this room until he returned to Charleville for a time in March. This room, 'pleine de jour sale et de bruits d'araignées,'[12] was the scene of many of the orgies of Rimbaud and Verlaine which led to the former's temporary exile from the capital. When he returned in May he lived in the Rue Monsieur-le-Prince and in the sordid little Hôtel de Cluny in the Rue Victor Cousin, near the Sorbonne; he remained there until he left for Brussels in July, in company with Verlaine.

CHAPTER II

PARIS

PARIS was a disappointment to Rimbaud for he was not a success with the literary people with whom he wished to stand well. Even Verlaine's boon companions, bohemians though they thought themselves to be, would never have descended to the depths of debauch to which Rimbaud was willing to descend. And moreover, there was all the difference in the world between La Bohême at the end of the Second Empire and during the first years of the Third Republic, and that of the 'nineties. In the later period dirt and depravity were considered the hallmark of genius and many a respectable 'fils de famille' ceased to wash and adopted dissolute habits in order to simulate the genius which he did not possess. Baudelaire, on the contrary, no matter to what depths of poverty he sank, always prided himself on spending at least two hours each day on his toilet, and he once fiercely arraigned his mother for daring to suggest that straitened means might have brought about a degradation of his person. In the 'nineties Baudelaire would have flaunted his poverty with pride and have gloried in it. In 1871, literature still remained a respectable and highly considered calling. The authors themselves took their position seriously as being that of men who were the depositories of truth and entrusted with the duty of helping in the 'redressement moral' of France after the disaster of the Franco-Prussian war and the tragedy of the Commune. A strange situation arose a few years later, in 1875, when Verlaine's poems were black-balled for inclusion in the third series of Le Parnasse Contemporain on grounds concerning only the moral character of their author. Poems from his pen had been printed in the issue of 1866 and in that of 1870 and these had been greatly admired and praised. He was in England in 1875 when he heard that a further series was being projected and he submitted certain of his verses for inclusion, some of the beautiful poems published later in Sagesse. However, between the second series of Le Parnasse Contemporain and the third, his relationship with Rimbaud had occurred, the trial in Brussels, and his subsequent term of imprisonment. As a result of this his poems were refused by the selection committee.[1] This committee consisted of three of his former friends, Banville, Coppée and Anatole France. Banville and Coppée abstained from voting, priding themselves that in so doing they were giving proof of tolerant generosity, but they were, in fact, merely throwing the brunt of the decision on to

Anatole France. He, however, was restrained by no scruples of affection, generosity or pity for his former friend and he wrote on his voting slip, 'L'auteur est indigne et ses vers sont les plus mauvais qu'on ait vus.'[2]

Anatole France was here giving proof neither of loyal friendship nor of literary acumen for the poems were amongst the finest that Verlaine had ever written. And so it came about that the third series of Le Parnasse Contemporain appeared without any contribution from the pen of Verlaine.

It was literary men with similar opinions and principles whom Rimbaud met in Paris, and it could not be expected that they would approve of his professed absence of moral standards, of his dirt and of his total lack of a sense of responsibility. They could not, moreover, endure his arrogance which they considered completely unjustified. He, on his side, made no effort to hide the scorn he felt for all those whom he met, and he did not disguise from them the fact that he considered them antediluvian in their theories of art. He went amongst them with a perpetual sneer of contempt on his face.

The war and the Commune had, as yet, made little difference in the æsthetic ideals of the literary world in Paris. It was the Parnassian conception of art which generally prevailed, as it had prevailed all through the Second Empire. The writers and artists professed to worship beauty, and beauty for them meant harmony and serenity. Above all else they worshipped the beauty of the human body, particularly of the female body; not the realistic beauty portrayed in Courbet's and Manet's paintings, but an etherealized and sexless beauty which could rouse no low desires. 'Le nu harmonieux' they called it. It can be imagined that Rimbaud's *Vénus Anadyomène*, 'belle hideusement d'un ulcère à l'anus,' was not calculated to please them. Although Baudelaire had died in 1867, his work was not yet understood or appreciated, except by a few rare poets like Verlaine, and even then only imperfectly. The other poets, with their eyes turned towards the past where they considered the source of real beauty sprang, could not accept his new conception of beauty, with its urban types, city men and women instead of gods and goddesses, narrow, slummy streets instead of fresh green glades, apartment houses instead of classic palaces. The only point on which they agreed with him was in his worship for work well done. Leconte de Lisle was the leader of the poets in Paris at this time, though the most typical was perhaps Hérédia with his perfect and beautiful, cold and monotonous, verse. In Hérédia's work can most readily be seen how much poetry had lost of the freedom it had gained during the Romantic revolution. According to the Parnassian recipe it was quite possible to compose what was considered the highest poetry about almost nothing, and this led inevitably to the bankruptcy of poetry, for the conception of true poetry is not fulfilled 'by pure language and liquid versification'. Parnassian verse has been called a clever and ingenious arrangement of bric-à-brac. To these writers Rimbaud's vital and very personal form of art could not possibly make an appeal. One and all they solidly rejected him on account of what they called the chaos of his theories and his errors in grammar and syntax. In their attitude can be seen not merely dislike and disapproval but the primordial and instinctive terror of change. All the best considered poets of mature years cast him out, Leconte de Lisle and Banville; he was not even accepted by those of a generation younger, Coppée, Hérédia and Catulle Mendès, who imagined themselves progressive. Verlaine alone still had confidence in his friend's powers and his opinion was held of little account since it was believed that Rimbaud had cast an evil eye on him and had bewitched him.

By a strange coincidence, however, there had died in Paris in the previous November a poet with whom Rimbaud had much in common, a poet as fiercely individualistic and revolutionary as he, Isidore Ducasse, who wrote under the name of Comte de Lautréamont. He had died unknown and undiscovered at the age of twenty-four, but his *Chants de Maldoror* have become to-day a rich hunting-ground for Surrealist writers and painters. The richness and strangeness of Lautréamont's imagination in many ways recall that of Rimbaud, but there is less coherence in his vision and he is less of an artist. That is to say that although his imagination is in no way inferior to that of Rimbaud he possesses to a lesser degree the power of giving concrete shape to this vision, of communicating it to his readers, of taking from it what is unnecessary and which only overloads it. He did not know how to choose from amongst the wealth of visions that crowded in on him, he never learnt to separate the gold from the dross. Rimbaud's unerring artistic sense is clearly seen in the development of one draft of a poem to the next, in those poems of which several versions exist. If the rough draft of *Une Saison en Enfer*—of which only two fragments have come down to us—is compared with the final version which he himself passed for press, his method will be seen at work. In the second version he has simplified and pruned his work, ejecting what is merely exuberance of emotional feeling, the useless froth, and leaving only what is fully expressive.

It is regrettable that circumstances did not permit Rimbaud and Lautréamont to meet for they held many literary theories in common. In 1869 Lautréamont felt the same artistic needs and aspirations as Rimbaud felt in 1871, and then he wrote: 'A l'heure que j'écris, de nouveaux frissons parcourent l'atmosphère intellectuelle; il ne s'agit que d'avoir le courage de les regarder en face.' His æsthetic doctrine, expressed in *Poésies*, bears some similarity to that of Rimbaud set forth in *Les Lettres du Voyant*. It is, however, impossible for Rimbaud to have known Lautréamont's work before formulating his own theory. The first canto of *Les Chants de Maldoror*, privately printed in 1868, passed unnoticed and the complete work, published by Lacroix in 1869, was never sold, as Lautréamont refused to make the alterations which the publisher, at the very last moment, considered necessary in view of the disturbed political situation. Then came the Franco-Prussian War and, before that was over, the death of the poet.

Rimbaud was doing nothing to ingratiate himself with the literary men whom he met; on the contrary, feeling that he was not being a success, he did his utmost to make himself even more disliked. He silenced all good will amongst those prepared to be kind to him, fearing that they might be prompted by pity, and pity Rimbaud's pride was never able to accept. Restrained by no sentiments of kindness or sympathy he brutally hurt the most tender feelings of all those with whom he came into contact.

Lepelletier, Verlaine's close friend, had recently lost his mother to whom he had been devoted, and Rimbaud wounded him deeply by calling him contemptuously a 'salueur de morts' when he saw him raising his hat as a funeral passed. All those who met Rimbaud thought that his conduct was particularly offensive considering his extreme youth. They felt that it was not merely to be excused as the provincial awkwardness of a country bumpkin, but that it was insufferable insolence to his elders and betters. At the Café de Cluny, the meeting-place of the poets, he used to lie full length on the seats, pretending to be asleep if verses which did not please him were being read, or else emitting low grunts of disgust and scorn.[3] If ever he opened his lips it was to let loose a torrent of revolutionary opinions which were badly received by his hearers. It was little more than six months since the Commune and the memory of those terrible weeks had burnt deeply into the minds of all Parisians.

He became the *bête noire* particularly of the kind and gentle poet Albert Mérat. Mérat was to have figured amongst the poets in Fantin Latour's picture, *Le Coin de Table*,[4] but at the last moment he refused to sit, saying that he did not wish to go down to posterity in company with that young hooligan Arthur Rimbaud. Finally says Mathilde Verlaine, a vase of flowers was substituted for him. Posterity does not feel that it has greatly lost by the substitution, for who to-day remembers the name of the gentle Mérat? Indeed the only names in the picture which are known to-day are those of Paul Verlaine and his undesirable friend.[5]

At this time Mérat had just published a book of verse entitled *L'Idole*, a sonnet sequence to celebrate all the physical beauties of woman. Verlaine and Rimbaud wrote a disrespectful parody of this work in the *Album Zutique*, a poem entitled *Le Sonnet du Trou du Cul*. The poem is obscene and pornographic and may have been the chief cause of Mérat's hostility to Rimbaud.[6]

It is sad that Rimbaud should have antagonized Albert Mérat for he was one of the few poets whom, before coming to Paris, he had admired. He had said that modern literature had only two *voyants*, Paul Verlaine and Albert Mérat.[7]

One evening at the literary dinner called *Les Vilains Bonshommes*,

Rimbaud disgraced himself so that he was never again invited to attend. This dinner was held periodically at the Café du Théâtre du Bobino; it was attended by the principal writers of the day, including Banville, Hérédia, Coppée and Verlaine, and Rimbaud went several times as Verlaine's guest. This evening, however, Jean Aicard was reading a selection of his poems and Rimbaud, by the end of dinner more than a little drunk, was punctuating every line with the word 'merde' uttered in a loud and distinct voice so that all present could hear. At first the guests pretended not to be conscious of what he was saying, thinking that he would then eventually grow tired and stop of his own accord, but it soon began to get on their nerves, especially as his voice was growing louder and drowning the voice of the poet. Then Carjat, the photographer, took it on himself to silence the impudent boy. When Rimbaud insolently replied that he would be silent for no one, Carjat shook him roughly and told him to be quiet or he would pull his ears. Rimbaud, now completely out of hand, seized hold of Verlaine's sword-stick, dashed at Carjat and would have done him bodily harm had those present not taken hold of him and reft the sword from his grasp. After this one of the other guests took him home to sleep off the effects of his intoxication.[8]

It was decided, after the events of that evening, that he was never again to be allowed to be present at the dinners of the society.

Then Rimbaud withdrew more and more within himself, into the hot-house atmosphere of his quickly developing mind, and in that confined and unventilated space, his pride and arrogance matured with the astonishing rapidity of everything else in him. Gazing with ceaseless contemplation on himself alone, he became more conscious than ever of his own originality, of his superiority to others and of the essential soundness of all his views. He was fast growing exasperated with everyone and everything. Had he been a 'climber' he might have been able to curb his expressions of disgust and to flatter those whom he considered his inferiors, but he did not hide his contempt and soon all the men of letters left him severely alone. There was, nevertheless, besides

Verlaine, one man who recognized his originality and promise, and this was Léon Valade. In a letter to his friend, the literary critic, Emile Blémont, he describes the effect that Rimbaud had on him in his first days in Paris.[9]

You missed a great deal in not being present at the last dinner of *Les Affreux Bonshommes*. There a most alarming poet, not yet eighteen, was exhibited by Paul Verlaine his inventor, and indeed his John the Baptist. Big hands, big feet, a completely babyish face, like that of a child of thirteen, deep blue eyes! His temperament, more wild than shy. Such is the boy, whose imagination is a compound of great power and undreamt of corruption, who has fascinated and terrified all our friends. D'Hervilly said: "Behold Jesus in the midst of the doctors." "More likely Satan!" replied Maître, and so the more apt description occurred to me "Satan in the midst of the doctors." I cannot give you the life history of our poet. Suffice it to say that he had just come from Charleville with the firm intention of never going home again. Come and you will be able to read his verses and to judge for yourself.

If it were not for the millstone which Fate so often keeps in reserve to hang about our necks, I should say that we are here beholding the birth of a genius. This is the statement of my considered opinion, which I have reached after three weeks of reflection and it is not merely a passing whim.[10]

Nevertheless, by degrees Rimbaud dropped out of Paris literary life and spent his time in the company of Verlaine, of the artist Forain, nicknamed Gavroche,[11] and of Richepin, all wild, antisocial creatures like himself. With these he sat most of the day in the cafés of the *Boul' Mich* drinking absinthe and living in a more or less permanent state of intoxication. This was the time when Verlaine was dissipating, chiefly on orgies with him, the capital which he had inherited from his father. When the cafés closed and finally broke up their revelry they used to repair to Rimbaud's room in the Rue Campagne-Première, there to continue their carousing until the following morning was far advanced.

There is no doubt that with Verlaine Rimbaud was finally able to reach the 'long et raisonné dérèglement de tous les sens.'

'Il y a bien un lieu de boisson que je préfère,' he wrote to

Delahaye,[12] 'Vive l'Académie d'absomphe,* malgré la mauvaise volonté des garçons! C'est le plus délicat et le plus tremblant des habits, que l'ivresse par la vertu de cette sauge des glaciers, l'absomphe.'

He was not, however, unconscious of the resulting physical degradation in his person through intoxication—although he considered this degradation necessary—for he added, 'Mais pour après se coucher dans la merde!'

There is a great difference between Rimbaud and Verlaine in their attitude towards drunkenness and debauch. Verlaine never asked for more than a mere momentary satisfaction of his senses and he did not question the why or the wherefore. Rimbaud, however, who had much of the puritan in his composition, considered debauch a necessary æsthetic and spiritual discipline, and for him it was no self-indulgence. It became, on the contrary, in his inverted asceticism, a form of self-maceration, a form of self-flagellation. It was the hairshirt which he always wore, the scourge he always carried stained with drops of his blood. He obtained little pleasure from the mere gratification of his senses and this the simple, less reflective and more light-hearted Verlaine could never understand. In *Comédie de la Soif*, describing intoxication, Rimbaud writes:

> J'aime, autant, mieux même,
> Pourrir dans l'étang,
> Sous l'affreuse creme,
> Près des bois flottants.[13]

His life of debauch was for him one long martyrdom, but a martyrdom giving him all the ecstatic joys of a religious martyrdom, and to reach this sublime condition he was willing to sacrifice dignity, health and purity. When his poetic production of this period is studied it will be seen that this state of sacrifice and martyrdom was concurrent, in his case, with a state of triumph and exaltation, and that indeed the triumph and the exaltation depended on the martyrdom and the sacrifice. In later years when he realized the vanity of this form of martyrdom he treated his

* Absinthe.

body as hardly, but in the opposite direction, and did not allow it even the most legitimate and necessary comforts. Now he became a *supplicié du vice* and this explains how, in the midst of depravity and vice, his face kept the look of extraordinary purity which we see in the photograph taken by Carjat at this time; the eyes and brows have in them an astonishing and spiritual beauty. 'His eyes,' said Delahaye, 'were the most beautiful that I have ever seen, with an expression of courage and gallantry, as if ready for all sacrifices, when he was serious; with an expression of child-like gentleness when he smiled; and always with an astonishing depth and tenderness.'[14]

There was in Rimbaud's innocence and purity a platinum-like quality which no depravity could corrode. 'All the evil of the world passed through his being' said Rivière, 'but only as a purge.' Debauch was for him a doctrine, a religious aim, and it was as stony a path to travel as that of virtue. One guesses in him at times a regret for his early uncomplicated purity, for the innocence of the days which he had spent in the open air of his native Ardennes, when he did not yet know what vice was; when he had wandered free amongst the mountains and the rivers; when he had not yet assumed this heavy burden. One feels in him a craving for rest, a weariness of the spirit in his self-imposed martyrdom and a longing that the bitter cup might be taken away from his lips. But, as long as he believed in his ideal, his fanaticism did not allow him to weaken.

CHAPTER III

## ALCHEMY AND MAGIC

IT is known that Rimbaud was much interested in books of alchemy and magic at the same time that he was studying occult philosophy. He himself declared that he had attained a state of bliss through the practice of magic—'J'ai fait la magique étude du bonheur'—that magic had been one of his means for attaining 'le dérèglement de tous les sens', which was one of the essential points of his æsthetic doctrine.

Although the librarian at the Municipal Library at Charleville did not approve of such reading, considering it unsuitable for a boy of his age, and believing that his interest in such literature could only be obscene and pornographic.

Yet, in the nineteenth century, sorcerers, wizards, and witches were no longer regarded, by those who took a pride in their progressive ideas and freedom of mind, as evil. Rimbaud, as a reader and follower of Michelet, would have learnt from the medieval portions of his *Histoire de France* and from *La Sorcière*, how important a part witches and sorcerers had played in the liberation of the human mind and spirit. Michelet declared that it was they who had first carried on research in science and mathematics, but that they had been persecuted by the Church which felt that such knowledge was a danger, since it might lead its flock to rebellion and to seek freedom. He considered that it was the Church which had delayed for so long the reconciliation between Christ and Satan. For him Satan represented intellectual curiosity and he claimed that it was he who had invented chemistry, physics and mathematics. Satan was the greatest magician— he used the word here in its original meaning of heir to the wisdom of the Magi, the wise men of the East—it is he who lights up the darkness of chaos, of life, with the torch of learning and discovery. He is the great teacher, the great healer, and it was he who invented—as well as chemistry, physics and mathematics— medicine. Magicians and witches were the first doctors and they were persecuted by the Church for their discoveries since it was considered that disease, ignorance and dirt were sent by God to test man. Michelet declared that the Renaissance was not in truth found amongst the great Churchmen such as Abelard but amongst the despised and hounded sorcerers and witches who achieved more in reality for the liberation of the human mind.

Thus when Rimbaud began the study of magic and alchemy it was with no sensation of wrong-doing, but rather with a feeling of high purpose. His aim was to help and to liberate others. 'Il faut que j'en aide d'autres,' he said in *Une Saison en Enfer*. The

RIMBAUD IN 1871
*a photograph by Carjat*

'LE COIN DE TABLE' BY FANTIN-LATOUR

alchemist receives the fruit of the eternal tree not for himself alone but for others and for the perfection of the question of the precious substance. His aim is not to attain moral perfection for himself alone, but to procure the mysterious essence and to create the incorruptible. Thus it is of small moment if he were himself destroyed physically and spiritually, it matters little whether he suffers—he would certainly be persecuted as all other prophets had been before him—and he must be prepared for this self-appointed martyrdom. The alchemists say that there is no light without shadow and no psychic completeness without imperfection. Sin and suffering are needed for this—the suffering of imperfection without which there is no movement upwards.

The real aim of magic is—as Eliphas Lévi says[1]—the conquest of the 'point central'. Those who reach this point are the 'thaumaturges' of science and they are masters of the riches of this world and of all other worlds. Nature obeys them because what they wish is the law of Nature, they are Nature itself, and they have reached the real Kingdom of God, the *Sanctum Regnum* of the Cabala. They have, on their own, attained in a certain measure, the omnipotence of God. Rimbaud came to believe that he too had been granted the privilege of reaching this stage, that he had been able to tear away the veil which hid the mysteries from view, and that he had lived 'étincelle d'or de la lumière *nature*'.[2] Nature obeyed his behest and he was able to invent new flowers, new worlds, new colours. He imagined that he was to be granted the power of reconciling Christ and Satan, and of cutting down the tree of good and evil, in order to bring in universal love and brotherhood. In *Illuminations* he said: 'On nous a promis d'enterrer dans l'ombre l'arbre du bien et du mal . . . afin que nous amenions notre très pur amour.'[3]

There is no evidence to show in what consisted Rimbaud's practice of magic. It does not seem that he ever dabbled in the evil experiments of black magic—demonology, black masses, witches' Sabbaths, or any obscene ceremonies. There is no proof that any of these things interested or attracted him. There is no indication that he experimented actively in alchemy, or that he believed in it in the literal sense, but only that he read alchemical texts and was influenced by their spiritual doctrine. He seems to have been more drawn towards the philosophic side of magic than the pornographic or blasphemous; and it was the religious aspect of alchemy, with its mysterious symbolism, which seems to have inspired him, and from which he drew images and suggestions which greatly enhanced the evocative power of his poetry. He found in alchemical texts and dictionaries an inexhaustible repertory of symbols and myths which gave the impression of mystery and hidden depths to his writings.

When he conceived his *Lettres du Voyant* his aim had been to create a new form of poetry, and to become a new kind of poet. The artistic aspect had then prevailed. Now his search—symbolically—for the 'philosopher's stone' was more important to him than poetry as an art. Now poetry became for him less an art than a magical exercise which would enable him to reach the regions beyond the world. Therefore his ideas became more significant for him than anything else; the search for wisdom and a philosophy more vital than the quest for mere beauty. This will explain how, later, he was able to abandon poetry when he thought that there were other and quicker ways of reaching his objective.

Alchemy is the science the object of which is the production of the philosopher's stone, or the philosopher's gold, and for this certain specific substances are used. For most people alchemy is merely the transmutation of baser metals into gold. To achieve this the base metals are broken down into their separate component parts through the action of fire, purified, blended and finally fixed at the appropriate stage, the stage of gold. Alchemists claim that by doing this they are working in the same mysterious way as Nature does, and with the same substance. Hermes Trismegistus was the first alchemist—hence the name hermetic philosophy.

There are seven stages, or processes, in the production of the gold: calcination, putrefaction, solution, distillation, sublimation, conjunction and finally fixation. They produce, during the processes, and in their correct progression, the various colours which are proof that the experiment is proceeding satisfactorily:

There are three main colours. First the black—the indication of dissolution and putrefaction—and when it appears it is a sign that the experiment is going well, that the calcination has had its proper effect of breaking down the various substances. Next comes the white, the colour of purification; and the third is the red, the colour of complete success. There are intermediary colours as well, passing through all the shades of the rainbow. Grey is the passage from black to white; yellow from white to red. Sometimes the gold is not produced even when the red appears, then, says Philalèthe,[4] it moves on to green, remains there for a time and turns blue. Care must be taken at this point that it does not return to black, for then the process would have to be begun all over again. If success comes then the gold should appear after the blue, grains of philosopher's gold. Sometimes the gold is in grains, but sometimes in liquid form, *aurum potabile* it is called, the elixir of long life. The whole process is sometimes described as the four ages, or the four seasons.

The colours are, as it were, the language, the shorthand, of the alchemists which they can all read and understand, and there are many images, metaphors and allegories to express them—or to disguise them. Dom Pernety, the eighteenth-century Benedictine alchemist, considers that all the Egyptian and Greek legends are in reality alchemical experiments expressed allegorically.[5] On the other hand, there are some who claim that the experiments of alchemy were never intended to be more than symbolism; that the quest for the philosopher's stone, the philosopher's gold, is only the symbol for endeavour to attain perfection of soul, for endeavouring to reach the fullness of vision; that human longing for purity and salvation is all that is expressed in all works of alchemy. Dom Pernety compiled a dictionary of alchemical symbols, entitled *Dictionnaire Mytho-Hermétique*, which is a repertory of poetical images.

Here is the place to mention Rimbaud's famous and notorious poem, *Sonnet des Voyelles*, since it was probably written just before he came to Paris, or soon after, at the time when he began the study of magic and alchemy. This poem was given prominence above all his other poems by the Symbolist Movement, and it was the point of departure of René Ghil's scientific *Instrumentation Verbale*.

It is fashionable to-day to believe that this poem was composed as a hoax, and that Rimbaud was merely mystifying his readers. Many people, including his close friend Izambard, were never certain when he was in earnest. Izambard made the mistake of seeing in *Cœur Supplicié* a joke in doubtful taste. Yet the more Rimbaud is studied, the more convinced one becomes that he misled his public less frequently than has been imagined, and that his poems—this sonnet in particular—were written in all seriousness. In *Une Saison en Enfer*, a work the sincerity of which cannot be doubted, he declared, criticizing what he then considered had been his greatest error and delusion, 'I invented the colour of vowels.'[6]

There was nothing startling or new in this conception of the connexion between colours and sound since Ballanche, Hoffmann, Gautier, Baudelaire—and even Balzac—had all described the sensation of colour being identical with that of sound, and of the possibility of stimulating one particular sense by appealing to another. It had been observed that the confusion of sensation became more marked for those in a state of hallucination or under the influence of certain drugs, and it has moreover, since then been proved scientifically that, at such times, the centres which experience the sensation of light can be stimulated by impressions received, not on the retina but in the organ of hearing. The patient will then, in fact, see what has no existence. This confusion of sensation can be due to the results of narcotic poisoning, or of venereal disease. From imagining one is seeing what in reality one is hearing there is, especially for a man with Rimbaud's passion for absoluteness, but one step to believing that the intimate connexion existing between sight and sound could be set down as a formula. It is unlikely that, when he composed the poem, he had worked out a regular system of vowel coloration, that he had tested his theory, or even that he knew precisely what he was doing. It is obvious that no strict or logical application of the sonnet is possible. Only a man very simple and obstinate could have gone to the lengths to which René Ghil went in his *En Méthode de l'Oeuvre*.

One theory is that Rimbaud used, in the composition of the poem, an alphabet which had been his as a child. The article putting forward this claim propounds—in other respects—many erroneous views which it is not profitable to discuss here,[7] but the theory is a possible one since there was an alphabet with coloured letters which was used extensively amongst French children during the Second Empire.[8] This may have been the starting point of Rimbaud's sonnet. The first six pages are devoted to the vowels—one to each page—and each vowel is differently coloured. Each page has also a list of words the initial letter of which is the vowel of that page. Only one of the vowels differs from Rimbaud's notation—the letter E. With Rimbaud it is white, whereas in the alphabet, it is yellow. It is possible that the colour of this letter, in the copy used by the Rimbaud children, had become so faint as to seem, in Rimbaud's memory, a creamy white, the white of old ivory. If this alphabet is indeed the starting point of Rimbaud's poem, then the memory of it was probably subconscious, and the poet himself unaware of it.

However, another explanation is possible, and indeed more likely. The poem was written at a time when he was studying magic and drawing some of his imagery from the doctrine of alchemy.

The colours here used are in the correct alchemical sequence during the process of producing the philosopher's gold, the elixir of life. The first colour to appear in the retort is black. That is the colour of dissolution, of putrefactions—as the alchemists say—when the chemicals are broken down into their several component parts, so as to obtain the elements in an unadulterated state, for without this it is not possible to produce the gold. In this state of putrefaction, dissolution or cadaver—there are many epithets for it—the gold is latent though not visible. During the next stage the colour gradually lightens until it becomes white, the state of purity when all extraneous and impure elements have been removed. Next comes the red when, if fortune favours the alchemist, the gold appears. But according to Philalèthe, the experiment is not always so rapidly successful, the red turns to green, remains there for a few days and

then turns to blue. This is the last colour, the omega, before
the blackness is again reached, and care must be taken that this
does not happen, for then the process must be started again from
the beginning. If the correct temperature and moisture have been
sustained then after the hyacinth blue the gold begins to appear,
grains of the purest gold bearing no resemblance to ordinary
metal gold, the philosopher's gold, perfect gold, the universal
medicine which prolongs life.

> A noir, E blanc, I rouge, U vert, O bleu: voyelles,
> Je dirai quelque jour vos naissances latentes.
> A, noir corset velu des mouches éclatantes
> Qui bombinent autour des puanteurs cruelles,
>
> Golfes d'ombre; E,candeurs des vapeurs et des tentes,
> Lances de glaciers fiers, rois blancs, frissons d'ombelles!
> I, pourpres, sang craché, rire des lèvres belles
> Dans la colère ou les ivresses pénitentes,
>
> U, cycles, vibrements divins des mers virides;
> Paix des pâtis semés d'animaux, paix des rides
> Que l'alchimie imprime aux grands fronts studieux.
>
> O, suprême Clairon plein des strideurs étranges,
> Silences traversés des Mondes et des Anges . . .
> O l'Oméga, rayon violet de Ses Yeux![9]

It will be seen that, in this poem, Rimbaud suggests that the poet
is a practiser of alchemy, and 'A', the colour of black, evokes
the images of dissolution and putrefaction. In alchemy one of the
symbols for the white colour is the letter 'E', and also the word
'vapeur'; and the images which the poet links to the vowel 'I'
are amongst those which Dom Pernety gives in his *Dictionnaire
Mytho-Hermétique*, to designate the alchemical experiment which
has reached the stage of the red colour. Green is the colour of
Venus, and she was born of the sea—hence the 'vibrements
divins' of the green seas. Finally, last of all, comes the blue, the
suspense before the gold appears, the sound of the trumpet
announcing victory. In alchemy the final achievement of the

gold is often taken as a symbol of attaining the vision of God. Rimbaud writes, 'Ses Yeux' as if to indicate the Divinity. The blue eyes also suggests the God in *Fleurs* from *Illuminations*, 'un dieu aux énormes yeux bleus et aux formes de neige,' a mystical figure which appears again in *Being Beauteous*, of the same collection.

It is possible that both sources inspired Rimbaud in the composition of the sonnet. From his memory of the alphabet he got the idea of giving each vowel its own individual colour; and from the doctrine of alchemy their sequence and meaning.

In his writing Rimbaud uses many alchemical symbols and metaphors—a large number of these are to be found in the *Dictionnaire Mytho-Hermétique*. He does not, however, use them, as did many alchemists of olden times, to disguise experiments, but rather to give the impression that a mystery exists and is hidden; and also to evoke a state of mind. He uses alchemical terms to suggest moods, from the blackness of the first stage expressing depression through the second of whiteness, to the extreme joy and ecstasy of the red. There are many images to render these stages—most of them poetic—and the sensitive use of them—alone or in combination with others—gives him the single evocative line, or the short 'illumination', which are amongst the greatest beauties of his work.

Avivant un agréable goût d'encre de Chine, une poudre noire pleut doucement sur ma veillée,—Je baisse les feux du lustre, je me jette sur le lit et, tourné du côté de l'ombre, je vous vois, mes filles! mes reines![10]

This passage has a beauty of image and harmony which does not depend on the meaning, yet this is further enhanced if the alchemical suggestion is perceived. The term 'encre' is one used to symbolize blackness, the first stage of dissolution, which is a time of melancholy as well as of hope, for when the blackness appears, it is proof that the experiment is safely begun, and there is the possibility of the gold—the vision of God. Rimbaud uses the term 'Chinese ink' for Chinese ink is the blackest of all black inks. Then he turns down the lights, throws himself on his couch and gives himself up to the vision. Finally, out of the darkness come the 'filles' and the 'reines', the alchemical name for the colours in their progression towards the completion of the elixir, the full vision.

In another poem there is the image, 'Je vois longtemps la mélancolique lessive d'or du couchant'. The word 'lessive' which is literally 'washing', has no particular beauty in isolation, though the whole line has harmony and evocative power. This is still further enhanced if we know that the term 'lessive' is used to denote the secret substance of the hermetic philosopher, so called because it is used to purify or wash the metals. It is also called Azoth, a word which has great importance for alchemists, since it contains the first and the last letters of the Hebrew, Greek and Latin languages. The *aleph* and *thau* of Hebrew, the *alpha* and *omega* of Greek, and the *a* and *z* of Latin. It serves also as the monogram of Hermetic Truth, the perfect sign of the absolute. This 'lessive' joined with gold—fire—is all that the alchemist needs to begin the *Grand Oeuvre*. All this adds an undertone of meaning to the lovely line.

The poem *Larme*[11] loses none of its beauty, but acquires a new meaning, if we realize that it may refer to the alchemist's *aurum potabile*, liquid gold, which is the universal panacea, the draught which gives longevity, and this potion can only have its full effect if it produces profuse perspiration.

> Que pouvais-je boire dans cette jeune Oise,
> Ormeaux sans voix, gazon sans fleurs, ciel couvert?
> Que tirais-je à la gourde de colocase?
> Quelque liqueur d'or, fade et qui fait suer.

This poem, however, was written during a time of discouragement and despair when the poet felt no desire to drink, no wish for long life on earth.

> Pleurant je voyais de l'or—et ne pus boire.

At other times the alchemical imagery is used to suggest a spiritual experience, as in the poems *Chanson de la plus Haute Tour* and *O Saisons, ô Châteaux*; and in the *Illumination, Matinée d'Ivresse*, but these poems will be discussed in a later chapter.

In *Barbare*, *Mystique*, *Fleurs*, and *Being Beauteous*, we have the imagery borrowed from the books of magic and alchemy without being certain what it actually symbolizes, suspecting that even the poet himself is not quite sure either and minding little since the poems—like music—have an evocative meaning of their own which has little to do with the logical sense of the words. They have the power to suggest but not to state their meaning. In *Fleurs* the title might surprise since the only flowers mentioned are the foxglove and the rose, but, for alchemists, the term 'flower' is the pure substance in the metal, the spirit of matter.

D'un gradin d'or,—parmi des cordons de soie, les gazes grises, les velours verts et les disques de cristal qui noircissent comme du bronze au soleil,—je vois la digitale s'ouvrir sur un tapis de filigranes d'argent, d'yeux et de chevelures.

Des pièces d'or jaune semées sur l'agate, des piliers d'acajou supportant un dôme d'émeraudes, des bouquets de satin blanc et de fines verges de rubis entourent la rose d'eau.

Tels qu'un dieu aux énormes yeux bleus et aux formes de neige, la mer et le ciel attirent aux terrasses de marbre la foule de jeunes et fortes roses.[12]

Here we have most of the alchemical images, the colours, the precious stones which symbolize the various stages of the work: the emerald of the hermetic books, the pure whites of the purification, the rubies of complete success. There are also the roses—symbol of Venus—while at the end, there arises the figure which appears several times in *Illuminations*, the God who is a synthesis of all the elements of nature in the perfection of whiteness in the state of purity which alchemists call 'la parfaite sublimation en dépuration'. It is the figure which we meet again in *Being Beauteous*. This title incidentally seems to be the translation—the inaccurate translation—of the 'être de beauté' of the first line and this imperfect rendering has mysteriously acquired a strange power of suggestion of its own which it could not have had in the mind of the writer. In this poem the alchemical intention is clearer than in *Fleurs*. The 'être de beauté' would appear to be a symbol of the completion of the experiment, the reaching of the philosopher's stone. The 'blessures écarlates et noires' occur as images in alchemy. Dom Pernety says what when Ovid uses the term 'black wound' out of which the poison flows, he is intending to express the blackness of putrefaction, the alchemical process. The 'trois couleurs propres de la vie' of which Rimbaud speaks must be the three important colours, the black, the white and the red. We have the impression that momentous events are taking place here, which are too deep for the expression of the poet.

Devant une neige, un être de beauté de haute taille. Des sifflements de mort et des cercles de musique sourde font monter, s'élargir et trembler comme un spectre ce corps adoré; des blessures écarlates et noires éclatent dans les chairs superbes.—Les couleurs propres de la vie se foncent, dansent, et se dégagent autour de la vision, sur le chantier.—Et les frissons s'élèvent et grondent, et la saveur forcenée de ces effets se chargeant avec les sifflements mortels et les rauques musiques que le monde, loin derrière nous, lance sur notre mère de beauté.—Elle recule, elle se dresse. Oh! nos os sont revêtus d'un nouveau corps amoureux.[13]

This 'être de beauté' is reminiscent of the being which Arthur Gordon Pym saw, in the tale by Edgar Allan Poe, translated by Baudelaire, just as he was about to be annihilated by the cataract: some supernatural creature made of whiteness and snow. As Gordon Pym and his companions approached the cataract a sullen darkness hovered over them, but from the milky depths of the ocean a luminous glare arose and stole up along the bulwarks of the boat. They were nearly overwhelmed by the white ashy shower which settled upon them and upon the canoe, but melted in the water as it fell. The summit of the cataract was lost in the dimness and the distance. At intervals there were visible wide yawnings and momentary rents and from out of these rents, within which was a chaos of flitting and indistinct images, there came a rushing and mighty but soundless wind, tearing up the ocean. Then there arose, in their path, a shrouded human figure, but very far larger in its proportions than any human being. And the hue of the skin of the figure was of the perfect whiteness of the snow. This large figure rising at the extreme limits of the world, on the brink of eternity, a universal mother figure, a goddess, is very like Rimbaud's 'mère de beauté' at whose sight 'nos os sont revêtus d'un nouveau corps amoureux.'

Rimbaud undertook his experiments in search of spiritual and not of material gold and we find that his experience of the Almighty is now expressed in the same terms as in the writings of occult philosophers. Eliphas Lévi says that the *logos* of supreme power—logic or reason he calls it—is God![14] This *Reason* throws light on all the darkness and doubt and nothing can touch it. It speaks through the mouth of wise men, it is incarnate in one being which is called the *logos* made flesh, 'la grande raison incarnée'. Thus 'Une Raison' is God. Rimbaud entitles one of his poems,

### A une Raison

Un coup de ton doigt sur le tambour décharge tous les sons et commence la nouvelle harmonie.

Un pas de toi, c'est la levée des nouveaux hommes et leur en-marche.

Ta tête se détourne: le nouvel amour! Ta tête se retourne: le nouvel amour!

'Change nos lots, crible les fléaux, à commencer par le temps' te chantent ces enfants. 'Élève n'importe où la substance de nos fortunes et de nos vœux,' on t'en prie.

Arrivée de toujours, qui t'en iras partout.[15]

It is possible that, at this time, Rimbaud, seeing himself in terms of the magician Merlin was inspired by the reading of Quinet's *Merlin l'Enchanteur*.[16] It is not the ideas or the writing of this turgid and monotonous pseudo-romance which could have influenced him, but merely the biographical details. Quinet's symbolism is prosaic and materialistic and he has little religious feeling; obviously he does not believe in the story he is telling but is only using it to relate, in a conventionally allegorical form, what he imagines to be the destiny of France. But this two-volumed Idyll contains many circumstances and scraps of legends which were useful to Rimbaud as he saw his own career in terms of that of Merlin.

Merlin was the son of a virtuous Christian woman and of Satan—we have seen that Rimbaud's birth was described by his first biographer in similar terms to that of Merlin. Madame

Rimbaud had always made her children feel that they had inherited all their bad qualities from their father. In a child's imagination he could have represented Satan and his mother the virtuous Christian woman. Through his mother Merlin felt drawn towards Heaven and through his father towards Hell. God or Satan, which would win in the end? There are two temperaments at war in him. One day he heard his father and mother discussing his future. His mother hoped that he would be a good Christian while his father hoped that he would eat of the tree of good and evil, the tree of knowledge. Then Merlin, who was listening, interrupted them and said: 'I'll be a magician!'

Thus Merlin became a magician and he had many talents. He could, at his own volition, invent new flowers, new animals and new insects. Rimbaud followed him in this and felt that he had acquired the same powers. These powers came to Merlin through the possession of the magic ring. Once, on his travels—and these were later emulated by Rimbaud—he came to a place where Venice now stands and where there was then nothing but sea marshes. He fell in love with a fisher-girl and through the aid of his magic ring, he was able to grant her all her wishes. He built for her the most beautiful city in the world, with lovely squares, canals and the finest church in Christendom, Saint Mark's. But she was not satisfied and she said that she wanted a ship large enough to carry a whole nation. In answer to her wish he built for her the *Buccentaure*, 'pavoisé d'or, d'argent et de soie', very similar to the ship which Rimbaud was to see in the heavens above him as he said farewell to the magician phase of his life.

But still these gifts did not satisfy the fisher-girl and when he asked her what she wanted to make her happy, she answered that she wanted his magic ring. He slipped it from his finger and handed it to her. She, after taking it from him, flung it into the sea, and the magician 'est resté seul, dépouillé, pleurant sur la rive déserte.' Rimbaud writes in *Enfance*, in *Illuminations*,[17] 'Je serais bien l'enfant abandonné sur la jetée partie à la haute mer, le petit valet suivant l'allée dont le front touche le ciel.' Later, when he felt that his practices had been sinful, when he believed his powers were waning, then he thought of the ring at the bottom of the sea, a ring which he might recover and then recapture the powers he had once possessed. In the rough draft of *Alchimie du Verbe* from *Une Saison en Enfer*, he wrote 'la mer, *anneau magique sous l'eau lumineuse*', and italicized the words himself to indicate that they had importance for him. While, in *Nuit de l'Enfer*, he said:[18] 'J'ai tous les talents . . . Veut-on que je disparaisse, que je plonge à la recherche de *l'anneau*? Veut-on? Je ferai de l'or, des remèdes'. This would lead to the supposition that he had indeed practised alchemy.

Merlin had a fairy wife, his constant companion, called Viviane, and together they studied the books of magic—it was their main occupation—and learned together the magic charms. Afterwards they used to sing little songs, not noble or complicated music, but little songs like folk music which recall somewhat the little songs of Rimbaud himself.[19]

> Tout est divin!
> L'amour commence!
> Puis vient la fin,
> Douleur immense,
> Mort ou démence.

Unfortunately, unlike Merlin, Rimbaud was never to find his Viviane, and he remained to the end 'une âme veuve'.

Merlin, being son of Satan, could not bear the thought that his father should remain permanently the prince of darkness and evil. He had been promised that he would, one day, be able to convert him. This wish was finally granted and we have the humorous picture—unconsciously humorous—of Satan retiring to a monastery to repent his sins in peace, and there he lives in company with Pan, now also a monk. Rimbaud also, at the height of his spiritual pride, imagined that he would be able to resolve the old struggle between good and evil.

When Rimbaud reached Paris and began to feel confidence in his magical powers, a great change took place in him. There was a sudden growth of self-confidence, a sudden blossoming of arrogant pride. As a child and as a youth he had been considered of no importance; he had been under the complete control of his mother; he had been pushed hither and thither, slapped and cuffed. From his earliest years he had been told again and again that he was no one, only a child who must do what he was bid, and that others knew better than he what was good for him. He had never been allowed any pocket-money; he had never possessed the means of cultivating, even simply and modestly, his personal tastes, and to develop his personality; he had been reduced to the illicit borrowing of books from book-stalls, to satisfy his craving for reading. There was nothing which was veritably his own, not even privacy—except what he could find in the open-air when he stole away to the woods. Now all that was over. Now, all at once, this humiliating condition—doubly humiliating to a youth of Rimbaud's pride—came to an end. Now he entered into possession of riches which no one could take from him; he was a chosen being, set apart, and all the heavenly regions were open to him. He was to become the channel for the voice of the Almighty. His pride was all the greater since his importance was not recognized by those around him; he could imagine that he was a divine voice crying in the wilderness, whom the common herd did not hear, and whom they persecuted as they had persecuted Joan of Arc. Like Faust, he no longer thought of himself as a mere magician, he thought himself the equal of God. 'J'ai cru acquérir des pouvoirs surnaturels', he said in *Une Saison en Enfer*.[20] Like Faust, he thought that he himself had become the image of the divinity, that his powers were greater than those of the Cherubim, that he even enjoyed the life of a God. Rimbaud reached the same arrogance and pride, though he was, later, to believe that this had been only a drug addict's delusion and megalomania. Verlaine understood this pride and, in a poem, *Crimen Amoris*, he described a young man —scarcely more than a boy—who had said that he would make himself God; he describes also the retribution which overtook such overweening arrogance. It is clear that the youth in the poem is intended for Rimbaud as Verlaine knew him first, in the autumn of 1871, when he was sixteen.

Verlaine stated, in *Mes Prisons*,[21] that he had composed *Crimen Amoris* while in custody in Brussels, where he was serving the first part of his sentence for having wounded Rimbaud. It was written, in July or August 1873, some weeks only after his trial. A few months later, in November, he wrote to his friend Lepelletier, who was his literary executor while he was in prison, to inform him of what he had been writing—several poems, amongst them *Crimen Amoris*, which he said was in Rimbaud's possession.[22] Rimbaud had probably been moved by the poem, which was very close to him, for he made a careful copy of it for himself, and this is the only one which has come down to us.[23] Ten years later, in 1884, Verlaine published a very much modified version of the poem in a collection entitled *Jadis et Naguère*. The version, which was in Rimbaud's possession, came to light very much later and was published on 9 January 1926 in *Le Figaro*. Jules Mouquet, in *Rimbaud raconté par Verlaine*, has printed the two stages of the poem side by side. The Dutch Rimbaud scholar, Daniel De Graaf, compared the two versions and came to the conclusion that the first was not merely transcribed by Rimbaud but composed by him, and later appropriated by Verlaine and amended. He published the results of his investigation in an article entitled *L'Auteur Véritable de Crimen Amoris*,[24] but his arguments are not very convincing. It is true that the first version has many more similarities with Rimbaud's style than the second, but this could be attributed to other grounds than authorship. In July 1873, so soon after the Brussels drama, Verlaine was very much more preoccupied with him and very much more under his influence than ten years later, when his impact had faded through absence. It is not very likely that Verlaine would have sent the poem to Rimbaud, would have got a copy made for his mother, and have asked Lepelletier to have a look at it, if it was not, in fact, by him. There are no adequate grounds for depriving Verlaine of what is, after all, his finest poem. Arthur Symons is nearer to the truth when he says[25] that there would have been no *Crimen Amoris* if Verlaine had not read *Le Bateau Ivre* by Rimbaud. However, he adds, with less discrimination, that this was Rimbaud's great work, to inspire Verlaine and that, having helped to make him a great poet, he could go.

In Ecbatane—so the poem relates—in a palace resplendent with gold and silken hangings, it was the feast of the Seven Deadly Sins. The softest music could be heard through the lofty halls, and a host of beautiful young devils, adolescent Satans, were to be seen bearing aloft the litter of the Seven Deadly Sins. Around them, as pages serving food and wine, crowded all human desires and appetites; there was dancing and music, and in the distance rose choirs of blended voices—men's and women's—surging like the waves of the sea. Now it happened that the most beautiful of all these wicked angels was only sixteen and stood apart from the others, dreaming, with his eyes full of tears. He stood alone and beautiful in his silken garments with a garland of flowers encircling his brow. The dance surged round him, but in vain; in vain all the Satans, his brothers and sisters, tried to cheer him, holding out towards him their welcoming arms, trying to rouse him from the gloom that weighed him down. He resisted all entreaties and would only answer, while despair clouded his brow: 'Oh! leave me in peace!' Then kissing them gently, he escaped with rapid steps and they saw him climb to the highest of all the citadels, to the topmost pinnacle, and there he stood, with a flaming torch in his hand. He waved it on high—it was as if dawn were suddenly breaking—and they heard his deep and tender voice, his voice which mingled with the crackling of the flames, and it cried: 'I am he who will create God!'

Then he began to relate how he would put an end to the tragic dilemma of right and wrong. 'We have suffered long enough' he cried, 'angels and men, from the eternal conflict between Good and Evil. Oh! all you sinners and saints, why this obstinate struggle? Why have we not made, as skilful artists should, of our work our sole virtue? There has been enough—indeed too much—of the too evenly balanced struggle! You know well that there is no difference between what you call Good and Evil, and that in both there is nothing but suffering. I shall break up this abnormal contest. There must be no more Hell, and no more Heaven. There must be only Love. Let God and Devil perish! There must be only happiness, I tell you! As a reply to Jesus who thought that he did well to maintain the balance equalized in this duel, I shall forthwith sacrifice Hell to Universal Love.'

As he spoke these words, he flung the torch from his hand; and the flames sprang up forthwith and began to devour the palace. The gold melted and flowed away in a stream, the marble pillars cleft asunder, and the whole building became a furnace full of splendour and fire. All the young Satans began to sing amongst the devouring flames; they understood and were resigned, and the chorus of their mingled voices rose up in the midst of the storm and the rage of the fire. But the boy stood proudly, with his arms folded against his breast, murmuring to himself a kind of prayer, which died away and was lost in the waves of song. His eyes were fixed on Heaven and he offered up all the destruction as a sacrifice to put an end to Good and Evil.

Those who know what thoughts and plans filled Rimbaud's mind at this time will have no doubt that Verlaine must frequently have heard him speak in some such fashion. They are the ideas contained in *Matinée d'Ivresse*. Verlaine also understood how much love and charity there was in the young poet's conception of his mission, for he called the poem *Crimen Amoris*—crime of love. The poem ends with the destruction of the arrogant young Satan. Suddenly a bolt of thunder burst from the darkened heaven and that was the end of the singer and the song.[26]

> Les bras tendus au ciel comme vers un frère,
> Un grand sourire aux lèvres, il s'exaltait,
> Quand retentit un affreux coup de tonnerre. . . .
>
> On n'avait pas agréé le sacrifice.
> Quelqu'un de fort et de juste assurément,
> Au nom du Ciel provoqué, faisant l'office
> De justicier, envoyait ce châtiment.
>
> Du haut palais aux cent tours pas un vestige,
> Rien ne resta dans ce désastre inouï,
> Afin que par un formidable prestige
> Ceci ne fût qu'un vain rêve évanoui.

Then, when the storm had died away, the calm night descended on the world, like a soft coverlet. It was a deep blue night with a thousand stars, and the peaceful celestial countryside spread out beneath the sky, while the branches of the trees, as they swayed in the breeze, seemed like a beating of angels' wings. The streams ran along their bed of pebbles singing their gentle song, and the owl hovered quietly in the still air which was full of mystery and the sense of prayer. Over all this peace a soft mist hung like a blessing, and everything seemed embalmed in ecstasy. All the previous turmoil and anguish were forgotten.

> Le rossignol épanchait sa triste plainte
> Répercutée au gazouillis des ruisseaux;
> Ce paysage, était d'une paix si sainte
> Qu'on se fût mis à genoux dans les roseaux,
>
> Sur les cailloux, parmi le sable des routes,
> Attendri sous le ciel immémorial,
> Pour adorer dans toutes ses oeuvres, toutes,
> Le Dieu clément qui nous sauvera du mal.

This poem makes it clear that for Verlaine Rimbaud had seemed, in the Paris days, like Lucifer who had tried to make himself the equal of God, and who had suffered the same downfall. It is clear also, from all the accounts, that the other writers in Paris had the same impression, and this explains how they never felt sure whether it was with Christ or Satan they had been speaking. 'Behold Jesus amongst the doctors' said one of them one day. 'More likely Satan!' replied another.

Later Rimbaud, like Faust, came to believe that he had been arrogant and had usurped powers that were not his by right, and that he had, thereby, been brought near to madness and destruction.

<br>

#### CHAPTER IV

## L'EPOUX INFERNAL ET LA VIERGE FOLLE

RIMBAUD had arrived in Paris in a state of feverish mental exaltation, with his sexual curiosity aroused and his senses stimulated but not yet satisfied. He was totally inexperienced, yet willing and anxious to learn, but there was distress and uneasiness mingled with his curiosity—this distress and uneasiness always manifest themselves when he thinks or writes of love. A poem, discovered not many years ago, *Les Remembrances du Vieillard Idiot*,[1] and written shortly after he reached Paris, shows this anguish. Even in its unfinished state, it is a magnificent poem, but more in the vein of the *Voyou* period than that of *Illuminations*.

> Oh! personne
> Ne fut si fréquemment troublé, comme étonné!
> Et maintenant que le pardon me soit donné:
> Puisque les sens infects m'ont mis de leurs victimes,
> Je me confesse de l'aveu des jeunes crimes!
> Puis!—qu'il me soit permis de parler au Seigneur!
> Pourquoi la puberté tardive et le malheur
> Du gland tenace et trop consulté! Pourquoi l'ombre
> Si lente au bas du ventre? et ces terreurs sans nombre
> Comblant toujours la joie ainsi qu'un gravier noir?
> Pardonée?
> Mon père,
>   o cette enfance! . . .

There was also *Les Déserts de l'Amour*, an interesting document in prose, which is generally believed to have been composed in 1871, but which is more in keeping with the period under present review, and which has some resemblance with a prose poem by Charles Cros published in *La Renaissance Littéraire et Artistique*, on 21 September 1872, entitled *La Distrayeuse*. The resemblances are in the style, for the spirit of the two poems is very different. Rimbaud had been closely associated with Cros since he arrived in Paris, and he may well have seen this poem before it was published. Bouillane de Lacoste claims that the manuscript is not in Rimbaud's writing of 1871 but in that of 1872.[2] And moreover, Rimbaud gave it to Forain in that year.

### PREFACE[3]

These writings are those of a young man, a very young man, whose life has been unfolded anywhere; without mother, without native land, heedless of all that is known, and fleeing from every moral force, like

many another pitiable young man. He was, however, in such a state
of *ennui* and distress that he only brought himself close to death.
Never having loved women—although full of strength—his heart
and soul were lifted up towards strange and sad errors. From the
following dreams—of his loves—which came to him, in bed, in the
streets, from their persistence and their end, there arise perhaps sweet
and moral considerations. But since that peculiar suffering possesses
so disturbing a power, we must ardently hope that this poor soul,
strayed amongst us and longing for death, may find, at the last, great
consolation, and that he may be found worthy of it.

### PART ONE

That time it was the Woman I saw in the town to whom I spoke
and who spoke to me. It was in my room without light. They came to
tell me that she was at my home, and I saw her in my bed, completely
mine, and it was dark; I was very much moved, especially because it
was in my parents' house. But infinite distress seized hold of me. I was
in rags and she who was giving herself to me, was richly dressed. She
had to leave! Then, Oh! indescribable distress, I took her and let her
fall outside the bed, half naked. And in my great weakness, I fell on
top of her, and crawled with her amongst the rugs, without light. And
the glow of the family lamp lit up each of the neighbouring rooms, in
turn, as it passed. But the woman disappeared! Then I wept more tears
than God could ever have wished.

I went into the town that never seemed to end. Oh! fatigue and
weariness! I was drowned in the dull, silent darkness and in the flight
of happiness. It was like a winter's night, with snow to stifle the world.
The friends to whom I cried: 'Oh! where is she gone?' answered me
falsely. I stood in front of the windows of the house where she goes
every evening. I ran into the sunken garden! But they all repulsed me.
And I wept bitterly on account of all this.

At last I went down into a place full of dust, and, sitting on a heap of
timber, I let all the tears of my body flow out with that night. My
complete exhaustion, nevertheless, always returned. And I understood that She was engrossed in her normal life, and that her kindness
would take longer to return to me than a star to this world. She never
came back to me, to my own house, which I would never have dared
to ask. Verily that time I wept more tears than all the children of the
world.

### PART TWO

It was certainly the same landscape, the same rustic house of my parents! . . . I was forsaken in that endless country house, reading in the kitchen, drying the mud from my clothes in front of my hosts, as they conversed in the living-room. I was moved to death by the sound of the morning milk, and the whispering night of the last century.

I was in a very dark room. What was I doing? I do not know. A maid-servant came to me, and I can say that she was a darling, although she was very beautiful, with a maternal nobility of countenance that I could never describe—pure, familiar, and completely charming. She pinched my arm. I do not clearly remember her face; it is not sufficient to recall her arm, and its skin which I gently pinched between my two fingers; nor her mouth which mine seized hold of, like a desperate little wave endlessly undermining something. I flung her down on a basket of cushions and linen sails, in a dark corner of the room. I can only remember her drawers with their white lace.

Then, oh! infinite despair, suddenly the wall of the room became vaguely the shadow of the trees, and I was engulfed in the loving sadness of the night. [Fragment.]

From the depths of Rimbaud's subconscious self there surged up these half, or wholly, forgotten memories of his childhood, in the descriptive details of the poem, which now rose to the surface of his mind and mingled with his present distress.

He may have assigned to woman a high and noble place in his æsthetic doctrine, nevertheless, in practice, he seems to have held the conviction that woman, as he knew her, was loathsome and repulsive, and that love, like everything else, needed renovating. This did not necessarily mean that the only alternative was homosexuality, but rather that the relations between the sexes needed to be changed. It is the materialism of women which offended him. In *Délires I*, from *Une Saison en Enfer*, he writes:[5]

Je n'aime pas les femmes; l'amour est à réinventer, on le sait. Elles ne peuvent plus que vouloir une position assurée. La position gagnée, cœur et beauté sont mis de côté; il ne reste que froid dédain, l'aliment du mariage aujourd'hui.

He intended to be above sin and condemnation and to experience everything; his sensuality was as yet only latent and cerebral

—there is no doubt about its intensity—but he was ready to be initiated and ready for 'le divin final anéantissement'. It was chance which made him meet Verlaine at this crisis of his development, and, although this was probably the most intense emotional experience of his life—perhaps even the only occasion on which he was ever passionately stirred—it seems that he was not naturally a homosexual and that he was never able to overcome his sense of guilt or inferiority in this relationship. Nevertheless there is no doubt that with him Rimbaud, for a time, experienced complete physical and spiritual ecstasy and complete freedom from all inhibitions. This deep experience was, at first, a stimulus, before he became disillusioned when, finding it a burden, he sighed, 'Quel ennui, l'heure du "cher corps" et du "cher cœur."'![6] It was during the time of the height of his passion for Verlaine that he produced the largest part of his work and this period coincided with his belief in himself and in his doctrine of art. There is also no doubt that at this time he was very much under the influence of Verlaine. A graphological comparison of his handwriting at this time with his earlier script reveals what mastery and self-confidence he has gained since his friendship with him; it also reveals that his writing has become identical with that of his friend.[7] Isabelle was to mistake the writing of Verlaine for that of her brother, and later critics have fallen into the same error. It is now admitted that most of the alleged Rimbaud manuscripts in the Barthou Collection are in Verlaine's handwriting.

Verlaine was, by nature, weak and vicious, with a love of perversity and a propensity towards self-indulgence in every form. He was what Oscar Wilde calls a 'bi-metallist'—moved passionately by both men and women—and there had been alleged rumours of adventures of various kinds in his early life. At the time when he first met Rimbaud he was starved for physical satisfaction by the delicate state of his wife's health; he was, moreover, weary of married respectability and he found in his new friend the boon companion after his own heart. Rimbaud was ready, as none of his other friends were, to try every form of sensual gratification, and he was restrained by no fear of retribution—physical or moral—by no kind of prejudice. He was inexperienced when he met Verlaine, but he was a willing and apt pupil and soon, by his strength of purpose, his single-mindedness towards his self-appointed task—his martyrdom—he was to outstrip his mentor and to obtain over him eventually unlimited influence and ascendancy.

It was Verlaine who initiated him into a life of depravity but he soon led his teacher further than he would have gone on his own account, and plunged him into depths of vice he would not have explored alone. Verlaine soon became convinced that life with Rimbaud was worth the sacrifice of everything he had hitherto held dear, and that life without him was not to be contemplated. With his new friend he felt freed from all inhibitions and restraints, freed especially from the overwhelming sense of guilt he had always experienced and which, sometimes, had restrained him. 'I am damning myself!' he had said at one time. Now, on the contrary, he could, on the most noble grounds, defend his worst aberrations, which in the past had seemed to him only weakness. Now he had become persuaded by a stronger character than his own that all his appetites were legitimate, that a life of debauch was the best incentive for a poet, and he could, thereby, excuse all his lowest actions. Rimbaud seemed to him at first the angel who had opened for him the gates of his prison, though he was later to appear as the devil who had tempted him to eat from the Tree of Knowledge.

In the early part of their relationship each found in the other perfect happiness and perfect fulfilment, the compensation for their suffering elsewhere. For Rimbaud, moreover, the rapture he experienced with Verlaine and the joy he had in literary composition were the reward and natural result of his terrible martyrdom, and he was ready and willing to pay their price.

It is impossible to prove conclusively whether Verlaine and Rimbaud actually practised sodomy, or whether their relationship was merely a violent form of sentimental and romantic friendship with its less extreme physical manifestations. When Verlaine was arrested in Brussels after he had turned on Rimbaud, wounding him by shooting, the medical report stated that he showed in his person recent signs of active and passive sodomy.

Indeed he owed the severity of his sentence—the maximum for a case of assault—to the facts revealed in this report. Certain medical practitioners, however, now allege that no reliance should be placed on the facts claimed to be revealed by such an examination.[8] Nevertheless this attitude of scepticism seems unnecessarily cautious. And, moreover, if the poems written by Verlaine are taken as further evidence, little doubt can remain in a reasonable reader's mind that sodomy must indeed have been practised.

Of the physical rapture felt by both the men no doubt can be entertained and Verlaine was of too simple a nature to attempt to disguise it in his writings; he wished all to know of it and to share with him his bliss. This desire was, however, coupled with the fear of consequences—a residue of his latent respectability—and he invariably gave a twist to the poem to make his intention less obvious; he was extremely adept at seeming to reveal everything and then finally leaving his readers in doubt as to his precise meaning. Nevertheless the meaning is clear for those who are not too obstinate to admit it, although some critics—witness Fontainas[9]—succeed in discovering an innocent interpretation in the poems which seem most pornographic.

In *Læti et Errabundi*,[10] Verlaine writes of their 'passions satisfaites absolument outre mesure,' of their freedom from women and from the 'last of the prejudices' and he addresses Rimbaud as 'mon grand péché radieux!' While of the room in Rue Campagne-Première, the scene of so many of their orgies, he writes:

> Seule, ô chambre, qui fuis en cônes affligeants,
> Seule, tu sais! mais sans doute combien de nuits
> De noce auront dévirginé leurs nuits, depuis.[11]

There is also *Le Bon Disciple*, a poem found in Rimbaud's pocket-book after the arrest of Verlaine in Brussels, and this leaves little doubt as to the nature of their relationship. The last verse runs:

> Toi le jaloux qui m'as fait signe,
> [Ah!] me voici, voici tout moi!
> Vers toi je rampe, encore indigne!
> —Monte sur mes reins et trépigne.[12]

Fontainas, however, sees in this poem a symbolical rendering of the fight between the Archangel Michael and Satan and the final downfall of the latter.[13]

And finally it seems only puerile innocence and futile quibbling to interpret otherwise than obscenely the poem *Ces Passions*.[14]

When Mathilde Verlaine made her legal demand for divorce from her husband, Paul Verlaine, one of the chief grounds for this demand was his alleged immorality with a young man, Arthur Rimbaud, and her lawyer asserted that deeds of the most monstrous immorality had been disclosed to the claimant.[15] Letters from Rimbaud to Verlaine said to afford conclusive proof of the allegation had been shown to the lawyer, but these letters were, however, not used as evidence against Verlaine since the charge of physical cruelty was finally considered sufficient. These letters were unfortunately destroyed at a later date by Mathilde Verlaine, since she did not wish them ever to fall into the hands of her young son.[16] 'There were many things in these letters,' she writes, 'that I will not repeat even here!'

No lover of literature can fail to regret that this valuable correspondence is irretrievably lost to us. Apart from the interest they might have concerning the relationship between Verlaine and Rimbaud, they would otherwise have thrown much light on Rimbaud's state of mind and on his artistic preoccupations in the most vital period of his literary career, at the time when his poetic talent was at its highest peak. It is impossible to conceive that he did not discuss with his friend the poems he had just composed, some of the finest he was to write. Mathilde Verlaine confesses that she destroyed between thirty and forty letters from Rimbaud to Verlaine.[17] And now the only letter of this period which has come down to us is the one written to Delahaye in June 1872 and which will be quoted in a later chapter. The beauty of its writing makes one regret still more the loss of this inestimable correspondence.

Everyone in the literary world in Paris was firmly convinced of the immorality of the relations of Verlaine and Rimbaud, even those most friendly with them; there were not two opinions on the subject. One evening, at the first performance of a new

Coppée play, when all literary Paris was present, the two friends walked in the *foyer* during the interval, with their arms around each other's necks, to the great horror and disgust of the rest of the audience. Verlaine's close friend, Lepelletier, writing an account of the first night for a daily paper, said:

> Amongst the men of letters to be seen at Coppée's first night was the poet Paul Verlaine giving his arm to a charming young person, Mademoiselle Rimbaud.[18]

Against all these arguments must be put the violent denials of both men, although these may have been due to caution and to a desire for self-preservation. 'Ce n'est pas ce que l'on pense,' Verlaine would frequently repeat, while Rimbaud used to say that he would not stoop to deny such allegations.

Whatever may have been the nature of the relationship, it brought them at first great joy and a sense of fulfilment, as well as literary stimulation, but it was eventually to prove for both of them the source of deep suffering, bitterness and all the devouring jealousy that such a relationship seems fated to produce. Only two members of the same sex have power to wound one another so deeply, when things go wrong between them, and to wound one another where hurt is most intolerable. The chapter in *Une Saison en Enfer* entitled *L'Époux Infernal et la Vierge Folle*, shows clearly the tension and suffering resulting from such a situation. It is generally felt that here is a picture of the relationship between the two men though some critics claim that this is not a correct interpretation and that, on the contrary, the *Époux Infernal* and the *Vierge Folle* are the two conflicting sides of Rimbaud's nature struggling together; that it is in fact a conversation between the poet and his soul. Good arguments can be adduced to support this theory yet it is hard to accept it as the truth, not so much because one is convinced that Rimbaud and Verlaine had immoral relations together and that the chapter called *L'Époux Infernal et la Vierge Folle* is an account of them, as because the second view would seem to make nonsense of the plan of *Une Saison en Enfer* and deprive the work of much of its coherence. It does not seem likely that Rimbaud had no ulterior intention when he numbered the *Délires* I and II respectively, calling the first *L'Époux Infernal et la Vierge Folle*, and the second *Alchimie du Verbe*. It seems probable that he wished to prove the vanity of physical *délire* in the first and of literary *délire* in the second. In other respects *Une Saison en Enfer* has a strict and coherent plan and the other interpretation of *Délire I*, a dialogue between Rimbaud and his soul, would bring in a new conception which would not harmonize with the scheme as it now stands. The interpretation might have been defended had the two chapters formed entirely different and separate sections. This chapter, at all events, gives what can be taken as a subtle picture of the relations of the two poets and greatly helps in the understanding of the psychological situation. It shows how much ascendancy Rimbaud came finally to exercise over Verlaine by his stronger and more violent character, by his greater intelligence. Rimbaud has cleverly succeeded in giving a picture of himself as seen through the eyes of Verlaine, of his conduct as it would strike his friend, and of the bewilderment and the distress that were its natural result. He has given proof here, not only of an acute power of self-analysis but—what is rarer still—of the faculty of seeing himself, with his qualities and his faults, as others must see him. The Foolish Virgin, with her lamentations, is a faithful picture of Verlaine at this time, weeping over the loss of her former purity and begging God for mercy, yet unwilling to make any attempt to end a state which she believed humiliating and sinful. It was precisely the weeping and wailing of Verlaine, his constant confession of sin, his lamentable weakness that, eventually, proved beyond Rimbaud's power of endurance.

'Oh! yes I was once upon a time serious-minded,' cried the Foolish Virgin, 'and he was little more than a child, but his strange delicacy of nature carried me away so that I left all my human obligations to follow him. What a life! Real life is absent and we are not of this world! I go wherever he goes, I must! But often he gets angry with me, poor wretch that I am! The Devil! For he is a Devil, you know, and not a man!'

By degrees, however, Verlaine came to rely and depend more and more on him, to feel hungry and thirsty for his love, and starved if he did not enjoy it. 'With his kisses and his embraces he made me free of Heaven!' he said. 'But it was a dark Heaven, where I would have liked, nevertheless, to remain forever even, poor, deaf, dumb and blind. His caresses were becoming a necessity to me!'

At first Rimbaud had hoped great things from his relationship with Verlaine. There was to have been between them complete harmony and understanding, perfect unity. His love for Verlaine and Verlaine's for him were to be the full explanation of everything. And he would tell him in touching and beautiful language how he had dreamt of bringing him back to his previous exalted state of 'fils du soleil'. As long as he had confidence in his love for his friend all went well with him and he had belief in himself and his powers.

Verlaine, however, could not always understand or follow him, nor enter with him into his world. Sometimes, unable to sleep, he would get up in the night and stand, looking down in bewilderment on the sleeping Rimbaud, and wonder why he longed so much to escape from reality, as if the pleasures they shared together were not sufficient. 'Perhaps he is right,' he used to think, 'when he says that he knows secrets that will change the world.' But he could not really believe that this was true and he would then add: 'Oh! no, he only thinks that he knows these secrets, but he is only looking for them!'

Sometimes he would try to imagine what the world would be like when Rimbaud had transformed it. 'Perhaps he really speaks with God,' he wondered to himself. Then, for a time he would try to follow him in his descriptions of his visions and in desperation he would say: 'I understand! Yes! I understand!' But Rimbaud knew well that this was not true, that it was merely to please him he said these words. He would not answer, but only shrugged his shoulders. How indeed could Verlaine understand what he saw, when all he could do was weep and lament his sins and his fall from grace? How could he understand what it was to enjoy God, and to be beyond the reach of sin?

By slow degrees the rapture faded, disillusionment came to Rimbaud and finally disgust, leaving nothing but a taste of ashes in his mouth. His consciousness of the failure of his relationship with Verlaine, his consciousness of the vanity of that experience was part of his spiritual failure and his ultimate débâcle.

As love began to fade and his nerves became affected, the streak of sadism in Rimbaud's nature began to appear. Then he would take delight in hurting Verlaine by professing admiration for all that his friend's more simple nature instinctively disliked, by pretending to be more cynical and hard-bitten than he was in reality. He would make a mock of all the things which Verlaine admired and which were dear to him; then, when goaded into desperation, the latter would burst into tears, he would turn on him in anger and disgust, and abuse him.

With true sadistic pleasure he delighted in terrifying him, by making of cruelty a virtue, and of infamy a glory. 'I am of Scandinavian extraction,' he would cry. 'My forebears used to pierce their sides and drink their own blood. I shall make cuts all over my body, I shall tattoo myself all over, for I want to become as hideous as a Mongol. You'll see! I shall shriek with a loud voice in the streets for I want to become mad with rage!'

Sometimes, when he was in a wild and savage mood, he used to fight with Verlaine and do him bodily harm. Once, at the Café du Rat Mort, in the presence of several friends he said to him: 'Put your hands flat on the table, I want to try an experiment.' And when his friend had complied with his request, he drew a knife from his pocket and slashed at the hands so trustingly laid before him. Verlaine immediately got up and left the café, but Rimbaud followed him into the street and wounded him again, in several places, with his knife.[19]

Yet nothing could make any difference to Verlaine nor keep him away from the friend whom he adored.

Sometimes, when Rimbaud was intoxicated, he would stand hidden in the dark corners near the entrance to the house where they lived, to jump out on Verlaine as he came home, never too steady on his feet. He used to recount to him what crimes he would commit and describe how, in the end, he would be executed with great and disgusting flow of blood.

Sometimes, on the contrary, after his irritation with Verlaine had driven him to the utmost limits of cruelty, he would regret his hardness and there would then be a reconciliation as passionate as the quarrel. For a time he would be overwhelmingly kind and speak in gentle and simple language that was intensely moving. Then tears would rise to his eyes, as he gazed at those around them in the low pub where they sat and drank. 'Bétail de misère!' he called them all. He would, with the most gentle care, lift up the drunkards whom he found lying insensible in the gutters and he had for all of them the tender pity of a mother for her children.

There seems to have been in Rimbaud's behaviour towards Verlaine all the uncertainty of temper, the intermittent sadism, that such a relationship seems fated to rouse, the alternating changes from kindness to cruelty which we see so clearly depicted in the monologue of L'Époux Infernal et la Vierge Folle

While the passionate relationship between Verlaine and Rimbaud was progressing, matters were going very badly between the former and his wife. She was accusing Rimbaud of demoralizing and depraving her husband; for since he had taken up with Rimbaud he had grown neglectful of his appearance; he had taken to wearing, at all hours of the day, a filthy old muffler and a soft felt hat, instead of the silk hat which she considered suitable for the son-in-law of Monsieur Mauté de Fleurville. Often he let a whole week go by without changing his under-linen or cleaning his shoes.[20] There was one evening, she remembered with particular horror, the first night of Coppée's play, L'Abandonnée, when Paul had brought shame on them by appearing in the filthy clothes in which he had slept the previous night. There, in the midst of the other literary men, with their white ties and their opera hats, to all of whom he was well known, in the midst of the glittering array of smart women, with their feathers and their jewels, their low-cut evening gowns, he walked in the foyer in his dirty crumpled suit, with his soft hat on his head, with his filthy muffler slung round his neck, and his uncleaned shoes. Leaning on his arm, swaggered Rimbaud who was even more disreputable, for at this time he had nothing else to wear but the putty-coloured overcoat which hung on him in tatters and was several sizes too large, and a shapeless hat, greasy and discoloured.

The impression created by the two friends was, from every point of view, deplorable.

In Rimbaud's company Verlaine was drinking more than was good for him, more than he could stand, and he was rarely sober. It was absinthe they drank chiefly and absinthe was poison to Verlaine, it always brought out the latent cruelty in him and this he vented on the nearest defenceless creature at hand, his unfortunate wife. She used to lie awake in bed at night, waiting with terror for his home-coming, and knowing immediately from the sound of his step on the stairs, whether he was returning drunk or sober.[21] On the nights when he came home drunk his fixed idea was that he must set fire to a cupboard in which her father kept his ammunition; this cupboard was in the room next to hers against the wall that touched her bed. She used to lie in bed terrified—she was after all only eighteen—when she heard her husband's drunken step stumble on the stairs.

Nothing can be said in defence of Verlaine's conduct to her, but it will, however, be readily admitted that she must have been the most infuriating wife with whom a man of his temperament could have been blessed. She took a pride in her self-control and in mildly turning the other cheek whenever she was hit. 'I never open my lips,' she used to say. But it only added further fuel to her husband's unreasonable anger to be invariably put in the wrong. If only she had sometimes retaliated and had shared with him some of the blame of loss of temper and control, he would, in the end, have been kinder to her. But she always suffered in silence, and there is nothing more calculated to bring out the worst in man or woman, than the behaviour of those who suffer in silence and turn the other cheek.

'Whenever he came home drunk,' she writes,[22] 'he used to abuse me in a low voice, but I never answered a word. Sometimes he used to hit me, and I did not try to defend myself. And I was never angry or bitter, but only horribly sad.'

One evening he said to her: 'I'm going to burn your hair!' and he lit a match and put it close to her head without her making, she says, the slightest movement to prevent him. But happily the match went out, singeing only the loose strands. Another time he split her lip open with a blow; another time he held a sharp knife to her throat, and yet again he slashed her hands and wrists.

Rimbaud was urging him on to further drinking and debauch, persuading him that there was nothing more ridiculous in the world than a good family man, and that, moreover, such discipline was degrading to a man of spirit. He was doing everything in his power to put him against his wife, for he hated her and could not forgive her for having humiliated him on the evening of his arrival in Paris. Rimbaud, like his mother, was incapable of forgetting.

In the meantime Rimbaud had left the house of Mauté de Fleurville. As we have seen, he lived in various places until, at the end of December 1871, Verlaine rented for him the room in Rue Campagne-Première. Verlaine left Paris for Christmas on a visit to relations, and only returned home on 13 January. Then occurred one of the sordid quarrels with his wife which, eventually, led to their separation. She was in bed when he arrived as she had not yet regained her health. As soon as dinner was over he went up to her bedroom. After some angry words, he complained of the coffee, saying that he was going to a café with his friends where he would get something worth drinking. As he was already far from sober, she was frightened and did not answer him, but continued to shame him by her long-suffering, by her patient endurance which, in his present state, drove him into such a frenzy that he shouted at her: 'Your calm and your coolness drive me wild, and I'm going to finish it all once and for all.'[23]

Then he seized his infant son and threw him against the wall, so that he was only saved from death through the thickness of the swaddling clothes. Next he took hold of his wife, and tore her hands with his nails; then he flung her onto the bed and, kneeling on her, began to strangle her. Hearing her cries for help, her parents dashed into the room and had the greatest difficulty in separating them and tearing him away.

The following day he did not come in for dinner, but when he returned home at midnight, he made another scene, and left the

SKETCH OF RIMBAUD BY FANTIN-LATOUR

RIMBAUD IN PARIS
*a drawing by Verlaine*

house saying he was never coming back. He alleged that he was going to stay with his mother, but, in reality, he went to live with Rimbaud in Rue Campagne-Première, the scene of the orgies described in *Le Poète et la Muse*, from Verlaine's collection of poems entitled *Jadis et Naguère*.

Her father now tried to insist on her applying for a separation, and wrote to Verlaine to inform him of this. Verlaine, for his part, was terrified of what he had done, and was in a chastened frame of mind. He begged Mathilde for forgiveness, with tears in his eyes, promising to mend his ways. She agreed to return to him after her convalescence, but only on the condition that Rimbaud was to be sent back to Charleville and her husband to have no further communication with him. Verlaine readily agreed to all her conditions, and managed to persuade Rimbaud to leave Paris for a time.[24] But, after he had gone, Verlaine did not abide by what he had promised his wife, and it was from Charleville that Rimbaud, furious at having been sacrificed to the whims of a mere woman, wrote the letters which Mathilde later destroyed. He was not, however, writing unbidden but encouraged by Verlaine, who gave him an accommodation address where correspondence could be sent in safety, and who begged him to be patient for a time, to have confidence in him, promising that, after a few weeks of separation, as soon as his marriage had been patched up, they would be together once more, and never again be parted.[25]

CHAPTER V

# LA CHASSE SPIRITUELLE

IT was during the time between his departure from Charleville in March 1872 and his arrival in England in September the same year, that, as far as we know at present, Rimbaud composed the last of his poems in verse. He was undoubtedly going through a period of intense creative productivity, and it is said that it was then also that he wrote *La Chasse Spirituelle* which Verlaine claimed was his greatest work, surpassing in beauty of conception and expression all his previous writings, full as it was of 'étranges mysticités, et les plus étranges aperçus psychologiques.'[1] Judging from the mystical poems in *Illuminations* which we believe to have been written then, we can only regret that we have been deprived of this masterpiece, a kind of *Hound of Heaven*—perhaps the fine flowering of all that he had hitherto only sporadically expressed.

Many texts of Rimbaud have come to light during the past twenty or thirty years, and it has been the most fervent hope of Rimbaldists all the world over that *La Chasse Spirituelle* should also be unearthed. Great therefore was the joy, in 1949, when a text bearing that name was published by *Le Mercure de France*, but these hopes were soon dashed to the ground when it was discovered that it was only a hoax which had been perpetrated by two students, Akakia Viala and Nicolas Bataillet.[2]

A large number of the poems in verse which Rimbaud composed during this period are dated, but, unfortunately not all. It would be particularly valuable to know the date of *Mémoire* which is one of his most original in form; and although it is in Alexandrines, the traditional French metre, it is one of his most advanced technically. It conjures up memories of childhood impressions rather than precise facts, and its beauty lies in its imagery and not in its harmony, for its unelided 'e' mutes make a somewhat clumsy rhythm; but its visual impact recalls that of impressionist painting.

### MÉMOIRE

L'eau claire; comme le sel des larmes d'enfance,
L'assaut au soleil des blancheurs des corps de femme;
la soie, en foule et de lys pur, des oriflammes
sous les murs dont quelque pucelle eut la défense;

l'ébat des anges;—Non . . . le courant d'or en marche,
meut ses bras, noirs, et lourds, et frais surtout, d'herbe. Elle
sombre, ayant le Ciel bleu pour ciel-de-lit, appelle
pour rideaux l'ombre de la colline et de l'arche.

## II

Eh! l'humide carreau tend ses bouillons limpides!
L'eau meuble d'or pâle et sans fond les couches prêtes.
Les robes vertes et déteintes des fillettes
font les saules, d'où sautent les oiseaux sans brides.

Plus pure qu'un louis, jaune et chaude paupière
le souci d'eau—ta foi conjugale, ô l'Épouse!—
au midi prompt, de son terne miroir, jalouse
au ciel gris de chaleur la Sphère rose et chère.

## III

Madame se tient trop debout dans la prairie
prochaine où neigent les fils du travail; l'ombrelle
aux doigts; foulant l'ombelle; trop fière pour elle;
des enfants lisant dans la verdure fleurie

leur livre de maroquin rouge!—Hélas, Lui, comme
mille anges blancs qui se séparent sur la route,
s'éloigne par-delà la montagne! Elle, toute
froide, et noire, court! après le départ de l'homme!

## IV

Regret des bras épais et jeunes d'herbe pure!
Or des lunes d'avril au coeur du saint lit! Joie
des chantiers riverains à l'abandon, en proie
aux soirs d'août qui faisaient germer ces pourritures!

Qu'elle pleure à présent sous les remparts! l'haleine
des peupliers d'en haut est pour la seule brise.
Puis, c'est la nappe, sans reflets, sans source, grise:
un vieux dragueur, dans sa barque immobile, peine.

## V

Jouet de cet oeil d'eau morne, je n'y puis prendre,
ô canot immobile! oh! bras trop courts! ni l'une
ni l'autre fleur: ni la jaune qui m'importune,
là; ni la bleue, amie à l'eau couleur de cendre.

Ah! la poudre des saules qu'une aile secoue!
Les roses des roseaux, dès longtemps dévorées!
Mon canot, toujours fixe; et sa chaîne tirée
Au fond de cette oeil d'eau sans bords,—à quelle boue?

It is possible that Rimbaud also composed at this time the spiritual and mystical *Illuminations*, but this problem will be discussed in the following chapter.

Rimbaud left Paris in a state of discouragement and distress. He knew that he had not been a success with the literary men of the capital, and he realized that the fair hopes with which he had left home so few months before, lay broken at his feet. He was returning not as a conqueror, but as a discredited prophet. No one had understood his message, and he had been persecuted, but this was the fate of all great prophets and magicians. This had been the fate of Joan of Arc. In *Une Saison en Enfer* he would write: 'Je me voyais devant une foule exaspérée, en face du peloton d'exécution, pleurant du malheur qu'ils n'aient pu comprendre, et pardonnant!—Comme Jeanne d'Arc.' He had sacrificed himself for others, had enslaved his youth, and, through altruism, had wasted his life:

Oisive jeunesse
A tout asservie,
Par délicatesse
J'ai perdu ma vie.[4]

He felt an enveloping sadness and futility, doubt of the goodness of the world and of the value of his alchemical researches.

Ces mille questions
Qui se ramifient
N'amènent, au fond,
Qu'ivresse et folie;

Le monde est vicieux,
Tu dis? Tu t'étonnes?
Vis! et laisse au feu
l'obscure infortune.[5]

There is sadness and discouragement too in the lovely poem *Larme*, where he sees the possibility of drinking the *aurum pota-*

*bile*, the philosopher's gold, the liquid gold, which will bring immortal life, and he felt no desire or thirst.[6]

> Loin des oiseaux, des troupeaux, des villageoises,
> Que buvais-je, à genoux dans cette bruyère
> Entourée de tendres bois de noisetiers,
> Dans un brouillard d'après-midi tiède et vert?
>
> Que pouvais-je boire dans cette jeune Oise,
> —Ormeaux sans voix, gazon sans fleurs, ciel couvert!
> Boire à ces gourdes jaunes, loin de ma case
> Chérie? Quelque liqueur d'or qui fait suer.
>
> Je faisais une louche enseigne d'auberge.
> —Un orage vint chasser le ciel. Au soir
> L'eau des bois se perdait sur les sables vierges,
> Le vent de Dieu jetait des glaçons aux mares;
>
> Pleurant, je voyais de l'or,—et ne pus boire.

The same sad mood is expressed in *La Rivière de Cassis*.[7]

> La Rivière de Cassis roule ignorée
>     En des vaux étranges:
> La voix de cent corbeaux l'accompagne, vraie
>     Et bonne voix d'anges:
> Avec les grands mouvements des sapinaies
>     Quand plusieurs vents plongent.
>
> Tout roule avec des mystères révoltants
>     De campagnes d'anciens temps;
> De donjons visités, de parcs importants:
>     C'est en ces bords qu'on entend
> Les passions mortes des chevaliers errants:
>     Mais que salubre est le vent!
>
> Que le piéton regarde à ces claires-voies:
>     Il ira plus courageux.
> Soldats des forêts que le Seigneur envoie,
>     Chers corbeaux délicieux!
> Faites fuir d'ici le paysan matois
>     Qui trinque d'un moignon vieux.

Cut off from congenial companionship, in his dreary home town he began to think of the problem of love and of his loneliness. There would never be anyone to love him, no woman to console him. 'L'orgie et la camaraderie des femmes m'étaient interdites,' he says in *Une Saison en Enfer*, 'pas même un compagnon!' There was always some barrier or inhibition. In the rough draft of *Alchimie du Verbe* from *Une Saison en Enfer* he wrote 'Sommeil de toute la virginité! Je m'éloignais du contact! Étonnante virginité.'

In the doctrine of magic it is said[8] that when a man, either through deliberate celibacy, or for some other cause, is denied or has denied himself the companionship of women, he is a widowed soul, 'une âme veuve'. Rimbaud too felt that he was such a soul. In *Chanson de la plus haute Tour* he talks of the 'mille veuvages de la si pauvre âme'—this poem, when quoted in *Une Saison en Enfer*, follows immediately after the passage where he discusses his astonishing virginity—and of the Blessed Virgin as the only woman in his life.

Most of the poems which we know to have been written at this time reflect distress and loneliness and the acceptance of his solitary destiny.

Such a poem is *Michel et Christine* the title of which has led to much speculation, since the only reference to these two characters occurs in the last line.

The first three stanzas of the poem describe a thunderstorm and the havoc caused by it. The flocks on the mountain-tops, the sheep-dogs and the shepherds are bidden flee from the heights where the storm is raging to find, in the valley below, 'des retraits meilleurs'.

> Zut alors, si le soleil quitte ces bords!
> Fuis, clair déluge! Voici l'ombre des routes.
> Dans les saules, dans la vieille cour d'honneur,
> L'orage d'abord jette ses larges gouttes.
>
> O cent agneaux, de l'idylle soldats blonds,
> Des aqueducs, des bruyères amaigries,
> Fuyez! plaine, déserts, prairie, horizons
> Sont à la toilette rouge de l'orage!

Chien noir, brun pasteur dont le manteau s'engouffre,
Fuyez l'heure des éclairs supérieurs;
Blond troupeau, quand voici nager ombre et soufre,
Tâchez de descendre à des retraits meilleurs.

The poet, however, does not seek refuge with the lambs, the sheep-dogs and the shepherd for he is carried away in imagination by the storm.

Mais moi, Seigneur! voici que mon esprit vole,
Après les cieux glacés de rouge, sous les
Nuages célestes qui courent et volent
Sur cent Solognes longues comme un railway.

La Sologne is the marshy plain along the River Loire and it may seem strange that Rimbaud should have used this image since he had never been to that district. But it is likely that he is referring to the fields which run along a stream in his own home-land of Roche, which the local inhabitants call 'La Loire' or 'L'Alloire'.[9] This would be in keeping with his usual method of artistic creation, of adding mystery to his poems, by unexplained allusiveness.

Then the picture changes; the image of the natural storm expands into that of war and merges with it. The storm—war—carries along with it 'comme mille graines sauvages,' a pack of savage wolves over the old continent of Europe where a hundred wild hordes will sweep.

Voilà mille loups, mille graines sauvages
Qu'emporte, non sans aimer les liserons,
Cette religieuse après-midi d'orage
Sur l'Europe ancienne où cent hordes iront!

'Les liserons' is a reference to the evil effect of that plant—convolvulus—on crops. The storm—or war—favours the co-operation of the weed in the work of destruction.

Finally the storm dies down and the moon shines out. The warriors, on their chargers, ride proudly and calmly away from battle. And all is peace.

Après, le clair de lune! Partout la lande,
Rougis et leurs fronts aux cieux noirs, les guerriers
Chevauchent lentement leurs pâles coursiers!
Les cailloux sonnent sous cette fière bande!

The poet identifies himself with one of the soldiers riding away and the poem ends.

—Et verrai-je le bois jaune et le val clair,
L'Epouse aux yeux bleus, l'homme au front rouge, ô Gaule,
Et le blanc Agneau Pascal, à leurs pieds chers,
—Michel et Christine—et Christ—fin de l'Idylle.

This is the only reference to Michel and Christine. In this last verse it is clear that the young man is wondering whether he will ever see the autumn woods and the fair valleys of France again, whether the Paschal Lamb eaten by the Jews, at the feast of the Passover, to commemorate their escape from captivity, will ever be slaughtered to celebrate his own safe return. The image of the 'Paschal Lamb,' combined with the girl's name suggests Christ, 'The Lamb of God, without sin'. Perhaps Rimbaud may even have thought of the prayer from the Mass 'Lamb of God who takes away the sins of the world have mercy on us, give us peace!' At the time of composition he may well have felt that he himself was in need of mercy and peace. These allusions and suggestions seem clear, but who then were 'l'épouse aux yeux bleus' and 'l'homme au front rouge'? Who were Michel and Christine? The fact that their names give the title to the poem indicate that they have some bearing on the meaning of the poem taken as a whole.

There is a vaudeville by Scribe called *Michel et Christine* and this may well have been the starting point of the poem. Later, when explaining his method of composition, Rimbaud wrote in *Délires II* of *Une Saison en Enfer*

Je m'habituai à l'hallucination simple; je voyais très franchement une mosquée à la place d'une usine . . . les monstres, les mystères; un titre de vaudeville dressait des épouvantes devant moi. Puis j'expliquai mes sophismes magiques avec l'hallucination des mots!

*Michel et Christine* was a play which enjoyed great vogue during the Second Empire—particularly in the provinces and it was here that Hortense Schneider, the famous interpreter of the musical comedies of Offenbach, Meilhac and Halévy, was first noticed —and it is unlikely that Rimbaud did not know it. *Michel et Christine* is a sentimental little play of no great interest telling how Stanislas, a Polish soldier, returning from the wars, comes down from the mountains into the valley to seek Christine with whom he had fallen in love when he had passed through the valley on his way to battle. He finds her—in the meantime she had become the owner of the inn in which she had formerly served as maid—she promises to marry him and he makes plans for an idyllic life with her. However, at the end he nobly renounces her when he discovers that she really loves Michel, a simple country youth much given to blushing—perhaps that is why Rimbaud calls him 'l'homme au front rouge'—who returns her affection. He rejoins his regiment, when it passes through the village, fully convinced that he will be killed in the ensuing battle, but he begs his hosts to keep a corner for him at their hearth in case he comes back. The play ends with the vision of the happy idyll of Michel and Christine. The two lovers symbolize perfect and simple happiness in mutually requited love.

At the end of this poem Rimbaud expresses a mood of sad longing, awareness that, for some reason, he is cut off from normal happiness. His distress resembles that of the Polish soldier going back into the storm and stress of war, lonely and leaving behind him simple happiness for ever.

Then in his loneliness and shut away from everything which made life precious, Rimbaud longed for the time to return which he could love and enjoy.

> Qu'il vienne, qu'il vienne,
> Le temps dont on s'éprenne!

He longed for the high tower which could be a refuge, the tower built on Justice as Merlin's tower had been. Merlin said: 'I inhabit the wonderful Tower of the King of Magicians. In this tower I need not fear the treachery of the men of darkness. My tower is built on the rock of Justice and who could shake it?'[10]

## Chanson de la plus haute Tour

Oisive jeunesse
A tout asservie,
Par délicatesse
J'ai perdu ma vie.
Ah que le temps vienne
Où les cœurs s'éprennent!

Je me suis dit: laisse,
Et qu'on ne te voie:
Et sans la promesse
De plus hautes joies
Que rien ne t'arrête,
Auguste retraite.

J'ai tant fait patience
Qu'à jamais j'oublie;
Craintes et souffrances
Aux cieux sont parties
Et la soif malsaine
Obscurcit mes veines.

Ainsi la Prairie
A l'oubli livrée,
Grandie, et fleurie
D'encens et d'ivraies;
Au bourdon farouche
De cent sales mouches.

Ah! mille veuvages
De la si pauvre âme
Qui n'a que l'image
De la Notre-Dame:
Est-ce que l'on prie
La Vierge Marie?

Oisive jeunesse
A tout asservie,
Par délicatesse

J'ai perdu ma vie.
Ah que le temps vienne
Où les cœurs s'éprennent!

In the meantime, in spite of the promise he had given to his wife, Verlaine had been writing to Rimbaud and a regular correspondence began between them. These are the letters of Rimbaud which Mathilde Verlaine subsequently destroyed. Verlaine was planning and plotting to bring his friend back to Paris unbeknown to his wife and her family. He implored Rimbaud to take him in hand and not to allow others to dictate to him any longer. 'Écris-moi et me renseigne sur mes devoirs, la vie que tu entends que nous menions, les joies, affres, hypocrisie, cynisme qu'il va falloir. Moi tout tien, tout toi,—le savoir? Dès ton retour, m'empoigner de suite, de façon qu'aucun secouisme—tu le pourras bien.'[11]

Finally Verlaine sent Rimbaud the money for his fare and begged him to come immediately; he told him of all the debauch which they would share together, while Rimbaud was to save him from the wrath of his family.

Rimbaud returned to Paris in May 1872 and Verlaine rented for him a room, first in the Rue Monsieur-le-Prince, and later in the Hôtel Cluny in the Rue Victor Cousin, near the Sorbonne. Then the life of drinking, pub-crawling and literary discussions began again.

In Paris, with encouragement and stimulation, Rimbaud recovered from his dejection and depression, and regained his feeling of power and ecstasy. He wrote further poems in verse, such as *Est-elle almée*, *Éternité*, *O Saisons, ô Châteaux*. These were not poems of depression, like those written recently in Charleville, but expressions of ecstasy and success, when he believed that he had reached perfect bliss, that he had attained 'raison et bonheur', the *Sanctum Regnum*, the centre point of Nature where he could command all powers. In *Délires II* of *Une Saison en Enfer* he wrote:

Enfin, ô bonheur, ô raison, j'écartai du ciel l'azur qui est du noir, et vécus, étincelle d'or de la lumière *nature*. De joie je prenais une expression bouffonne au possible.

Baudelaire, in *Paradis Artificiels*, describes the hilarity of expression caused by the pleasure of smoking hashish. Rimbaud's ecstasy reached similar outlet when he composed *Éternité*.

> Elle est retrouvée.
> Quoi? L'Eternité.
> C'est la mer allée
> Avec le soleil.
>
> Ame sentinelle,
> Murmurons l'aveu
> De la nuit si nulle
> Et du jour en feu.
>
> Des humains suffrages,
> Des communs élans
> Là tu te dégages
> Et voles selon.
>
> Puisque de vous seules,
> Braises de satin,
> Le devoirs 'exhale
> Sans qu'on dise: enfin.
>
> Là pas d'espérance,
> Nul orietur.
> Science et patience,
> Le supplice est sûr.
>
> Elle est retrouvée.
> Quoi?—L'Eternité.
> C'est la mer allée
> Avec le soleil.

Pascal, after many long nights of struggle with his soul, reached complete certainty and ecstasy, and recorded his experience on the paper which was found close to his heart after his death. In the same way, Rimbaud seems, after long nights of watching, to have reached his same state of total bliss. He used to work and read all night in his little room in the rue Monsieur-le-Prince—a whole section of *Illuminations* is entitled *Veillées*—and there is, as a record, a lovely passage from his letter to Delahaye, in June 1872, which is worthy of being placed beside a prose poem from Baudelaire's *Spleen de Paris*.[12]

Maintenant c'est la nuit que je travaince (travaille). De minuit à cinq heures du matin. Le mois passé ma chambre, rue Monsieur-le-Prince, donnait sur un jardin du lycée Saint-Louis. Il y avait des arbres énormes sous ma fenêtre étroite. A trois heures du matin, la bougie pâlit; tous les oiseaux crient à la fois dans les arbres; c'est fini! Plus de travail! Il me fallait regarder les arbres, le ciel, saisis par cette heure indicible première du matin. Je voyais les dortoirs du lycée, absolument sourds. Et déjà, le bruit saccadé, sonore, délicieux des tombereaux sur les boulevards.—Je fumais ma pipe-marteau en crachant sur les tuiles, car c'était une mansarde, ma chambre. A cinq heures je descendais à l'achat de quelque pain. C'est l'heure de se soûler chez les marchands de vin pour moi. Je rentrais manger et me couchais à sept heures du matin, quand le soleil faisait sortir les cloportes de dessous les tuiles. Le premier matin en été, et les soirs de décembre, voilà ce qui m'a ravi toujours ici. Mais en ce moment j'ai une chambre sur une cour sans fond, mais de trois mêtres carrés.—Là je bois l'eau toute la nuit. Je ne vois pas le matin, je ne dors pas, j'étouffe. Et voilà!

To appreciate to the full the significance of this letter it should be read in conjunction with a poem entitled *O Saison, ô Châteaux*, and an *Illumination* called *Matinée d'Ivresse*, and these two poems take on a richer meaning when seen against the background of the letter. We do not know the date of the *Illumination*, but the poem was composed in May 1872, and Rimbaud, in his letter, dated June 1872, is describing events which took place the previous month. It is after the work and meditation of a Pascalian night that he must have written *Matinée d'Ivresse*, which is an almost hysterical expression of superhuman ecstasy. It is bliss finding vent in incoherent words, yet this spontaneous incoherence reflects more vividly the poetic and spiritual experience than would logical analysis. It is impossible that it could have been written at any other time than when this was a reality to him:

O *mon* Bien! O *mon* Beau! Fanfare atroce où je ne trébuche point! Chevalet féerique! Hourra pour l'œuvre inouïe et pour le corps merveilleux, pour la première fois! Cela commença sous les rires des enfants, cela finira par eux. Ce poison va rester dans toutes nos veines même quand, la fanfare tournant, nous serons rendu à l'ancienne inharmonie. O maintenant nous si digne de ces tortures! rassemblons fervemment cette promesse, cette démence! L'élégance, la science, la violence! On nous a promis d'enterrer dans l'ombre l'arbre du bien et du mal, de déporter les honnêtetés tryanniques, afin que nous amenions notre très pur amour. Cela commença par quelques dégoûts et cela finit—ne pouvant nous saisir sur-le-champ de cette éternité— cela finit par une débandade de parfums.

Rire des enfants, discrétion des esclaves, austérités des vierges, horreurs des figures et des objets d'ici, sacrés soyez-vous par le souvenir de cette veille. Cela commença par toute la rustrerie, voici que cela finit par des anges de flamme et de glace.

Petite veille d'ivresse sainte! quand ce ne serait que pour le masque dont tu nous as gratifié. Nous t'affirmons, méthode! Nous n'oublions pas que tu as glorifié hier chacun de nos âges. Nous avons foi au poison. Nous savons donner notre vie tout entière tous les jours.

Voici venir le temps des ASSASSINS.

Alchemists call their metals, in French, 'corps', and there are 'corps parfaits' and 'corps imparfaits' according to the degree of purity which has been achieved. It is possible that Rimbaud is referring, in the opening of the poem, to the perfection of the metal when he talks, alchemically, of 'le corps merveilleux'; and 'l'œuvre inouïe' may be the 'grand œuvre', the completion of the experiment.[13] This is the first time that he has attained it and he prays that his pride, awe and joy may not throw him off his balance. 'Fanfare atroce où je ne trébuche pas.' The 'chevalet' is a form of medieval torture and it is here used as a symbol for the suffering of the poet; it is a torture through magic, therefore a 'chevalet féerique'. Extreme suffering is part of Rimbaud's aesthetic doctrine; it is the price which must be paid for the final victory, the proof that one has been chosen for the triumph. Rimbaud was happy and proud to have been chosen for this torture, happy to have been considered worthy. The happiness he has achieved will remain his, even when the magic has faded away and he has returned to his former state of discord, when he will be 'rendu à l'ancienne inharmonie'. But he, who was held worthy of this suffering, will enjoy the super-human promise given to him, the unbelievable promise that the tree of good and evil will be cut down and buried for ever in darkness, so that he can establish his pure and universal love. Now he can praise and bless all the sleepless nights which have led up to this sublime experience. 'Sacrés soyez-vous par le souvenir de cette veille!' His method has been finally vindicated and he has been glorified in each of his ages. Alchemists believe that there are four ages which express the process of producing the philosopher's stone, or the gold—or the total vision which they symbolize—and each age is expressed by its colour, the colours following the usual alchemical progress. The first age is Saturn and its colour is black; the second Jupiter, its colour white; the third Venus, its colour yellow and the fourth Mars with its colour red. The symbolism of the use of the term 'ages' is similar to that of 'seasons' which will be discussed later in connection with the poem *O Saisons, ô Châteaux!* He had been right to have confidence in the poison. Now he will be able to sacrifice his life every day. The time of the 'Assassins' has come. Rimbaud is here using the word 'assassins' in a particular sense. He is probably referring to the Fatemite sect founded in Cairo in 1020 of which Michelet wrote in his *Histoire de France*.[14] The sect was founded by Hassan-ben-Sabah-Momairi and it was pledged to total and unconditional obedience. The members were astrologers, doctors and they became professional assassins. They could refuse no duty and they used to be engaged for difficult political murders. If one did not suffice, then others came along, one after the other, until the end had been achieved—regardless of the consequences. Before they embarked on their duties they used to be given hachich—hence the term 'hachichin' or 'assassin', according to Baudelaire —and when in this state of intoxication they became indifferent to suffering and to death—their own or those of others. Michelet further tells us that their leader declared that he was the *Iman*, the *Messiah* so long expected, the incarnation of the spirit of Ali. All this meaning is suggested by Rimbaud's use of the word.

*Matinée d'Ivresse* is the first and full expression of the spiritual experience; its quintessence and purified form is distilled in *O Saison, ô Châteaux*.[15]

The conception of the four seasons is an important one in the alchemical doctrine. It is not a season in the ordinary calendar sense. The seasons are spent in the 'philosophical vessel' and the four seasons are the period needed to perfect the *Elixir*, to produce the 'philosophic gold'. Each of the seasons is a necessary stage—each having its own peculiarities—and the length of the alchemical year cannot be measured by mere lapse of time. Each time the gold is produced makes a year and the process has to be begun each time afresh. Some periods of four seasons are much longer than others. Winter is the first season of the alchemical year, the age of blackness; it is also called the Golden Age, the age of Saturn, which has been discussed in a previous chapter. It is the time of dissolution, and—as alchemists say—of putrefaction —so that the elements can be broken up in order to make it eventually possible to produce the perfect gold. The season in which the blackness passes from black, through grey, to white is spring. The complete whiteness shading through yellow towards pink is the full summer; then when it reaches the red it is the alchemical autumn, the highest point of the year, the time when the magic fruits are garnered, the philosophic gold. This is the perfection of the *Elixir*.

Rimbaud uses the expression 'château' frequently in his poetry and the image is an important one for him. There were many famous castles in the Ardennes, one in particular near Charleville, called Le Château de la Fée which was believed to have been built first as a temple to the Emperor Julian the Apostate who was said to be a magician.[16] But in this poem the image has a fuller and deeper meaning than in the other poems. It seems as if Rimbaud were using it as a further symbol to express the perfection of his experience, the reaching of the spiritual gold. It is the inner core, the inner shrine of the spiritual experience. It is similar to the inner mansion of Saint Teresa, the interior castle. Those who have been granted the privilege of reaching that sanctuary enjoy total and perfect bliss. In the interior castle of the soul Saint Teresa describes the ineffable state of the Divine

Marriage and the new life which follows it. The presence of God is in the soul and the soul has become one with God. In the interior castle there is celestial happiness which compensates for the great spiritual suffering and tribulations which have preceded it. Saint Teresa's work was translated into French in 1859 and Rimbaud may well have read it. He reached the interior castle more quickly than she for he made use of magic charms and did not rely solely on the power of prayer.

Enjoyment of the poem does not, however, depend on these extraneous details.

> O Saisons, ô châteaux,
> Quelle âme est sans défauts?
>
> O saisons, ô châteaux.
>
> J'ai fait la magique étude
> Du bonheur, que nul n'élude.
>
> O vive lui, chaque fois
> Que chante le coq gaulois,
>
> Mais! je n'aurai plus d'envie,
> Il s'est chargé de ma vie.
>
> Ce charme! il prit âme et corps,
> Et dispersa tous efforts.
>
> Que comprendre à ma parole?
> Il faut qu'elle fuie et vole.
>
> O saisons, ô châteaux!

Rimbaud had reached this happiness by magic—'J'ai fait la magique étude du bonheur'—and he sang its praises at dawn each morning, when the cock crew, for it was after a long night's vigil that he had attained the full vision. At this time, in the summer of 1872, happiness through magic had seemed something to be grateful for and to praise. Later, when he repented of his practices, he came to believe that this pursuit of happiness through magic had been his curse, his temptation, his death. Then he saw happiness as a serpent with its 'dent douce à la mort'—as he was to say in the version of the poem used in *Une Saison en Enfer*—then it was a warning to him which he received each morning when the cock crew—just as Saint Peter had received his own remonstrance—and he added a couplet to the poem which did not exist in the first version.

> L'heure de la fuite hélas!
> Sera l'heure du trépas.

Happiness and peace would then come only through death. This stage will be treated in a later chapter.

There is little doubt that, at this time, Rimbaud was in a mystic and exalted spiritual state and that he was certain that he had been granted the vision of God. It seems very likely that it was then that he composed *La Chasse Spirituelle* which we are told he gave Verlaine in July 1872. It must have been before 7 July as it was on that date that the two friends left Paris for Belgium and England. It was amongst the manuscripts which were left behind with Verlaine's belongings at the house of his father-in-law, which would make it seem that Rimbaud had not had time to have copies made of it, or to show it to anyone else. This explains why no trace of it has ever been found.

Rimbaud's sublime experience in this period made him, for the greater part of the time, unconscious of neglect and oblivious of the squalor of his life. It is surely then that he wrote a large number of *Illuminations*, those which express confidence and belief in his doctrine, those which are dynamic and full of hope, those which are transcendental. Later there would be others which reveal a different vision of reality, a vision of material reality; they express doubt and resulting disgust with the life he had been leading, once it had been stripped of spiritual force and motive power. They show the withdrawal of the vision, and the fall from grace.

The poems in verse which we know that Rimbaud composed between March and August 1872, show a gain in technical freedom and originality, which is probably due to the influence and encouragement of Verlaine. In the poems written before he arrived in Paris, the daring lies less in the versification than in the conception and vocabulary. Up to that moment, even in *Le Bateau Ivre* and *Voyelles*, he had kept to the traditional forms, and it was almost as if he had been shocked by what he called the 'fortes licences' in Verlaine's *Fêtes Galantes*, when he had read it before he left Charleville, and found that its author had placed the sixth syllable of an Alexandrine in the middle of a word so that no pause was possible.[17] Verlaine, although he did not care for the form which Rimbaud's daring use of vocabulary took, nevertheless urged him on to greater freedom in prosody, and to the use of other metres beyond those of the traditional masters whom he had hitherto followed. Verlaine himself greatly favoured the 'vers impair'—that is to say the line with an uneven number of syllables, which had not been widely used since the eclipse of the Pléiade when Malherbe had come—'Enfin Malherbe vint' but, as Nodier irreverently remarked in the nineteenth century, 'qui aurait pu, sans grand inconvénient, se dispenser de venir'—after Malherbe had come and regulated poetry, eliminating the accomplishment of his immediate predecessors, and establishing the rule that only a line with an even number of syllables was correct prosodically. Sainte-Beuve, an admirer and follower of the poets of the Pléiade, reintroduced the 'vers impair' in 1828, in his *Poésies de Joseph Delorme*, but it did not take on seriously until Verlaine made it popular, declaring later, in his *Art Poétique*, that he preferred 'l'impair' to the regular line, for it gave greater vagueness and mystery to the verse.

Most of Rimbaud's last poems are in 'vers impairs'; *Michel et Christine*, *Chanson de la plus haute Tour*, *Éternité*, *Age d'Or*, *Larme*, *Honte*, and others. He uses various metres of 'vers impairs', either alone or in combination with others, often several different kinds in the same verse, interspersed with regular lines. As for instance, in *La Rivière de Cassis*,[18] *Comédie de la Soif*.[19] He also frequently makes use of the ten syllable line—not normally popular with French poets, even though it is the metre of their national epic, and also of *Le Cimetière Marin* by Paul Valéry—as in *Jeune Ménage*[20] or *Bruxelles*.[21] Like Verlaine, he also liberated himself from the tyranny of rhyme, using sometimes, 'rimes fausses', as in *Larme*,[22] or assonance as in the same poem and in *Jeune Ménage*.[20] Sometimes he omits to rhyme altogether. It is often as if he were impatient with versification as a whole, and did not wish to follow any rules—in *Age d'Or* and in *Honte*, he has, in each case, written a line with an extra syllable, and whether this is due to a deliberate act of rebellion, or to carelessness, is not clear. In the second, *Honte*, Paterne Berrichon, in the 1912 edition of Rimbaud's poems, has emended the line from 'Qu'à sa mort, pourtant, ô mon Dieu' to 'Qu'à sa mort, pourtant, mon Dieu', but recent editions have replaced it by Rimbaud's original line.[23] In *Éternité*, it is not clear whether he intends to count 'science' as one syllable, or whether he did not just mind again an extra syllable in the line:[24]

Science avec patience.

The freedom from the traditional rules of versification in Rimbaud's last poems is very daring for that period, when it is considered that it was at the height of the Parnassian movement, when nothing more daring than Verlaine's *Poèmes Saturniens* had yet appeared; when Mallarmé had not yet published any but his early poems—and those in a periodical—and when Charles Cros' *Coffret de Santal* and Tristan Corbière's *Amours Jaunes* had not yet come out—they are particularly daring considering that their author was only seventeen.

His impatience with, or disregard of, traditional versification, led him quite naturally to the poem in prose which we shall find in *Illuminations*, which we believe he began writing at this time. In this, as often, he was following Michelet who had said in his *Introduction* to *l'Histoire Universelle*,[25] 'Le triomphe universel de la prose sur la poésie qui, après tout, n'annonçait qu'un progrès vers la maturité, vers l'âge viril du genre humain, on crut y voir un signe de mort.' And again, in the same *Introduction*:[26]

La prose est la dernière forme de la pensée, ce qu'il y a du plus éloigné de la vague et inactive rêverie, ce qu'il y a de plus près de l'action. Le passage de la poésie à la prose est un progrès vers l'égalité des luminères; c'est un nivellement intellectuel.

## CHAPTER VI

# ILLUMINATIONS

HERE is the place to discuss *Illuminations* since it is possible that some of the poems which make up the collection were composed at this time. It is Rimbaud's most controversial and most widely discussed work, and, until we have formed some opinion concerning the date of its composition, it will be very difficult to reach any final estimate of him as a poet, and of the development of his art. It is considered by some—indeed probably by most people—as his noblest work and the highest peak of his achievement.

The first time we hear of the collection, under that name, is in August 1878, in a letter from Verlaine to his brother-in-law, Charles de Sivry, in which he says that he has reread '*Illuminations (Painted Plates)*', and that he will return the manuscript when he sees him after the holidays. This would mean that the manuscript was, or had been recently, in the hands of de Sivry, and that Verlaine had already read it on some previous occasion, before receiving it from him now. He must eventually have returned it, since he asks for it again later, in a letter dated 27 October. He does not seem to have been able to obtain it this time for, three years later, in January 1881, he repeats his request: '*Et ces Illuminations?*' Perhaps, in the meantime, his brother-in-law had mislaid it, for Verlaine seems to have grown weary of waiting and, when writing of Rimbaud in *Lutèce*, in 1883, he mentions a series of magnificent fragments, entitled *Illuminations*, which he fears are irretrievably lost. The following year, on 1 September 1884, he writes to Léo d'Orfer, begging him to try to extract the manuscript from de Sivry who certainly must have it in his possession. Another eighteen months seem to have elapsed before de Sivry finally unearthed it—or part of it—and sent it to Louis le Cardonnel, who was connected with the Symbolist periodical *La Vogue*.[1] At this time le Cardonnel was leaving Paris to enter a monastery and he entrusted the manuscripts to Louis Fière to pass on to Gustave Kahn, the editor of *La Vogue*.[2]

It is not known whether the title *Illuminations*, which seems to bear the hallmark of Rimbaud's genius, was certainly his—though this is highly probable. The word is written on one of the poems, *Promontoire*, but not in his handwriting, and it is not known who put it there. However, underneath that word, which is in the plural, can be faintly seen, in certain photographs, but not in all, the word *Illumination* in the singular, in another hand, and I agree with De Graaf in thinking that it is very similar to Rimbaud's.[3] The manuscript of the poem has disappeared.

*Illuminations* is not a title which Verlaine himself would have invented; it seems to be connected with illuminist doctrine and it suggests that the poems are intended to be the 'illuminations' of an 'illuminé'. Verlaine declared, however, that Rimbaud intended by *Illuminations*, 'gravures coloriées', which he translates 'coloured plates', in the preface of the first edition of the collection in 1886, thinking probably of medieval illuminated manuscripts, and he says that this was the sub-title which Rimbaud had chosen for the collection. But, in his letter to de Sivry, of August 1878, where he mentions the title for the first time, he used the term, 'painted plates', and this is the sub-title which Bouillane de Lacoste adopted for his edition published in 1949. It is hard to believe that Rimbaud could really have intended to use it, as it is pointless in this connection, and means nothing more than painted table plates. Bouillane de Lacoste believes that it must have figured on the manuscript which Verlaine received from de Sivry. If that is so it can only have been on a cover which has been lost, for there is no room for it on the pages of manuscript—'painted' or 'coloured plates' appears nowhere in writing, and comes to us solely from Verlaine.

A manuscript of *Illuminations* certainly existed in 1886, from which the poems were published in *La Vogue*, and it undoubtedly came from Charles de Sivry. But who its original recipient was, from the hands of Rimbaud, still remains a mystery. A note, published in *Le Mercure de France*, on 15 January 1939, states that the manuscript of *Illuminations* was given by Rimbaud to Charles de Sivry in February 1875 at Stuttgart, but does not produce any evidence in support of this assertion; and de Sivry's daughter declared categorically that her father had never been to Stuttgart, or to Germany at all, although he had often wanted to go there for the music—he was himself a musician.[4] The whereabouts of the manuscript, before 1878, when it is heard of in de Sivry's hands, is still unknown. Unknown also is the date when Rimbaud prepared it for publication—for the greater part of the manuscript has certainly the appearance of a fair copy. There are many contradictory views concerning the date of composition of the poems, and some modern critics are of the opinion that they were composed up to1878 or 1879; while others believe that there were none after *Une Saison en Enfer*, in 1873.

It is very probable that the manuscript of *Illuminations* which has come down to us, is the batch of prose poems which was in Verlaine's hands in 1875, which he mentions in a letter to Delahaye, of 1 May 1875, saying that Rimbaud had asked him two months previously—presumably when he met him at Stuttgart —to send to Germain Nouveau all the prose poems in his possession, so that he could negotiate their publication. He does not say that Rimbaud gave them to him then, but only that they were in his possession, and he does not mention a title. They might have been in his possession before he went to Germany; or else he might have obtained them in Stuttgart from Rimbaud himself. If he really had the manuscripts of the prose poems before he went there in February 1875, then they can only have come into his possession before July 1873, before he was imprisoned in Belgium, and they must have remained amongst his effects until he retrieved them on his release. If this is true then it would mean that all of the *Illuminations* had been composed before July 1873, and that the manuscript was then ready for publication. Charles Chadwick believes that the prose poems were in fact amongst Verlaine's effects, in his mother's custody, while he was in prison.[5] There are many difficulties connected with this view, which will be discussed later.

Verlaine, when writing of Rimbaud in 1888, in *Les Hommes*

*d'Aujourd'hui*, said that the manuscript of *Illuminations* had been given to someone at Stuttgart in 1875 who took good care of it. This can only have been either Charles de Sivry or himself, and the former appears to be ruled out by the testimony of his daughter, which leaves only Verlaine. It seems indeed likely that it was he who brought the manuscript back from Germany, in order to forward it to Germain Nouveau, and, subsequently, he seems to have considered it as his own property, when he believed that its author was dead. There is no doubt that he sent a batch of prose poems to Germain Nouveau in February or March 1875, who was then in Belgium.[6] After this nothing is known of the poems in prose until we hear of a manuscript entitled *Illuminations* in the hands of Charles de Sivry in 1878. What happened to the poems in the meantime, since 1875—for there can be no reasonable doubt that they are the same manuscripts—and how did they get from Nouveau to de Sivry? It may be that Nouveau had not been able to arrange their publication, and had sent them on to de Sivry himself, who seemed to have better and more influential connections in Paris—especially amongst the promoters of advanced periodicals such as *La Vogue*.

The poems which Le Cardonnel obtained from de Sivry and transmitted to Gustave Kahn, were published in *La Vogue* in 1886, in the fifth to ninth issues of the paper. It was Félix Fénéon who was responsible for establishing their order and, where this is indicated in the manuscripts—where the poems follow one another on the same pages—there is no room for doubt, but there are other cases where no direction existed, and the solution reached by Fénéon was purely arbitrary and has no special validity.

The fifth and sixth issues of *La Vogue*, of that year, contained only prose poems—except for one in *vers libre* entitled *Marine*. The seventh contained nothing but poems in verse. It is not stated where these came from, nor why they were added to the prose poems which are, undoubtedly, the only ones which should figure under the title *Illuminations*. They may have happened to be amongst the manuscripts in de Sivry's possession, but then how did they come to be there, and who gave them to him? Verlaine does not mention any verse amongst the poems which he sent to Germain Nouveau in 1875, and they are unlikely to have been given either to him or to Nouveau by Rimbaud himself at that time. They may have been in Nouveau's possession since the previous year, when he was in England with Rimbaud, and he added them for good measure. There is, however, no mention of them anywhere. They are the poems in verse—mostly dated by their author—known to have been composed in 1872, and Bouillane de Lacoste declares that the writing of the manuscripts is undoubtedly that of 1872. They were composed before Rimbaud left for England with Verlaine, and nearly two years before he met Nouveau. No later manuscripts have ever come to light, and where did they remain since 1872? It is certainly mysterious how they suddenly turn up here out of the blue. It is from their publication now in *La Vogue* that the tradition arose of their being two kinds of *Illuminations*, some in verse and some in prose, and this continued until the late War. Whereas it is now generally accepted that the collection should rightly contain only prose poems—except for the two in *vers libre*.

The eighth issue of *La Vogue* contained three poems in verse and three in prose; the ninth, three in verse, four in prose and one in *vers libre*, entitled *Mouvement*. At the end of this number a note stated that the publication would be continued in the following issue, and this would indicate that there were further poems to come—perhaps de Sivry had not yet been able to lay his hands on the whole batch of manuscripts at once. No further poems were to be published in *La Vogue*, but five poems in prose—as well as four in verse—did in fact turn up later, and they were all alleged to have come also from de Sivry. The prose poems were: *Fairy, Guerre, Génie, Jeunesse* and *Solde*, and all the poems—prose and verse—were published in 1895 in Rimbaud's *Poésies Complètes*. This does not necessarily mean that they were composed later than the poems published earlier, but only that they came to light later, after being mislaid for a time. These poems in verse, as well as the earlier ones, were certainly all written also in 1872, and Bouillane de Lacoste declares that the writing in the manuscripts is that of 1872, except in the case of *Mouvement* the poem in *vers libre*, which is that of 1874.

Vanier published *Illuminations* in book form, the same year as it had appeared in *La Vogue*, edited and prefaced by Verlaine, and this is the first edition of the work. Verlaine disregarded the manuscripts—perhaps he was not able to consult them again as he spent most of the year in hospital—and completely altered the order in which they had first appeared—notwithstanding that, in many cases, it was the one decided by the poet himself—printing prose and verse mingled according to no visible plan. Indeed he admitted, in the preface, that he could find no plan in the collection. 'There is no central idea' he declared 'or none, at all events, that we have been able to discover.' Since Rimbaud, then in Abyssinia, did not answer his request for information and further poems, he published the collection as the work of 'the late Arthur Rimbaud'. An unpublished letter, from Verlaine to Gustave Kahn, now amongst the Berès documents, and dated '12 June 1886' asks whether Rimbaud is really dead.

Verlaine republished this version, in the same order with the same preface, but with the addition of *Une Saison en Enfer*, in 1892. Then, in 1895, he published what he claimed to be Rimbaud's *Poésies Complètes*, in which were printed 'Autres *Illuminations*', the further poems, in verse and prose, alleged to have come also from de Sivry.[9]

In the meantime the manuscripts had all disappeared, divided up amongst the editors and publishers of *La Vogue*—chiefly, it seems, between Gustave Kahn and Vanier—and Verlaine appears never to have been able to recover what he considered his own property.[10]

All subsequent editions—until the manuscripts finally turned up again, at the end of the late War, had to be brought out without consulting the originals. Paterne Berrichon, who, after Rimbaud's death, married his younger sister, Isabelle, produced, in 1912, the version of the poet's complete works which for over thirty years, remained the model for all later editions. It was prefaced by Paul Claudel and, as no manuscripts were available, the editor discussed the poems—their composition and possible intention—with those who had known the poet, and, as a result, adopted a new order. In *Illuminations*, he separated the verse

218

from the prose and, in this respect at all events, this edition is an improvement on the first; and he grouped the poems in prose roughly according to the subject matter. He placed the collection before *Une Saison en Enfer*.

The manuscripts of *Illuminations* eventually came to light again. Except for a few odd pages, they were in two lots belonging, one to Lucien Graux and the other to Pierre Berès. Lucien Graux died in Germany, where he had been deported during the late War, in a concentration camp, and his manuscripts were eventually acquired by the Bibliothèque Nationale in Paris. They are in two volumes: the first consists of the complete set of poems in prose which served for the fifth and sixth issues of *La Vogue* in 1886, numbered in the order established by Félix Fénéon. The second volume consists of the 'Autres *Illuminations*'—the prose poems amongst them—which were first published in *Poésies Complètes* in 1895. One poem is missing, *Génie*, but it is now amongst the Pierre Berès documents; and another, *Jeunesse*, figures in one only of its four parts—the other three are still missing, but a facsimile was published in the centenary number of *Le Bateau Ivre* in September 1954. It was, however, published under the title *Vies* and it was stated that the manuscript from which the facsimile was made, had been lent by Henri Matarasso. The manuscript of *Vies* is, in fact, amongst the Lucien Graux manuscripts at the Bibliothèque Nationale. Henri Matarasso, when asked by the present author to describe the manuscript, of which he had published the facsimile, replied that he had never seen a manuscript of the last three parts of *Jeunesse*. When it was pointed out to him that the text published in *Le Bateau Ivre*, of which he was alleged to possess the manuscript, was wrongly entitled *Vies* and that, in fact, it consisted of the second, third and fourth sections of *Jeunesse*, he replied that he had never possessed more than the facsimile, which he had obtained from Messein, Vanier's successor. It is strange that the editors of *Le Bateau Ivre*, a paper devoted to Rimbaud studies, should not have noticed the mistake in 1954, and should not have been aware that here was an unknown facsimile of a text of which there existed no known manuscript.

The Lucien Graux manuscripts at the Bibliothèque Nationale are the bulk of *Illuminations*, thirty-four out of forty-two poems in prose.

The Piere Berès manuscripts consist of nearly all the poems—prose and verse—which were published in the seventh, eighth and ninth issues of *La Vogue* in 1886, but three of the prose poems are missing—*Promontoire*, *Dévotion* and *Démocratie*—the first has come to light separately in someone else's possession and a facsimile has been published, but the whereabouts of the other two is still unknown; and no known facsimiles exist. Berès later acquired *Génie*, but this fact does not seem to be generally known, for the editions of Rimbaud's works continue to state that there exists of it 'aucun manuscrit connu'. This accounts for all the manuscripts which served for the publication of *Illuminations* in *La Vogue* in 1886, and in *Poésies Complètes* in 1895—except for the two items which are still missing and of which there are no known facsimiles.

An examination of the available manuscripts and facsimiles of *Illuminations*—forty out of forty-two prose poems—reveals that, with a couple of exceptions, they have the appearance of fair copies which, despite insignificant inaccuracies—chiefly minor errors in spelling—seem to have been made ready for publication. In most cases there is more than one poem on each page, and frequently a poem is continued on another sheet, containing a further poem.

The first exception is *Après le Déluge*, placed number one by Fénéon—there being no indication of its position—the writing of which is so small as to be almost illegible, and it has obviously been cut—either to trim its edges, or to separate it from something else. If it has been cut from something else, then this must have happened before it reached *La Vogue*, for the printed order of the poems shows that it must have been alone on its sheet of paper, since there is nothing in the manuscripts to which it could have been joined. It may therefore not be a final copy, as its size is so much smaller than the other pages, most of which contain more than one poem.

The other exception is *Nocturne Vulgaire*, which is written on one side of the paper, with *Marine* and *Fête d'Hiver* on the reverse side. This is the only occasion when both sides of the paper have been used, and this would suggest that this page also might not be in its final form.

In 'Autres *Illuminations*' *Fairy* has a large 'I' under its title; *Guerre* has a large 'II' at the side of the page—there being no room under the title; and *Génie* has a large 'III' under the title. These figures would seem to be in Rimbaud's hand, and this would suggest some order, or that the three poems in question were intended to belong together to some section under a separate heading. They are the only poems to have these numbers under the titles, but no editor has taken any account of them—though Bouillane de Lacoste, in his edition of *Illuminations*, published in 1949, mentions two of them in the notes—he had not seen the manuscript of *Génie*.

*Guerre* has the same appearance as *Après le Déluge*, very small and cramped—obviously cut—with no room, under the title, for the number which, as stated previously, has had to be placed at the side of the page. It may also only be a rough copy.

*Dimanche*, the first section of *Jeunesse*—now in the Bibliothèque Nationale—is written on blue paper, and it has obviously been cut from something else. The word *Jeunesse* above *Dimanche*, to an inexpert graphologist's eye, does not seem to be in Rimbaud's hand, but Bouillane de Lacoste does not suggest that the writing is not his. *Génie*—now in the Berès manuscripts—is also on blue paper, the end of which must have been on the same page from which *Dimanche* has been cut—the shape of the edge is identical in both cases. The missing last three sections of *Jeunesse* appear, from the facsimile, to have been on one page, although the middle section seems to have been added at some different time, for the writing is much smaller and cramped, than the other two sections on the page. This page is likely to have been blue also. There would thus seem to have been three blue pages amongst the manuscripts—on the first of which was the beginning of *Génie*; on the second its continuation and the beginning of *Jeunesse*; and, on the third, the last three sections of *Jeunesse*.

The first edition to print only poems in prose under the title

*Illuminations* was that prepared by Bouillane de Lacoste for the firm of Hazan in 1945. This is now generally accepted by all modern editions, and the only difference between one and the other is where *Illuminations* is to be placed—before or after *Une Saison en Enfer*.

This leads to the most burning and controversial question in Rimbuad studies to-day, that of the date of composition of *Illuminations*.

Verlaine always declared that it had been written between 1873 and 1875, while Rimbaud was wandering round Europe—his real wanderings, however, did not begin until after that—but Verlaine varied very much in what he said about the collection, and he was always very evasive concerning the date. He was in prison during the largest part of the years he mentions—from July 1873 to January 1875—but he certainly never mentioned having known any of the poems before that. Yet he had, presumably, seen *La Chasse Spirituelle* in 1872, but was, nevertheless, unable to say anything precise about it—not even whether it was in prose or verse.

Delahaye, on the contrary, always claimed that it was composed in 1872 and 1873, and he declared that he had heard some of the poems read in 1872,[11] but he was never able to describe the nature of the poems he had heard, and they may have been other prose poems altogether—for there were certainly prose poems written in 1872, those described by Verlaine as having been left behind in his father-in-law's house when he and Rimbaud went to England,[12] but their title was not mentioned. Delahaye also said that, by the end of 1873, Rimbaud had long since given up writing both verse and prose.[13] He had, evidently, forgotten that Verlaine had told him, in May 1875, that he had just sent a batch of Rimbaud's poems in prose to Germain Nouveau.

Isabelle Rimbaud states categorically that *Illuminations* came before *Une Saison en Enfer* which, she says, was definitely his farewell to literature.[14] But, during his lifetime, she knew very little about what he had written, she was only thirteen when he composed *Une Saison en Enfer*, and she had never heard of *Illuminations* until after he had died.

Until comparatively recently it was generally accepted that *Illuminations* came before *Une Saison en Enfer*. Delahaye and Isabelle Rimbaud were believed and not Verlaine, who was usually considered incurably unreliable. Certainly what reliance could be placed on the opinions of a man who, although emphatically declaring that *Illuminations* had all been composed between 1873 and 1875 yet, nevertheless, in his own edition of the collection, included poems in verse which had been written—as he must well have known—in 1872, and which he must have read at the time? That opinion continued for many generations and it was generally taken for granted that Rimbaud, when writing *Une Saison en Enfer*, was deliberately abandoning literature, saying farewell to it, and that, after that, he wrote no more. That was a logical and neatly rounded-off plan.

Nevertheless even when writing my first *Arthur Rimbaud*, published in 1938, I was not happy about the simplicity of this conclusion. Why, I asked myself, if he intended to say farewell to literature, did he then publish *Une Saison en Enfer*; and why did he do his best to get it noticed by men of letters in Paris? Why also, when he went to Brussels, in October 1873, to collect the copies of his book, did he sign the police register as 'homme de lettres'?[15] Furthermore, why was he sufficiently interested in his prose poems, two years after his alleged abandonment of literature, and a longer time after he had composed them, to wish to have them published? There is no doubt about that. Why did he keep them, and why not try to publish his poetry in verse written at the same time? And finally, why did he want a copy of *Une Saison en Enfer*, in the summer of 1875, to present to the widow in Milan, who had been kind to him, if he had no longer any interest in his writings?

I came to the conclusion then—and I have not departed from it—that *Illuminations* was not written all at the same time; that it is a book of different spiritual climates—different 'états d'âme' as the Symbolists would say—composed at various periods. I did not see how such mystical poems as *Matinée d'Ivresse*, *Génie* or *A une Raison* could have been composed at any other time than when their author was an 'illuminé' and believed in his

223

visions; at any other time than when he was like the youth in *Crimen Amoris* by Verlaine; I did not see how the latter could have painted his picture of the young man in the poem without having known, at all events, *Matinée d'Ivresse*. Disillusionment with that phase of his life led eventually to his recantation in *Une Saison en Enfer*. But I believed also that there were other *Illuminations*, which were composed when the impact of the modern world began to make itself felt on him, when disillusionment with the visionary world set in; the beginning of the fall from grace. I believed, finally, that there were others, still later, which were more intellectual and less transcendental, written after his abandonment of magic and alchemy, when he was envisaging a new form of art; when his vision was more humanitarian and scientific. I believed then—and still do—that the mystical and transcendental *Illuminations* were composed at the end of his period in Paris, before he went to England, at the same time as his last poems in verse and *La Chasse Spirituelle*. There is no insuperable argument against his having, in fact, composed poems in prose at that time. While in London, Verlaine wrote to a friend in Paris to ask him to try to retrieve from his father-in-law's house the things which he had left behind when he set out with Rimbaud in July 1872, and amongst them he listed, as well as *La Chasse Spirituelle*, which was in a separate envelope, various poems in prose by his friend.[12]

The poems showing the impact of the modern city were certainly inspired by London, but it is true that they could equally have been composed in the year between 1872 and 1873, before *Une Saison en Enfer*, as in 1874, after it. Yet some must surely have been composed during the first period, for they are so similar in inspiration to what Verlaine wrote in his correspondence with his friends in Paris during the first winter in London. In this Rimbaud could not have copied Verlaine later, for he would not have seen the letters, but Verlaine might have put in his correspondence what he had heard his friend say—or what they had said together, as they both seem to have been much impressed —and in the same way—by their first vision of the large modern city, with its docks, its working-class quarters, its factories;

RIMBAUD DURING HIS MYSTICAL PERIOD
*a photograph by Carjat*

VERLAINE AND RIMBAUD IN LONDON
*a drawing by Régamey*

and the impact would have been stronger on a first visit than later.

I do not believe that, in *Une Saison en Enfer*, Rimbaud meant to say farewell to literature in general, but only to visionary literature; and I feel that he intended to compose, and did compose, further poems in prose—he had probably finished with verse—of a different nature. I believe that among such poems are *Soir Historique*, *Démocratie* and *Ville*—to commit oneself to some titles. They are more intellectual and hermetic, less emotional and passionate, than some of the earlier poems. They are composed more after a mathematical or musical pattern—musical contrapuntally that is, and not melodiously.

Since the late War there has been a general move in favour of placing all of the *Illuminations* after *Une Saison en Enfer*. The chief exponents of this thesis are first and foremost Bouillane de Lacoste, and then Daniel De Graaf and V. P. Underwood. When in 1949, Bouillane de Lacoste defended his doctoral thesis at the Sorbonne, *Rimbaud et le Problème des Illuminations*, he particularly seized on the imagination of most Rimbaud scholars, and few were able to withstand him, for he was persuasive in argument. He resurrected Verlaine's theory that all the poems had been written between 1873 and 1875—that is after *Une Saison en Enfer*. He was one of the first scholars to whom it had been possible to consult the manuscripts, and he came to the conclusion that their writing was that of Rimbaud in 1874 and 1875. Only a specialist is qualified to judge the validity of such graphological conclusions, but, even if they are reliable, they do not reveal anything about the date of composition, and Bouillane de Lacoste has failed to take into account the fact that the manuscripts may be—and most probably are—fair copies made from another text, the date of which alone is important. He claims also to have made the startling discovery that some of the writing is that of Germain Nouveau. As the latter is known to have been in London with Rimbaud in 1874, Bouillane de Lacoste concludes that the poems were written then. Another explanation is more likely, that Rimbaud and Nouveau were both copying from another script. It is in fact evident that Rimbaud has been transcribing from another text, for it can be seen that, in *Promontoire*, he had, in-advertently, at first left out a passage, so he crossed out what he had just written, and went back to add what he had omitted. As had been said before, it is clear that the manuscript, in most of its pages, is a fair copy—whenever it was produced—and it is unlikely to have been made over a long period of time. This would mean that its writing should be that of 1874 or 1875, but not of both.

Even if the graphological deductions are sound, they do not prove much and, moreover, some critics consider that the examples of handwriting are too few to allow any safe conclusions to be drawn from them. For 1874 only one undoubted specimen of Rimbaud's handwriting could be found, his signature on his application for a Reader's ticket to the British Museum. There are some also who deny that the writing on the manuscript, cited by Bouillane de Lacoste, is in fact that of Germain Nouveau.[15]

Bouillane de Lacoste has other arguments beside the graphological, as for instance, that the poem, 'Tu en es encore à la tentation d'Antoine' must have been composed after the publication of Flaubert's work of that title, in 1874. But Flaubert is not the only writer to have used the name of Saint Anthony—not to mention the various painters—and, in any case, extracts from the work had been published in *L'Artiste* in 1856 and 1857, and Rimbaud is likely to have known that review. Bouillane de Lacoste also believes that *Aube* must have been written in Germany in 1875, because it contains the German word 'wasserfall'. If he had really been in Germany at the time, he would probably have put a capital to this noun, as is correct in German. In any case, the word is in common usage in the Ardennes, Rimbaud's native country. But apart from these considerations, Bouillane de Lacoste has not taken the manuscript into account. In the arrangement on the pages, *Aube* must be considered together with *Veillées*, *Mystique* and *Fleurs*, since they follow one another on the same pages of the manuscript, and must therefore have been transcribed at the same time; but he does not claim that all these poems had been written in Germany. Although he discusses Rimbaud's handwriting of 1875—several long specimens exist for that year—he does not attempt to ascribe any of the pages of the manuscript to it and, in fact, the only evidence he produces for attributing any poem at all, to 1875, is the one of vocabulary in *Aube*.

*Aube* seems, on the contrary, to be a simple and straightforward poem and, from its style, would appear to be one of the earliest of the collection, for its attitude to nature is very similar to that of its author in his first poems, in such poems as *Soleil et Chair*. His response to nature is very characteristic of him, and it differs very much from that of most other poets of the nineteenth century. It is not the awe which we find in Hugo; nor the terror of Vigny at the heartlessness of nature; nor is it the condescension which Baudelaire expressed; nor the grudging admiration of Leconte de Lisle; nor yet the search for sympathy and comfort of Lamartine. There is something fiercely possessive and sensual in Rimbaud's love, as if it were lust rather than love that he felt; as if nature were a living woman whom he could worship sensually with his own body, and to whom he could give the surging passion and love which he had not given yet to any woman. And it is not merely desire and longing which he experienced, but the final ecstasy of orgasm. This gives an intensity to his nature poetry and a quality which is not found elsewhere.[16]

J'ai embrassé l'aube d'été.

Rien ne bougeait encore au front des palais. L'eau était morte. Les camps d'ombre ne quittaient pas la route du bois. J'ai marché, réveillant les haleines vives et tièdes, et les pierreries regardèrent, et les ailes se levèrent sans bruit.

La première entreprise fut, dans le sentier déjà empli de frais et blêmes éclats, une fleur qui me dit son nom.

Je ris au wasserfall blond qui s'échevela à travers les sapins; à la cime argentée je reconnus la déesse.

Alors je levai un à un les voiles. Dans l'allée, en agitant les bras. Par la plaine, où je l'ai dénoncée au coq. A la grand'ville, elle fuyait parmi les clochers et les dômes, et, courant comme un mendiant sur les quais de marbre, je la chassais.

En haut de la route, près d'un bois de lauriers, je l'ai entourée avec ses voiles amassés, et j'ai senti un peu son immense corps. L'aube et l'enfant tombèrent au bas du bois.

Au réveil il était midi.

De Graaf and Adam have tried to move the date of composition still further forward, right up to 1878 or 1879.[17] If this were true it would, naturally, completely demolish Bouillane de Lacoste's graphological deductions. Neither of these scholars discusses the manuscripts which certainly present the appearance of dating from one particular moment. They seem to assume that Rimbaud handed odd poems, at various times, as he composed them, to Verlaine, right up to the time when he left Europe for good—that is in 1879—even though there is no evidence of their having met after 1875. They deal mostly with internal evidence in the poems, and try to trace all the poet's journeys in them. As, for instance, when he mentions, in *Démocratie*, 'les pays poivrés' Adam believes that he is referring to his trip to Java, and there are many other examples. But just as many so-called references to these journeys could be found in *Le Bateau Ivre*, which is known to have been composed in 1871, when he had been, as yet, no further than Paris from home.

The strongest argument—and one very difficult to refute—in favour of all the *Illuminations* having been composed after *Une Saison en Enfer*, is that, in the latter, when Rimbaud quotes passages from his former work, which has proved so great a delusion, it is never a poem in prose that he cites, but always, on the contrary, one in verse, such as *Éternité* or *Chanson de la plus Haute Tour*, known to have been composed in 1872. Chadwick suggests,[19] that this is because they are easier to remember than passages in prose, and that he did not have any of his earlier manuscripts with him when he was finishing *Une Saison en Enfer*—these, according to him, being still amongst Verlaine's belongings. But he also believes that Rimbaud, even if he was not quoting verbatim from his prose poems, was, nevertheless, referring to them by implication.

On the other hand, one of the strongest arguments in favour of Rimbaud having composed some *Illuminations* before *Une Saison en Enfer*—at least in London between September 1872 and April 1873, when he began the latter work—is that there are, otherwise, no writings extant for that period, and it seems well nigh impossible to imagine that he would have written nothing then, when Verlaine was composing the bulk of *Romances sans Paroles*. It is hard to believe that Verlaine would have stayed at home to work if Rimbaud had been occupied elsewhere. Only his example would have encouraged his friend to creative effort.

The most recent arrival in the field of Rimbaud studies, Charles Chadwick,[5] wishes to reverse the new popular order, and to return to the first view, that *all* of the *Illuminations* were composed before *Une Saison en Enfer*, so that this work becomes once more Rimbaud's farewell to literature. The poems which he cites as illustrations for his thesis are precisely those which I have always placed amongst the earliest, but he seems to me to leave out of account those which do not support this theory—*Soir Historique* and *Ville*, for instance. He is also wrong, I think, when he suggests that Rimbaud told Delahaye in May 1873 that he was composing poems in prose. What Rimbaud in fact said, in a letter dated May 1873, was that Verlaine would probably give Delahaye some fragments in prose to return to him, Rimbaud. But these fragments in prose are most certainly passages from *Une Saison en Enfer*, which he was writing at that moment, and which he mentions in the same letter, calling it a 'Livre païen, ou Livre nègre'. He says, at the same time, that his fate depends on this book for which he has still six stories to write, and that he has already composed three. This cannot possibly have anything to do with *Illuminations*.

Chadwick also has not discussed the question when, and for what purpose, the manuscripts were prepared, for one cannot escape from the fact that they appear to have been got ready for publication. The poems in verse which have come down to us are on separate sheets, of which sometimes several copies were made to give away to friends; but they do not seem to have been collected, in the way that *Illuminations* was, in view of making a complete book. If this was really ready, in the summer of 1873— indeed before April that year, when he began writing *Une Saison en Enfer*—why did he wait until 1875 before considering publication?

Chadwick also believes that, in writing *Une Saison en Enfer*, Rimbaud meant to say farewell to literature, but he does not explain then why he should still continue to be concerned for his writings so long after that? He did not abandon interest in literary and intellectual pursuits until the middle of 1875, two years after he had finished *Une Saison en Enfer*.

Unfortunately the inescapable fact seems to be that there do not exist conclusive proofs for any one thesis, and that each is equally strong—or, more likely, equally weak. The best that can be hoped for are arguments which cannot be conclusively proved as wrong.

Bouillane de Lacoste's deductions from the handwriting prove nothing at all; and his arguments concerning the German word, and the mention of the temptation of Saint Anthony, do not carry any weight. Neither does Chadwick's view that *Ouvriers* must have been composed in 1873 since the poet writes as if it was February, mentioning floods of the previous month; and he discovered, from consulting the daily press, that there were, in fact, heavy floods in the London district in January 1873 but not in 1874. Nor is Guiraud's any stronger,[15] that, in *Phrases*, the sentence, 'Pendant que les fonds publics s'écoulent en fêtes de fraternité, il sonne une cloche de feu rose parmi les nuages' must refer to the fireworks for the Quatorze Juillet celebrations. As Rimbaud was in London on 14 July 1874, and in Brussels in 1873, he concludes that the poem must have been composed in 1872.

If an episode in a poem conclusively refers to one particular incident, the poem will, naturally, not have been written before the event. But afterwards there is no limit to the length of time which may have elapsed, and it is often years later that some trivial fact may reach fruition.

Chadwick draws attention to similarities of imagery between certain poems of Verlaine and Rimbaud, but these may not necessarily prove that the former was imitating the latter, but, on the contrary, might indicate the exact opposite.

Verlaine writes in *Kaleidoscope*, in *Jadis et Naguère*, 'cette rue . . . que traverseront des bandes de musique'; and Rimbaud in *Vagabonds*, 'la campagne traversée des bandes de musique rare'. Le Dantec, commenting on the poem in his notes to the *Oeuvres Poétiques Complètes* of Verlaine, declares that Rimbaud later borrowed the expression from Verlaine.[20] The poem was composed in prison, in Brussels, in October 1873, and it is very probable that Rimbaud knew of it, in the same way as he learned of *Crimen Amoris*, a few months earlier. Verlaine writes again, in *Luxures*, in the same collection, 'chair, ô seul fruit mordu des vergers d'ici-bas'; and Rimbaud, in *Sonnet*, the second part of *Jeunesse*, 'la chair n'était-elle pas un fruit pendu dans le verger'. This poem was written in May 1873, and Rimbaud must have known it then, and may even have possessed a copy of it. The first parallel seems more characteristic of Rimbaud and the second of Verlaine. The only certainty, in both cases, is the date of composition of Verlaine's poems, and Rimbaud might well have remembered the expressions and used them later; or Verlaine might have borrowed them from *Illuminations* if—a big if—the poems were composed at that time. At all events no conclusive deductions can be made from the similarities.

When Verlaine places a quotation from a poem of Rimbaud, at the head of one of his poems in *Romances sans Paroles*—'Il pleut doucement sur la ville'—Chadwick concludes, since there is no extant poem by Rimbaud containing this line, that he must have been thinking of a passage from *Veillées* in *Illuminations*, 'Une poudre noire pleut doucement sur ma veillée'. It is, however, far nearer to a very early poem which Rimbaud gave to his school-mate, Labarrière, who subsequently lost it and, trying to reconstruct it, could recall only one line, 'Il pleut doucement sur la plaine'. Verlaine, writing inspired by a rainy day in London, did not need an image from the countryside and he might have altered the quotation deliberately or inadvertently.[21] It can certainly not be used as any evidence in fixing the date of *Illuminations*.

The only strong argument in favour of the earlier dating of some at least of the *Illuminations* is that Verlaine must have known *Matinée d'Ivresse* when he wrote *Crimen Amoris*—or at all events the ideas which it contains. But there remains the awkward question why did Rimbaud still want to publish the poem two and a half years later—that is an undisputed fact—when it was part of the past which he had repudiated in *Une Saison en Enfer*.

I myself still believe—though without conclusive arguments

to support my contention—that, at some time in 1874, Rimbaud
decided to make a fair copy of *Illuminations*, which had been composed over a period of two years, in the hope of publishing the
collection. He did this either alone, or helped by someone else,
and gave the result to Verlaine at the end of February 1875, in
Stuttgart when they met, for him to transmit to Germain Nouveau, so that he could negotiate its publication. He could not do
this himself as he was in Germany—he may have discussed the
matter with him the previous year in England—he may also
have wished Verlaine to read what he had written since they had
parted; and also he was probably not loth to allow him to pay
the whole cost of postage—we know from Verlaine's letter to
Delahaye, that he considered it very heavy—several shillings.
Rimbaud was, as usual, in financial straits as his mother kept him
as short of money as possible. If the writing on the manuscript
is really that of Rimbaud in 1874, and if some of it is that of
Germain Nouveau, this adds weight to this argument. I believe
that, by the middle of 1875, when he was studying music and
mathematics, these took the place for him of poetry. There is no
proof that, after his meeting with the hospitable widow in Milan,
in the summer of 1875, he took the slightest interest in what he
had written. When his *Illuminations* was published in 1886, and
he was informed of this, he did not take the trouble to find out
how it had been produced, and to claim its authorship to obtain
royalties. But all this will be discussed in a later chapter. Here,
at this point, what interests us is the visionary stage of Rimbaud's
development and which of the *Illuminations*—if any—he may
have composed then. The poems which we believe that he wrote
at this time, were, as all his work had been up to then, an 'éva-
sion', something to help him to escape from sordid reality and
to find his own form of life. The poems express his manner of
escape, and his efforts to create a magic land of his own, where he
would be able to find what he calls 'la vraie vie'. And so he
viewed life as if it was a comedy enacted for his private delecta-
tion, which he could alter at will, and in which he was not obliged to play a part. Or else he saw the scenes before him as
pictures, living pictures, in which the depicted objects had an

independent life of their own, and were not bound by ordinary laws of logic. They were fantastic pictures in magic technicolour come to life, in which the known and the unknown mingle and blend; real and imagined things come together in a way which makes one wonder whether there may not be some deep alchemical or magical meaning involved.

One escape from the sordid world which he did not feel capable of accepting, was to return, in memory, to the days of his childhood, to the time of vivid impressions, when his mind was fresh and not yet vitiated by education. Now, in retrospect, since his sensitive nature had been bruised by the ugliness and coarseness of adult life, it seemed to him a fairyland of peace and beauty, like the land of Baudelaire's *Invitation au Voyage*.

> Là tout n'est qu'ordre et beauté
> Luxe, calme et volupté.

The two years which he had just spent had given him more of reality than he could endure, and now he began to look back on his childhood—which had once seemed to him dreary and restricted—as having been a time of plenitude, integrity and purity. He had been whole then, untouched and unmutilated by life. Now, consciously, he turned his thoughts towards those early years and tried to recapture that first state of mind. A study of *Illuminations* reveals how large a part childhood, and the memories of childhood, play in the visions of the poems, even of those which do not set out to describe that period of his life. It is Delahaye who first drew attention to the fact that many of Rimbaud's poems are built round the remembered experiences of childhood.[22] He claims that he never invented anything, that he always used real episodes which had happened to him, real things which he had seen, although he altered them, changing the chronology and using them in different connections. In his *Souvenirs Familiers* he has cited precise examples from *Illuminations* of the events which Rimbaud had seen and used in a transformed manner in the poems. Delahaye, although unquestionably right in his assertion, did not fully understand the way in which Rimbaud worked. Rimbaud realized clearly that he had experienced—as do all children—extraordinarily vivid impressions and sensations; that, in his childhood, everything had loomed much larger than in later years and that, by degrees, his senses had become blunted. He no longer looked at things he saw with the same wonder and awe; he was no longer poignantly moved, indeed he sometimes wondered whether anything now had power to stir his emotions any more. A child experiences the vivid sensations without knowing what they mean, without knowing how to use them, and without the language to express them. Rimbaud now imagined that there must be some hidden significance in these unalloyed and vivid sensations, that it would be valuable to recapture and make permanent that first untuitive state. He said to Delahaye: 'The whole of poetry is there. We have only to open our senses and then to fix, with words, what they have received. We have only to listen to our sensitiveness to everything that we feel, whatever it may be, and to fix with words what it tells us has happened.[23]

No one better than a child has his senses tuned to register without rational and conscious control, the most vivid sensations. With all his powers Rimbaud tried now to recapture the sensations which he had thought were lost or forgotten. He jotted down everything which he could remember, his most vivid and poignant memories, and leaves them, scattered, like beautiful images, in his work. He could not believe that such strong emotions could fail to be full of deep meaning or significance, but he did not try—any more than does a child—to explain, or even to analyse their significance, or to underlie it. The following is a section from *Enfance*.[24]

Au bois il y an un oiseau, son chant vous arrête et vous fait rougir.
Il y a une horloge qui ne sonne pas.
Il y a une fondrière avec un nid de bêtes blanches.
Il y a une cathédrale qui descend et un lac qui monte.
Il y a une petite voiture abandonnée dans le taillis ou qui descend en courant abandonnée.
Il y a une troupe de petits comédiens en costume, aperçus sur la route à travers la lisière du bois.
Il y a enfin, quand on a faim et soif, quelqu'un qui vous chasse.

And this poem stands without commentary:[25]

Une matinée couverte en juillet. Un goût de cendre vole dans l'air;—une odeur de bois suant dans l'âtre,—les fleurs rouies,—le saccage des promenades,—la bruine des canaux par les champs,—pourquoi pas déjà les joujoux et l'encens.

The literary critic would only destroy the poet's effects if he tried, ponderously, to comment on the passages. All Rimbaud's efforts have gone to preventing the control and the comment of his own rational mind, and that of the pompous critic would be no more welcome.

Rimbaud thought that a child was the same sensitive plate as the visionary, capable of receiving the impressions direct, without rationalizing them with his logic; the child receives the sensations with unquestioning wonder and amazement, which is nearer to wisdom and truth than the meditation of his elders. Rimbaud wished to recapture in himself the wonder of childhood and the power a child possesses of creating a world not bound by the limitations of possibility. And so we find in *Illuminations* all the things which had filled his imaginative life as a child—all the characters and stage properties of the fairy-tales and novels of adventure which had been his chief reading. These now mingled with his recent study of alchemy and magic, the subject-matter of which—apart from the occult meaning—was of the same legendary and mythical nature.

Another path of escape was into the land of dreams. Baudelaire had said that it was through dreaming that man entered into communication with the rich dark world which surrounds him, and Rimbaud used all known means of inducing in himself this state of perpetual dreaming—drugs, alcohol, even hunger, thirst and fatigue, all served to loosen the cramping grip of conscious thought, and they quickly brought on the state of semi-hallucination which he found most fruitful for composition. Then he could no longer distinguish, and no longer wished to distinguish, what was true vision and what was mere hallucination; what was dream or what was reality, since everything possessed the same blended solidity and vagueness. He admitted later, in *Une Saison en Enfer*, that he became accustomed to hallucination and saw a mere factory as an eastern mosque; saw carriages driving through the sky, and a parlour at the bottom of a lake. He could not distinguish—and neither can we, now—between what was real—although transposed and transfigured by his imagination—and what had no existence at all. And moreover, we do not know which is the hallucination—the mosque or the factory. This state of hallucination eventually became so frequent with him that he came to regard the world around him as a shifting spectacle the solidarity and truth of which must not be too seriously relied upon. Then he saw nothing strange in blending with these material objects those he had invented and he refused to be bound by ordinary rules of verisimilitude and reality. Reality was only the raw material for his creative vision with which he could take complete liberty. 'Ta mémoire et tes sens' he said 'ne seront que la nourriture de ton impulsion créatrice.' In this he reached, in a manner perhaps unforeseen by himself, 'le dérèglement de tous les sens', each sense receiving the impressions normally only received by another. We find associated together things which we do not usually connect. In *Enfance*:[26]

A la lisière de la forêt les fleurs de rêve tintent, éclatent, éclairent,—la fille à la lèvre d'orange, les genoux croisés dans le clair déluge qui sourd des prés, nudité qu'ombrent, traversent et habillent les arcs-en-ciel, la flore, la mer.

And again, in *Veillées*.[27]

Les lampes et les tapis de la veillée font le bruit des vagues la nuit le long de la coque et autour du steerage.

This will also be the method of the Symbolist Movement in the eighteen-eighties.

Hashish was, however, the most swift means of inducing this creative state. It has frequently been remarked that hashish addicts dream constantly, even when they are awake, and experience then all the manifestations of the dreams of sleep, but often in a much more vivid manner. The strangest and most grotesque ideas rush through their minds with astonishing rapidity, and these dreams mingle with their real life and become part of it. Many of

*Illuminations* read as if they had been composed in such a state of induced dreaming.

Rimbaud was not always able to achieve this happy state of magic receptivity, for he was still often bound by what he considered his besetting inhibition—a consciousness of guilt. He was unable to accept everything simply and naturally, for he had not yet completely uprooted the effects of his early training; he constantly felt that he was being submitted to temptation and was yielding to it; he was not able to achieve the instinctive certainty he wished to possess, that he was indeed above the reach of sin and condemnation. He believed that only when he had shaken himself free from what seemed to him no more than a foolish inhibition could he achieve full creative power. He endured moments of doubt and anguish, of unbearable suffering, when he was uncertain whether he would ever be able to rise up out of the depths, when he doubted his own powers of creation. He writes in a poem reflecting this mood, in *Angoisse*: [28]

Se peut-il qu'Elle me fasse pardonner les ambitions continuellement écrasées,—qu'une fin aisée répare les âges d'indigence,—qu'un jour de succès nous endorme sur la honte de notre inhabileté fatale.

Then, when he thought that he could endure the anguish and the doubt no longer, there came the flash of light, the full experience and the full vision. This is expressed in *Matinée d'Ivresse* which has been mentioned in an earlier chapter.

The greatest escape of all was in spiritual and visionary adventure. It is not surprising to find that a large number of *Illuminations* express transcendental experience and many are those who have found conversion to their own religious faith—in East and West—after reading his poems. 'It is to Rimbaud that I owe, humanly speaking, my return to the faith,' wrote Paul Claudel. [29] 'The little number of *La Vogue* of 6 May 1886, battered down the walls of the prison where I lay stifled, and brought me the tremendous revelation of the supernatural everywhere around us.'

Claudel, however, in his anxiety to prove that his 'mystique à l'état sauvage'—as he called Rimbaud—was a good and orthodox Catholic, compares *Illuminations* with the writings of Catholic thinkers, and, in this, forces his point, since little similarity can be found—except in so far as mystic experience of God finds the same expression all the world over.

Rimbaud had always been of an ardently religious nature; his religious feeling was very different in character from the whimpering piety of Verlaine. He had the passionate fervour of Saint Teresa. In his childhood, before he had begun to think independently for himself, his piety had been orthodox, but later he had turned against God because the only God he knew was the one supported by the bourgeoisie, the God of capitalism, the God who demanded eternal sacrifice and seemed to him more like a pagan idol gorging on human flesh and blood than a spiritual God.

> J'étais bien jeune et Christ a souillé mes haleines;
> Il me bonda jusqu'à la gorge de dégoûts.

But he was not satisfied to remain permanently separated from God, and he determined to find him for himself, in his own manner, and to force his way into His presence. We have the experience of this discovery in *A une Raison* and in *Génie*. The fullest expression is to be found in the latter. It refers probably to one of the seven Genii of the Cabala each of whom governed an age of the world and made it unto his own liking during the three hundred and fifty-four years and four months of his reign.[30]

Il est l'affection et le présent puisqu'il a fait la maison ouverte à l'hiver écumeux et à la rumeur de l'été—lui qui a purifié les boissons et les aliments—lui qui est le charme des lieux fuyants et le délice surhumain des stations. Il est l'affection et l'avenir, la force et l'amour que nous, debout dans les rages et les ennuis, nous voyons passer dans le ciel de tempête et les drapeaux d'extase.

Il est l'amour, mesure parfaite et réinventé, raison merveilleuse et imprévue, et l'éternité: machine aimée des qualités fatales. Nous avons tous eu l'épouvante de sa concession et de la nôtre: ô jouissance de notre santé, élan de nos facultés, affection égoïste et passion pour lui, lui qui nous aime pour sa vie infinie. . .

Et nous nous le rappelons et il voyage. . . . Et si l'Adoration s'en va, sonne, sa promesse sonne: 'Arrière ces superstitions, ces anciens corps, ces ménages et ces âges. C'est cette époque-ci qui a sombré!'

ILLUMINATIONS

Il ne s'en ira pas, il ne redescendra pas d'un ciel, il n'accomplira pas
la rédemption des colères des femmes et des gaietés des hommes et de
tout ce péché: car c'est fait, lui étant, et étant aimé.

O ses souffles, ses têtes, ses courses; la terrible célérité de la perfection
des formes et de l'action.
O fécondité de l'esprit et immensité de l'univers!
Son corps! le dégagement rêvé, le brisement de la grâce croisée
de violence nouvelle!
Sa vue, sa vue! tous les agenouillages anciens et les peines *relevés*
à sa suite.
Son jour! l'abolition de toutes les souffrances sonores et mouvantes
dans la musique plus intense.
Son pas! les migrations plus énormes que les anciennes invasions.
O Lui et nous! l'orgueil plus bienveillant que les charités perdues.
O monde! et le chant clair des malheurs nouveaux!
Il nous a connus tous et nous a aimés. Sachons, cette nuit d'hiver, de
cap en cap, du pôle tumultueux au château, de la foule à la plage, de
regards en regards, forces et sentiments las, le héler et le voir, et le
renvoyer, et, sous les marées et au haut des déserts de neige, suivre
ses vues, ses souffles, son corps, son jour.

Rimbaud's mystical poems are a manifestation of an experience trying to find expression in a medium which cannot contain
it. It is the spirit trying to incarnate itself in images which cannot
hold it adequately and the only possible way of suggesting such
an experience is to do so symbolically, not by description but by
evoking in the reader the poet's emotional state and spiritual
intuition. Each little group of words is then intended to suggest,
not the full experience, but one single flash of understanding. We
do not receive the whole vision at once, but in a series of these
flashes, of *illuminations*, which, in the end, force the impression
into our mind. We can feel that Rimbaud is often groping after
his experience, trying to express a sensation too deep to be rendered in mere words, and that these words will always remain
inadequate. *Illuminations* are often mere exclamations of joy, in
which the words mean little in themselves, and their real value
lies in their spontaneous power of suggestion. They are in the
nature of incantations, words strung together, without logical

order—just as a child strings odd words together, in an endeavour to express the overpowering ecstasy he had experienced but did not yet comprehend—beautiful words which he repeated over and over again, words the meaning of which he did not fully grasp, because they seemed to exteriorize his rapture. Just as Pascal, on the night of his revelation of God, could give no coherent expression to his experience, but could only cry again and again: 'Joies! Joies! Pleurs de joie!' Some of *Illuminations* seem to perform for Rimbaud the function of the Litany which Catholics have always found a valuable outlet as an expression of spiritual emotion and awareness of God, which they would have been unable to render in coherent speech.

*Illuminations* is a curiously solitary book. Rimbaud was right, when he said in *Une Saison en Enfer*, 'Pas même un compagnon!' and again 'Mais pas une main amie! où puiser le secours!'

Although most of the poems were written during the height of his friendship with Verlaine—if we are right in our theory of the composition—the presence of no one is felt beside him. He stands alone on his bare mountain, lit up occasionally at dawn by the radiance of sunrise, but more often enveloped in darkness. There Rimbaud stands alone, alone with his God, with his soul and his dreams.

It is certainly in the prose poem that Rimbaud reached his highest peak of originality, and it is the form best suited to his elliptical and hermetic style, since it allows of infinite freedom. It is, however, perhaps worth noting—in view of the claim of later writers—that he wrote the two first poems in *vers libre*, *Marine* and *Mouvement*, more than ten years before Kahn, Laforgue or Dujardin. But they are less interesting in achievement than his prose poems.

The prose poem had existed already before Rimbaud since it is a form which had been used by Gérard de Nerval, Aloysius Bertrand, Charles Baudelaire and Charles Cros. It had tended, hitherto, on the whole, to be narrative and descriptive—either of these characteristics being more or less marked according to the individual taste of the author. The *Gaspard de la Nuit* of Aloysius Bertrand had been descriptive rather than narrative; whilst both

Gérard de Nerval and Baudelaire had favoured the more narrative form, although the latter departed, at times, from this—in *Le Port* for instance—and composed the descriptive prose poem of the type later adopted by Mallarmé. With Rimbaud the prose poem is generally stripped of all its anecdotal, narrative or even descriptive content, and it becomes highly concentrated and short. Typical of his method is the very beautiful *Veillées I*. There is something to be said for Chadwick's view that this poem should be considered one in *vers libre* rather than in prose.[32]

> C'est le repos éclairé, ni fièvre ni langueur, sur le lit ou sur le pré.
> C'est l'ami ni ardent ni faible. L'ami.
> C'est l'aimée ni tourmentante ni tourmentée. L'aimée.
> L'air et le monde point cherchés. La vie.
> —Etait-ce donc ceci?
> —Et le rêve fraîchit.

Sometimes the function of the prose poem is to exteriorize one brief flash of sensation, one short *illumination*; then frequently one single line is the entire poem.[33]

> J'ai tendu des cordes de clocher à clocher; des guirlandes de fenêtre à fenêtre; des chaînes d'or d'étoile à étoile, et je danse.

A whole section of *Illuminations* is composed of these '*Phrases*' as Rimbaud entitles them.

Some critics have thought that Rimbaud owed his form of prose poem to his constant reading of the Bible as a child.[34] Other sources of inspiration are also possible. There is some similarity between his prose poems and Chinese poetry—that is Chinese poetry in French translation. Translations of Chinese poems were well known towards the end of the Second Empire—particularly in Parnassian circles. Laprade, in his *Sentiment de la Nature avant le Christianisme*, published in 1866, included French renderings of many lovely Chinese lyrics. It is highly probable that Rimbaud knew this work—interested as he was in all Parnassian productions. There is also *Le Livre de Jade* by Judith Gautier—the daughter of the poet—published in 1869 under the name Judith Walter, which is a collection of lyrics freely translated from the Chinese. It is impossible that Rimbaud should not have known this work, which Verlaine compared to *Gaspard de la Nuit* by Aloysius Bertrand,[35] and in which Catulle Mendès sees one of the sources of *vers libre*; it is, however, much nearer to the prose poem used by Rimbaud, and it is possible that it is from there that he drew his first inspiration. Judith Gautier deserves more recognition in the history of French poetry than she has yet received. Apart from *Le Livre de Jade*, which is the translation—adaptation would be nearer the truth—of Chinese poems, she composed also original prose poems of her own, which appeared fourteen years before those of Rimbaud were published in *La Vogue*. Although these owe something to Baudelaire—who, at the end of the nineteenth century does not?—they have their own originality, and bear some resemblance to certain poems in *Illuminations*. Many appeared in *La Renaissance Littéraire et Artistique* between June and December 1872, and Rimbaud must have read them for he knew the paper, in which he published himself his poem *Les Corbeaux* on 15 September 1872. Another possible source of inspiration is *Le Coffret de Santal* by Charles Cros, which contains prose poems very like his. It is true that the collection only appeared in 1873, but many of the poems were published first in *La Renaissance Littéraire et Artistique* in 1872. In any case Rimbaud had been in close touch with Charles Cros since his arrival in Paris in September 1871, and considered him indeed as one of his closest friends, the one with whom he had, artistically, most affinity.

The first half of 1872 was for Rimbaud, in spite of disappointment in Paris and his suffering, the richest and most productive period of his whole literary career. He might have floundered in disillusionment and discouragement had he not been upheld by his friendship with Verlaine, and the latter's admiration for him —particularly his genuine belief in his talent and future. This kept the flame alive which he had ravished, like Prometheus, from Heaven. At this time he still had confidence in his powers, in his doctrine, and so misunderstanding, poverty and outward failure, were of little account in comparison with the fire which burned in him.

In *Illuminations* there is a symbolical poem called *Royauté*,[36] and it describes how a man, one day, cried to all those whom he met, as he walked through the town, that he was King and that the woman by his side was his Queen. To all who would listen he recounted the story of his trials and their end, and of the revelations which he had received. For one whole day the man and the woman were in fact King and Queen because they believed this to be true. In the same way, for a short space of time, Arthur Rimbaud was a *mage* and a *voyant*, the equal of the Almighty, because he believed it, and in him burned the creative power of a God.

CHAPTER VII

# METROPOLIS

As the summer of 1872 wore on Paris became unendurable to Rimbaud and he longed for the fresh air of his native Ardennes. This was the first summer that he had spent in a city, for he had lived all his life in a little town on the edge of the country, with escape to the farm at Roche. 'I hate the summer,' he wrote to Delahaye,[1] 'It kills me when it begins to flare up. I have a gangrenous thirst! The Ardennes rivers and the Belgian caves, those are what I specially miss.'

He began now to find his hotel room unbearable, looking into its evil-smelling court. It was the type of sordid Latin Quarter hotel which, even to-day, houses countless generations of needy students. From the very entrance the stench of stale urine rises in the fusty stairs from water-closets never cleaned, and the squalid airless rooms are redolent, in the dark warm nights, of the smell of dust-bins—the very name 'poubelles' conjures up the decaying refuse—floating up through the narrow tube of the court. When daylight penetrates to these dim rooms, which no rays of the sun ever reach, the only noticeable change is that a grey darkness has taken the place of the black.

By July he felt that he could endure it no longer and he

decided to leave Paris for a time and to force Verlaine to accompany him. He knew by now that he had sufficient power to influence him. He went out to Montmartre to inform him of his plans and met him in the street, just as he was leaving the house to fetch his wife's medicine from a near-by chemist. At first Verlaine, restrained by scruples, refused to accompany him. 'And my wife?' he asked. But Rimbaud answered brutally. 'To Hell with your wife!' Finally Verlaine allowed himself to be persuaded and followed his friend.

They spent the day in a café and then when evening came, they took a train for Arras where an old aunt of Verlaine's lived. This was 7 July 1872 and Rimbaud little guessed that this was the end of his literary life in Paris. He was leaving the capital which he had meant to conquer when he had arrived, full of high hopes, from the provinces, the previous year; but he had conquered nothing; he was still unknown and was leaving only enemies behind him.

They travelled all night, arriving in Arras in the early morning, and they behaved like two irresponsible children on holiday.[2] To while away the time until they could suitably call on Verlaine's aunt, they sat breakfasting at the station buffet and decided that they would horrify the stolid bourgeois whom they saw drinking their morning *café au lait* with such smug satisfaction. They began conversing together in simulated whispers, but so that all could hear, of the burglaries they had committed, boasting even of attempted murder, but so pleased did they become with their inventive power that they overdid the piling up of detail. Suddenly they were stopped short in their narrative by the sight of two ferocious policemen whom the bar-tender had, surreptitiously, called in on overhearing their conversation. They were immediately arrested and marched off together to the Hôtel de Ville, and there they had the greatest difficulty in explaining to the magistrate that their conversation had only been a joke. There had been an execution in Arras a few days previously, and Verlaine's and Rimbaud's conversation had given rise to misconception, for it was thought that it might have some connection with the crime which had led to the guillotine. The magistrate, in any case, was very suspicious as to why the two friends had come to Arras at all. The matter ended by their being led by the police to the railway station and being put into the train for Paris. On arriving in Paris they did not, however, remain there; they merely changed from the *Gare du Nord* to the *Gare de l'Est* and took tickets for Charleville. Madame Rimbaud was by then with the family in the country cottage at Roche, and there was no danger of encountering her. The two friends spent a happy day drinking with Charles Bretagne and when evening came they hired a horse and cart to take them over the frontier into Belgium, at a quiet spot where they were not likely to meet customs officials, and once they were on Belgian soil, they took the train for Brussels.

In the meantime, in Paris, Mathilde Verlaine was left in a state of great anxiety on her husband's behalf, for she had received no news of him since the moment when he had gone to the chemist, meaning to be absent no more than a few minutes. It would never have entered her head to think that he might have gone on a journey, for he had set off without any luggage and people, she knew, did not travel without change of clothes. She thought that some accident must have happened to him and she made the police search for him, in all the hospitals, in all the police stations of the city, even at the morgue, but in vain, no one had any news of him.

Finally, a few days later, a letter arrived for her from Brussels, a pathetic letter, which shows how much Rimbaud had Verlaine under his influence.[3]

My dear Mathilde, don't be distressed. Don't grieve and don't cry! I'm in the middle of a nightmare! I'll return one day!

On receiving this letter, she decided that she would make one further effort to win her husband back from the scoundrel who had bewitched him. In company with her mother she set off for Brussels to find him and to persuade him to come back to her. In a poem dated 'Bruxelles-Londres.—Septembre–octobre 1872' Verlaine describes his meeting with her, when he went nervously to his hotel room hearing that she had arrived.[4]

Je vous vois encore. J'entr'ouvris la porte.
Vous étiez au lit comme fatiguée.
Mais, ô corps léger que l'amour emporte,
Vous bondîtes nue, éplorée et gaie.

Then he was suddenly overcome with love and remorse and his feeling of nervousness and apprehension vanished.

O quels baisers, quels enlacements fous!
J'en riais moi-même à travers mes pleurs.
Certes, ces instants seront entre tous,
Mes plus tristes, mais aussi mes meilleurs.


Je ne veux revoir de votre sourire
Et de vos beaux yeux, en cette occurrence,
Et de vous, enfin, qu'il faudrait maudire,
Et du piège exquis, rien que l'apparence.

He forgave her the trap she had set for his senses, and only thought of his love and her beauty.

But when she was dressed again and the lover vanished as the staid wife reappeared in her conventional clothes, with her innocent and spontaneous gaiety gone, then all the problems rose up, and he knew what his fate was to be.

Je vous vois encore! En robe d'été
Blanche et jaune avec des fleurs de rideaux.
Mais vous n'aviez plus l'humide gaîté
Du plus délirant de nos tantôts.


La petite épouse et la fille aînée
Était reparue avec la toilette,
Et c'était déjà notre destinée
Qui me regardait sous votre voilette.

It is said that he confessed to her the nature of his relations with Rimbaud, but she did not, at the time, fully understand what he meant.[5] She still counted on his love for her, of which she had just had proof, hoping to persuade him to return with her. She was, foolishly, making plans of what they would do when they were united again and how she would save him in spite of himself. They would go away, she thought—her father would be willing to advance the money in so good a cause. They would go away, just the two of them, to La Nouvelle Calédonie, and her mother would look after the baby in her absence. They would both grow strong again and forget the past; Paul would make a complete break with his present associations and would finish the book he had planned to write on the Commune which he seemed, in his present circumstances, unable to write.

After meeting his wife and mother-in-law Verlaine allowed himself to be persuaded to return to Paris with them but he begged to be permitted to say good-bye to Rimbaud in order to explain everything to him verbally, and he promised that he would meet them at the station. When he arrived at the train, just as it was leaving, the two women realized immediately that he was no longer in the same gentle frame of mind, that he was intoxicated and in a bad temper. However, he entered the carriage with his wife and mother-in-law, but sat himself down in the corner and remained sunk in gloom and despondency, refusing to answer a word when spoken to. At the frontier they were obliged to leave the carriage for the customs examination, but, in the flurry of the moment, the two women lost sight of him, and did not notice what had become of him. After they got back into their carriage they looked everywhere for him and, just as the train was about to leave, they saw him standing, at some distance, on the platform. 'Jump in!' cried Madame Mauté de Fleurville, waving excitedly to him, and speaking with false heartiness to conceal her anxiety. 'You'll get left behind if you don't take care!' But Verlaine only shook his head in answer, and the train steamed out of the station without him. This was the last time that Mathilde Verlaine was ever to see her husband.

The following day she received a letter from him which would be comic were the situation not so tragic.[6]

Misérable fée carotte, princesse souris, punaise, qu'attendent les deux doigts et le pot. Vous m'avez fait tout; vous m'avez peut-être tué le cœur de mon ami. Je rejoins Rimbaud, s'il veut encore de moi, après cette trahison que vous m'avez fait faire.

In the meantime, as we know from a letter from a Brussels police officer to the detective branch of the service, on 6 August

1872, Madame Rimbaud had asked the Belgian police to discover the whereabouts of her son who had left home with a
certain Paul Verlaine. It was disclosed that Verlaine was living at
a hotel in Rue de Brabant in Saint-Josse-ten-Noode, but that
nothing was known of Rimbaud who, presumably, was therefore living with his friend.[7]

Verlaine and Rimbaud remained for two months in Belgium,
wandering about the country, then, in September, they crossed
over from Ostend to Dover.

On their arrival in London they first went to their fellow-
countryman, the artist Régamey, who has given us a picture of
the dishevelled appearance of the two men which did not, as it
happened, strike a discordant note in the bohemian atmosphere
of Continental Soho.[8] With the exiles from the Commune—
politicians, journalists, writers and agitators—there was more
true bohemianism in Soho than there was, at that time, in the
literary world in Paris. Régamey helped the two Frenchmen to
find lodgings and they first rented the room which had once been
occupied by Vermersch at 35 Howland Street, an eighteenth-
century house in the style of Adam—off Tottenham Court Road.

At first the two friends felt lonely and home-sick. 'A flat black
bug, that is London,' wrote Verlaine to Lepelletier.[9] They missed
the light stimulating air of Paris, the welcoming cafés on the
boulevards with their tables set out on the pavement; they
missed above all the friendly waiters, with their cheeky humour
and their skill at pouring the icy water on the green absinthe,
drop by drop, to turn it into a snowy liqueur. Verlaine described
with disgust the small and narrow English public houses, where
standing at the counter, you hastily swallow drink after drink.[10]
You enter by a heavy door which is held ajar by a thick leather
strap, and the door treats you in a most unfriendly and unwel-
coming manner, striking you in the back as you go in, and often
knocking off your hat. The interior is dingy and mean, there are
no tables to be seen, only a zinc-topped counter in front of which
men stand, silently and solemnly drinking. In these bars, says
Verlaine, 'Oh! lamentable infériorité des Anglo-Saxons,' no one
ever talks. There is none of the bright, intelligent and literary

conversation which makes an hour in a French café an education as well as a pleasure. Behind the counter stand the bar-tenders, in their shirt sleeves, and sometimes blowsy barmaids, richly dressed in the worst of style.

Like all Continental visitors to London, Verlaine and Rimbaud were deeply impressed and depressed by the dreariness of the Anglo-Saxon Sunday, which, in these far-off Victorian days, must have been even more dreary than now. It was Sunday morning when they had arrived and they had found it almost impossible to discover a place open that would give them some sort of a meal. Until one o'clock everywhere was closed; from one o'clock until three a few public-houses and restaurants opened their doors, under the vigilant eye of a policeman, who stood, watch in hand, to see that the exact time limit was not exceeded; the same comedy was enacted again from six until seven. Even the shoe-blacks did not work on Sundays; one of these had dared ply his trade on the day of the Lord and he had been severely reprimanded by a passing 'copper.'[11] There were no theatres or places of amusement open and the sole recreation available to the citizens of the biggest city in the world was the open-air preachers in Hyde Park and the dismal music of the Salvation Army Band.

By degrees Verlaine and Rimbaud sank into the French atmosphere of the Soho quarter. There were there, at that time, many Parisian refugees who, after the Commune, had fled from France under penalty of death, or fearing reprisals, from the new and reactionary government; men like Andrieu and Vermersch, the latter of whom had been condemned, in absence, to death for the part he had played in the publication of that revolutionary paper *Père Duchesne*. These refugees lived in dingy lodgings round Leicester and Soho Squares, or in sordid rooms in the streets off the Tottenham Court Road. They used all to foregather at the *Cercles d'Études Sociales* in Francis Street and in a few public-houses in which they managed to create a certain Continental atmosphere. There was the Duke of York, near Gray's Inn Road, the *Café de la Sablonnière et de Provence* off Leicester Square and particularly the bar at 5 Old Compton Street. It was there that Vermersch delivered a lecture on Blanqui and read the poem written by Verlaine in honour of the revolt: O *Cloître de Saint-Merry.*

The lot of these refugees was wretched in the extreme for they found it almost impossible to obtain work. There was, at that time, a very close co-operation between the London and the Paris police, the former keeping the latter well informed of all the activities of French nationals, and on the request of Paris, putting all obstacles in the way of their earning a livelihood. England, then as now, had a horror of violence and revolt and these unfortunate men were considered dangerous anarchists and revolutionary agents, and not upholders and martyrs of liberty; they were consequently submitted constantly to the most irritating and humiliating surveillance. Amongst these poor wretches Verlaine and Rimbaud with their dishevelled and disreputable appearance seemed in their element. After they had settled down to a more or less regular life Verlaine was completely happy in London and wished that this existence could continue for ever; he was able then to finish his lovely collection of poems, *Romances sans Paroles.* 'Here I devote myself entirely to poetry,' he wrote to Lepelletier,[12] 'to intellectual considerations, to purely artistic and serious conversations amongst a small circle of artists and literary men.'

It is said that in London Verlaine and Rimbaud met members of the English literary movement—writers such as Rossetti and Swinburne. But the acquaintanceship, if indeed acquaintanceship there was, cannot have been very deep, for on neither side— English nor French—have we any mention of it. In a letter to Émile Blémont[13] Verlaine says that he is soon to make the acquaintance of Swinburne, but we hear no more about it, and we can only surmise that they must have met, for later, from prison in Belgium, he requested Lepelletier to send a copy of his recently published work, *Romances sans Paroles,* to Swinburne.[14]

It is true that Swinburne had always been much interested in French literature, that he had been one of the earliest admirers of Baudelaire; this interest had increased since he had met Taine at Balliol College, Oxford, during the previous summer of 1871.

It seems probable that Rimbaud may have met Oliver Madox

Brown, the son of the painter, Ford Madox Brown, whom Gosse calls 'that marvellous boy'. He may be the poet mentioned by Verlaine to Blémont, whose name he had forgotten. 'I'm shortly to meet Swinburne and also a poet whose name I can't remember, as unknown as astounding. In a few days I'll send you news about this interesting fellow.'[15]

Oliver Madox Brown was a pupil of the French refugee, Andrieu, from 1871 until the boy's death in 1874 and was instructed by him in French and Latin. Andrieu was also a close friend of Rimbaud's, and one of his constant companions, during the winter he spent in London from 1872 until 1873. Oliver Madox Brown and Rimbaud were of much the same age—Rimbaud being the elder by a year—and it would have been natural had Andrieu brought together these two literary prodigies who shared so many interests in common. Both were poets, both shared a passion for classical poetry—particularly for Lucretius—and both had been greatly stirred by the events of the Commune. It seems likely that Madox Brown would have wished to meet a young revolutionary poet straight from Paris. Ever since his earliest childhood he had been considered a genius and his talent had been sympathetically fostered and encouraged by his family. At the age of eight he had completed his first picture, a water-colour, which was highly praised by artist friends of his father. At the age of fourteen, in 1869, a picture of his, *Chiron receiving the Infant Jason from the Slave*, was exhibited at the Dudley Gallery, his *Mazeppa* at the New British Institute in 1871, and his *Prospero and the Infant Miranda* at the International Exhibition at South Kensington in the same year. During the winter of 1871 he had been writing what Ingram calls[16] 'one of the imperishable works which, once read, imprint the reader's memory'. This was the *Black Swan* and the novel was published in a mutilated form to conform to the British moral prejudice in 1873, under the title *Gabriel Denver*. Nevertheless, in spite of Ingram's praise, and although the death of its author at the age of nineteen was considered at the time to be a tragedy for literature, the work strikes the modern reader as being sadly dated and without any intrinsic merit. Indeed all the compositions of Madox

Brown reflect a fleeting taste which is no longer ours, and they have little more to them than the promise of a brilliant youth, tragically cut off too soon; they have none of the power and the genius shown by Rimbaud's work composed at the same age.

It seems, however, possible that he and Rimbaud may have met, though he might have considered the French youth too unkempt to invite to his father's house at Fitzroy Square, where the élite of London literary and artistic society used to gather. It may have been that he found the lack of discipline and absence of principles distasteful in Rimbaud, for, though Madox Brown was in some ways a bohemian he was essentially refined and cultured, whilst Rimbaud was deliberately ill-mannered, insolent and coarse.

Verlaine and Rimbaud spent the greater part of their time learning English as they wandered from pub to pub, chatting with all manner and classes of people. They gave French lessons when they could find pupils but unfortunately these were rare. A study of the advertisements columns of *The Times* of that year reveals the fact that there were scores of other Frenchmen, equally well qualified, seeking the same kind of work. In order to inspire confidence in his prospective employers, Rimbaud bought a top-hat of which he was inordinately proud. It remained for some years his symbol of riches and respectability, and he wore it proudly in his return to Charleville. 'He loved it like an old and venerable friend,' wrote Delahaye,[17] 'and he used to smooth its silky surface tenderly with his elbow, with a gesture of naïve and touching pity.'

In London Verlaine and Rimbaud made no attempt to disguise the nature of their friendship and it is said that they openly boasted of it, so that even the refugees were somewhat shocked. Eventually rumours of their behaviour trickled back to Paris and to Mathilde Verlaine's lawyer, who was collecting material for the demand for separation, so that these rumours were welcome evidence. News, however, of what was being projected in Paris reached Verlaine in London and he began to grow frightened. He did not wish to be legally separated from his wife whom he still professed to love, nor from his little son, now a year old. He wrote to Madame Rimbaud to inform her of what was being said about her son, hoping that she might be able to do something to check the rumours, and soon he began to entertain an active correspondence with her. Strange to relate she seemed well disposed towards him.[18] Then Rimbaud himself wrote to his mother in November, asking her to make efforts to obtain from the Mauté de Fleurville family the return of his papers which he had entrusted to Verlaine when he was still in Paris and which Verlaine, in the rush of departure for Brussels, had left at Montmartre. He told her that these papers could be printed and that they might bring in much money; he knew that the prospect of financial gain would always stir her to action. Now she planned to go to Paris immediately. She first placed her two daughters as boarders in the convent of the Saint-Sépulcre—Vitalie was then fourteen and Isabelle twelve—and set off for the capital.[19] On her arrival in Paris she called on old Madame Verlaine and the mothers soon understood each other perfectly. Both disapproved of the nature of their sons' friendship, but each was, at first, inclined to blame the son of the other. Eventually they commiserated with one another and struck up a friendship, both of them agreeing to dislike the Mauté de Fleurville family. Madame Verlaine gave Madame Rimbaud a letter of introduction to Madame Mauté de Fleurville, but the mother of Verlaine's evil genius was badly received by the mother of his injured wife. The Mauté de Fleurville did not like the dour-faced countrywoman with her provincial clothes and manner, and moreover they wished to have no dealings whatsoever with any member of the Rimbaud tribe. They were prepared to make no concessions or agreements because they wished nothing to prevent, at the last moment, the separation of their daughter from the scoundrel Paul Verlaine. They would not discuss the question of the rumours concerning Verlaine and Rimbaud and how these were to be checked and they refused to hand over any papers that were in their possession. Amongst these were, as already mentioned, *La Chasse Spirituelle* and some poems in verse and prose. Madame Rimbaud left the rue Nicolet burning with suppressed fury and indignation, more determined than ever to separate her son from his friend; but, at the same time, feeling more kindly disposed towards Verlaine himself in the matter of his relations with his wife. She wrote to Arthur telling him of her lack of success and of what the Mauté de Fleurville family intended to do. She advised him to return immediately to Charleville if he did not wish to be implicated in the proceedings which Mathilde, on her father's instigation, was about to take against her husband. At the same time she told Verlaine, who relied on her advice, that, by ceasing to see her son, he might be able to alter his wife's resolve.[20]

Rimbaud followed his mother's advice; he left Verlaine in London and went back to Charleville for Christmas 1872. Verlaine however, alone in London and deprived of his friend, became gloomy and depressed. The little room in Howland Street, which had been so happy a home when Rimbaud had been there, now seemed dismal in the winter weather, with thick yellow fog outside; or else the rain endlessly falling. Alone and lonely he composed one of the poems from *Romances sans Paroles*, one of his most characteristic pieces.

> Il pleure dans mon cœur
> Comme il pleut sur la ville.
> Quelle est cette langueur
> Qui pénètre mon cœur?
>
> O bruit doux de la pluie
> Par terre et sur les toits!
> Pour un cœur qui s'ennuie,
> O le chant de la pluie!
>
> Il pleure sans raison
> Dans ce cœur qui s'écœure.
> Quoi! nulle trahison?
> Ce deuil est sans raison.
>
> C'est bien la pire peine
> De ne savoir pourquoi,
> Sans amour et sans haine,
> Mon cœur a tant de peine![21]

As has been said before, in the previous chapter, the poem was inspired by a line from Rimbaud, which is quoted at the head of the poem: 'Il pleut doucement sur la ville.' The line is however, not in any extant poem, unless it is the one given to his school-mate, Labarrière who, having lost it, tried to reconstruct it from memory, but could only recall this single line.[22]

Il pleut doucement sur la plaine.

Verlaine was alone for Christmas and in the dreary solitude of Boxing Day he wrote to Lepelletier, 'Christmas yesterday! And to-day an even worse Sunday and almost as canting! I'm very sad and alone. Rimbaud, whom you don't know well, and whom I alone perhaps fully understand, is no longer here. There's a horrible emptiness and all the rest is nothing to me.'

Then in January, in the damp weather, he fell ill, a mere attack of influenza, but in his depressed state he began to exaggerate the seriousness of his condition. He sentimentalized over himself, wept tears of self-pity on his loneliness and, in his habitual manner, began to dramatize the situation. In imagination, he saw himself as dying alone and far away from everyone, with no one to look after him or to receive his last breath, no one to care for him. He then wrote to his mother, telling her that he was dying, begging her to come immediately and to send a couple of pounds to Rimbaud so that he too could come and bid him a last farewell before the end.

Madame Verlaine and a niece set off immediately for London and Rimbaud followed two days later; he had been gone scarcely a month.

If I did not write to you for so long [wrote Verlaine to Lepelletier],[25] It's because I didn't know your new address. Otherwise you'd have received a week ago—as well as all my close friends—a letter of farewell. At the same time I wired to my wife and to my mother telling them to come quickly, for I really felt that I was dying. Only my mother came. Two days later Rimbaud, who had left here a month ago, also arrived and his care—added to those of my mother and cousin, succeeded in saving me, if not exactly from death, at least from an attack which might have proved fatal in this solitude.

As soon as Verlaine's health was restored the two friends took up once more their life of pub-crawling and debauch which Verlaine was later to call 'our shameful life in London in 1873'. In between times they used to wander on foot through the town in order to get to know it thoroughly. 'Every day we take enormous walks in the suburbs and in the country round London,' wrote Verlaine to Blémont.[24] 'We've seen Kew, Woolwich and many other places, for London is by now well known to us. Drury Lane, Whitechapel, Pimlico, the City, Hyde Park, all these have no longer any mystery for us.' Rimbaud used to drag Verlaine away to visit the Docks. 'The docks are impossible to describe,' wrote Verlaine,[25] the city dweller who had rarely left Paris. 'They are unbelievable! Tyre and Carthage all rolled into one!' In the docks they saw all types of humanity, swarming from all the four quarters of the world, black, brown and yellow faces; coarse, bestial and beautiful faces, beneath their multi-coloured and variously shaped headgear. They saw, piled up in rich profusion, crates, boxes, and baskets of goods from the furthest ends of the earth; they heard strange languages spoken, and saw printed on the bales of goods mysterious signs they could not read. Rimbaud spent in the docks more and more time, examining the various types of goods and talking, when he could make himself understood, to the sailors whom he met, making them describe what they had seen in their far-flung wandering, trying to understand and penetrate the mystery of their restless and nomadic life.

This was his first experience of big ships and they brought back to him, with a new poignancy, the dreams of his childhood—before he had embarked on his spiritual mission—when, in his imagination, he had travelled to the ends of the earth, and had only needed his mother's rolls of linen cloth to feel that he was on his *bateau ivre*. Now the same dreams began to crowd into his mind once more, the same longings. Perhaps it was then that he began to wonder whether a life of action might not be, after all, preferable and more worth living than a life of contemplation and mystical experience. He had begun by being an adventurer of the worldly regions before he became an adventurer

1873

March 28th

25/7

I have read the "DIRECTIONS respecting the Reading Room,"

And I declare that I am not under twenty-one years of age.

ss. 1351  Arthur Rimbaud  34 Howland street Fitzroy square W

4/5

I have read the "DIRECTIONS respecting the Reading Room,"

And I declare that I am not under twenty-one years of age.

9. 2335  Jean-Nicolas-Joseph-Arthur Rimbaud. 178 Stamford street, Waterloo Road S.E.

A FACSIMILE OF RIMBAUD'S ENTRIES IN THE REGISTERS OF THE BRITISH MUSEUM

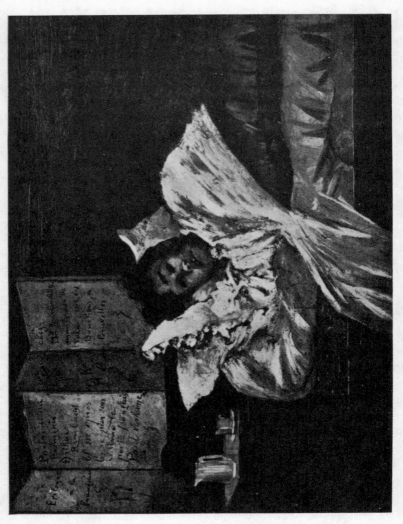

RIMBAUD WOUNDED, IN BRUSSELS
*a portrait by Jef Rosman, lent by Henri Matarasso*

of the beyond and he was to return finally to his first manner. Jean Aubry says,[26] that it was in London that Rimbaud formed a connection amongst sailors who came from all quarters of the globe, that he discovered from them what were the commercial possibilities in those distant lands, and what lay before those who ventured there.

Verlaine and Rimbaud used to wander as well through the poorer districts, through Whitechapel and Poplar, and Verlaine in his correspondence describes the picturesque, leprous little hovels, on which hang signs written in Hebrew, and the Jews, whom he saw wandering amongst the dark lanes and who seemed to him figures from a picture by Rembrandt, with their livid yellow skin, their drawn and haggard features, their straggling beards and their skeleton-like claws.

Tout est petit, mince et émacié, surtout les pauvres [he writes],[27] avec leur teint palôt, leurs traits tirés, leurs longues mains de squelettes, leur barbiche rare, leurs tristes cheveux blondasses, frisottés naturelle-ment par la floraison des choses faibles, telles que les pommes de terre énervées dans les caves, que les fleurs de serres, que tous les étiole-ments. Rien ne pourra dire la douceur infame resignée jusqu'à l'assas-sinat, de ces très peu intéressants, mais très beaux, très distingués misérables.

The sight of the weight of misery in this modern metropolis moved Rimbaud to a new form of compassion and charity, not merely compassion towards the individual but for the struggling and submerged masses.

Parfois il parle, en une façon de patois attendri, de la mort qui fait repentir, des malheureux qui existent certainement, des travaux pénibles, des départs qui déchirent les cœurs. Dans les bouges où nous nous enivrions, il pleurait en considérant ceux qui nous entouraient, bétail de la misère. Il relevait les ivrognes dans les rues noires. Il avait la pitié d'une mère méchante pour les petits enfants.[28]

His inspiration was now turning away from pure mysticism to-wards more materialistic subjects. It is probably then that he began to compose *Illuminations* such as *Villes*, a new form of prose poem. In these he made concrete, with uncanny skill, the horror of the modern industrial capital, with its dreary streets, straggling on in sordid never-ending lines towards the horizon; the suburbs with each mean little house entrenched behind its mean little garden. Over all this hangs, like a dark pall, the London fog and smoke, through which flit sinister figures, the Furies of the modern world. None of this is realistically painted, but is conjured up with an evocative power which is more suggestive than mere description.

These *Illuminations* could certainly not have been composed in France for they are too suggestive of the English atmosphere, but, as none are dated, it would be impossible to state conclusively whether they were written now or a year later.

It is said that Verlaine and Rimbaud visited the Chinese dens in the east-end by the docks, and learned to smoke opium. This might explain the distortion of Rimbaud's vision of reality which we find in the *Illuminations* dealing with the town. He sees the city almost as an archaeologist might, with all the strata laid bare at once in sections. Or else like a primitive picture painted without perspective, with the different 'grounds' set one above the other. Baudelaire, talking of his hashish dreams, says, in *L'Homme Dieu* from *Les Paradis Artificiels*, 'Ces villes magnifiques où les bâtiments superbes sont échelonnés comme dans les décors'. Rimbaud's view of the modern city is similar, and it is also like Baudelaire's in his adaptation of the *Confessions of an Opium Eater* by De Quincey. One passage from *Les Tortures de l'Opium* will show the resemblance, but there are many others:

D'étonnantes et monstrueuses architectures se dressaient dans son cerveau, semblables à ces constructions que l'œil du poète aperçoit dans les nuages colorés par le soleil couchant. Mais bientôt à ces rêves de terrasses, de tours, de remparts, montant à des hauteurs inconnues et s'enfonçant dans d'immenses profondeurs, succédèrent des lacs et de vastes étendues d'eau. . . . Les eaux changèrent bientôt de caractère, et les lacs transparents, brillants comme des miroirs, devinrent des mers et des océans.

Rimbaud describes London in a similar fashion:

Par le groupement des bâtiments, en squares, cours et terrasses fermées, on a évincé les cochers. Les parcs représentent la nature primitive travaillée par un art superbe. Le haut quartier a des parties inexplicables: un bras de mer, sans bateaux, roule sa nappe de grésil bleu entre des quais chargés de candélabres géants. Un pont court conduit à une poterne immédiatement sous le dôme de la Sainte-Chapelle. Ce dôme est une armature d'acier artistique de quinze mille pieds de diamètre environ.[29]

Here we seem to see the West End, with its squares and terraces, its parks and artificial lakes. Then we move towards Piccadilly, towards the business centre and the markets.

Sur quelques points des passerelles de cuivre, des plates-formes, des escaliers qui contournent les halles, et les piliers, j'ai cru juger la profondeur de la ville! C'est le prodige dont je n'ai pu me rendre compte: quels sont les niveaux des autres quartiers sur ou sous l'acropole? Pour l'étranger de notre temps la reconnaissance est impossible. Le quartier commerçant est un circus d'un seul style, avec galeries à arcades. On ne voit pas de boutiques, mais la neige de la chaussée est écrasée; quelques nababs, aussi rares que les promeneurs d'un matin de dimanche à Londres, se dirigent vers une diligence de diamants, Quelques divans de velours rouge: on sert des boissons polaires dont le prix varie de huit cents à mille roupies. A l'idée de chercher des théâtres sur ce circus, je me réponds que les boutiques doivent contenir des drames assez sombres. Je pense qu'il y a une police; mais la loi doit être tellement étrange, que je renonce à me faire une idée des aventuriers d'ici.

And finally we reach the outskirts, the smarter suburbs, towards the West.

Le faubourg, aussi élégant qu'une belle rue de Paris, est favorisé d'un air de lumière: l'élément démocratique compte quelques cents âmes. Là encore, les maisons ne se suivent pas; le faubourg se perd bizarrement dans la campagne, le 'comté' qui remplit l'occident éternel des forêts et des plantations prodigieuses où les gentilshommes sauvages chassent leurs chroniques sous la lumière qu'on a créée.

Another source of inspiration—or similarity—besides Baudelaire is, however, possible. It may be *Les Beautés des Spectacles de la Nature* by l'Abbé Pluche, which Paterne Berrichon tells us was in the library of the Pension Rosset which Rimbaud attended from the age of eight to ten.[30] This image may have fixed itself in his mind without his knowledge, and he drew on it later. L'Abbé Pluche writes:

La structure de cette ville est tout à fait ingénieuse, quoique très différente des nôtres. La muraille n'est pas une simple enceinte qui entoure la place, mais c'est une grande voûte qui la couvre en entier et l'environne de toutes parts. Après avoir bien creusé, on ne trouve que deux portes; et comme l'obscurité était grande sous cette voûte, on en avait abattu une partie pour voir clair dans les différentes places de la ville. Mais voici bien un autre sujet d'étonnement, les rues ne sont pas, comme chez nous, rangées à côté l'une de l'autre; elles sont posées les unes sur les autres, par étages, et les étages séparés par plusieurs rangs de colonnes. Ce sont moins des rues que des portiques, dont le premier est appuyé sur le second, le second sur le troisième, et ainsi de suite en descendant. Les maisons sont toutes égales et serrées les unes contre les autres dans l'épaisseur des voûtes. Toutes les maisons qui composent un même ordre, et qui sont toutes de niveau dans un étage sont couvertes par une terrasse ou par un toit commun tout plat, fait avec un massif très ferme et uni comme le pavé d'une chambre carrelée. Les habitants se promenaient sur cette place, entre les piliers qui soutiennent une autre voûte et un autre rang de maisons. Il y a jusqu'à onze portiques ou voûtes semblables, où l'on trouve tout bien symétrisé et bien entendu. Il n'y a que l'obscurité qui défigure cet ouvrage. Je n'y ai vu aucun vestige de fanal ni de lanterne.

It is only after this long description that we are informed that this town has been constructed by a swarm of wasps.

This vision of the material world replacing visions of the spiritual world is symptomatic of a radical change in Rimbaud. Now he began to realize that all the things on which he had based his life and art were false. False had been his belief in the dynamic value of debauch; from debauch he had reaped nothing but bitterness, disgust and a deeper loneliness. Baudelaire had said: 'Après une débauche on se sent toujours plus seul, plus abandonné.'[31] This too had been Rimbaud's experience: 'La débauche est bête, le vice est bête' he says in Une Saison en Enfer,[32] 'Il faut jeter les pourritures à l'écart'. False too had been his theory of art, and false especially his conviction that he had become the equal of God.

Une Saison en Enfer is the key to Illuminations—those of the first period. It is a merciless indictment of all his previous hopes and beliefs, the most cruel criticism of his former life. From the

beginning to the end of its burning pages he looks back, through
his blinding tears, on his plan to change the world, to invent a
new language, a new form of art, and realize how fantastic have
been his previous pride and arrogance, his spiritual pride—one
of the seven deadly sins. He had staked everything on this one
card, of penetrating into eternity, of forcing his way into the
presence of the Almighty; he had tried to enter Heaven before
his appointed time, by the means of magic, alchemy and drugs,
and had not waited to win promotion—as Baudelaire said—
through long and patient effort. He had imagined that poetry
was the magic key to that kingdom, that he had acquired supernatural powers, that his poetry had been God's voice speaking
through him. But his card had been worthless. As Baudelaire
said in *Morale* which ends his *Paradis Artificiels*, he who wishes to
be God, by virtue of an inexorable moral law, finds himself
fallen lower than his own nature. Now everything broke up in
Rimbaud as he discovered that he had done no more than the
poets whom he despised, that he had drawn only on what was
in himself. Poetry had been for him, with all his fine hopes and
ambitions, what it had been for the others—a mere vehicle for
self-expression. And since poetry, his own particular brand of
poetry, could not help him to reach absolute truth, 'la vraie vie',
then he would have none of it, and he would cast it away. He
would cast aside all that he had hitherto achieved, all that he had
dreamt of achieving. He wrote on the rough draft of *L'Alchimie
du Verbe*, in *Une Saison en Enfer*: 'Maintenant je puis dire que
l'art est une sottise.'

Whether Rimbaud succeeded for a time in his art, or failed
to achieve his aim, is not here in question. He certainly believed
that he had failed, and that it was a general rout for him. Then he
sold up, at bankrupt prices, all his former spiritual and artistic
stock, all his dreams, his beliefs and his aspirations. He was ready
now to start on something else, on a new venture.

Assez vu. La vision s'est rencôntrée à tous les airs.
Assez eu. Rumeurs des Villes le soir, au soleil, et toujours.
Assez connu. Les arrêts de la vie. O Rumeurs et Visions!
Départ dans l'affection et le bruit neufs.[33]

## CHAPTER VIII

# PARADISE LOST

PATERNE BERRICHON wrote—and almost every biographer after him has repeated it—that in February 1873 Rimbaud left Verlaine in London and returned to Charleville, where he was in March, and from where he made several journeys to Brussels to find a publisher for his work, and that it was returning from one of these trips that he arrived at his mother's farm at Roche on Good Friday.[1] Paterne Berrichon claims that he was at Charleville during the whole of February and March. But it is highly improbable that, having been home for Christmas 1872, and back again in London in January 1873 at Verlaine's request, he should have returned home in February, to remain there, and only making a trip to London on 25 March to apply for a permanent Reader's Ticket at the British Museum. On that date he signed the register in company with Verlaine, stating, although he was only eighteen at the time, that he was over twenty-one.[2] Furthermore the description of his arrival at his mother's house, given by his sister Vitalie, in her *Journal*,[3] is not that of someone who has been absent only for a few days and has come home after a short trip to Brussels, to rejoin the family who have gone on ahead to the country. It is that of someone who has returned after a considerable time of absences, from afar and whom the family were not expecting just then.

Ce jour là devait faire époque dans ma vie [wrote Vitalie], car il fut marqué d'un incident qui me toucha particulièrement; sans en être pour ainsi dire prévenus, l'arrivée de mon second frère vint pour mettre un comble à notre joie. Je me vois encore, dans notre chambre où nous restions habituellement, occupés à ranger quelques affaires; ma mère, mon frère et ma sœur étaient auprès de moi, lorsqu'un coup discret retentit à la porte. J'allai ouvrir et . . . jugez de ma surprise, je me trouvai face à face avec Arthur. Les premiers moments d'étonnement passés, le nouveau venu nous expliqua l'objet de cet événement; nous en fûmes bien joyeux, et lui bien content de nous voir satisfaits.

Furthermore, in the full letters which Verlaine wrote to his friends in France from London, he mentions Rimbaud's departure in December 1872 and his return the following month, but says nothing about his leaving in February. It is very unlikely that he would not have mentioned it if it had in fact happened. It is probable that Rimbaud left London in his company early in April. Verlaine left hurriedly—when undoubtedly he expected to remain longer—because his friends in Paris told him that his wife was about to start legal proceedings to obtain her separation from him. He was afraid to go directly to France in case he was arrested on account of the part he had played during the *Commune*. He went to Belgium whence he wrote to Lepelletier on 15 April. A poem by him—*Beams* from *Les Romances sans Paroles* —dated 'Douvres—Ostende, à bord de *La Comtesse de Flandre*, 4 avril 1873' gives the exact date of their departure for Belgium. It is probable that it is after some days spent in Brussels with Verlaine that Rimbaud returned unannounced to Roche on Good Friday, 11 April.

Roche is a little farming village in the Ardennes, belonging to the commune of Chuffily comprising about a dozen farming families. There had been once, in the days when Attigny was one of the King's residences, a royal shooting lodge at Roche, but this glory had departed from the village with the Revolution. Madame Rimbaud's farm which had been in the possession of the Cuif family for several generations, was a little eighteenth-century house, built directly on the roadside, but a large and nobly planned gateway opened into the farm courtyard. A portion of the house and most of the outhouses, had been destroyed during the Franco-Prussian War and, since Madame Rimbaud always found great difficulty in spending ready money, the family was, even at this late date, still camping amongst the ruins. But since they occupied the house only during the summer months this did not greatly matter. Whenever Rimbaud wished for solitude for his writing he was obliged to retire to the barn.

This was the first visit of the family to the cottage since the war and Vitalie describes how she with her brother and sister showed Arthur the beauty and extent of the lands. Easter Sunday was spent by the whole family making a tour of inspection of the whole demesne. Hunger for land was Madame Rimbaud's ruling passion, and she had been able to come into possession of the shares of both her brothers. Later, when Rimbaud sent her back money from Abyssinia for the purchase of books and scientific instruments, she did not heed his requests, thinking them only foolish, and invested the money in increasing the property at Roche, but he did not live to enjoy these fruits of his labour.

Paterne Berrichon describes the poor state of health of Rimbaud at this time—though falsely attributing it to an earlier period[4]—which did not show any improvement until nearly autumn. His complexion had become grey and livid and on his cheek-bones stood out two red patches of colour. His eyes, which had always been of a startling vivid blue, seemed now to have faded, and the pupils were constantly dilating and contracting so as almost to disappear, giving his eyes a vague and dying appearance. For hours he used to lie stretched on his bed, with half-open eyes, not saying a word. When the time for the meals came round his sisters used to call him to the table, but when he arrived he would refuse to eat. Nevertheless, whenever he was questioned about his health, he used to answer that there was nothing wrong with him and that all he asked was to be left in peace. Paterne Berrichon wrote this description more than twenty years later, from the testimony of Isabelle who was only twelve at the time. Nevertheless it reads like a description of someone suffering from the effects of narcotic poisoning, or the aftermath, when he was deprived of drugs or was trying to cure himself.

This was April and May, when the farm needed all the manual labour which it could obtain, yet Rimbaud did not help his family. In *Mauvis Sang* from *Une Saison en Enfer*—written at this time—he said, 'J'ai horreur de tous les métiers. Maîtres et ouvriers, tous paysans, ignobles.' One can feel in the irritation of these lines the protest against the demands on his time and energy to which he did not mean to accede. One can sense much of the family drama. Vitalie only mentions him once more after his arrival, in her *Journal*—much later, in July, when she remarks on

his not helping with the harvest. One can believe that she felt—
or was made to feel by her hard and inflexible mother—that here
was a subject too serious for light discussion.

Rimbaud was certainly going through a period of stress and
strain. Isabelle says that he was unable to sleep at night, that his
light was often to be seen burning into the early hours of the
morning, and that he was groaning as if he were struggling with
some devil. Often he was to be seen wandering alone through the
fields and woods, a poignant figure of desolation and despair.
He was making, in his mind, a General Confession, having a full
'examen de conscience', and reviewing his past life and all its
errors. *Une Saison en Enfer*, which was begun soon after his arrival,
is the explanation of his poetry of the magician period, an indictment and repudiation of it. In the violence of self-analysis and
self-criticism he shows the same exaggeration as in everything
else. Yet, mingled with the self-accusations, are regrets for the
past which had been so fair when he had believed in it. He had
thought himself a *mage* and a *voyant*, an angel, the messenger
from God; he had thought that he had invented new colours,
new flowers, new rhythms to express his new sensations. He had
created new worlds. He had tried to reach complete·happiness
and satisfaction through magic, to tear back the veil from the
heavenly mysteries. He had thought that he had penetrated into
the *Sanctum Regnum* of the occultists, that he had become part of
the 'lumière nature'. But he had been mistaken. What he had
thought were *Illuminations* were only *Hallucinations* after all, yet
he had deliberately continued, knowing this to be so, and had
found explanations for his 'sophismes'.

He asked himself what had been the cause of his failure. First
his idleness. In *Mauvais Sang* he writes, 'Mais! qui a fait ma langue
perfide tellement, qu'elle ait guidé et sauvegardé jusqu'ici ma
paresse? Sans me servir pour rien de mon corps, et plus oisif que
le crapaud, j'ai vécu partout.' Idleness was the most fatal vice
for anyone aiming to be a *mage*. Eliphas Lévi says that an idle
man can never hope to become a magician.[5] And again that the
most fatal enemy of the soul is laziness, 'Inertia is an intoxication
which puts to sleep, but the sleep of inertia is corruption and

death.'[6] Laziness prevented him from reaching true wisdom and sainthood and yet one can only attain magic powers if one is a wise man and a saint.[7] If not, and one tries to use these powers, then one will be broken by them. A terrible death awaits those who profane the sanctuary of Nature.[8] But wisdom itself is not sufficient, the magician must also be sober, chaste and free from prejudice and terror. Rimbaud's life had not fulfilled any of these conditions and now he cried, 'La débauche est bête, le vice est bête.' He had thought once that vice and degradation were necessary material for art and that from them he would be able to distil beauty. Just as the fly gorging on filth and putrefying matter does not realize the nature of the substances on which it feeds and revels. 'O le moucheron enivré à la pissotière de l'auberge, amoureux de la bourrache et que dissout un rayon.'[9]

According to Lévi there are two kinds of men—the free and the slaves—and magic is only for the free.[10] But Rimbaud now thought that he had never been free, that he had belonged to a slave race, from the dawn of time. In *Mauvais Sang*, he writes, 'Il m'est évident que j'ai toujours été race inférieure. Je ne puis comprendre la révolte. Ma race ne se souleva jamais que pour piller: tels les loups à la bête qu'ils n'ont pas tuée.'

He had also been led astray because he had not realized that there were two forms of magic—the true and the false, that of darkness and that of light—the heavenly and infernal.[11] The magicians of light were Orpheus and Mercury and they were revered as Gods after their death. Magicians of darkness were Merlin and Julian the Apostate, who were, as Lévi says, 'des suppôts de l'enfer'.

Lévi had said that one might be able to reach a magic state by the gradual use of narcotics and drugs, but that their use was a crime against nature which eventually led to illness, to madness or death. Rimbaud had not taken heed of his advice nor of that of Baudelaire, and this had led him to a state of hallucination which had threatened his health and his sanity. As he lay dying and his sister asked why he had given up poetry he answered that it was because it was wrong, because he would have gone mad. He wrote in *Une Saison en Enfer*, 'Ma santé fut menacée. La terreur venait. Je tombais dans des sommeils de plusieurs jours, et, levé, je continuais les rêves les plus tristes. J'étais mûr pour le trépas, et par une route de dangers ma faiblesse me menait aux confins du monde et de la Cimmérie, patrie de l'ombre et des tourbillons.' While on the rough draft he wrote 'Je ne pouvais plus rien. *Les hallucinations tourbillonnaient trop.* Un mois de cet exercice: ma santé s'ébranla.' This passage follows after one in which he describes himself as conversing with men during other incarnations and this would make one wonder whether he might not have practised necromancy and the evocation of spirits which Eliphas Lévi describes, saying also that these exercises are highly dangerous since they can induce psychological and physical disturbances.

These practices of false magic had separated him from God and a soul which is cut off from God can do nothing for others, for Satan turns against him all his best endeavours. Yet Rimbaud had gone into magic and alchemy in order to help others.

It is interesting to note that at this time he was reading Goethe's *Faust* for there are many similarities between it and *Une Saison en Enfer*.[12]

Faust had thought that he had become the image of the divinity, the mirror of eternal truth; he believed that he too could create and enjoy the power of a God. Then he discovered the emptiness of his pride and he cried in anguish, 'I am not the equal of God! I am only like the worm which the foot of the traveller crushes underfoot and buries in the earth.'

Rimbaud too had thought himself the equal of God. but now he discovered that, like *L'Homme-Dieu* of Baudelaire, it was only the distorting fumes of opium which had made him magnify his own image. He too was cast down to earth, 'Je suis rendu au sol avec un devoir à chercher!'

Faust, to escape his torment, to expiate his sin, was preparing to drink the poison and so end his days, when he was restrained, at the last moment, by hearing the choir of angels sing, on Easter Sunday, for the Resurrection of Christ who had died, taking on himself all the sins of the world, and who had descended into Hell to liberate the damned.

Rimbaud's actions had brought him to the same pass as Faust. He too was ripe for death and felt himself sliding down the slope towards the realms of darkness. He tried to distract his mind from 'les magies religieuses' through travel, and on the sea 'que j'aimais comme si elle eût dû me laver d'une souillure.' But the sea reminded him of the magician's ring which had been flung into it, the source of all his power. 'Anneau magique sous l'eau lumineuse.'[13] And further he wrote, 'J'avais été damné par l'arc-en-ciel et les magies religieuses.'[14] The rainbow is generally accepted as a symbol of hope, but this one must be connected with magic and is probably the one of which Lévi speaks,[15] which shone in the house of the old magician Jechiel when he was working at his spells. But on the horizon of the sea Rimbaud saw the cross rising, like the early morning sun, 'la croix consolatrice.' It is not for him the cross of salvation, but only the cross of consolation and he was never able to accept mere consolation.

He had sought happiness and satisfaction through the agency of magic, but now he realized that this pursuit of happiness, of the Artificial Paradise, had been his fatality, his temptation and remorse. Earlier, at the time of Matinée d'Ivresse, the first crow of the cock had made him cry out, 'Long live happiness!' He had achieved the 'Grand Œuvre,' the Philosopher's Stone. Now happiness, with its temptation, its sweet tongue, had led him to the brink of the pit of death, and the first crow of the cock was only now a warning to him, as it had been to Peter. 'Le bonheur, sa dent douce à la mort, m'avertissait au chant du coq.' And just as Faust had heard in his despair the chorus of angels sing out in praise of the Resurrection, so Rimbaud now heard the sound of Matines, 'Ad matutinum' and 'Christus venit.' But Christ brought salvation and hope only through death. Then Rimbaud added to the poem, O Saisons, ô Châteaux, which had been one celebrating undiluted joy when he had composed it, the two lines:

L'heure de la fuite, hélas!
Sera l'heure du trépas!

Then, as he finished copying out the poem, remembering the interior castle, the inner sanctuary, the refuge he had once enjoyed, he wrote on the rough draft, 'Quel cloître possible pour ce beau dégoût!' And further, 'Je hais maintenant les élans mystiques et les bizarreries de style. Maintenant je puis dire que l'art est une sottise.'

All this Rimbaud wrote before the events in Belgium, before what is called the Brussels Drama. It is certain that the work on which he was engaged during April, after he got home to Roche, was *Une Saison en Enfer*. This is the book which made him impatient with his family, and withdraw from the work of the farm. He remained shut up in the barn while the rest of the family worked in the fields.

At this time he was contemplating a literature of a new kind and indeed the *Illuminations* composed in England—*Villes*— show signs of the changed inspiration. Now he was expressing disgust for all the ideas which he had hitherto held—both artistic and spiritual. There can be little doubt that in the portion of *Une Saison en Enfer* on which he was now engaged he was liquidating all his previous dreams and aspirations, but he had not yet begun to formulate his positive beliefs for the future, nor his plans for his work. But he was certainly working. In a letter to Delahaye early in May he said, 'I'm working fairly regularly. I'm writing little prose tales and the title will be something like, *Livre Païen* or else *Livre Nègre*. It's all very innocent.' There can be little doubt that this book is *Une Saison en Enfer*. On publishing it he dated it 'Avril—Août 1873.' By May he had composed three of the chapters and he said that he still had six more to write.[16] This would mean that *Une Saison en Enfer* must, from the very beginning, have been planned in its general lines, for the completed work has in fact nine chapters.

In writing to Delahaye Rimbaud said, referring to the work which was occupying him, 'My fate depends on this book!' Much has been written in an endeavour to explain the statement. Some critics claim that it means that his mother has imposed on him the task of finishing the work, refusing to allow him to leave Roche until this has been achieved. This is manifestly absurd, for she had never succeeded, since her son left school, in making him do what he did not wish to do, and moreover he did leave Roche before the completion of the book. Some say that he felt he would only be free spiritually when he had succeeded in sloughing off his past completely, in exorcising it through the writing of the book, through saving himself as the Opium Eater had claimed that he had done, at the end of his *Confessions*. But a simpler explanation is possible. He may have meant that his literary fame and future depended on the success of the book. He may have been abandoning the old ways of poetry and thought, but this did not necessarily mean—as many critics claim—that he was giving up all thoughts of literature. During the composition of the book and on its publication he was far from being disinterested in its fate and he counted very much on its success. It is the only work—besides three poems already mentioned—which he himself published and we are told that already in April 1873 he had made arrangements with a Belgian firm for its printing.[17]

He did not, however, finish *Une Saison en Enfer*, his *Livre Païen ou Nègre* as quickly as he had hoped. Verlaine was at this time at Jehonville, not far from Roche, on a visit to relations and also at a loose end. He had not been able to see his wife or her parents. He had written to her pointing out how unnecessary were the legal proceedings which she was threatening in order to obtain a legal separation, telling her that he had parted from Rimbaud, and that they could still be happy together if she would give him one more chance. He received a letter from her, dictated by her father, informing him that he was no longer to pester her. Then he abandoned all hope of domestic happiness and decided that he would take up again his relationship with Rimbaud. It was then he went to stay with his relations at Jehonville and wrote several times to Rimbaud. The two friends met on various occasions during the latter part of April and in May, then Verlaine finally managed to persuade Rimbaud to accompany him once more to England, where he hoped that they might be as happy as they had been when first they arrived in London the previous year. There was no bone of contention or source of worry between them, no feeling of guilt on Verlaine's side, drawing him back towards his wife.

It is fatal to go back on a decision and to retrace one's steps into the past and Rimbaud made a great mistake in weakening and allowing himself to be persuaded by Verlaine. Perhaps he was exhausted through the efforts of literary creation, perhaps he needed relaxation and alcoholic or drug stimulation—he had been accustomed to compose under the fillip of drugs and drink, and perhaps he was finding it difficult to write without them, for his weaning had been too drastic and too sudden, since he could obtain nothing at Roche. In his letter to Delahaye he said that he had not a penny in his pocket, that in any case there were no pubs within reach and that one was obliged to walk six miles for a drink. 'Quelle horreur que cette campagne française.' Perhaps there were other reasons—sexual, or emotional or charitable. Perhaps it was compassion for Verlaine's loneliness and need— he had never been proof against appeals to his kindness of heart. Perhaps it was his own will deliquescing under the corroding effect of Verlaine's clinging. Whatever may be the reason—personal need, compassion or weakness—on 27 May 1873 he accompanied Verlaine to England. He had been home at Roche little more than a month.

CHAPTER IX

## THE BRUSSELS DRAMA

ON arriving in London Verlaine and Rimbaud rented temporarily a room at 8 Great College Street—now Royal College Street—in Camden Town until they could find more comfortable accommodation. From the very first, however, things began to go badly between them. Rimbaud felt humiliated at having, once more, yielded to Verlaine; he felt diminished in his own eyes at having sacrificed the liberty which he had conquered after so hard a struggle. He felt also a return of his guilt complex. His relationship with Verlaine had been one of the things from which he had wanted to escape. Now Verlaine's stranglehold was tightening round him again and he felt that he was being dragged back again into vice, that he was being drained of all vitality and of will-power. He felt that he could no longer endure Verlaine's sentimentality, his accommodating conscience, his feeble tears of repentance, his 'songe de chagrin idiot'. He wrote in *Vagabonds* from *Illuminations*.[1]

Pitoyable frère! que d'atroces veillées je lui dus! Je ne me saisissais pas fervemment de cette entreprise. Je m'étais joué de son infirmité. Par ma faute nous retournerions en exil, en esclavage. Il me supposait un guignon et une innocence très bizarres, et il ajoutait des raisons inquiétantes.

Je répondis en ricanant à ce satanique docteur, et finissais par gagner la fenêtre. Je créais, par delà la campagne traversée par des bandes de musique rare, les fantômes du futur luxe nocturne.

Après cette distraction vaguement hygiénique, je m'étendais sur une paillasse. Et, presque chaque nuit, aussitôt endormi, le pauvre frère se levait, la bouche pourrie, les yeux arrachés—tel qu'il se rêvait! et me tirait dans la salle en hurlant son songe de chagrin idiot.

And so, in self defence, to prove that he still was strong, and to ease the tension of his nerves—his health was still far from good —he was driven into acts of cruelty which he afterwards bitterly regretted. He was cruel without willing it, often without knowing it, as he hit out against the soft thing which clung to him. There was a streak of sadism in him which was more often directed against himself than against others, and this now came into play against Verlaine. He was often as hard as he knew how to be, rarely permitting himself a kind or gracious word lest it should release the flood of sentimentality that always burst from Verlaine if he were ever allowed to show his affection. He would humiliate him in every possible way, pointing out to him how degraded was his state, making fun of his ugliness and a mock of all the ideas and principles that he still held dear. Yet he could not bear his own hardness. He would then, by extra gentleness, try to wipe out his previous hardness, feeling at the same time ashamed of his readiness to make up these quarrels and disgust at the necessity of disguising his real feelings from his friend. They were verily, as Rimbaud said in '*L'Époux Infernal et la Vierge Folle*,' 'des compagnons d'enfer'. Rimbaud felt that he must, at all costs, escape. He describes himself as preparing his friend for their ultimate separation. He used to say, 'Comme ça te paraîtra drôle, quand je n'y serai plus, ce par quoi tu as passé. Quand tu n'auras plus mes bras sous ton cou, ni mon cœur pour t'y reposer, ni cette bouche sur tes yeux. Parce qu'il faudra que je m'en aille, très loin, un jour. Puis il faut que j'en aide d'autres: c'est mon devoir.' Then the *Vierge Folle* said, 'Tout de suite je me pressentais, lui parti, en proie au vertige, précipitée dans l'ombre la plus affreuse: la mort. Je lui faisais promettre qu'il ne me lâcherait pas. Il l'a faite vingt fois, cette promesse d'amant. C'était aussi frivole que moi lui disant: 'Je te comprends.'[2]

Both of them were desperately unhappy. Verlaine's only escape from his grief seems to have been to write long letters to his mother, telling her how unhappy he was and that he did not think that he could endure any longer the misery of his life. When he wrote he attributed his unhappiness to his wife's cruel treatment, to his separation from her and from his child—his mother would not have understood his distress concerning his relationship with Rimbaud—believing this to be true, or trying, to deceive himself, for Verlaine had an unlimited faculty for self deception.

It is said that at this time Rimbaud fell in love with a girl whom he met in the Underground. This may have been an added cause—or the main cause—of the strain between the two friends. Yet the episode need not have grieved Verlaine, for Rimbaud seems to have undergone the same anguish and sense of frustration which he had experienced as a boy of seventeen in Charleville in his earlier encounters with girls. *Bottom* from *Illuminations* reflects the same sense of longing, distress and unfulfilment which we found in *Les Déserts de l'Amour*.

Mme. Méléra who knew Isabelle Rimbaud writes in her biography[3]—though she does not say how she came by her information—that the girl lived in a fine house in the West End and that Rimbaud used to follow her but never dared speak to her. One evening he remained until very late sitting on a seat in the square near her house, from whence he could see the light shining from her window.

## Bottom

La réalité étant trop épineuse pour mon grand caractère,—je me trouvai néanmoins chez ma dame, en gros oiseau gris-bleu s'essorant vers les moulures du plafond et traînant l'aile dans les ombres de la soirée.

Je fus, au pied du baldaquin supportant ses bijoux adorés et ses chefs-d'œuvre physiques, un gros ours aux gencives violettes et au poil chenu de chagrin, les yeux aux cristaux et aux argents des consoles.

Tout se fit ombre et aquarium ardent.

Au matin—aube de juin batailleuse,—je courus aux champs âne, claironnant et brandissant mon grief, jusqu'à ce que les Sabines de la banlieue vinrent se jeter à mon poitrail.

René Silvain imagines that Rimbaud has called the poem *Bottom* because in it he reached, 'le fond de l'abîme'.[3] He may have in this poem, reached rock bottom of desolation, but that is certainly not the reason for the title. The ending of the poem where the ass is described as running away 'claironnant son grief,' shows that he was thinking of Bottom from *Midsummer Night's Dream*, of Bottom who was, despite his ass's head, nevertheless loved by the Queen of the Fairies—albeit through the agency of a magic charm. But there was now no magic charm for Rimbaud.

The poem is an interesting example of Rimbaud's method of artistic gestation, showing how atoms from different sources become attracted together and fuse round the core of his personal experience to form an entity which is his alone. As he sits beneath the window of the girl he loves but cannot reach, his imagination conjures up possibilities which might bridge the gulf which separates them. He could, if he were a bird, fly up to her room, a blue bird flying round the moulding of her ceiling, a sad blue bird nevertheless whose wings droop with disappointment. Did he then perhaps think of a book he must have read as a child, the story of *Fleurine et Truiton*, a legend of the Ardennes which was retold and sold for a few pence in Charleville at the end of the Second Empire under the title *L'Oiseau Bleu*.[4] It is the tale of a beautiful girl called Fleurine who is loved by a prince but whom her sister imprisons in the tower of the castle because she herself wishes to marry him, but his Fairy-Godmother enables him, each evening, to take on the shape of a blue bird so that he can fly to the room of the girl he loves, and spend the night with her.

Or else, if there is no magic charm which will metamorphose him into a bird, he could perhaps disguise himself in order to reach her. There was the hero in the vaudeville by Scribe, *L'Ours et le Pacha*, who, in order to be able to penetrate into the secret precincts of the palace to reach the presence of his lady love, disguised himself as the Pacha's favourite tame bear. In the usual fashion of the imbroglios of Scribe's plays there are the pelts of two bears—one black and one white—and the hero, inadvertently, puts on the body of the black bear and the head of the white. When the Pacha asks in astonishment what has happened to his bear, the Grand Vizir answers that it has grown white in a single night through grief at his absence. The bear's head brings to Rimbaud's mind the ass's head in *Midsummer Night's Dream* hence the name *Bottom* for the poem. While the poor fool sitting outside and unnoticed by the woman he loves brings to his mind the prose poem from Baudelaire's *Spleen de Paris*, *Le Fou et Vénus*, in which he describes the poor buffoon at the foot of Venus, amidst the universal joy, whose duty it is to make others laugh while his own heart is breaking. He is dressed in his ridiculous motley and bells but his eyes seem to say, as he sits at the foot of the beautiful woman, 'Je suis le dernier et le plus solitaire des humains, privé d'amour et bien inférieur en cela au plus imparfait des animaux. Cependant je suis fait, moi aussi, pour comprendre et sentir l'immortelle beauté. Ah! déesse! Ayez pitié de ma tristesse et de mon délire!' But implacable Venus only looked away into the far distance with her unseeing eyes of marble.

Then morning came and the poet was left, a poor ass braying his grief, and the street-walkers returning home at dawn, eager for one last client, assail him but he only turns away in disgust. 'Je m'éloignais du contact. Étonnante virginité!'

All these images fuse around the core of Rimbaud's experience —longing and distress—and become a poem which is characteristic of him alone.

Baudelaire, when he finished his adaptation of De Quincey's

*Confessions of an Opium Eater*, wrote a final chapter of his own which he called *Faux Dénouement* because he did not believe that the author had been telling the truth when he claimed that he had been cured—Baudelaire's intuition in this was correct— he thought that De Quincey had only said this to satisfy, what he called, English 'cant' and hypocrisy. He believed that no man could ever escape from the thrall of opium. Rimbaud first called the chapter of *Une Saison en Enfer* which he wrote at this time in London *Fausse Conversion*, though he was later to alter the title to *Nuit de l'Enfer*. His had indeed been a false conversion for he had succumbed again and it was verily a night of Hell, his experience in England. The anguish of the experience is better apprehended in the rough draft of the chapter than in the finished and more artistic product.

Jour de malheur! J'ai avalé un fameux verre de poison. La rage du désespoir m'emporte contre tout, la nature, les objets, moi, que je veux déchirer. Trois fois béni soit le conseil qui m'est arrivé. Les entrailles me brûlent, la violence du vénin tord mes membres, me rend difforme. Je meurs de soif. J'étouffe. Je ne puis crier. C'est l'enfer, l'éternité de la peine. Voilà comme le feu se relève. *Va, démon, va diable, va Satan*, attise le. Je brûle bien. C'est un bel et bon enfer!

This poison is, metaphorically, the same poison which Faust was about to take in his anguish when he was guilty of the sin of despair. In the midst of his own despair Rimbaud remembers how he had seen salvation and conversion and he tries to express his vision.

C'étaient des millions de créatures charmantes, un suave concert spirituel, la force et la paix, les nobles ambitions, que sais-je?

But now he has only the same old life again, 'l'existence enragée; la colère dans le sang, *la vie bestiale*, l'abêtissement du *malheur des autres qui m'importent le plus*'. That was what he minded most of all, the harm he was doing to others as well as to himself, to Verlaine whom, in all sincerity, he had hoped to bring back to his first state of 'fils du soleil'.[5]

This *Fausse Conversion* or *Nuit de l'Enfer* is the beginning of the tragic and desperate note in *Une Saison en Enfer*.

In the meantime the life of quarrelling and bickering between the two 'compagnons d'enfer' continued. Finally, one day Verlaine, at the end of his tether, broke away, feeling that he could not endure the torture any longer. After a quarrel—not more violent than the others, but merely the futile culmination of much previous irritation—he walked out of the house, without any luggage and without saying where he was going. At his cross-examination in Brussels Rimbaud stated that Verlaine had become angry because he had reproached him with being lazy and treating badly some of their friends. Later in life Verlaine gave his friends a different account of the quarrel. He had gone out shopping, he said, and was returning with a salted herring in one hand and a bottle of salad oil in the other, when Rimbaud, who had been waiting for him and looking out of the window, began to roar with laughter as he saw him arrive. Then, when he came into their room, he said to him, 'If you only knew how fucking silly you look with that herring in your hand!'

Without another word Verlaine left the house, abandoning Rimbaud alone and without money in London. When the latter finally realized that Verlaine had really gone he fell into a state of great distress and bitterly regretted the conduct which had goaded his friend too far. He must have guessed what Verlaine intended to do—perhaps he had frequently threatened it—for he went to London Docks and arrived breathless at the quayside just as the gangway was being hoisted on the Antwerp boat, and he made excited signs to his friend who was standing on deck, to leave the boat and to come and join him. Verlaine, however, only shook his head and looked away. When the boat had left and nothing further could be gained by waiting, he went home to his lodgings in a state of great distress.

On board the boat which was taking him to Antwerp Verlaine wrote to his wife informing her that he had left Rimbaud for ever and that if she did not come to him to Brussels he intended to blow his brains out. Mathilde, however, did not receive this letter until five years later, for all communications from her husband were intercepted by her father and not allowed to reach her.

In the meantime Rimbaud, alone in the dingy lodging-house

room, composed the letter to Verlaine which some critics have considered mere play-acting and which cynics have said was written for purely mercenary motives. Fair-minded readers will, however, feel the sincerity of the distress and Rimbaud's regret at having goaded his friend too far. They will also see in it an interesting psychological document for the understanding of the emotional relationship existing between the two friends.

Come back! Come back! dearest friend! [wrote Rimbaud].[6] My only friend come back! I swear to you I shall henceforth be kind! If I was nasty to you it was all a joke, a joke in which I persisted. I am more sorry than I can ever say! Come back and everything will be forgotten! How unfortunate that you should have taken that joke seriously! For two whole days I have been doing nothing but weep! Be brave! Nothing is lost! You have only got to cross over again and we shall live together bravely and patiently. I implore you! It's in your own interest as well! Come back and you will find all your things here! I hope that you realize that there was nothing really in our quarrel! That awful moment! But you, when I beckoned to you to leave the boat, why didn't you come? Have we lived together for two years to come to such a pass? What will you do now? If you don't want to come back here, would you like me to join you wherever you are?

Yes! I know it was I who was in the wrong! Oh! Say you won't ever forget me! No! You can't forget me!

For my part you are always in me! Do answer at once! Are we no longer to live happily together? Be brave and answer quickly! I can't remain here much longer. Only follow the feelings of your heart. Quick! Tell me if I am to go to you. Yours for all life.

RIMBAUD.

PS. If I can't see you again I shall enlist in the army or the navy. Oh! Come back! At all hours of the day I weep! Tell me to come to you and I'll come! Tell me! Wire to me immediately.

The letter shows traces in the handwriting of having been composed under intense nervous excitement and in a state of mental instability.[7] There are, also, visible traces on the paper of what must have been tears.

In the meantime Verlaine's state of exaltation had fallen and he began to regret what he had done. From the boat that was bearing him to Antwerp, he wrote to Rimbaud a letter that is typical of his habit of self-dramatization and his power of self-deception.

I don't know whether you will still be in London when this reaches you. I want, however, to tell you that you must absolutely understand that I had to leave, that I damn well couldn't stand any longer the violent life we have been leading lately, full of scenes and quarrels, with no other cause than your warped temper. Only, as I love you greatly (honi soit qui mal y pense!) I want to tell you that if at the end of three days I'm not reconciled with my wife, in perfect amity, I'm going to blow my brains out. This will explain to you my meanness of this afternoon. You must forgive me! If, which is very likely, I'm obliged to perform this last pitiable act, I shall, at least, do it bravely. My last thought will be for you, for you who were beckoning to me, this afternoon, from the quayside, when I wouldn't go back, because it's necessary that I should die. Nevertheless! I embrace you before I die.

Your poor VERLAINE.

Rimbaud's feelings of remorse and regret evaporated on receiving this letter. He felt that here was once more the same old Verlaine from whom nothing could ever be expected, in whom there was nothing solid and stable. The same old sentimental slush oozed up once more and he felt nauseated. Verlaine could keep to no decision and he had gone soft and cringing again, contemptuously soft. He was, moreover, dramatizing an ordinary situation, play-acting and wallowing in self-pity.

Rimbaud's moment of regret and remorse was over and it was in a very different frame of mind that he answered the letter the following day. He no longer begged his friend to come back to him; it was an ultimatum that he sent him and he made no attempt to hide his contempt.

I've just received your letter written on board. You're wrong this time, terribly wrong. Firstly there's nothing positive that one can get hold of in your letter. Your wife will either not come at all, or else she'll come only after three months, three years, what do I know!

And as for dying! I know you well! You'll get all worked up in a great state of excitement. you'll wander about in a great pother and bore a whole lot of people. What! Haven't you yet recognized that anger was as wrong on your side as on mine. But it's you who are to blame in the last resort, since, even when I beckoned to you, you would persist in your wrong ways. Do you imagine that your life with others will be happier than with me? Think it over carefully! Certainly not! With me you're free. And since I swear henceforth to be kind and admit that I regret all the wrong I did! I'm very fond of you and if you don't wish to come back to me or for me to come to you, you're doing wrong and you'll regret it for many a long year, because of the loss of your liberty and all the horrible annoyances, perhaps even worse than those you've already endured. Remember what you were before you knew me!

As for me, I shan't go home to my mother. I'll go to Paris and I'll try to be gone by Monday evening. You'll have obliged me to sell all your clothes. I can't help it. They're not yet sold, they won't be sold until Monday morning.

Certainly if your wife returns to you, I shan't compromise you by writing to you. I'll never write again. The only truth is—come back! If you listen to that you'll be showing courage and a sincere mind. Otherwise I pity you! But I love you. I embrace you and we'll meet again.

RIMBAUD.

In Brussels, however, Verlaine had written to his mother, giving her his address and telling her that he was going to shoot himself in three days if his wife did not come back to him, and he signed the letter, 'Your poor son, who loved you very dearly.'

This letter had, naturally, the desired effect, and Madame Verlaine *mère*, arrived post haste in Belgium to prevent her only child from committing suicide. Verlaine was indulging to the full his propensity for self-pity in writing to all his friends to inform them, in the strictest confidence, of his intention of putting an end to his miserable life. To each he said that he wished him to be the only person to know beforehand of his resolve. To Lepelletier, his oldest friend, he said,[3]

I'm going to kill myself! Only I don't want anyone to know that until the thing is done and until, moreover, it's certain that my wife, for whom I'll wait until to-morrow afternoon, has been informed three times by wire and by post, and so it will be her obstinacy that will have caused everything.

I want everyone to know that it's not the fear of the lawsuit, which in any case wouldn't take place before ten months, but the abuse of my affection by such a creature. . . . Look after my little book.[9] And not a word to anyone. My mother, knowing my state, is here trying to dissuade me from my resolve, but I don't think that she'll succeed. I'm waiting for my wife.

He had also written to Madame Rimbaud, the same day that he wrote to his own mother and he received from her a letter that is extremely moving; it reveals more power of feeling than one would have expected from one who is always reputed to be so hard, and it makes one wonder whether critics may not have been unjust in their estimation of this reserved and inflexible woman, in seeing her devoid of any other emotion but that of gain. She was a woman of no education, indeed almost illiterate, yet she was here able to express her feelings in a manner that a trained writer would not have surpassed.[10]

Monsieur! Now as I write to you, I hope that calm reflection will have come back to your mind. What! Kill yourself, unfortunate man! To kill one's self when one is overwhelmed by misfortune is an act of cowardice, but to commit suicide when one has a tender and loving mother who would give her life for you and who will die of your death, and when, moreover, one is the father of a little boy who already stretches out his arms towards you, who will later smile up at you and who will, one day, need your help and advice, to commit suicide in these conditions is an infamous act. The world rightly despises those who thus die and God, himself, cannot forgive such a sin and casts the sinner out of his bosom. I do not know the nature of your quarrel with Arthur, but I always expected that your relationship would end disastrously. Why? You'll ask me? Well! simply because what is not authorized by good and honest parents cannot possibly bring happiness to the children. You young men all laugh and make fun of everything, but it is none the less true that we parents have experience on our side, and each time you do not follow our advice you'll be unhappy. You see I don't flatter you; I never flatter those of whom I am fond. You complain of your unhappy life, poor child! But how can you know what to-morrow will bring? Have hope then! You're too sensible to imagine that happiness can merely exist in the successful carrying out of a plan, or the gratifying of a whim. No indeed! A man who would find all his desires fulfilled would not be happy, for as long as the heart has no aspirations no emotion is possible and so no happiness. And so the heart must be moved at the thought of goodness, of the good one does or that one hopes to do. I too have been desperately unhappy. I have suffered and wept but I have been able to turn my misfortunes to my profit. God has granted me a strong heart, full of courage and energy. I've struggled against adversity and I've thought very deeply. I've looked around me and I've become convinced, yes utterly convinced, that each of us has a wound in his heart, more or less deep. My own wound seemed to me deeper than the wounds of others and that was quite natural. I could feel my own wound but not those of others. And then I said to myself—and I see every day that I am right—that true happiness consists solely in the fulfilling of one's duty, however painful it may be. Do as I do, be strong and courageous against affliction. Banish from your heart all evil thoughts. Fight! fight with all your might against what is called the injustice of Fate, and you'll see that misfortune will grow weary of pursuing you, and you'll become happy once more. You must also work a good deal and find an aim to your life. You'll, naturally, have many bad days still to go through. But however much wickedness you find in man never despair of God. He alone knows how to comfort and to heal, believe me.

Your mother would give me great pleasure if she would write to me some time. I say good-bye to you and not farewell, for I hope to meet you again one day.

V. RIMBAUD.

But in the meantime Verlaine had altered his plans, he had abandoned the idea of suicide. The limit he had set himself for waiting for his wife had by now expired and she had not replied, so on 8 July he sent a wire to Rimbaud asking him to come to Brussels to say good-bye to him, since his intention now was to go to Spain as a volunteer to fight in the Carlist ranks. Rimbaud arrived in Brussels the same day and found Verlaine in a state of great excitement and intoxication. His plans had once more been altered; he was no longer going to Spain but wanted to return to London with Rimbaud, but this time it was the latter who would not go with him for he was determined to stick to his own plan of going to Paris. He suddenly felt disgust at the sight of the weak, slobbering, intoxicated figure before him and felt that he could not bear to take up their relationship again. He wanted, at all costs, to be free, to go alone, to shake off the clinging octopus that was strangling him, and whom he must finally destroy or else be stifled. Nevertheless, he felt as he always did, pity at the sight of his friend's distress, and he could not bring himself to take the irrevocable step of leaving. All Tuesday night and the whole of Wednesday he spent arguing with Verlaine, trying to persuade him to allow him to go willingly, and he was growing more and more nervous and exasperated. On the Wednesday evening, Verlaine drank so much that he finally fell into a drunken stupor. On the Thursday morning he got up early, went out and did not return to the hotel until lunch time. He was by then once more intoxicated and he showed Rimbaud a revolver which he had just purchased, saying that with it he intended to shoot everybody. Rimbaud then informed him that he was leaving that afternoon for Paris. Verlaine, blind with fury, locked the door of their room and sat on a chair against it. 'Now try to go,' he cried, 'and you'll see what will happen!' He whipped the revolver out of his pocket and fired three times at his friend. He was only three yards away from him and the first shot hit him in the wrist, while the second and third went wide and embedded themselves in the wall. Then Verlaine, suddenly realizing what he had done, broke down. He wrenched open the door, dashed into his mother's room telling her that he had shot Rimbaud; he flung himself on the bed and began to weep violently. Then seeing Rimbaud appear, he handed him the revolver and begged him to shoot him. Madame Verlaine and Rimbaud managed, eventually, between them, to appease him, and Rimbaud's wound was temporarily bound up. But, strange to relate, neither of them thought of seizing the revolver and putting it in a safe place.

That afternoon Verlaine and his mother accompanied Rimbaud to the hospital, but the bullet could not be extracted that day. Madame Verlaine wished Rimbaud to remain in Brussels with them until this could be done and until his wound had healed, but he preferred to return to his mother at Roche and he accepted twenty francs for the journey. However, as the time approached for his departure, Verlaine once more showed signs of growing excitement and was doing all he could to persuade his friend to change his plans, but Rimbaud was adamant. Finally, as they were all going to the station, Verlaine again completely lost control of himself, he threatened to shoot Rimbaud, saying that this time he would not miss his mark, and as he spoke he had his hand in the pocket which concealed the revolver. Rimbaud was by now completely unnerved, he ran away and asked a policeman for protection, and the policeman had no other course open to him but to arrest Verlaine. Madame Verlaine said in her evidence that her son had not threatened Rimbaud, but there is no doubt that the latter imagined that his life was once more in danger. Verlaine was arrested in the afternoon of 10 July 1873. Rimbaud made his first statement that evening at the police station as a result of which Verlaine was taken to L'Amigo prison and later to the Prison des Petits Carmes. The charge was at first one of attempted murder.

After making his statement, Rimbaud went to hospital and there he remained over a week since the bullet could not be immediately extracted on account of his feverish condition. It was in hospital that he gave his evidence on 12 July as the doctor did not consider him in fit condition to go to court and had written on the summons: 'This young man is in a state of fever which demands complete rest and he is in no fit condition to go to the court.' Rimbaud stuck to what he had said on the evening when he had given an account of Verlaine's first attack and of his fear of a second, but, on a further interrogation on 18 July he added that Verlaine had been in so intoxicated a state as to have completely lost his reason.

The bullet was extracted on 17 July and two days later Rimbaud was permitted to leave the hospital. He had, by then, had time to consider all the implications of Verlaine's arrest and of what the charge of attempted murder would mean. On 19 July, on coming out of hospital, he went to the law courts and declared that he did not wish to bring any charge against Verlaine who had by then been a week in prison, that he was convinced that it was all a mistake and an accident, that the revolver had not been purchased with the intention of doing him bodily harm and that moreover, Verlaine had not been in a condition to know what he was doing.[12] By this time, however, all the machinery of law had been set in motion and it was impossible to stop it. Mathilde's lawyer had come to Brussels to see what evidence he could collect to make her demand for divorce from her husband more certain, and his presence did not help Verlaine. The case was continued but the charge was reduced to one of criminal assault instead of one of attempted murder. It came up on 8 August and, very unjustly, what was known or suspected of the relations of Verlaine and Rimbaud was dragged up, and the medical report on Verlaine's physical condition, which had nothing to do with the case, was produced and read in court. The effect of this report was to make the judge and jury show no leniency to Verlaine and to pay no heed to Rimbaud's evidence and particularly to his last statement. Verlaine was given the maximum sentence, two years' hard labour and a fine of two hundred francs. The following year, in April 1874, Mathilde Verlaine obtained a separation from her husband on the grounds of his physical cruelty and his intemperate habits; his alleged immoral relations with a young man was a subsidiary reason.

It is said by Paterne Berrichon that Rimbaud was summarily ejected from Belgium and led by the police to the frontier, without being given time for complete recovery from his wound.[13] It is certain that he was shattered by his interrogation by the police and the judge, when all their questions made it clear what was their opinion of him.

'On what did you live in London?' they said to him and he was forced to answer, 'Chiefly on the money that Madame Verlaine sent her son.' Next they asked him whether he was not one of the chief grounds of Mathilde Verlaine's grievances against her husband. 'Yes!' he answered, 'she accuses us of immoral relations together, but I shall not even take the trouble to contradict such slander!'

Suddenly he was brought face to face with himself and saw himself with new clarity. He was only eighteen and far from being self-assured and confirmed in his ways. During his week in hospital, in the pure whiteness of the ward, where the nuns, gliding in their silent shoes, between the beds, appeared to his fevered brain like angels from another world, where the smell of antiseptic seemed to his confused, drugged mind the incense of the church services of his early years, Rimbaud felt like a child again and thought how good it would be to lay down his arms, to give in and to believe.[14] In his weakness it was not freedom that he needed, but comfort and help; help to escape his past life and all the desolation it had brought him.

He left hospital on 19 July but by then the twenty francs which Madame Verlaine had given him had evaporated, and he was obliged to return home on foot. The family was at that time at Roche. When he arrived at the farm he found them all sitting round the lunch table, his mother, Frederick and the two young sisters. His arm was in a sling, his face was thin and ravaged by suffering, and at the first expression of sympathy he laid his head down on the table and burst into tears. Suddenly finding sympathy and unexpected gentleness in the mother whom he had always thought so hard, in the woman who had found kind words to write to Verlaine in his distress, he confided to her his unhappiness and his plans for finishing the book already begun, his last hope. He wanted to exorcise his past and to take from his mouth the taste of ashes. His mother now promised to give him financial help towards the publication of the book and to leave him in peace until it was completed.

That day, and many days thereafter, when Arthur came to table he looked depressed and worn, more silent than ever. But when members of the family went by near the barn where he shut himself away to work, they could hear sobs and groans issuing forth from it as if he were in agony, and shouts and curses of rage as if he were in battle with an enemy.[15]

Vitalie observes the same silence about this crisis in her brother's life as she had done about the other. She only mentions him once at this time in her *Journal*. After talking about the heavy farm work of the season, she adds, 'My brother Arthur did not share our agricultural pursuits. He found sufficient occupation with his pen to prevent his taking part in the work of the farm.' She does however give a hint of abnormal circumstances in the home circle. 'This month of July, this month which was so extraordinary for me was the cause of many sensations and many determinations.'

The following month, after many weeks of great anguish of mind, Rimbaud finished *Une Saison en Enfer*. And to his mother who, having read the book with bewilderment and amazement, asked him what it all meant, he answered, 'It means exactly what I've said, literally and completely, in all respects.'

## CHAPTER X

## UNE SAISON EN ENFER

WITH *Le Bateau Ivre*, *Mémoire* and certain poems from *Illuminations*, *Une Saison en Enfer* ranks as Rimbaud's greatest work. It contains some very lovely passages of writing which are prose poems in themselves, and could be printed as such, taken from their context.

In August 1873, after many weeks of anguish, he finished the work. We do not know how much there was still left to write when he returned wounded from Belgium at the end of July, nor how much he had written in London, nor yet how much he re-wrote of what he had already written, after his tragic experience. From the comparison of the rough draft—of which we have only two chapters—with the final version, we suspect that any changes he made must have been stylistic with a view to simplifying his vision and taking from it what was not necessary, rather than to altering the initial inspiration.

We know definitely—of this there can be no doubt—that *Une Saison en Enfer* was the book on which he had been at work since April, the 'Livre Païen ou Livre Nègre,' which he had mentioned in his letter to Delahaye in May, and of which three chapters were already written when he went to England with Verlaine. He might subsequently have scrapped these three chapters, but this supposition is unlikely since he would then scarcely have dated the finished work 'April–August 1873'. It can therefore safely be assumed that *Une Saison en Enfer* was begun in April and that even as early as that he intended to make a complete break with his past, with everything that he had hitherto prized and on which he had built his hopes. This point needs emphasizing since it is tempting to believe that it was the Brussels drama that drove him into relating his season in Hell and to say farewell to literature. It is naturally very probable that the events in Belgium gave a new poignancy and a fresh anguish to the struggle. Yet one of the more tragic chapters, *Nuit de l'Enfer*, was written in London in July.

*Une Saison en Enfer* is composed of nine chapters of varying lengths, each, with the exception of the first, *Mauvais Sang*, relating some single aspect of the struggle. There is no justification for printing—as Paterne Berrichon has done in the 1912 edition for *Le Mercure de France*—the prose poem describing Christ's first miracle, as an introduction, on no better grounds than that it was written on the reverse side of the rough draft of a chapter of the work. Rimbaud himself published *Une Saison en Enfer* and had he wished the poem to serve as a prologue he would have included it. Delahaye tells us in any case that this was a poem in the series he was projecting under the title *Photographies du Temps Passé*.[1]

For alchemists the descent into Hell was symbolical for the descent into oneself. This is a terrifying experience and there is the psychological danger of the complete dissolution of the human personality, disintegration. Rimbaud's *Saison en Enfer* was the record of such a descent into himself and with him there was the danger of this disintegration of his personality, but he rose in the end victorious. According to the alchemists the Hermetic Philosopher makes this descent as a 'redeemer'. Rimbaud hoped that he might be such a redeemer.

*Une Saison en Enfer* is difficult to interpret as a whole for Rimbaud has described, simultaneously, the past, the present and the future and he has omitted all the connecting links. The *leit motiven* of the various problems which are besetting him surge each in turn and subside, only to burst out again with renewed force,

Roche, 7 Août 97

THE BARN AT ROCHE, WHERE RIMBAUD COMPOSED 'UNE SAISON EN ENFER'

VITALIE RIMBAUD
*from a photograph lent by Henri Matarasso*

at a later part of the work; or else they mingle together so as to form an intricate and bewildering fugue. The nature of the problems is mainly spiritual for it was spiritual aspiration which had driven him to adopt his particular form of art and so his failure was a spiritual rather than artistic failure. Thus the problem on which so many critics concentrate—the question of whether or not he intended to continue being a poet—pales into insignificance beside the greater spiritual problem. What was chiefly occupying him was his attitude to God and his previous doctrine of art had been closely linked with his religious conceptions. When he discovered that all his aspirations and hopes had been based on falsehood, he cast aside the art and the philosophy which had deceived him, but there was nothing to prevent his still being a poet, if a poet of a different kind.

The three important *leit motiven* in *Une Saison en Enfer* are the problem of sin, the problem of God—his personal need to believe in God—and finally the problem of life, the acceptance of life. These thread their way backwards and forwards through the texture of the work, and only, at the very end, are brought to full conclusion.

Rimbaud had previously imagined that with his art he had soared into the beyond, but he discovered now that it was not Heaven into which he had penetrated, but Hell; it had verily been a season in Hell. It was his pride and arrogance which had brought him to such a pass and had led him into the deepest state of sin. This brought him face to face with the problem of evil. What was sin and did it really exist? At the time of the first *Illuminations* he had thought that the tree of Good and Evil could finally be cut down.

But this had been an illusion like all his other illusions, for the tree had sent out sucker shoots that had grown big enough to destroy him. 'Le vice qui a poussé ses racines à mon côté, dès l'âge de raison,—qui monte au ciel, me bat, me renverse, me traîne.'[2]

One of his main reasons for beginning to write *Une Saison en Enfer* was to solve, once and for all, the problem of this conflict between Good and Evil. He had meant by his first title, 'Livre

Païen ou Livre Nègre,' to indicate that his intention was to return to the days before the advent of Christianity, before there had existed the tragic dilemma of right and wrong. Pagans and Negroes can still live in blissful ignorance knowing nothing of the problem of good and evil; the tree of knowledge, with its heavy sickly shade, does not yet darken their lives. Rimbaud refused to accept the ideals of Christianity and intended to return to the real kingdom of the children of Ham.[3] 'Prêtres, professeurs, maîtres, vous vous trompez en me livrant à la justice. Je n'ai jamais été de ce peuple-ci; je n'ai jamais été chrétien; je ne comprends pas les lois; je n'ai pas le sens moral, je suis une brute, vous vous trompez.

'Oui, j'ai les yeux fermés à votre lumière. Je suis une bête, un nègre. Mais je puis être sauvé.'[4]

This was in the early days of composition. But, as he worked at the book and pondered on the problem, he discovered—to his great anguish—that he was, after all, like all the others, that he could not escape his hereditary taint, that he could not wipe out the traces of his baptism, that no one of the west could ever eradicate the imprint left by two thousand years of Christianity. His whole nature, his mind and soul, had been formed and moulded by the civilization from which he had thought he could escape. With the food he ate, the water he drank, the very air he breathed, he absorbed into his being the tainted ideals of Christianity. Long before he had been conceived it had been decreed that he should be born a westerner and there was no way of escaping this fatality however passionate might be his longing. The characteristic sign of westerners, of Christians, is their consciousness of sin. Baudelaire's poetry had been the expression of the conflict between *Spleen* and *Idéal*. Rimbaud's work now becomes the expression of a similar conflict—between God and Satan, between good and evil. The two voices rise one after the other, sometimes in unison, sometimes mingling in a strange duet. With Baudelaire we have no doubt on which side he would wish to weight the scales; but with Rimbaud we do not know which voice is stronger, nor which is divine, that of God or Satan, and even he himself is uncertain.

The second *leit motif* is that of Rimbaud's longing for God, for a belief in God. His need of God was one of the fundamental needs of his nature and when he found that he could no longer accept the God of his Catholic teaching he could not rest until he had found a God which would satisfy his spiritual aspirations. He had staked everything on expressing God and the infinite, on becoming like unto God himself. When this conviction failed he was left bewildered and lost. His problem was now whether he could return to the humble Christian position in front of God. From the beginning to the end of *Une Saison en Enfer* we find expressed his burning longing for a religion in which to lose himself, but his longing is damped down by his inability to accept the loss of personality and liberty, by his desire to keep '*la liberté dans le salut*'. He was incapable of the simple trusting faith of Verlaine; he would not be God's humble servant, nor the patient little donkey of the Lord. And seeing in himself the longing and the desire for faith he cried, 'Je reconnais là ma sale éducation d'enfance.'[5]

In spite of what Catholic critics allege, Rimbaud came out of his season in Hell determined to leave God's love behind him and to keep his personal freedom at all costs. That was part of the victory on which, at the end, he prided himself; he had not yielded in spite of his longing to give in; God fought him with all His powers of persuasion, with all the weight of His arm, but he had stood firm till the end and kept himself intact. Nevertheless his later career was to prove that his victory had left him mutilated and that by stifling the voice of God in himself he condemned himself to live out his life spiritually maimed and crippled.

The third big problem is that of the acceptance or endurance of life as we have to live it in the world. The manner in which Rimbaud approached this problem and tried to solve it reveals his fundamental inability to accept life as it is and to live like all those ordinary human beings whom he so deeply despised. *Une Saison en Enfer* is, for the greater part, an acute expression of the idealism of youth hurt by the ugliness which it encounters and which it cannot explain, since it has not yet learnt—the bitterest of all the lessons which we have to learn—to make concessions with our ideals and principles, and to accept the second best. Rimbaud never learned to make concessions and since he was not able to possess what he believed was *la vraie vie* he would have nothing. In the days of his pride and his belief in his powers he refused life as it was given to him; he intended to create his own life, on his own conditions. He would destroy everything that existed naturally in himself; he would build everything again and transform life. And so he spurned and refused all the things which made life sweet for ordinary simple human beings—work, love and hope. 'Quant au bonheur établi, domestique ou non. . . . Non je ne peux pas!'[6] he exclaimed. Slowly, and by degrees he destroyed all the things in him which had made him a human being, and in this struggle he became willingly, with masochistic delight, a new kind of martyr. But this martyrdom eventually led him only to the dead end of the acceptance of the inevitable, to the grudging acceptance of reality, of perpetual slavery. He belonged to the slave race and so it did not behove him to curse life. 'Esclaves, ne maudissons pas la vie!'[7]

Rimbaud's *bateau ivre*, instead of bearing him into the centre of the ocean of infinity, or as Baudelaire's boat to the shores at least of that endless sea, had merely described a complete circle, bringing him back to the reality from which he had fled, from which he had imagined he had escaped, to revolting reality. That was the final port into which his boat sailed after all the storms and the return was not easy. Whatever he might say or think, reality was what Rimbaud was never able—and never would be able—to accept. 'L'automne déjà, notre barque élevée dans les brumes immobiles tourne vers le port de la misère, la cité énorme au ciel taché de feu et de boue.'[8]

He was left now with the imperative necessity of finding some philosophy which would make the past comprehensible, give some meaning to the chaos around him and some direction for the future. But this will be studied later.

These briefly are the chief problems that were occupying Rimbaud during the composition of *Une Saison en Enfer*. It must be remembered that this work was not written by a man who had reached a definite point, and, knowing he had reached it, had retraced the steps to show how this had been achieved. When he started writing he had reached no point whatsoever; his only certainty was his anguish and distress and his conviction that all his past life and art had been a delusion. Thus in *Une Saison en Enfer* we live the struggle with the poet, with him we contemplate the problems, dropping them partially solved, only to take them up later, casting aside the early abortive solutions. *Une Saison en Enfer* is a moment of Rimbaud's life with all the burning intensity of a struggle whose end is not known to the writer. It is not, as is most art, an attempt to recapture a past state, it is not 'emotion recollected in tranquillity'. This leads to contradictions and inconsistencies and to a certain indecision at times; the author himself does not always know in what direction he is steering.

The opening chapter which serves as an introduction was written in the fevered and anguished state of mind of his return from Brussels in July 1873. It sets out to explain how and why he had reached the point of reviewing his past existence. It is written with tragic bitterness and is a merciless judgment of that life, of his illusions and of his colossal pride. From his present disillusionment and despair he looks back at the days of his childhood and sees them as having been beautiful and fair before he knew the meaning of evil and vice. 'Jadis, si je me souviens bien, ma vie était un festin où s'ouvraient tous les cœurs, où tous les vins coulaient.' Then, when he was a mere boy, he fell in love with Beauty—with Art—and, seating her on his knee made love to her. His passion for her made him forget all else. But this love proved bitter and disappointing and then he turned on her and abused her. This was his break with traditional beauty. He revolted against all the fairness that had deceived him, against goodness, against law and order, and became a law unto himself. But he squandered all his treasure of youth, of trust, of idealism, and flung all that wealth to the witches. He thought that he could do better than others, that he had no need of the things that made life sweet for them, and he tried a life of crime and vice. 'Je parvins à faire s'évanouir dans mon esprit toute l'espérance humaine. Sur toute joie pour l'étrangler, j'ai fait le bond sourd de la bête féroce. J'ai appelé les bourreaux pour, en périssant, mordre la crosse de leurs fusils. Le malheur a été mon dieu. Je me suis allongé dans la boue. Je me suis séché à l'air du crime.' But the life he had made for himself had brought him nothing but bitterness. Then, recently, as he lay on his hospital bed, thinking of the death which he had just escaped, he wondered whether he could find once more the key to his early happiness. 'La clef du festin ancien où je reprendrais peut-être appétit.' Charity was perhaps this key, he thought. In the religious instruction which he had received at the Collège de Charleville Charity had been lauded above all the other Christian virtues.[9] Charity the greatest of the theological virtues, which was love of God and love of one's neighbour, the movement by which we love God on account of himself. All those who did not attain to Charity were said to be led, inevitably, into a state of sin, for Charity conditioned a state of purity. Charity was not mere kindness and altruism. To rise to a state of Charity it was essential to sacrifice something of oneself, it was necessary to attain self-effacement and self-abnegation. Rimbaud had thought that he had practised Charity but he found that this was an illusion as well as all the rest. But he might be able to achieve it now, Charity might be the key which would open for him again the gates of the Garden of Eden. But he did not feel prepared yet to sacrifice his personal freedom, nor ready to reach that state of complete self-effacement, and so he said 'La Charité est cette clef—Cette inspiration prouve que j'ai rêvé.' No return for him was possible since he would not grasp the only available key. 'Tu resteras hyène, se récrie le démon qui me couronna de si aimables pavots. Gagne la mort avec tous tes appétits, et ton égoïsme et tous tes péchés capitaux.'

This preface was written at the end of July 1873. Then Rimbaud, taking up work on the book already begun, was convinced that no salvation was possible, but he changed this opinion before the end. It was probably then that he chose the title for what was, earlier, intended to be a composition of a somewhat different nature. The chapters which he had previously written to express his disillusionment with love, art and philosophy, now took on a new significance and since he saw himself as irretrievably

damned, he called all the chapters which follow the Introduction, 'Quelques hideux feuillets' of his 'carnet de damné'.

Each 'feuillet' of this 'carnet' is a separate chapter, a separate
entity. The first, *Mauvais Sang*, is the longest and was probably
intended originally to be the centre and core of the whole composition, and it might indeed make a work in itself, for it is more
comprehensive and covers more ground than any of the other
chapters. Taken by itself it is logical and coherent and it becomes
contradictory only when fitted into the texture of the whole
work. In it Rimbaud analyses himself and all that had formed
him in an effort to understand the causes of his failure. He studied
himself in his hereditary past as well as in the present, and especially at the time of his greatest pride. He saw himself as verily the
son of his own race, 'les plus ineptes de leur temps.' Wherever
he looked—in many previous existences—he saw himself as never
belonging to anything but an inferior cast. He saw in himself all
the vices of his forefathers—their lying, their deceit and above all
their great sloth. He felt in himself the fatality of this sloth, sloth
for manual work, sloth even for intellectual work. Hitherto he
had succeeded in safeguarding that idleness, in doing nothing and
in finding good grounds to defend it. That sloth, however, was
only further proof that he belonged to an inferior race—inferior
in the past, in the present and the future, inferior for all eternity.
His present overwhelming consciousness of worthlessness was the
swing of the pendulum, the reaction from his previous certainty
that he was the equal of God.

The clearest sign of his inferiority was his thirst for God which
nothing could quench. Whatever he did, wherever he went, he
still relied on God, and counted on Christ who had died to save
all men and had thus pauperized them, spiritually, for all eternity,
by taking on Himself all the sins of the world. 'J'attends Dieu
avec gourmandise. Je suis de race inférieure de toute éternité.'

He had tried to escape the doom of inferiority in the pursuit of
knowledge, of philosophy and science; all these things had,
however, only proved 'des remèdes de bonne femme'. His
thirst for God was not assuaged.

At one time he had imagined that he might escape if he fled

from the civilization penetrated and rotted by Christianity. Nothing further could be hoped from Europe since the coming of Christ and the Gospels had warped it; it would be better to leave it, with its 'anciens parapets' and go to other regions, returning later with renewed vigour. He dreamed of escaping from the foul and decaying swamps of Europe and of sailing away where something new could be found. 'Me voici sur la plage armoricaine'—Merlin had been a Breton—'Que les villes s'allument le soir. Ma journée est faite; je quitte l'Europe. L'air marin brûlera mes poumons; les climats perdus me tanneront. Je reviendrai avec des membres de fer, la peau sombre, l'œil farouche; sur mon masque on me jugera d'une race forte, j'aurai de l'or.'

The dream, however, faded as he was brought back to reality: 'Maintenant je suis maudit, j'ai horreur de la patrie. Le meilleur c'est un sommeil bien ivre sur la grève.'

No escape for him was possible. Especially no escape was possible from the problem of evil which he had hoped to flee in the new world. There was nothing for him but to continue his weary tramp along the well-worn paths, weighed down by the burden of sin; sin which, since his earliest childhood, had grown its roots into his very being and was now rising to heaven, impeding him at every step, overpowering him and strangling him. To attain peace and rest he would, at this moment, have accepted any creed, sacrificed all his own freedom and his own beliefs. 'Ah!' Je suis tellement délaissé que j'offre à n'importe quelle divine image mes élans vers la perfection. Oh! mon abnégation, ô ma charité merveilleuse! De profundis, Domine!' Then the old irony broke out again as he added, 'Dieu suis-je bête!'

He wondered then if salvation lay in sacrificing everything voluntarily. If he had given up everything of his own accord no one would ever again be able to take anything from him. Even, as a child, he had admired the confirmed convict on whom the gates of the prison were always closing; everything he had once possessed was gone from him, even his liberty; there was nothing more that could be taken from him. If he too were to give up everything, like the convict, he would have more strength than a saint and alone he would be witness of his power and his glory.

When he looked back into his past he saw himself as having been alone and solitary, as deserted as a convict; when he looked into the future he saw nothing but loneliness ahead of him. No one had ever really understood his ideas or appreciated his dreams and he had been persecuted like Joan of Arc and Merlin. No man had ever truly been a friend to him and friendship with women had been impossible. All those who had come into contact with him had seen nothing but vice and had not looked any further —none had looked into his heart. It was only they who had called it vice, it had not been vice to him. His beliefs had not been their beliefs, nor his dreams theirs, but they had never allowed him to keep his own convictions, they had wished to convert him to theirs. It was the old story of the ignorant white man baptizing at the point of the bayonet those whom he considered heathens.

But now he knew that the life he had led had been foolish and wrong, that vice was stupid and so was debauch, that it had all brought him nothing but remorse, regret and ill-health. Perhaps another opportunity will be allowed to him to repair all the mistakes he had made; perhaps another world will be granted to him where all his errors will be set right, where all his dreams will be fulfilled; perhaps he will be taken away, like 'a child, 'pour jouer dans l'oubli de tout malheur'.

With the thought of the possibility of another world hope sprang up again in his heart, and from the ship which was bearing him to safety—a ship like the one described by Michelet,[11] the ship of the *Libre Esprit* carrying those that sailed on it to a new world of freedom and hope—the voices of the angels rose singing the praises of divine love. 'La raison m'est née. Le monde est bon. Je bénirai la vie. J'aimerai mes frères. Ce ne sont pas des promesses d'enfance, ni l'espoir d'échapper à la vieillesse et à la mort. Dieu fait ma force et je loue Dieu.'

With this temporary submission to life, this temporary acceptance of the divine love of God, it was as if the whole burden were suddenly lifted from his shoulders. 'Les rages, les débauches, la folie, dont je sais tous les élans, et les désastres,—tout mon fardeau est déposé. Apprécions sans vertige l'étendue de mon innocence.' In the midst of the serenity of faith doubt, however, once more assailed him, and his pride and reason began to revolt. 'J'ai dit Dieu! Je veux la liberté dans le salut! Comment la poursuivre?' Each person has his own reason and he must use it himself, and Rimbaud would not sacrifice his but intended to keep his place at the top of 'cette angélique échelle de bon sens.' And, moreover, when he considered them, peace and contented happiness did not attract him; he will have none of them nor of the work which is alleged to produce them. 'Quant au bonheur établi et domestique ou non . . . non je ne peux pas. Je suis trop dissipé, trop faible, la vie fleurit par le travail, vieille vérité; moi, ma vie n'est pas assez pesante, elle s'envole et flotte loin au-dessus de l'action, ce cher point du monde.' But his courage flinched at the prospect of the hard life of independence without succour which lay before him; he knew well that he was frequently cowardly, too ready to raise aloft the white flag of defeatism and to beg for the 'coup-de-grâce' to end his misery. 'Feu! feu sur moi! Là ou je me rends,—Lâches!—Je me tue! Je me jette aux pieds des chevaux! Ah!'

The chapter ends, 'Je m'y habituerai!' He, like everyone else, will grow accustomed to the meaningless farce in which we all, willy-nilly, play a part. 'La vie est la farce à mener par tous.'

This is the longest section of the work written in the spring of 1873, before he took up his relationship again with Verlaine and it sets out the problems in their full complexity, without envisaging any solution. The subsequent chapters will analyse the separate moments and aspects of the conflict.

The next chapter is the one written in London, in June or July, called first *Fausse Conversion* but later *Nuit de l'Enfer*. When he began his *Livre Païen* he had thought that he had sloughed off his past, banished his obsession of evil and returned to a primitive state of innocence. But it had been only an abortive conversion, and with Verlaine he had drunk again from the poisoned draught.[12] Even if there is no Hell, even if this Hell is only in his imagination, it is none the less Hell. 'Je me crois en Enfer; donc j'y suis!' He had thought that he had found wisdom but his parents had neutralized all his efforts. By the act of baptism, by confirming the belief in the necessity of eradicating original sin, they condemned him to his hell, they sowed in him the seeds of the tree of right and wrong whose roots now spread through his whole being. Hell cannot touch pagans since they do not admit its existence; pagans do not suffer from the hell of this dilemma, the conflict of good and evil.

The whole chapter is a frenzied expression of intolerable anguish and explains the strained relations existing between Verlaine and Rimbaud during the agonizing weeks in London of June and July 1873.

La peau de ma tête se dessèche. Pitié! Seigneur, J'ai peur. J'ai soif, si soif! Ah! l'enfance, l'herbe, la pluie, le lac sur les pierres. Le clair de lune quand le clocher sonnait douze. Le diable est au clocher à cette heure. Marie! Sainte Vierge! Horreur de ma bêtise!

Then the life he had led rose up before his mind. 'Ma vie ne fut que folies douces, c'est regrettable.' And he enumerates all the talents he had possessed. 'J'ai tous les talents! . . . Veut-on des chants nègres, des danses de houris? Veut-on que je disparaisse, que je plonge à la recherche de l'anneau? Veut-on? Je ferai de l'or, des remèdes.'

But all that had been sinful and he was now in Hell, not one hell but several hells, a hell for each of his vices. In occult doctrine there are Seven Tabernacles in Hell—each indeed a separate hell —in charge of a demon representing one of the vices and this demon has the function of tormenting those who were addicted to his particular vice in the world. Furthermore each Tabernacle is subdivided into lesser houses in charge of demons representing other sins. Rimbaud says: 'Je devrais avoir mon enfer pour la colère, mon enfer pour l'orgueil,—et l'enfer de la paresse; un concert d'enfers.'

In his despair, he who had thought that he had kept his liberty, that he still clung to the topmost rung of the ladder of common sense, he offered up a desperate prayer, imploring an end to his sufferings. 'Je meurs de lassitude. C'est le tombeau, je m'en vais aux vers, horreur de l'horreur! . . . Je réclame! un coup de fourche, une goutte de feu. . . . Et ce poison, ce baiser mille fois maudit. Ma faiblesse, la cruauté du monde! Mon Dieu, pitié, cachez-moi, je me tiens trop mal!—'

And the chapter ends, 'C'est le feu qui se relève avec son damné.'

But as the flames surged upwards, from the centre of the fire a voice arose, that of the *Vierge Folle*, his companion in Hell, and it is her confession that next we hear.[13] The two *Délires* chapters are the relation of the two main causes of his downfall, love and art. In *Délires I*, through the mouth of the foolish virgin, he analyses his conduct; it is at times as if he were pleading his own case, although he spares himself no blame. At the close of the chapter he, as well as his companion, is uncertain whether it is to Heaven or to Hell he is to be translated. 'Un jour peut-être il disparaîtra merveilleusement; mais il faut que je sache, s'il doit remonter à un ciel, que je voie un peu l'assomption de mon petit ami.'[14]

In *Délires II* he criticizes his artistic follies and errors, the greatest cause of his fall.[15] He had thought that vice and degradation were necessary material for art and that from them he would be able to distil beauty. Just as the fly gorging on filth and putrefying matter does not realize the nature of the substance on which it feeds and revels. 'O le moucheron enivré à la pissotière de l'auberge, amoureux de la bourrache, et que dissout un rayon.'[16] And, moreover, it was believed by alchemists and occultists that demons and evil spirits were in the habit of haunting places of putrefaction.

All his experiments in art had been folly and madness; folly which had endangered his health and brought him near to madness. 'Aucun des sophismes de la folie—la folie qu'on enferme —n'a été oublié par moi: je pourrais les redire tous, je tiens le système.'[17]

Next follows the chapter called *L'Impossible* and there we are shown the failure of his philosophical and religious beliefs. One of the central conceptions of his literary doctrine at the time of the early *Illuminations*, had been that childhood was the most precious period in life and that all possible methods should be used to recapture that time of instinctive wisdom when God speaks directly to the human soul. But that belief, like all the others, had been only a delusion. 'Ah! cette vie de mon enfance, la grande route par tous les temps, sobre surnaturellement, plus désintéressé que le meilleur des mendiants, fier de n'avoir ni pays, ni amis, quelle sottise c'était.—Et je m'en aperçois seulement.'[18]

In that flash of clarity he realized, all at once, that he had been mistaken in thinking that one could go back to the time of child-hood or recapture that instinctive attitude to life, any more than one could return to the state of mind which had existed before the coming of Christ, any more than one could, as he had tried, adopt the wiser philosophy of the East. Now he could scorn the beliefs which had once attracted him—even the doctrine of Eastern religious thought. 'Il paraît que c'est un rêve de paresse grossière.'

Suddenly now he felt as if his mind were freed from every-thing which had, hitherto, bound it down, and it seemed to him that if his mind had always thus been free he would by now be soaring in the midst of light and he would not have yielded to his lower instincts. 'S'il était bien éveillé toujours à partir de ce moment, nous serions bientôt à la vérité, qui peut-être nous entoure avec ses anges pleurant! S'il avait été éveillé jusqu'à ce moment-ci, c'est que je n'aurais pas cédé aux instincts délétères à une époque immémoriale! S'il avait été éveillé, je voguerais en pleine sagesse! O pureté! pureté!'

In this moment of the vision of perfect purity he realized that it is through the spirit alone that one can reach God, and the chapter ends: 'Déchirante infortune!' It is indeed 'déchirante infortune' since he cannot and will not yet accept that solution.

Another solution suggests itself to him, in a flash, in the chapter *L'Éclair*. Work may perhaps be his salvation as it has been to many others before him. 'Le travail humain c'est l'explosion qui éclaire mon abîme de temps en temps!'[19] This, however, seemed to him a poor and slow remedy—he had wanted everything to go so fast. 'Que la prière galope et que la lumière gronde!' he said. His pride would not accept so commonplace a solution for his problem. 'Je connais le travail. . . . C'est trop simple, et il fait trop chaud; on se passera de moi. J'ai mon devoir; j'en serai fier à la façon de plusieurs, en le mettant de côté.' No! work was too light a thing for his pride, too great a confession of weakness and failure. He did not intend to yield so easily and, at the last moment, he would attack, right and left. This may mean, however, that eternity will be lost to him forever. 'Alors!—Oh!—chère pauvre âme, l'éternité serait-elle perdue pour nous!'

Here Rimbaud reached the darkest moment of his season in Hell, the moment before dawn. He had exhausted all his words in the relation of his fall and he had none left; he could no more express himself than the beggar with his eternal 'Pater et Ave Maria'.[20] Up to this moment we have only the relation of the failure, we have no hint of what the solution may be. But in the last two chapters—*Matin* and *Adieu*—if we know how to read them aright—we find the escape and hope which Rimbaud reached and which will explain his subsequent conduct.

Morning came and with the dawn the long night in Hell was over, but the light found him weak and spent. There is no fight in *Matin* only infinite lassitude and weariness. But hope rose with the sun and his eyes, glancing upwards, saw the silver star, the last star of night slowly paling, a silver star like the star at Bethlehem on that first Christmas so long ago, sent as a messenger, a symbol of eternal hope, a new rebirth. Then follows one of the loveliest passages in *Une Saison en Enfer*.

Du même désert, à la même nuit, toujours mes yeux las se réveillent à l'étoile d'argent, toujours, sans que s'émeuvent les Rois de la vie, les trois mages, le cœur, l'âme, l'esprit. Quand irons-nous, par delà les grèves et les monts, saluer la naissance du travail nouveau, la sagesse nouvelle, la fuite des tyrans et des démons, la fin de la superstition, adorer—les premiers!—Noël sur la terre?

If the transformation which Rimbaud has undergone is not appreciated the implications of this passage—and also of the following chapter *Adieu*—will not be understood. Without reasons for hope and confidence in it the morning constellation would have been no more to him than a mere silver star in the dark sky.

He had been, since his boyhood, a follower and admirer of Michelet and now, when abandoning magic and alchemy, it was to his ideas that he turned for support and hope. Michelet had believed in a continuous ascension towards a higher form of humanity through science and the application of science in industry. This would culminate in the *Libre Esprit*, the *Saint-Esprit*, in an age of science. In the *Conclusion* to the *Bible de l'Humanité* he wrote:[21]

Il faut faire volte-face, et vivement, franchement, tourner le dos au moyen-âge, à ce passé morbide, qui même quand il n'agit pas, influe terriblement par la contagion de la mort. Il ne faut pas combattre, ni critiquer, mais oublier. Oublions et marchons!

Marchons aux sciences de la vie, au musée, aux écoles. Marchons aux sciences de l'histoire et de l'humanité, aux langues d'Orient. Interrogeons le *genius* antique dans son accord avec tant de récents voyages. Là nous prendrons le *sens humain*.

Soyons, je vous prie, *hommes*, et aggradissons-nous des nouvelles grandeurs inouïes de l'humanité.

He described humanity moving away from the fatalistic conception of destiny of Eastern philosophy and, by examining natural phenomena through the light of science, creating a world based on liberty; liberty for the human soul freed from the shackling belief in fatality.[22] Michelet owed much to Vico. 'I have no other master but Vico' he wrote,[23] '*L'Humanité qui se crée* was my book and my teaching.' Through his translation of *La Scienza Novella*, *La Science Nouvelle*—Rimbaud came into contact with the theories of Vico, but it does not seem that he went further than the *Introduction*, in which Michelet summarizes, in picturesque language, the main points. The work, in its entirety—even in Michelet's translation, which has clarified the Italian—was too colourless, legalistic and dry to appeal to him; too complicated and involved in its argument; too much filled with legal bias. But Michelet made the ideas living and accessible. Vico believed that there were three stages in the evolution of mankind: the first was poetic and creative; this was the time of the theological poets, the oldest wise men of pagan times. The second stage was the heroic; and the third was an age of humanity, of reasonable beings, kindly beings who recognized the laws of conscience, reason and duty. Michelet called the third stage the civilized or human age, and he believed—in the middle of the nineteenth century—that it was about to begin for humanity. Elsewhere he writes,[24] that the new world was not merely one of industry, that progress meant love and sympathy, and that the future was to be based on universal love.

Rimbaud was now giving up magic and alchemy, was giving up the idea of returning to the East, was facing the materialistic nineteenth-century future, and he saw in the silver star, shining in the sky, the symbol of the new birth, the new Christmas, when tyrants would be abolished and superstitions dead; when there would be only scientific certainty and reasonable belief. He hailed the new work and the new wisdom—*La Science Nouvelle*—this was the hope with which he took up life again. Michelet had said,[25] that the new world was to be faced with entirely modern ideas, that all traces of the old world were to be effaced: 'Soyons nets, purs des vieux mélanges, ne pas boiter d'un monde à l'autre.' Rimbaud says, similarly, 'Il faut être absolument moderne. Point de cantiques, tenir le pas gagné'. Michelet, in his *Introduction* to *La Science Nouvelle*, says that here on earth, with goodwill, the great city of nations could be built, governed by God himself, the 'Républiques de l'Univers'. This, in other words, is 'les splendides villes' of Rimbaud.

It was autumn when day broke for Rimbaud, autumn the prelude to winter, and the time to seek out shelter. As he looked up at the early morning sky, he saw that his boat had taken him back once more to the reality from which through his art, he had hoped to escape:

L'automne. Notre barque élevée dans les brumes immobiles tourne vers le port de la misère, la cité énorme au ciel taché de feu et de boue.

Ah! les haillons pourris, le pain trempé de pluie, l'ivresse, les mille amours qui m'ont crucifié. . . . Je me revois la peau rongée par la boue et la peste, des vers pleins les cheveux et les aisselles, et encore de plus gros vers dans le cœur, étendu parmi les inconnus sans âge, sans sentiment. . . . J'aurais pu y mourir. L'affreuse évocation! J'exècre la misère.[26]

His thoughts then turned once more to the hopes that he had cherished, to the dreams that had been his escape from that reality, to the dreams which he had thought a reality of a higher order:

Quelquefois je vois au ciel des plages sans fin couvertes de blanches nations en joie.

Un grand vaisseau d'or, au-dessus de moi agite ses pavillons multi-colores sous les brises du matin, J'ai créé toutes les fêtes, tous les triomphes, tous les drames.

He had thought that he could invent new flowers, new stars, a new language; he had imagined that he could acquire super-natural powers. But this had been an illusion, and all he had now left to do was to bury his imagination and his dreams, even though this might be 'une belle gloire d'artiste emportée!' He who had thought himself a prophet, a messenger from the beyond, he was cast down to earth again, even lower than Lucifer. 'Moi! moi qui me suis dit mage ou ange, dispensé de toute morale, je suis rendu au sol, avec un devoir à chercher et la réalité rugueuse à étreindre! Paysan!'

With these words he reached the charity, the self-abnegation, which he had found impossible when he had written the *Intro-duction*. As he wrote, however, doubt assailed him once more, and fear of sacrificing everything for no return. 'Suis-je trompé?' he asked 'la charité serait-elle sœur de la mort pour moi?' But he cast aside that doubt and in his new-found humility begged for forgiveness for having fed so long on falsehood and self-deception. 'Enfin, je demanderai pardon pour m'être nourri de mensonge. Et allons!'

The battle had been hard but victory was his. Merlin had fought with his father Satan for possession of the world, to save it from evil, had fought hard the whole of one night, a battle fiercer than the battle which Jacob had fought with the angel. This too had been Rimbaud's fate. 'Dure nuit! le sang séché fume sur ma face, et je n'ai derrière moi que cet horrible arbrisseau'— the shrivelled-up tree of good and evil which would not flourish in the new world. 'Le combat spirituel est aussi brutal que la bataille d'hommes; mais la vision de la justice est le plaisir de Dieu seul.' Yet victory was his in spite of the harshness of the hour. The weeping and wailing, and gnashing of teeth were past, and the crackling fire had subsided; all obscene memories had faded, all regrets, all jealousies. 'Je puis dire que la victoire m'est acquise.' It was a victory over his arrogance and pride, over his desire and longing for faith; a victory over his obsession with sin and his inability to accept life. He was no longer going to make an exception of himself; he was not going to try to be God, nor try to penetrate into the beyond. The vision of righteousness was the pleasure of God alone. He was going to remain satisfied with the ordinary human condition—he did not yet know how impossible this was to be for him—as a slave he was not going to curse life; he was not going to try to escape from reality. He was going to lay aside his pride and egoism, and become one of the herd of modern men, no longer taking on himself the arrogant charge of other souls. He was going to live out his allotted span as an ordinary man, 'aller mes vingt ans si les autres vont vingt ans!' It turned out to be only eighteen in the end. His victory over himself was to have sacrificed the lovely dream in which he was God, and to have accepted the lowly position of a small unit in a long line of coarse peasants. And, hardest victory of all, he had conquered his desire for faith, had stilled the voice of intuition, and given the last word to reason. He had kept 'la liberté dans le salut'. But he was full of joy and hope that the 'splendides villes' would open their gates to him, and, why wait for the hand of a friend, he asked himself; he could afford to scorn lying friendships and the old form of human love 'Je puis rire des vieilles amours mensongères'—perhaps a reference to his homosexual period—'et frapper de honte ces couples menteurs,—j'ai vu l'enfer des femmes là-bas; et il me sera loisible de *posséder la vérité dans une âme et un corps.*' These are the last words of *Une Saison en Enfer*, italicized by the poet himself, and they have puzzled many readers: 'I shall be able to possess truth in *one* soul and *one* body.' Many conflicting interpretations have been brought forward. When one recalls that, hitherto, he had considered himself a widowed soul, half a soul, it is possible to imagine that he now felt that he was at last going to be whole. Now he would be able to scorn ordinary love and friendship, the 'amours mensongères', the love which he had said earlier in his confession, 'est à réinventer'. Amongst all the other hells which he had seen in the Seven Tabernacles of Hell—a hell for each vice—he had seen the hell of women, of these women who had been deprived of their soul-mate, the other half without which they were incomplete and widowed. We have seen that, in occult doctrine, the 'woman-soul' of a man who had embraced celibacy—or been forced to it—is condemned to a hell of suffering, of debauch and vice, the prey of evil spirits. Rimbaud was now going to rescue his 'soul-mate' from that fate and become whole himself.

It is tempting, as we lay down *Une Saison en Enfer*, to think that here we have Rimbaud's farewell to literature, to the life of the mind, and that henceforth he intended to lead a life of action. It would be pleasant—or at least it would round off the account neatly—to believe that this had been his intention when he wrote *Adieu*, that the victory of which he had talked was the sacrifice of his 'gloire de conteur'. that there was nothing further for him to do, to close the chapter, but burn his books and papers.

This is a picturesque story but the truth is not so dramatic. He did not, in fact, burn his manuscripts until three months after he had finished *Une Saison en Enfer*, after he had printed the book —his mother paying for its publication—and after he had sent copies to his friends. Those who believe this and who think that he never wrote another line, work back from this result, see the intention in *Une Saison en Enfer*, and intrepret it accordingly. The book is, in many ways, so far from clear, that passages can be found to use as proof. Nevertheless, it is possible that what they read as Rimbaud's farewell to poetry may only be his farewell to the kind of literature he had practised during his 'magician' period, and it does not necessarily mean that he will never write again, or that a literary career is at an end for him. It will only mean that his poetry will be of a different quality and mood.

There is no evidence whatsoever that he intended to say a final and definitive farewell to art. It was only to be a farewell to frenzied inspiration, to the 'théorie du voyant', to 'l'Alchimie du Verbe'. In the rough draft of this chapter had he not written; 'Je hais maintenant les élans mystiques et les bizarreries du style', and, in the final version: 'Cela s'est passé. Je sais aujourd'hui saluer la beauté'. Delahaye tells us that Rimbaud had spoken to him, during the winter of 1872 to 1873, of the new prose poems he was about to compose, not the short poems of the previous year, but poems on a grandiose scale, something more vivid than Michelet.[27] The general title was to be *L'Histoire Magnifique*, and it was to open with scenes called, *Photographies des Temps Passés*. Some of these were already written, according to Delahaye, who had heard them, but who could later recall only an impression of the Middle Ages flooded with light and colour. He remembered a seventeenth-century picture where French Catholicism appeared symbolized, at the zenith of its triumph, by a splendid figure wearing a golden mitre and standing against a background of great magnificence. Delahaye claims that the poem describing Christ's first miracle was to belong to this series.

If Rimbaud had intended, after composing *Une Saison en Enfer*, to abandon literature why then did he print the work? This was the only complete work which he himself published, and he corrected the proofs with care. Why did he send copies to his friends and to men of letters in Paris, whom he admired, hoping that they would review it favourably in the press? The truth is that, when the book was ready, he was anxious concerning its reception and success as any author. 'Mon sort dépend de ce livre' he had said to Delahaye[28] when he had written three chapters, and he did not depart from that opinion, for he did everything in his power to get the book known and well received, and he was bitterly disappointed at its reception.

If he had intended to abandon literature, why was he sufficiently interested in his poems in prose to make copies of them the following year, in London in 1874; and why, in 1875, did he try to get them published? If he intended to abandon literature why did he, in October 1873, sign himself 'homme de lettres' in the police records in Brussels, where he had gone to collect the copies of *Une Saison en Enfer*?[29] And finally why, in the summer of 1875, was he sufficiently interested in his reputation as a writer, to ask Delahaye to return him the copy of *Une Saison en Enfer*, which he had given him on publication, so that he could impress a widow in Italy who had been kind to him?

It is clear that in writing *Une Saison en Enfer*, he intended to examine his past and to make a complete break with it; with his previous forms of art; with his way of living and his beliefs. All this had undermined his health, his spiritual nature, and his mind. His relationship with Verlaine was now at an end, and he was never to renew it. He had given up magic, alchemy and superstitions. His idea of the future was of a materialistic and reasonable world, in which he was to further the cause of democracy. He had given up Eastern philosophy; he was going to be modern, 'tenir le pas gagné' and sing no hymns of farewell. He was returning to ordinary life, very humbly as an ordinary human being, asking for no privileges, and thinking himself as humble as a slave. What he had tried to achieve was not granted to a slave, but only to the free, and he was not of these. Magic could not be imparted to those who were weak and unable to govern themselves. But there was the hope of emancipating oneself from slavery—Joseph had done so and he owed his emancipation from slavery to his knowledge and his learning. The following year in London, Rimbaud, when applying for a new Reader's ticket at the British Museum, signed the register 'Jean. Nicolas. Joseph-Arthur Rimbaud.' The name Joseph does not figure on his birth certificate and this is the only time we see it. Rimbaud rarely did a thing without some hidden meaning and he must have had some reason for this addition; it is interesting to notice that the name *Joseph* is hyphened to the name which was most his own name, the name by which he was always known, *Arthur*. Occultists believe that a name has a mysterious effect on those who bear it and Rimbaud may have thought that the name *Joseph* would eventually succeed in freeing him, the name of the slave who had liberated himself through study, and had become a prophet.

Ruchon says[30] that if Rimbaud has written anything after *Une Saison en Enfer* then the work would lose all meaning. No doubt, if he had written *Illuminations* of the transcendental kind, for this was the form of art which he was repudiating. But it is probable that he intended to compose—and indeed did compose, if not after *Une Saison en Enfer* certainly at the same time—poems which would set forth his new view of life. His theory now was that literature was to be prosaic and rational, devoid of symbolism, that was the form most suited to the modern world. Michelet had said in the Introduction to *L'Histoire Universelle*, that prose is the latest and most highly perfected form of thought, the one which is furthest away from vague dreaming, the one nearest to action. He thought that the transition from silent symbolism to poetry, then from poetry to prose, was a progress towards light and equality; it is an intellectual levelling—'un nivellement intellectuel' and he meant this as praise. He thought that the democratic genius of a country was never better seen than in its prosaic qualities and believed that it was by this that France was destined to raise the whole intellectual and equalitarian standard of the world. Rimbaud was moved by this conception at the time though he was later to be disillusioned by democracy.

Believing in the significance and importance of his new beliefs and how they would save the world, knowing the sincerity and purity of his intentions, he could not believe it possible that others would misunderstand them. He thought that everything he had written was crystal clear and self-evident. He did not realize that to understand it one much have a knowledge of the background of his mind. If anyone had asked him what it signified he would have answered as he had answered his mother when she asked him in amazement what it all meant. 'It means exactly what I've said, literally and completely, in all respects.' If the book had been favourably received perhaps he would not have become so easily discouraged and disillusioned the following year. But perhaps his renunciation, at the end, was not entirely voluntary, perhaps his new form of poetry led him to a dead end, perhaps he could no longer write when he ceased to believe that he saw God face to face. It had been the overwhelming mystic confidence which had given so much power to his writing. Perhaps he could not find material worthy of his talent—he was never to be able to acclimatize himself to this world in spite of all his efforts. Perhaps he had nothing further to say when he could no longer relate what he discovered in his own soul. Literary expression had seemed, in his greatest period, a sort of spiritual orgasm, and possibly he was incapable of composing without this release.

Rimbaud carefully superintended the printing of his book and went in person to collect the copies in Belgium in October 1873. An entry in the records of the police in Brussels states that 'Rimbaud Arthur, man of letters, residing at No. 1 rue des Brasseurs, departed furtively on 24 October, without giving his new address.' Perhaps he left the copy of his book, inscribed to Verlaine, at the prison at Petits Carmes where he was incarcerated, and from which he would be transferred to Mons the following day.[29]

After dispatching the copies of *Une Saison en Enfer* to those whom he knew, Rimbaud set out for Paris to find out what kind of reception the book was getting, and it is probable that he was very coldly received. It was only four months after the affair in Brussels, and few literary men were unaware of the nature of the doctor's report on Verlaine, or that this report was responsible for the severity of his sentence. Few approved of Verlaine's conduct, though many were fond of him, but all considered Rimbaud a monster who was his evil genius and who had brought him to this pass. In 1875, when he came out of prison, Verlaine was to be considered 'indigne' by many of his close friends, how much more infamous must Rimbaud have seemed in 1873, just after the tragedy, to those who, in any case, had never liked him and thought his work that of a lunatic? It is very probable that he was received with hostility and snubs, and that his book was not even read. Rimbaud's pride and sensitiveness gained thereby a wound that he was never afterwards able to forget. He had come to them in all humility—even if proud humility—confessing his past errors and renouncing all that hitherto he had held dear, and they had repulsed him. There are few things more easily wounded than proud humility.

Albert Poussin, the poet, relates how on 1 November 1873, he saw Rimbaud sitting in the little literary café Tabourey, where Verlaine and he had once spent so many happy evenings together. It was a holiday and the café was thronged with writers chatting merrily together, but Rimbaud sat alone, sunk in the deepest despair. All the other tables were crowded, but there was no one with him, though most of those present must have known him at least by sight, for his was a striking face not easily forgotten, even if he had not been notorious. Poussin had only recently come from the provinces, he did not then know who Rimbaud was, but, seeing this pale and gloomy young man sitting alone, he went up to him in a friendly way and offered him a drink. Rimbaud looked at him with vacant unseeing eyes, and then turned away without answering. Poussin left him, not wishing to intrude further on a grief which was too deep for his comprehension.[31]

Later, when the café closed, Rimbaud went silently away, without saying a word to anyone. This was the dawn of All Souls' Day, and he returned forthwith on foot to his native Charleville. When he arrived, we are told, he made a holocaust of all the manuscripts in his possession, and of the whole edition of his book.

This gesture of sacrifice has led to much conjecture and comment. It is highly probable that he burned his manuscripts and papers—that story seems authentic for Isabelle remembers the blaze—but it is not likely that he burned any books. These do not burn easily nor blaze, and it is inconceivable that his mother would not have prevented the outrage. Furthermore the whole edition, except for the author's copies, was found by the printer in the attics of his press in 1901, which Rimbaud had never claimed or paid for.[32] And Bouillane de Lacoste, in his critical edition of *Une Saison en Enfer*, has accounted for the author's copies which Rimbaud is likely to have received. What is possible —and it would be very characteristic of Rimbaud—is that he burned his papers as a gesture of repudiation and loathing of the literary circles of his day, and, in so doing, he was modelling himself once more on Baudelaire. In an addition which he made to the *Suspiria* of De Quincey in his *Paradis Artificiels*, Baudelaire wrote—at a moment when he was much tempted himself to make such a gesture to show his loathing of the literary public of his day:

Un homme de génie, mélancolique, misanthrope et voulant se venger de l'injustice de son siècle, jette un jour au feu toutes ses œuvres encore manuscrites. Et comme on lui reprochait cet effroyable holocauste fait à la haine, qui d'ailleurs était le sacrifice de toutes ses propres espérances, il répondit: "Qu'importe? Ce qui était important c'était que ces choses fussent créées; elles ont été créées, donc elles sont."[33]

Or perhaps Rimbaud had heard of James Thomson's similar gesture—he who was to publish *The City of Dreadful Night* the following year, in 1874. He was in London from January to July 1873 and he and Rimbaud who were kindred spirits, may well have met. Thomson records that, on 4 November 1869, he burned all his papers. 'Burned all my old papers, manuscripts and letters, save the book mss which have been already in great part printed. It took me five hours to burn them, guarding against chimney on fire, and keeping them thoroughly burning. I was sad and stupid—scarcely looked in any; had I begun reading them I might never have finished their destruction. . . . I felt myself like one who, having climbed half-way up a long rope, cuts off all beneath his feet; he must climb on and can never touch the old earth again without a fatal fall. . . . After this terrible year I could do no less than consume the past. I can now better face the future, come in what guise it may.'

<br>

CHAPTER XI

# SOLDE

It is interesting to speculate on whether Rimbaud's literary life would have been different if he had not as a gesture of disgust and revolt against his fellow-men of letters, felt impelled to destroy his manuscripts and papers. This action increased his feeling of loneliness and isolation, and cut him off still further from others. The world had not appreciated his recantation, nor had it understood his great plan for humanity, his great work, and it had spurned it. His pride and tenderest feelings had been wounded past healing, and he developed a dislike for literary men and their ways, which he was never to lose. The gentle feelings of good-will with which he had emerged from his sojourn in

313

Hell were turned to bitterness, and he determined that he would never again seek the approval of others.

We do not know what he was doing from November 1873 to February 1874. Some say that he lived in Paris but, if that is so, we do not know on what he lived nor how he was occupied. In February he was certainly in Paris and it is said that it was then that he made the acquaintance of Germain Nouveau, a wild bohemian poet a couple of years older than himself with whom he had much in common. However, he might have known him earlier for Germain Nouveau was a contributor to the *Renaissance Littéraire et Artistique* which Rimbaud had known since its foundation in 1872, and to which he also had contributed. What is certain is that, in February or March 1874, they went over to London together and shared a room in a boarding-house at 178 Stamford Street. As neither of them had any money they were forced to earn their living as best they could. They looked for pupils to instruct in the French language, but these were hard to find since the market was still glutted with French teachers, as a study of the advertisement columns in the daily papers makes abundantly clear. It is said that they worked in a cardboard box factory at starvation pay, and that they eventually gave up the employment as they found the life a senseless waste of valuable time. This was probably Rimbaud's first experience of the real life of a working man, and this may have inspired the poem *Ouvriers* in *Illuminations*. On his previous visits to London he had lived at Verlaine's expense. Nothing further is known of their manner of living and spending their time, but they must have been engaged in intellectual pursuits as well as manual labour, for both applied for Readers' tickets at the British Museum on 4 April 1870—Rimbaud must have lost his permanent ticket, obtained the previous year, or else he burned it in the holocaust in November—and it was then that he signed the register 'Jean. Nicholas. Joseph-Arthur Rimbaud' and again certified that he was over twenty-one although he was only nineteen.[1]

Rimbaud must also have shown some interest in his compositions for, if Bouillane de Lacoste is correct in his contention that the writing on the manuscript of *Illuminations* is partly Rimbaud's of 1874 and 1875, and partly that of Germain Nouveau,[2] then the poems must have been transcribed in 1874, and Rimbaud must have been sufficiently interested in them to make fair copies of them.

Germain Nouveau and Rimbaud eventually separated and went their different ways—the former was back in Paris by the month of June. Perhaps the latter then set up house with a girl, as the aforementioned poem *Ouvriers*, might suggest, for he mentions 'ma femme'. The whole poem is a vivid evocation of the desolation of life together in the sordid conditions in which they found themselves, and it does not seem likely that it could have been composed the previous year when he was living with Verlaine.

One Sunday in February—the month might apply to either year—as they were taking a walk in the suburbs, a premature south wind of spring suddenly awoke sleeping memories in him, and showed up the dreariness of their youthful poverty. She wore a checked skirt, long out of fashion, a bonnet trimmed with ribbons and a silk scarf—sad finery, sadder even than mourning. The day was clouded over and the south wind stirred up the stench of decay in the ravaged gardens and the parched fields. But she did not seem to mind it as much as he did. She was young and foolish, and could take pleasure in meaningless trifles. Wherever they went the town seemed to be following them, the terrible town, with its smoke and factories; and he thought of other places blessed by Heaven. He remembered his childhood and all his despairs, which he had thought gone forever. He could not bear the thought of his longings and failures. He knew that he could not spend the summer in this mean country, where they would never be anything but orphan lovers.[3]

O cette chaude matinée de février! le Sud inopportun vint relever nos souvenirs d'indigents absurdes, notre jeune misère.

Henrika avait une jupe de coton à carreaux blanc et brun, qui a dû être portée au siècle dernier, un bonnet à rubans et un foulard de soie. C'était plus triste qu'un deuil. Nous faisions un tour dans la banlieue. Le temps était couvert, et ce vent du Sud excitait toutes les vilaines odeurs des jardins ravagés et des prés desséchés.

Cela ne devait pas fatiguer ma femme au même point que moi. Dans une flache laissée par l'inondation du mois précédent à un sentier assez haut, elle me fit remarquer de très-petits poissons.

La ville, avec sa fumée et ses bruits de métier, nous suivait dans les chemins. O l'autre monde, l'habitation bénie par le ciel, et les ombrages! Le Sud me rappelait les misérables incidents de mon enfance, mes désespoirs d'été, l'horrible quantité de force et de science que le sort a toujours éloignée de moi. Non! nous ne passerons pas l'été dans cet avare pays où nous ne serons jamais que des orphelins fiancés. Je veux que ce bras durci ne traîne plus une *chère image*.

The last line would suggest that the relationship might be about to come to an end.

We do not know where Rimbaud lived after he and Germain Nouveau separated.

Rimbaud seems to have suffered some sort of crisis during the summer of 1874—perhaps the reflection of it is contained in this poem; or perhaps it was merely his poverty. Whatever may have been its cause—poverty, illness or despair—is impossible now to determine. The biographers say that he fell ill and that his mother came over to London to look after him. He cannot have been ill in the ordinary sense—in bed or in hospital—for he went to meet his mother and sister at Charing Cross station, and was well enough during the whole of their visit to show them the sights of London, and also to go every day to work at the British Museum. Yet something serious must have been amiss to have persuaded that hard, realistic and practical woman to put her youngest daughter as a boarder in the convent, and to set off for London, on that expensive expedition, with her elder daughter Vitalie. We have a full account of the visit in the *Journal* of the girl, and in her letters to her sister.[4]

Rimbaud rented for them a room at 12 Argyle Square, a finely built house, looking out onto the gardens, which Vitalie calls a park. It was a better locality than Stamford Street. 'Underneath the windows of our room' wrote Vitalie to her sister, 'there are large quantities of flowers, shaded by enormous trees.'

Vitalie's *Journal* is a complete record of the visit to London and we learn that Rimbaud shepherded his mother on tours round the capital, but he seems also to have spent much time studying at the British Museum. Vitalie's childish and sentimental reflections on London and the English way of life are not edifying reading. Her chief emotion was one of home-sickness, a longing to return home and irritation against her brother who, by not finding a job, obliges them to remain so long in England. The *Journal* is full of sentimental regrets for Charleville, expressions of despair at her long enforced stay in London. The main interest it has for us to-day is in the picture that it conjures up unconsciously of Rimbaud and it should be read by those who persist in seeing him only as a hooligan, an anarchist and a sadist who brought nothing but unhappiness to his family. Without conscious effort Vitalie gives us the impression of an older brother good-humoured, willing and kind, who, seeing how distressed she was, tries to make things happier for her. She is cross and overcome by the summer heat and longs for an ice or lemonade. He seems to guess her silent wish and procures them for her. 'Arthur is so kind,' she writes, 'he guessed my wish and gratified it. An ice-cream, how delicious that is!' He even accompanied his mother to show her the best shops and helped her in her purchases for she did not know a word of English. But Vitalie, still disagreeable and cross, followed them at a short distance behind. He, seeing how bored and disgruntled she was at this expedition, suggested that they should—when the shopping was over—visit Kensington Gardens and he gave her a drink from one of the fountains. She describes it as 'simple et naïf' and in these words can be heard the echo of an ironic description by Rimbaud himself.

Another time, after she had been very disagreeable to her mother, Arthur coming in, guessed the tenseness of the atmosphere and he smiled at her, trying to make her laugh, then offered to take her to see the British Museum. One can imagine that in her mood she was not an enlivening companion for him, she was such a child moreover, only fifteen. It is interesting to note that she mentions that her brother showed her the relics of the Emperor Theodore of Abyssinia and says that this is what interested her most. There were tunics decorated with silver bells and real diamonds, shoes belonging to his queen, set with silver and precious stones; their coloured wooden spoons and bowls. This was Negus Theodore who was defeated at Magdala by the English in 1868 and then committed suicide; his relics were brought to the British Museum in 1874. It is interesting that Rimbaud, as early as this, should already be attracted by Abyssinia.

The reason why Madame Rimbaud and Vitalie were kept so long in London was that the mother wanted to see her son settled in a job before she left. Vitalie tells us that her mother wore her best clothes—her grey silk dress and her Chantilly lace mantle—so that she could go with him well dressed as proof of respectability. According to Vitalie her brother receives letters every day which offer him posts, but the offers never seem to come to anything. On 11 July he received a letter—probably from some agency since it contained the offer of three jobs. 'I'm glad for his sake and for ours,' wrote Vitalie, 'for the sooner he is fixed up, the sooner we can return to France. Although I think London wonderful, I'm bored.' But these hopes were again disappointed and on 16 July Arthur was still without a job. 'Nothing yet for Arthur,' she wrote that day. 'Oh! if only he could get fixed up. If he doesn't get anything it will be most unfortunate. Maman is so sad and so withdrawn and close.' On 18 July he put a fresh lot of advertisements in the papers and applied to another agency. With so many disappointments Vitalie was beginning to doubt the good faith of her brother, but she is ashamed of her petulance. Madame Rimbaud then says that she will allow one week more.

During that week Rimbaud became progressively gloomier and more irritable—he was no longer described by Vitalie as kind and smiling. At last, on 29 July, as he went out in the morning to work at the British Museum, he said that he would not come home for lunch. At ten o'clock, however, he returned saying that he had found a job and that he would be leaving to take it up the following day. His mother and sister spent the day shopping for themselves and for him. Finally he did not leave on 30th, as the laundry had not sent back his linen, but only on 31st. He left at half-past-four in the morning, and he seemed sadder than ever. His mother was in tears after his departure. Why was he so sad as he left, and why did his mother, who should have been pleased that he had, at last, found employment, weep so bitterly after he had gone, as she wrote letters? And where did he go so early in the morning?

All the biographers—presumably basing their statements on family testimony—say that he went to Scotland to teach in a school, and that he stayed there until Christmas. But this claim cannot be substantiated by evidence. He did not, in fact, go to a post in a school in Scotland, but to a coaching establishment at Reading, opened by a certain Frenchman called Camille Leclair, in July 1874, and there he remained until the end of the year, when he left England never to return.[5]

It has not been possible to discover anything concerning his activities in Reading, nor whether he kept up his intellectual pursuits, he certainly did not read at the Bodleian Library at Oxford.

It is impossible to be sure when he can have composed the remaining *Illuminations*, which have not yet been mentioned. V. P. Underwood makes out a good case for *Promontoire* having been inspired by a visit to Scarborough, but he is not so strong in the matter of date, for it could as easily have taken place in 1873 as 1874.[6] However, from its style it gives the impression of being a late poem, and, on these grounds, we are tempted to ascribe it to 1874. Our opinion is that no further poems were composed after the middle of 1875, when he began to study music—and probably none after he left England, and started his life of far-flung wandering early in 1875. But he certainly kept some interest in his literary works for he sought, that year, to publish his prose poems, and he asked Delahaye to return him the copy of *Une Saison en Enfer*, which he had given him in 1873, so that he could present it to a kind widow in Milan, who had given him hospitality when he had fallen ill there, and was without means, in the summer of 1875.

It would seem probable that he composed *Jeunesse* in England in 1874, as one of the sections is headed *Vingt Ans*, and he reached the age of twenty in October that year—he may, of course, have made himself out older than he was, as he had had the habit of doing when he was a child. It would not seem possible that the poems reflecting cynicism, pessimism and disillusionment with democracy, should have been written either at the time of his mystical inspiration, or at the moment when, after *Une Saison en Enfer*, he was marching towards a new modern world of humanity. In these further poems concerning modernity we find the deepest disillusionment with progress and democracy. It is a dreary picture of the modern world that he now paints, a dehydrated and sanitary world, which has much similarity with our planned mechanical world of to-day. It is indeed 'a brave new world'.

Je suis un éphémère et point trop mécontent citoyen d'une métropole crue moderne, parce que tout goût connu a été éludé dans les ameublements et l'extérieur des maisons aussi bien que dans le plan de la ville. Ici vous ne signaleriez les traces d'aucun monument de superstition. La morale et la langue sont réduites à leur plus simple expression, enfin! Ces millions de gens qui n'ont pas besoin de se connaître amènent si pareillement l'éducation, le métier et la vieillesse, que ce cours de vie doit être plusieurs fois moins long que ce qu'une statistique folle trouve pour les peuples du continent. Aussi comme de ma fenêtre je vois des spectres nouveaux roulant à travers l'épaisse et éternelle fumée de charbon—notre ombre des bois notre nuit d'été!—des Erinnyes nouvelles, devant mon cottage qui est ma patrie et tout mon cœur puisque tout ici ressemble à ceci,—la Mort sans pleurs, notre active fille et servante, un Amour désespéré et un joli Crime piaulant dans la boue de la rue.[7]

*Métropolitain* is another and more sordid vision of the town, of the poorer quarters. It is a view of what can be seen as the train passes through the city, and the traveller looks out at the scenes— at different levels—sometimes the houses and streets are above him, and sometimes he overlooks dreary little back gardens and old bald-headed men working at their vegetables; sometimes dreary rows of suburban houses, all the same.

Du détroit d'indigo auc mers d'Ossian, sur le sable rose et orange qu'a lavé le ciel vineux viennent de monter et de se croiser des boulevards de cristal habités incontinent par de jeunes familles pauvres qui s'alimentent chez les fruitiers. Rien de riche.—La Ville!
Du désert de bitume fuient droit en déroute avec les nappes de

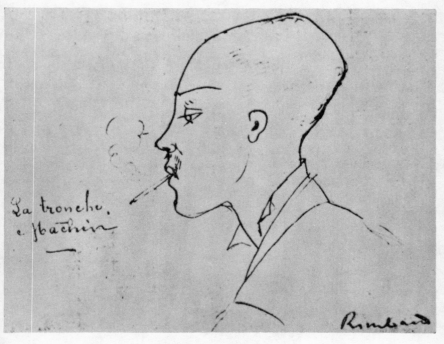

La tronche.
e ßachein

RIMBAUD IN 1875
*a drawing by Delahaye*

RIMBAUD IN 1877
*a drawing by Isabelle Rimbaud*

brume échelonnées en bandes affreuses au ciel qui se recourbe, se recule et descend formé de la plus sinistre fumée noire qui puisse faire l'Océan en deuil, les casques, les roues, les barques, les croupes.—La bataille!

Lève la tête; ce pont de bois arqué; les derniers potagers de Samarie; ces masques enluminés sous la lanterne fouettée par la nuit froide; l'ondine niaise à la robe bruyante, au bas de la rivière; les cranes lumineux dans les plants de pois,—et les autres fantasmagories,—la campagne.

Des routes bordées de grilles et de murs, contenant à peine leurs bosquets, et les atroces fleurs qu'on appellerait cœurs et sœurs, Damas damnant de longueur,—possessions de féeriques aristocraties ultra-Rhénanes, Japonaises, Guaranies, propres encore à recevoir la musique des anciens,—et il y a des auberges qui pour toujours n'ouvrent déjà plus;—il y a des princesses, et, si tu n'es pas trop accablé, l'étude des astres,—le ciel. [8]

James Thomson published his *City of Dreadful Night* in March 1874, and, in many ways, his view of the modern town corresponds with Rimbaud's—though his means of rendering it are very different. The two poets had much in common temperamentally, and both were, in the same way—as Verlaine would say—'Poètes Maudits'. It is interesting to imagine that they might have met in London during one of Rimbaud's visits, but no information exists of any such meeting.

Rimbaud's picture of the modern world is painted with cold objectivity and detachment, but, in *Démocratie*, he gives expression to the overflow of the disgust and nausea at all the picture implies. [1]

Le Drapeau va au paysage immonde, et notre patois étouffe le tambour.

Aux centre nous alimenterons la plus cynique prostitution. Nous massacrerons les révoltes logiques,

Aux pays poivrés et détrempés!—au service des plus monstrueuses exploitations industrielles ou militaires.

Au revoir ici, n'importe où. Conscrits du bon vouloir, nous aurons la philosophie féroce; ignorants pour la science, roués pour le confort; la crevaison pour le monde qui va. C'est la vraie marche. En avant, route!

Michelet had seen the history of the sixteenth and seventeenth centuries as a multi-coloured pageant, the parade 'of the marionettes', he calls it, the comedy of the 'dieux crevés' and the 'rois

pourris', in which they appeared without any disguise, and unashamed. He claimed that he was writing a new form of history,
very different from the conventional and prudish record which
had hitherto satisfied the public. He brings into his pageant the
whole succession of the Valois debauchees. Henry IV and Sully
gave a short respite, Henry was assassinated and Sully degraded,
then France fell once more into the hands of the marionettes—
the spendthrifts, the greedy, the avaricious, the fanatics. Rimbaud,
who likewise considered life as a sort of comedy of which he was
a spectator, has a similar pageant for the nineteenth century, only
his is a 'parade' of democracy, of sturdy rogues, exploiting their
former superiors and prostituting themselves for gain. In im-
provised costumes of nightmarish taste, they play tragedies of
scoundrels, or of demi-gods—it matters little which—and alter-
nate between sophistication and simple naïvety. It is indeed a
'parade sauvage' as he calls it in the *Illumination* entitled *Parade*,
and he feels nothing but disgust as he contemplates it.[10]

Vico and Michelet had both seen what deterioration might
come with democracy, since democracy in weakness, inevitably
leads to anarchy. If the community is to survive then something
must come to conquer this lawlessness. Vico said that a new ruler
would arise and order could be instituted under the leadership
of a strong man. But if this remedy did not prove efficacious,
then a more radical one would have to be tried. The country
would have to be subdued, become the slave of a stronger, more
virile and better country. This conquest could infuse new blood
into it, and it might yet rise to great heights, though it would no
longer be the same country. But if it could be saved neither by
a new ruler, nor by the conquest of a stronger and better country,
then Providence would have to apply a still more drastic remedy
to conquer this new form of barbarism which, with its scientific
and intellectual development, was a worse form of barbarism than
the first, since it was degenerate and deliberately cruel, while the
first had been merely natural and ignorant. Then destruction
must come from Heaven by act of God. Michelet exclaims.[11]

Qu'elle périsse donc cette société par la fureur des factions, par
l'acharnement désespéré des guerres civiles; que les cités redeviennent

forêts, que les forêts soient le repaire des hommes, et qu'à force de siècles, leur ingénieuse malice, leur subtilité perverse disparaissent sous la rouille de la barbarie.

When society had sunk back once more into primitiveness then it would be ready to be civilized again.

Rimbaud, following the pattern of nineteenth-century historians of mankind, opens his *Illuminations* with the Deluge. This does not mean that this poem is first in chronological order—in fact it seems a late poem—but only that, when he was establishing the plan of the collection, he placed it as the opening. After the Fall of Adam the earth gradually became a sorry place of vice, and God sent the Deluge to wipe away all traces of the decadence of the human race, and to give a few chosen men the chance of starting afresh, in a world washed clean of corruption and sin. For a short time everything was beautiful, everything was pure. 'Oh! les pierres précieuses qui se cachaient,—les fleurs qui regardaient déjà.'[12] Very soon, however, the same squalor and vice sprang up again, just as if the world had never been cleansed. The same old towns with their old sordidness; their vulgar boulevards and their monstrous hotels; the same old errors. The world was ripe for a new Deluge which should sweep away and wipe out everything as we know it now. One by one, since the first Flood subsided, all the magic flowers and precious stones have hidden themselves away, and the Witch will no longer tell us all the things which we do not know- and which she alone knows. 'Sourds, étang;—écume, roule sur le pont et par-dessus les bois; draps noirs et orgues, éclairs et tonnerre, montez et roulez;—eaux et tristesses, montez et relevez les Déluges.'[12]

Rimbaud had now a hatred of the man-made world and the so-called civilization in which we are called to live. He saw the same sordid things springing up everywhere, wherever the mail-train set him down. And, just as Baudelaire had seen in every country where his ship reached port, 'le spectacle ennuyeux de l'immortel péché',[13] he saw 'la magie bourgeoise', and he felt that this was something beyond his powers of endurance.[14] Was it to reach this state that he had sacrificed all his dreams and ambitions. Once he had thought that he possessed 'la clef de l'amour', that he was an 'inventeur bien autrement méritant que tous ceux qui m'ont précédé'.[15] But he had nothing left now but his 'atroce scepticisme'. He did not believe any longer in humanity or democracy, or in the possibility of saving or improving the world. All that was left to him was to find some new path, some new idea, though this too might prove only a delusion in the end. 'Et comme ce scepticisme ne peut désormais être mis en œuvre, et que, d'ailleurs, je suis dévoué à un trouble nouveau,—j'attends de devenir un très méchant fou.'[16]

This is the final liquidation of his poetic theories, of his democratic beliefs; the final bankrupt sale, the bargain-basement clearance sale, of all his previous ideas.[17]

A vendre ce que les Juifs n'ont pas vendu, ce que noblesse ni crime n'ont goûté, ce qu'ignore l'amour maudit et la probité infernale des masses! ce que le temps et la science n'ont pas à reconnaître.

Les Voix reconstituées; l'éveil fraternel de toutes les énergies chorales et orchestrales et leurs applications instantanées; l'occasion, unique, de dégager nos sens!

A vendre les Corps sans prix, hors de toute descendance! Les richesses jaillissant à chaque démarche. Solde de diamants sans contrôle.

A Vendre l'anarchie pour les masses; la satisfaction irrépressible pour les amateurs supérieurs; la mort atroce pour les fidèles et les amants!

A vendre les habitations et migrations, sports, féeriques et conforts parfaits et le bruit, le mouvement et l'avenir qu'ils font.

The only hope might perhaps lie with the primitive people who had no need of Deluge, who had not yet been corrupted. It will be noticed that, in the poem generally called *Vertige*, in which he calls down destruction on all the countries of the world, and on all the continents, he omits Africa from his general condemnation.

Quinet had written of the descent into Limbo of Merlin to visit the souls of those as yet unborn, and he describes the procession of negro souls before the magician.[18] After the hosts of the pale larvae have gone by, then a procession of black passes, slow and sad, as if weighted down with chains. These negro souls go by and they do, what none of the other larvae had done, they fall at Merlin's feet and cry to him: 'Save us from this burden which is beyond our powers of bearing.'

Rimbaud, in *Une Saison en Enfer*, had expressed the desire to go to the kingdom of Ham, the founders of the negro race, and, in *Vertige*, he prays for destruction to come which will bring in a new era to mankind. He cries:[19]

Qu'est-ce pour nous, mon cœur, que les nappes de sang
Et de braise, et mille meurtres, et les longs cris
De rage, sanglots de tout enfer renversant
Tout ordre, et l'Aquilon encor sur les débris;

Et toute vengeance?—Rien! . . Mais si, toute encore,
Nous la voulons! Industriels, princes, sénats:
Périssez! Puissance, justice, histoire: à bas!
Ça nous est dû. Le sang! le sang! la flamme d'or!

Tout à la guerre, à la vengeance, à la terreur.
Mon esprit! tournons dans la morsure: Ah! passez,
Républiques de ce monde! Des empereurs,
Des régiments, des colons, des peuples: assez!

Europe, Asie, Amérique, disparaissez.
Notre marche vengeresse a tout occupé,
Cités et campagnes!—Nous serons écrasés!
Les volcans sauteront! Et l'Océan frappé. . .

Oh! mes amis!—Mon cœur, c'est sûr, ils sont des frères:
Noirs inconnus, si nous allions! Allons! allons!
O malheur! je me sens frémir, la vieille terre,
Sur moi de plus en plus à vous! la terre fond.

Then Rimbaud, wishing to go out East, put an advertisement in *The Times* on 9 November 1874.

A Parisian (20) of high literary and linguistic attainments, excellent conversation, will be glad to accompany a Gentleman (Artist preferred) or a family wishing to travel in southern or eastern countries. Good references. A.R. No. 165, King's Road, Reading.

After Verlaine's death the rough draft of this advertisement, somewhat differently worded, was discovered amongst his papers. In the catalogue of the Magg's exhibition of autographs in Paris in 1937, this rough draft was shown with the caption, 'Annonce autographe au crayon de la main de Rimbaud corrigée par Verlaine.' Since the advertisement was alleged to have been corrected by Verlaine, and since it was discovered amongst his papers, it was natural to believe that it had been drawn up during the period when he and Rimbaud were together in England, some time between September 1872 and July 1873. How the correct advertisement was finally brought to light, and how this led to the discovery that Rimbaud had taught at the coaching establishment in Reading, is told elsewhere.[20] But how the rough draft of this advertisement, which appeared in England while Verlaine was in prison in Belgium, fell into the hands of the latter remains a mystery. It is possible that the scrap of paper, with the rough draft, may have been amongst the manuscripts of *Illuminations* when they came into Verlaine's hands—however this may have happened. Or perhaps he may have been given it by Germain Nouveau when they met. At all events it is impossible that it was, as the catalogue declares, corrected by Verlaine. It is true that Verlaine's writing has frequently been taken for that of Rimbaud—even Isabelle Rimbaud was sometimes mistaken.

The advertisement, however, did not bear any fruit, and Rimbaud was home in Charleville for Christmas 1874. He never went back to England.

CHAPTER XII

# L'HOMME AUX SEMELLES DE VENT

FOR the next five years Rimbaud became a wanderer over the face of Europe, venturing even as far as Cairo, Alexandria and Java. He was as restless as the English occultist whose name is unknown, but who called himself 'The Wanderer on the face of the earth', and who could strike roots nowhere. Never did

Rimbaud seem—to those who did not know his inner thoughts—more unstable as he moved restlessly from country to country on the continent. He was training to become Michelet's man of action of the future, preparing to take his part in the new world which was appearing on the horizon, not forgetting that progress must be based on Charity. Michelet wrote, in his Introduction to his *Histoire de France*,[1] that passive resignation, so useful to tyrants, was being replaced by active love which wanted to establish here below on earth God's justice, which acts, fights and accomplishes a miracle very different from that in the Gospels. It is a new, a superior love, love in action. He symbolized this by Joan of Arc who felt 'la pitié qui est au royaume de France', and this innocent heroine did more, he claimed, than merely to deliver France, she liberated the future, and gave birth to a new kind of hero, the contrary of the passive hero of the Christian ideal, the modern hero who is the hero in action. Now Rimbaud felt that all time which he spent inactively was time wasted. That is what gave the impression of restlessness. 'Why must so much precious time be lost' he said to Delahaye.[2] Verlaine called him 'l'homme aux semelles de vent'. and, in a poem written somewhat later, he described the 'wanderlust' of his friend.[3]

> La malédiction de n'être jamais las
> Suit tes pas sur le monde où l'horizon t'attire. . .
> Maintenant il te faut passer devant les portes
> Hâtant le pas de peur qu'on ne lache les chiens,
> Et si tu n'entends pas rire, c'est encor bien. . .
> Malheureux! toi Français, toi Chrétien, quel dommage!
> Mais tu vas, la pensée obscure de l'image
> D'un bonheur qu'il te faut immédiat, étant
> Athée—avec la foule—et jaloux de l'instant.

Verlaine did not appreciate what it was that was impelling Rimbaud forward. He thought that he was walking ceaselessly in order to stifle in his soul his longing for higher things. He describes him as destroying the powers of his mind, and becoming incapable of intellectual effort. All that was left of his former self, according to Verlaine, was the pride which made him unconscious of degradation. He ended his poem with a prayer on behalf of his former friend, 'Dieu des Humbles, sauvez cet enfant de la colère!'

After his Christmas rest at Charleville the first state of Rimbaud's wandering in search of a new language took him to Germany in January 1875. He went to Stuttgart as a paying-guest to a family called Wagner. The name, which is a common one in Germany, led Isabelle to relate later a fantastic story of her brother's having gone to Stuttgart for the Wagner season. He worked diligently, acquiring a thorough knowledge of the language and hoped to have finished his studies by the spring. He was very gifted for languages and the facility which had been evident, when he was a small boy, in Latin, he showed now in every language he chose to learn. We know that he was also spending long hours in the library—perhaps he was continuing his study of occult philosophy, for Germany was one of the countries richest in hermetic literature. His mother, careful as ever, would not send him sufficient money and, to supplement his allowance, he was obliged to take menial work. In Germany, as in England, he did not find it an easy job to earn his living.

That year, in January, Verlaine was released from prison—his sentence being reduced on account of his good conduct. On leaving prison he remained, at first, for a time, with his mother in the country to rest and to grow acclimatized to ordinary life. In February he went to Paris, hoping, foolishly, for a reconciliation with his wife who had obtained her separation from him the previous year, when he was in prison. He was not permitted to see either her or the child. Deeply depressed by this disappointment, he was suddenly seized with the conviction that he had a vocation, and, with the intention of becoming a monk, he went for a probationary period as a novice to the Trappist monastery at Chimay. There the superior soon made it clear to him that his was not a genuine vocation, and that the life of a monk was not for him. He departed again after a few weeks. Now completely without plans for his future, he thought again of Rimbaud, and of picking up once more the broken threads of his relationship with him. He extracted his address in Germany from Delahaye, and wrote him an edifying and highly moral letter which he said that he had meditated upon at great length during his years in prison. This letter, in which he begged Rimbaud to become reconverted to Catholicism, ended with the words, 'Let us love one another in Jesus Christ.'

Rimbaud, apparently, received the letter with blasphemous language, but agreed, nevertheless, that Verlaine might visit him. 'The other day' wrote Rimbaud,[4] 'Verlaine arrived in Stuttgart, with a rosary in his paws, but three hours later he denied God, and made the ninety-six wounds of our Blessed Lord bleed again'. The attempt at conversion failed lamentably. It must have been a sad and unedifying spectacle, the reunion of the two 'compagnons d'enfer'. It was a repetition of the last months of their life in London in 1873. They trekked from bar to bar, Rimbaud becoming, with intoxication, violent and blasphemous, and Verlaine pious and sentimental. Finally they went for a walk on the banks of the Neckar, where a violent quarrel took place. It is possible to imagine that Verlaine—who never, for the rest of his life and in the midst of his other and various adventures, forgot his first passion for Rimbaud—made advances to him which he repulsed. Then Verlaine, excited by the now unwonted alcohol, attacked Rimbaud and struck him.

Rimbaud was also in an advanced state of intoxication, he was the stronger and the tougher of the two, he hit back and ran away, leaving him unconscious on the ground, where, on the banks of the river, he was found the following morning by some peasants going to their work. They picked him up and bore him in their cart to the town.

Verlaine, now sobered and repentant, bewailed, with bitter tears, his fall from grace, and the way in which Satan, in the shape of Rimbaud, had so easily tempted him, and taken possession of him again. He remained two further days in Stuttgart, then, on the advice of Rimbaud, returned to Paris, with the intention of going over to England to take up a post as a teacher of French in a Grammar School. This is generally supposed to be the last time that Verlaine and Rimbaud ever met.

By the summer of 1875, Rimbaud had grown tired of Germany and he felt that he knew the language sufficiently well to leave, that it was now time to add Italian to his stock. He was also vaguely planning to join a man whom he knew, at Paros, the owner of a soap factory. Since his mother would not give him the money for his trip, he sold his trunk and all his belongings, and set out from Germany. By the time he had reached Altdorf his money had given out, and he was obliged to cross the Alps on foot. He arrived in Italy in an exhausted state, and almost starving, but it is said that, in Milan, a charitable widow, recognizing in him a cultivated and educated man, gave him shelter for some days.[5] It was for her that he asked Delahaye to return him the copy of *Une Saison en Enfer*, which he had given him two years before, so that he could present it to his hostess, as evidence of his competence as a writer. This means that he must, therefore, have discussed literature with her and what he had done himself.

Most biographers give the impression that Rimbaud wandered from country to country like a vagabond, and looking like an inveterate tramp. This is far from being the truth. There is a drawing of him by Verlaine, at this time, which shows him looking almost like a dandy, elegantly dressed in a smart suit, with a top-hat—probably the London hat—and the caption says: 'Les voyages forment la jeunesse! M. . . à la Daromphe!'—one of his irreverent names for his mother—'Je fous le camp à Wien.' Delahaye says that he had had visiting-cards engraved while he was in Germany—'gravées sur du joli bristol'—and that he sent him one from Milan, with his address on it.

After leaving the kindly *signora* Rimbaud set out, on foot, for Brindisi where he was to take the boat for Paros. It was then midsummer and, being unused to southern heat, he was struck down on the road by sunstroke. He was carried in a serious condition to hospital, and, when he was released, he was repatriated to Marseilles, through the offices of the French Consul.

On arriving in the French port he felt restored and, not wishing to return home, he lived for some weeks on the proceeds of odd jobs which he picked up in the *Vieux Port*; loading and unloading ships; clearing away rubble; in fact doing anything which might bring in a couple of francs. Then one evening, in a bar, he was offered drinks by a foreigner who seemed to have unlimited money to spend. He was an officer recruiting volunteers to fight in Spain for the Carlists, and he managed to enrol Rimbaud. But he, as soon as he received his bonus, bolted for Paris. It is only fair to add that Isabelle Rimbaud denies that this event ever took place.[6] She states categorically that her brother was with the family in Paris in June, July and August 1875 and that when she, her sister and mother went back to Charleville he had just taken up a post as tutor at Maisons-Alfort near Paris. She said that he liked to 'mystifier' his friends by telling them, with an air of great seriousness, the most horrifying and unbelievable stories about himself, and then afterwards to make fun of them because they had been so gullible.[7] Certainly he was in Paris in August for Germain Nouveau, writing to Verlaine, said that he had seen him with Mercier, Cabaner and Forain, who were—according to Nouveau—becoming disgusted with his lack of discipline and his habits of intoxication.[8] But Nouveau's testimony is always subject to caution.

By the end of August his money was exhausted and he returned to Charleville on foot. The family no longer lived in the pleasant apartment on the Quai de la Madeleine, but in a depressing house in the narrow little Rue Saint-Barthélemy. The elder daughter Vitalie, then seventeen, who had never been strong, was desperately ill, and the home atmosphere was very gloomy.

The mother's temper had of late become very much soured through anxiety for her daughter's state of health and disappointment in her sons. Frederick was completely hopeless and seemed determined to sink into a class lower than the one in which he had been born. In 1872, to her great shame, he had sold papers in the streets of Charleville where the family was well known, and now he had no more lofty ambition than to become a carter. This she could have borne with resignation, had Arthur fulfilled his promise and it was against him she nourished most bitterness; on him she had centred all her hopes and she could not now forgive him the squandering of his talents, and his total disregard for his future—or so it seemed to her. When he was at home she grudgingly allowed him board and lodging, but she would not give him any pocket-money.

Rimbaud, like so many whose minds are occupied with cosmic visions, had no inhibitions where money was concerned, and he saw no reason why he should not 'sponge' on his friends when he was short of cash for drinks or smokes. Delahaye, his oldest friend, now a careful and rather mean 'fonctionnaire', used to accuse him, in letters to Verlaine, of practising petty frauds to extract from the few remaining friends he still possessed, small sums of ready money. He used to call him 'l'œstre' or the gadfly.[9] But it seems that it was on Verlaine that he hoped most to sponge. He remembered his former weakness and his recklessness where money was concerned; he had moreover noticed that he seemed loth to lose his friendship, that he clung to it as to one of the beautiful things in his sordid and shipwrecked life, and he hoped that he would be willing to pay for the luxury of this sentiment. He tried to borrow money from him for what he considered a vital and legitimate cause, for preparing himself for high office in the new world, for the study of the piano and music. But Verlaine did not believe his pretext. If we are to credit the letter which Verlaine wrote to Delahaye in October 1875, there was some half-hearted attempt at blackmail. But it is very probable that Verlaine misunderstood Rimbaud's letter which he said was written in 'charabia'. Verlaine, however, except for his one lapse at Stuttgart, had not yet begun to fall from grace; he was still upheld by religion and the habit of frequent confession, which he had formed in prison, and he did not think that he had anything now to fear from Rimbaud. Ever since his visit to Germany he had been reflecting on the past and on their friendship, and he had come to the conclusion that Rimbaud had exercised a pernicious influence on him. He was now of the opinion that, in the past, he had been too generous and that it was time to show him that he could no longer be imposed upon. There is very little evidence of affection towards Rimbaud in the letter which he wrote Delahaye, but signs only of deep-rooted grudge and resentment—and signs also that he is not as free from his influence as he pretends. What can one expect, he said, from a man who imagines that insolence is strength and that swindling is clever—except that he will become, very soon, a dirty cad who will be a very nasty customer by the time he is thirty? He added that Rimbaud had verily killed the goose that lays the golden eggs, but that he was, nevertheless, ready to offer him his affection and his friendship, 'prêt chrétiennement, bien entendu,' at the first signs of change of heart. He asked Delahaye to make these sentiments known to Rimbaud. This Delahaye did with alacrity, nothing loth to stir up mischief between the two friends, and he reported to Verlaine the remarks which he said Rimbaud had made about him. Delahaye, whose own relations with Verlaine would appear to have been very questionable, did not play a very elevated part between the two former friends. He said in a letter to Verlaine that if Rimbaud persisted in his present mode of life, he would undoubtedly end up in a lunatic asylum.[10]

When Rimbaud heard of Verlaine's offer of Christian friendship he thanked Delahaye for the kind information and said, 'I make no comment on the latest insolence—"grossièretés"—of Loyala—Verlaine—for I have no energy to spare at the moment in that direction. Je n'ai plus d'activité à me donner de ce côté là à présent.'[11] Carré, when publishing this letter of Rimbaud's, did not take into account Verlaine's previous letter to him, and he says that Rimbaud intended by the 'grossièretés' to refer to Verlaine's collection of poems called *Sagesse*, and that his answer meant that he had, for the time being, no thoughts for literature. Yet the 'grossièretés' are far more likely to be the information which Verlaine requested Delahaye to convey to Rimbaud, and his hope that his friend would now turn his thoughts to religion, to Catholicism. Verlaine's offer of a Christian friendship was not of a nature to appeal to Rimbaud in this drifting period of his life, and he certainly had no energy to spare for Christianity. Besides Rimbaud's thoughts were not so far, in 1875, from literature as Carré's note would lead us to expect, witness his desire to have his poems published, and his wish to give a sample of his work to the kindly widow in Italy. This does not mean that he was still writing—that is most unlikely. The poem *Poison Perdu*, alleged to have been composed by him at this time, seems, when the evidence has been sifted, not to be by him, but possibly

333

by Germain Nouveau.[12] There were, later, many pastiches of his more obscene verse, and the doggerel, *Le Rêve*, enclosed in a letter to Delahaye, is obviously only intended as a joke.[13] There is little doubt that by 1875 he had ceased to write. Delahaye, in a letter to Verlaine at this time says: 'Verses of his? His inspiration has long since run dry.'[14]

Rimbaud did not answer Verlaine's appeal for Christian friendship and Verlaine, who could never really leave him alone, wrote to him from London in December.[15]

I did not write to you because I was waiting for a satisfactory letter from you. As I received nothing, I answered nothing. But to-day I break my long silence to repeat what I said to you two months ago.

I am still the same. Strictly pious, because it is the only intelligent and good thing to be. The Church has fashioned modern civilization, science and literature; she has also made France what she is, and France is now dying because she has broken with her. That is quite clear! And the Church also forms men. I'm astonished that you especially, do not realize that, for it's striking. I've had ample time, during the last eighteen months to ponder on all these things and I assure you that I'm clinging to all this as to the only plank. The last seven months spent amongst Protestants has only confirmed me in this conviction.

I'm resigned for the excellent reason that I see myself as justly punished and humiliated, and the severer the lesson the greater the grace in accepting it. You can't think that this is a pose or a pretence on my part. And so I'm still the same towards you. The same affection (somewhat modified) for you. It would give me much pleasure to see you enlightened. It's a source of great sorrow to me to see you persisting in such idiotic ways, you so intelligent and so ready for conversion —although this may strike you as strange—you have only to notice your disgust of everything, which indeed is fully justified, though it's unconscious of its true cause.

As for the question of money. You can't seriously fail to recognize that I'm generous. It's one of my few qualities—or one of my many vices—whichever you prefer. But, on account of the necessity of building up again my little capital which was seriously eaten into by our absurd and shameful life three years ago, and also taking into consideration my son, and finally on account of my new and firm principles, you must understand that I can't possibly keep you. Where indeed would the money go? To pubs and prostitutes! And as for piano lessons? What a question! Wouldn't your mother agree to pay for them if you really need them? Last April you wrote such nasty and self-revealing letters, so full of the vilest intentions, that I can't now risk giving you my address. Although all your plans to harm me would be vain, I tell you in advance, and besides I warn you that these would be answered legally, with evidence. But I put aside all these odious thoughts, and I'm convinced, in any case, that this is only a passing whim of yours, a brain storm that a little calm reflection will soon clear away. However, prudence is mother of security and you will have my address only when I'm sure of you. That is why I begged Delahaye not to give it to you, and I asked him to be kind enough to forward all your letters.

Come! Show a little kindness, consideration and affection for some-one who will always remain your, PAUL VERLAINE.

P.S. Later I'll explain to you, via Delahaye, the life I would like to see you lead—religion apart, although this is my chief advice—as soon as you've answered properly.

Rimbaud did not sense the genuine affection in the letter; he felt only the smug piety, the insulting caution and the condes-cension. His satisfactory answer was never written and the friends never met again.

All that winter Rimbaud remained at Charleville and seemed undecided what to do next. He did not, however, remain idle, but appears to have been employed intellectually, learning Arabic, Hindustani and Russian. His studies were somewhat hampered through lack of means and the only Russian book he possessed was a Russian-Greek dictionary, this he cut into strips to fill his pockets and he used to learn them from memory as he walked through the woods round Charleville.[16] For a time also he toyed with the idea of finally sitting for his *baccalauréat*. Delahaye was now a schoolmaster at the Collège de Notre-Dame at Réthel—the post which Verlaine was later to fill—and Rimbaud wrote to him for advice as to how he should proceed to work for the *baccalauréat* in science, what books he should read, what teaching he should procure and what standard of achievement would be expected of him.[17] From a stray remark in a letter from Verlaine to Delahaye,[18] it would seem as if he had considered the possi-bility of entering L'École Polytechnique; this would explain why he wished to prepare the examination in science. Verlaine who used, sneeringly, to call him at this time the 'philomathe', expressed the utmost scorn of this scheme. 'Who is the fool, more fool than a dog, who is advising the École Polytechnique?' he said.[18] Possibly then Delahaye gave Rimbaud no encouragement, for we hear no more of the project. This was unwise since he might, with training and qualifications, have made a sound engineer and, technically equipped, he would have found it easier later to find congenial employment abroad.

It is at this time that one of the strangest of Rimbaud's vagaries occurred, his determination to learn music, and to play the piano. The story is authenticated in two sources, and is not merely one of the wild rumours that were always current about him. We know that he tried to borrow money from Verlaine for this purpose, although the latter thought that it was only a pretext to obtain a loan. One of the sources of information was Charles Lefèvre, son of the landlord, who was taking German lessons from him at this time.[19] and he vouches for the truth of the story. He also relates—though it is difficult to credit such behaviour in a man of twenty-one—that, his mother having refused to hire a piano, Rimbaud cut out a keyboard on the dining-room table, and that on this he used to practise scales and exercises by the hour, as he corrected his pupil's translations. To prevent the same fate overtaking the rest of her furniture his mother finally consented to hire an instrument, and it is said that he soon became a proficient pianist, if the volume of sound which issued from the flat could be taken as evidence. There is a drawing by Verlaine which depicts Rimbaud at the piano, playing with great vigour, the sweat pouring from his forehead, and the caption says: 'La musique adoucit les mœurs.'

Our second source of information is a certain Louis Létrange who, at this time, lived in the same house as the Rimbaud family.[20] He was the conductor of a chorale society, also the choir master at the church of Notre-Dame at Charleville, and he used to give piano and organ lessons. Rimbaud went to him for help and advice in his musical studies, borrowing from him Mademoiselle Charpentier's manual of pianoforte exercises, and discussing with him 'des sonorités nouvelles'—this would seem to indicate that he had not yet abandoned all interest in literature and art. Létrange as well as Lefèvre saw the piano cut out on the table. It was only in December 1875 that Madame Rimbaud finally consented to hire the piano, and, up to that, he had practised for months on the 'silent instrument'.

Delahaye alleges,[21] that, although Rimbaud had not gone very far in actual performance on the piano, he had acquired a considerable amount of theoretic knowledge. This was, as a man of letters, far more important than mere proficiency as a performer. He was probably learning the piano as part of his acquisition of a knowledge of music. Music is closely linked with mathematics and, for the Greeks, mathematics comprised music as well as astronomy. They believed that music was a universal language which could be understood by all peoples and that its study—like that of mathematics—prepared for the study of philosophy. Pythagoras, who was a famous magician, as well as a mathematician, based much of his system and calculations on the musical scale. By this he measured the distance which separates the fixed stars from the earth, and filled in the intervals with the Moon, Mercury, Venus and other moving bodies. All these were placed in respect of one another at distances equal to the tones and semitones of the musical scale. It is from this that he deduced the harmony of the world and the spheres, and the 'music of the spheres' was not with him merely a figure of speech. The relationship between the bodies depends on their distance from the centre, the slower and nearer bodies giving forth deeper notes; and the swifter, a higher note; the combination of the whole yielded the cosmic octave. The reason why, according to him, we do not hear this music is that our ears are deafened by the louder noises around us, but if we could obtain perfect silence then we should become conscious of it—unfortunately we are not usually in the position to contrast it with silence. It is probable that Rimbaud was learning music as a part of mathematics, since mathematics were to be the most important branch of learning in the new world.

This seems, however, to be the last occasion on which Rimbaud showed any interest in artistic or literary topics.

The ailing Vitalie died on 18 December 1875, and Madame Rimbaud locked herself more tightly into her rigid austerity. The wound in her heart, of which she had written to Verlaine two and a half years previously, had spread now so widely as to leave little of her heart intact and whole.

When the winter was over and spring had come, Rimbaud set off once more on his wanderings. This time his intention was to reach Russia and it had been with this journey in view that he had been learning the language all the winter. However, he did not reach any further than Vienna. On arrival in that city he took a carriage and, most ill-advisedly, struck up a friendship with the driver, who proved a scoundrel who robbed him of all his money and his luggage. To obtain food he was obliged to beg in the streets. He was then arrested for vagrancy and led to the frontier as an undesirable alien; there he was handed into the custody of the German police, and in this way, was finally deposited, without a penny in his pocket, in French territory on the borders of Alsace. From there he tramped on foot to Charleville. He had by this time, says Delahaye,[22] grown enormously strong and tough, and in his whole appearance, he had the hardened look of the habitual tramp.

His long legs calmly covered the ground in enormous strides, like a horse; he held himself well, but he had a look of resigned defiance, the look of a man ready for anything, without anger and without fear.

He soon found the family atmosphere intolerable and he stayed at home only a short time. It was still spring and he was always on the road until autumn, coming home to roost in the winter like a bird. 'Je redoute l'hiver,' he had said in *Une Saison en Enfer*, 'parce que c'est la saison du comfort.'[23] (*sic*)

His idea was now to find some means of reaching the East and he toyed with a plan, for a short time, of becoming a priest in order to travel as a missionary.[24] But he abandoned this project and merely made his way to Holland where he enlisted in the Dutch army to go to Java. He signed on for a term of six years and was given a bonus of twelve pounds. He sailed on 10 June 1876, on board the *Prince of Orange*,[25] and the journey took six weeks. As the boat sailed down the Red Sea he saw the Sudan, the Arab coast and the whole stretch of the Somali coast which he was later to know as well as he knew his own home town. At the time all was quiet on the western shore of the Red Sea and there were, as yet, no signs of European activity. The boat docked at Batavia on 23 July. Rimbaud was attached to the first battalion of infantry, but he soon grew weary of the rigours of army routine. For six years now he had done little else but follow his own inclinations, and he had left school at fifteen before he had had time to form habits of discipline. From his barracks he saw all around him wonderful countries waiting to be explored and he deserted on the first opportunity, three weeks after his arrival. We know that he deserted on 15 August but we do not know whether he deserted from Batavia or Salatiga. There were many deserters at that time from the Dutch Colonial Army—Europeans who had enlisted merely to escape from Europe.

After his desertion, according to the first biographers, he wandered through the jungle for weeks, even months, and eventually returned to England as an able-bodied seaman on board a British sailing ship freighting sugar. But whatever happened he cannot have wandered very long nor very far in the jungle since he was back in Charleville on 31 December 1876 and the journey, by sailing-ship round the Cape, took a minimum of three or four months. According to Delahaye, he wandered with delight through the island, until finally he reached a port where a British sailing-ship carrying sugar signed him on as a seaman. This ship, after encountering a fierce storm as it sailed round the Cape, brought him to Liverpool whence he returned to France. The story told by Houin and Bourguignon is similar except that the ship, after having stopped at Liverpool, sailed along the coast of Britain, along Scandinavian, Danish, Dutch and Belgian coasts, the coast of France, until it reached Bordeaux whence Rimbaud returned by train to Charleville. According to Paterne Berrichon, Rimbaud proceeded straight from Liverpool to Dieppe, thence home.

None of these accounts can be absolutely accurate, and Delahaye's does not at all tally with what he said in the letter to his friend Millot, published by De Graaf,[26] which was written on 28 January 1877 and so contemporaneous with the events described. In this he said that Rimbaud had told him that he had returned on a ship which had put in at Saint Helena, the Azores, Queenstown in Ireland, Liverpool, and finally landed him at Le Havre. From there he had gone to Paris, where he spent a few days before returning to Charleville, and, according to Delahaye, he had remained in hiding there from 9 to 31 December, when he rejoined his family.

Before the publication of this letter an attempt was made by the present author to discover on what ship Rimbaud might have returned from Java. After arduous research it was established that, of the twenty-four ships which left Java between 15 August and 31 December 1876, only fifteen arrived in England or France before January 1877.

*The Register General of Shipping and Seamen*, which used to be in London, preserved the papers and documents concerning all British ships in its archives. The records are complete and contain a copy of the contract of each individual member of every crew, his nationality, his wages, a report on his state of health and conduct during the voyage; the name of the port at which he joined the ship and of that at which he left it. The papers of all the crews of seven of the possible ships were investigated—the other eight not being British their papers were not in the Register. The name of Rimbaud does not figure in any of these contracts, or on any of the lists of seamen, or in any of the reports. A specimen of his writing was compared with the signatures in the contracts, in case he had joined under an assumed name, but no writing remotely resembling his was found. It follows therefore that he cannot have returned to Europe from the Dutch East Indies as a seamen on board a British ship.[27] He may well, of course, have returned as a passenger—or he might have returned as a passenger or seaman on board a ship not flying the British flag. Yet the friends and early biographers have always asserted that it was as a seaman and on board a British sailing ship carrying a cargo of sugar, that he came back to France.

Another fact emerges from these investigations, that no British ship, coming from Java, arrived at Liverpool in the period under review. One ship *La Léonie*, coming from the East Indies, did put in at Liverpool some time before 23 December, but it was not a British ship and it has not been possible to discover anything further about it.

The ship most likely to have brought Rimbaud back to Europe is a British ship, *The Wandering Chief*—a name worthy of association with *L'Homme aux Semelles de Vent*. It was carrying a cargo of sugar, and it left Samarang on 30 August. At that time there were several ports of call in Java and Rimbaud might have joined the ship at any of them. *The Wandering Chief* called at Saint Helena, and encountered a violent storm as it rounded the Cape, during which it lost its mast and almost foundered. All these details correspond with Isabelle's account of her brother's journey. It arrived at Le Havre on 17 December and this would have permitted him to spend a few days in Paris and to be home in Charleville well before New Year's Eve. He was not employed on board as a seaman, but he might have returned on it at his own expense, and he was quite capable of inventing a romantic story of his exploits. Germain Nouveau describes him, on his way through Paris, as dressed in a British sailor's uniform, which he said he had been given by the crew because his own clothes were in rags after his trek through the jungle—it may however, have been because he was still in his Dutch soldier's uniform, which it was not safe for him to wear since he was a deserter. The fact of his being dressed as a British sailor may have given rise to the rumour that he had been a seaman on board a British ship. Henceforth Germain Nouveau always called him 'Rimbaud the Sailor' on the analogy of 'Sinbad the Sailor' from the *Arabian Nights*.[28]

Most of the particulars concerning *The Wandering Chief* tally also with those of Delahaye's letter to Millot—except in the matter of the date of arrival in France. If Rimbaud had landed at Le Havre only on 17 December, he could not possibly have been at Charleville—as Delahaye asserts—by 9 December. But was he really there by that date? There is no proof of it, and no one seems to have seen him. Delahaye did not meet him personally until after the New Year—his letter to Millot is dated 28 January—and he may well have been mistaken in the matter of the actual date. He may also perhaps have written '9th.' instead of '19th.' by mistake; or De Graaf may have read it incorrectly for he had difficulty in deciphering the letter. Three weeks is a very long time for Rimbaud to have remained incognito in his native town, without anyone being aware of his presence, for the first that is heard of him was on New Year's Eve when he reached home.

De Graaf suggests that he returned on a ship called *The City of Exeter*,[26] which left Samarang on 17 September, but he gives no further particulars and brings no arguments in support of his theory.

The records of the *General Register and Records of Shipping and Seamen*, preserved in Cardiff, contain all the details of the journey of *The City of Exeter*.[28] It was a steam ship and not as ailing vessel, and there is no information regarding its cargo. The ship set out with a crew of twenty-four, however, with subsequent substitutions, the agreement bears seventy names, but it did not sign on any crew between Hongkong and Malta. It went straight from Samarang to Malta, thence to Marseilles where it arrived on 15 November 1876. None of these circumstances agree with the accounts of either the family or the early biographers, nor with the facts related by Delahaye in his letter to Millot at the time. The vessel did not go near Queenstown or Liverpool, and these places would hardly have been invented by Rimbaud or Delahaye. All the available evidence seems to disprove the theory that it was *The City of Exeter* on which Rimbaud returned from Java, and *The Wandering Chief* still remains the most likely.

On reaching Le Havre, Rimbaud seems to have gone to Paris for a few days, or to have passed through the capital on his way to the north. Then he returned to Charleville for his annual winter rest. He looked now far older than his twenty-two years, with his thick fair beard and his skin tanned the colour of old leather. His mother now accepted his vagaries as her mortal cross, with stoic and Christian resignation, but not with amiability. She was more silent and dour than ever, and, in the home, scarcely a word was exchanged between the various members of the family.

Spring saw Rimbaud on the road once more. This time he went to Hamburg looking for employment on a ship sailing east. He could not find what he wanted and—according to the early biographers—accepted the post of interpreter-manager in the Loisset circus, now on its way for a tour of the northern capitals. According to the story, this Loisset had two beautiful daughters; one of them eventually married a Russian prince, and the other died as the result of an accident during her equestrian turn.[29] But even their charms were not sufficient to compensate Rimbaud for the restrictions of circus life and the boredom of the shows that were always the same. He found, moreover, that he could not endure the cold of the northern capitals, he who had always gone south or east in search of the sun. Finally, being unable to find work which would take him home, he is said to have got himself repatriated through the services of the French Consul at Stockholm at the expense of the State. Isabelle Rimbaud declared[30] later, that she had never heard of this circus and that, when he was in Sweden, he had worked in a saw-mill. And investigations, by the present author, at the French Consulate at Stockholm, proved that he was never repatriated from Sweden at the expense of France.[31]

It is, however, very likely that he did in fact visit Scandinavia for a caricature by Delahaye shows him drinking with a white polar bear, and it was said that he had been seen in Copenhagen and Stockholm.[32] The letter which includes the caricature does not mention any circus.

After he got home Rimbaud felt that he could not endure the whole stretch of the winter in company with his silent mother. It was still early autumn, and he set out for Alexandria in search of warmth. It was at this time that the conception of the wild Rimbaud crystallized amongst his friends. Delahaye, in a letter to Verlaine, calls him the 'hottentot',[33] and he has also left a drawing representing him staggering amongst a group of negro women, with a bottle of brandy in his hand, and a dictionary slung by a cord round his waist.[34] He did not however, reach Alexandria this time; unfortunately he was taken ill on board the ship and was landed on the Italian coast. When he had sufficiently recovered to leave hospital, the winter had set in and it was too late to start on any further journeys, so he was forced to return home. His illness had left him in a feeble state of health, and he remained almost a year at home, until the following autumn. His mother, however, refused to keep him in idleness, and he worked on the farm at Roche, all through the spring and summer. In September of that year he was seen in the Latin Quarter in Paris, but it is not known what he was doing then.[35]

He left home in October 1878, and went again to Hamburg, hoping once more for a ship that would take him out east. There he met a man who promised him work in Alexandria if he went immediately to Genoa to join the boat that was leaving for Egypt. He quickly crossed the length of France, but discovered, on reaching Altdorf, that the pass across the Alps was already closed to vehicular traffic for the winter, and that, if he wished to reach Italy, he would be obliged to cross the mountains on foot.

He set out on foot in a violent snowstorm.[36] From Altdorf the way began immediately to rise and twist, skirting precipices, then, gradually, the climb grew even steeper. The road, which was only eighteen feet wide, was bordered all along one side by a fall of snow six feet high which sometimes stretched across the whole extent of the path, and he was obliged to dig his way through while the hailstones beat upon his face. There was not a shadow to be seen, neither at his side, nor in front of him, nor below him; no precipices were now visible, no mountains; nothing but the blinding whiteness to see, to touch, to feel, and to think about. He could not lift his eyes from the dazzling whiteness before him, for the wind cut into him like a sharp knife. His eyelashes, his eyebrows, his moustache, were covered with stalactites of ice, and his ears were flayed by the wind, while his neck was swollen from the effort of the climb. There was nothing by which he could distinguish his direction, except by the intermittent telegraph poles, for the wires, overhead, were totally invisible in the pervading whiteness. At one point of his ascent he was obliged to dig his way through a snowdrift three feet deep, along a length of a mile.

As he mounted higher the wind grew stronger, the cold more intense and he stumbled on, sinking into the snow up to his armpits, realizing that if the storm further increased it would completely bury him. Suddenly, when he thought that he had reached the limits of his powers of endurance, he saw what he imagined was a pale shadow at the side of a precipice. It was the Hospice and now he was safe.

When he pulled the bell a disagreeable young man opened to him, and he was conducted to a dirty, low room and provided with the usual meal: a bowl of soup and some bread and cheese, and a glass of wine. Later still further stragglers arrived, half paralysed with cold. Then hard mattresses and insufficient blankets were doled out to everyone and late in the night—wrote Rimbaud irreverently—the monks could be heard breaking forth into sacred hymns to celebrate their joy at having, once more, robbed the various governments which subsidized their hut.

The following morning, after a collation of bread and cheese, with a glass of wine, Rimbaud set off, invigorated by his night's rest. It was a fine day, the wind had fallen, and the mountains were resplendent in the brilliant winter sunlight. There was no more climbing, for it was down the mountains all the way. Down and down he tramped, until he came to warmer air; then he saw vineyards and meadows, farms and cows and pigs. Finally he reached Lugano where he could take the train for Genoa to board the boat for Alexandria.

High up on a pillar in the temple of Luxor, near Alexandria, the name 'Rimbaud' has been deeply carved in the stone. No one nowadays could do this as a practical joke, or unnoticed and without the aid of a tall ladder and scaffolding. But sixty years ago—or thereabouts—before the temple had been completely excavated, when only the top of the pillars emerged from the sand, it would have been an easy task, and so all the old signatures appear at the top of buildings. At that time Rimbaud was virtually unknown and it would not have occurred to anyone to do such a thing as a joke. Did he possibly visit Luxor, when he was in Alexandria, or is it only a coincidence of name?[37]

At Alexandria Rimbaud first worked for a man farming on a

large scale, but he did not intend to remain long in that employment. He had heard that well-paid work could be obtained at Cyprus,[38] and his plan was to make his way thither as soon as he had saved sufficient money. He went first to Suez, where a fellow-countryman, Suel, the owner of a hotel, often had odd jobs of a more or less disreputable nature to bestow. Suel had his finger in every local pie—from plans for building lighthouses to save ships from disaster, as the Foreign Office records show—[39] to employing ship-breakers to rob unfortunate vessels that were wrecked on that dangerous coast of Gardafui, and whose safety his lighthouse was to safeguard. It was to collect loot from one of these ships that he employed Rimbaud in the first fortnight of December 1878.[40]

When that lucrative piece of work was completed, Rimbaud crossed over to Cyprus. The island had recently been acquired from Turkey by the British, and they were carrying out all manner of improvements in the ports, in the canals and in the roads. He was engaged as foreman of a gang of men working in a quarry, in the desert, at an hour's walk from the nearest village. There was nothing there to be seen, he said, but a chaos of tumbled rock, the river and the sea. There was no earth, no flowers, no grass, and, even in winter, the heat was intense. He gives this information in a letter to his family.[41] However, his remarks seem to have been exaggerated, for a present-day correspondent declares that no place on the island can be so described. 'There is no true desert in Cyprus, and no place which is hot in winter, let alone intensely hot. If Rimbaud stayed from January to June, he is more likely to have suffered from cold than from heat. During March, April and May flowers abound everywhere.'[42]

Rimbaud says that he was the only European not to catch fever, and that three or four of the patients died from it. He was placed in charge of the native workmen; his duties being to pay them and to dole out the stores and the food. His wages were thirty shillings and he had to find his own clothes and food.

He spent the minimum on himself and managed to save a portion of his meagre wages. He hoped later to find more remunerative work for there were many plans on foot for the laying down of railways, digging of canals and building hospitals.

In April 1879 he was still in Cyprus, still employed at the same work and finding it almost unendurable. The conditions of life were intolerable; he and the men in his charge had not even the merest necessities; they were short of food and no shelter was provided for them, so that they were tortured by mosquitoes which also gave them malaria. At one time he had difficulties with his men and he was obliged to ask his employers for arms to protect himself and the stores. One day some of the men rifled the money-chest containing the pay, and he is alleged to have taken them aside and to have explained to each one separately his predicament, how he was responsible for all those under him and how they all counted on their wages without which they would only starve. It is said that with few exceptions he managed to touch them so that they restored what they had stolen.[43]

He remained in Cyprus until June 1879, when he fell ill with typhoid and he returned home to recuperate. When Delahaye saw him after his six months abroad this time he did not, at first, recognize him so changed was he. All that he recognized were his eyes, those extraordinarily beautiful eyes which had not yet lost their colour. But his cheeks, which formerly had been round and full, were now hollow through illness, hollower than they had been even in his starving Paris days; all the bony structure of his face was now clearly visible. The fresh complexion had entirely gone; the rosy colour that had once made him look like an English baby had been replaced by the dark, tough skin of an Arab. His hair was beginning to turn grey and he wore a bleached frizzy little beard and moustache—these had come very late to him—which gave him an even more exotic appearance. His voice had lost the boyish timbre it had kept for so long, it was now deep and grave.

He was ill most of that winter and, after the heat of Cyprus and in his debilitated condition, he suffered intensely from the cold, especially as his mother would never allow the house to be sufficiently heated. When the family was at the farm at Roche, the only place where he could keep warm was in the stable with the pony.

Home that winter was drearier than ever, for there only remained Isabelle—now eighteen—and her mother. Frederick had completed his military service, but having no ambition, he had done what he had threatened to do, become a carter. His mother now treated him in the same manner as she was treating her own brother—she disowned him, never permitting him to cross her threshold, and whenever the firm which employed him sent him with parcels to deliver she refused to receive them. Captain Rimbaud died that year in Dijon and although his death made little difference to his wife and children, it brought back to her more forcibly than ever the hopes that she had once built on their children—his and hers—how these children were to make up to her for all her matrimonial disappointments. Now all these hopes were shipwrecked; Vitalie was dead, Frederick had sunk back into the working-class, and Arthur, from whom most had been expected, was at home in complete idleness and with no prospects that anyone could see. There was only Isabelle, now rising nineteen, who had as yet shown no positive qualities or defects.

In October 1879 Rimbaud reached his twenty-fifth birthday, and his friends began to notice a change in him. Delahaye describes him at the end of 1879 as having considerably calmed down and sobered. He seemed to have lost all taste for alcohol and for excitement, and there was, in the expression of his eyes, something gentle and spiritual once more. The possession of which he was then most proud and which he valued most was the good 'reference' which his employer at Cyprus had given him.[44] During this visit to Roche, Delahaye went over several times to visit him and the two old friends talked of many things—of the past and the future. Rimbaud told Delahaye that his days of wandering were over—it was as if he had suddenly come to new decisions— and he told him of his ambitions for the future. He talked now of it as if he saw some direction and pattern in it, but he did not mention any of his old interests—neither history, philosophy, nor literature. 'And what about literature?' Delahaye asked suddenly. 'Oh! I never think of that now!' he answered gruffly. Then he hastily changed the subject.[45]

Then he said that he was going away, this time for a long period, and that he would not be seen again for several years. Before he left for abroad this time some of his old cronies— Millot, Pierquin and Delahaye—invited him to spend the evening with them at a little café in the Place Ducale at Charleville. When he arrived he was dressed in new clothes from top to toe, looking very smart and spruce. He told them that he had bought the new suit and all the rest on account and that the bills were to be sent to his mother after his departure. All the evening he was very gay, in better form than they had seen him for many years. It was as if he had shaken off a heavy load. He had come to some momentous decision about his future.

Twenty-five is an important milestone in the life of a man. He could no longer consider himself a youth; it was time to take on a man's estate and responsibilities, and to see the pattern of his life. He was now going to settle down and build for the future, taking the world as it was, with its disappointments and limitations. He was not going to wait for a new world. His years of vaga-bondage were now at an end. He was going to work for a career, like any ordinary man; he was going to climb up the ladder of commonsense, slowly, and by his own painful efforts. He intended to reach the topmost rung, and to cling there.

At eleven o'clock he left his friends and none of them was ever to see him again.

# PART III

## CHAPTER I

# THE COFFEE EXPORTER

RIMBAUD went back to Cyprus, this time to the town of Limasol, for there the English were spending large sums of money on the improvement of the port, and he hoped to obtain employment.[1] He eventually found work as a foreman of a gang of men engaged in building the Governor's summer residence which was quickly rising on the heights of Mount Troodos. In his letter to his family Rimbaud calls it the palace of the Governor-General, although it was little more than a cottage.[2] A plaque in memory of this event has now been fixed to the house, which states:

ARTHUR RIMBAUD

poète et génie français
au mépris de sa re-
nommée contribua de
ses propres mains à la
construction de cette
maison MDCCCLXXXI

But the date is incorrect for it should be 1880.

Rimbaud had fifty men under his command, and he earned about two pounds a week, but the standard of living was too high for his taste, since he was living chiefly amongst English people. Food was also dear and he had many expenses; he was obliged to go everywhere on horseback, and it was he who provided this transport. Then, up on the heights of the mountains, it was cold, and he needed extra clothing which was expensive to buy locally. Nevertheless, by stinting himself in all possible ways, he was able to save money. He was henceforth to devote to the laying by of money the fanatical ardour he had always given to everything which he had undertaken.

He had expected to remain in Cyprus until the month of September, and he could, eventually, have reached a good position, if he had not quarrelled with his employer. Quarrels between Rimbaud and those who employed him became a striking characteristic of his activities in the East. At the end of June he left with his savings—sixteen pounds all told—and travelled down the Red Sea, calling in at the ports on both sides of the coast, to look for work. This was the time when the various European countries were beginning to struggle for positions on the Somali coast, and he hoped to pick up some well-paid employment, but none was forth-coming. Finally, in August he was discovered in Aden, ill with fever—thrown up like a wreck on the torrid desert sands—by a coffee exporter called Pierre Bardey, who had pity on him and gave him a post in his store at Aden.[2] It was no very grand position, he was paid three shillings a day and his keep, and his work consisted chiefly in book-keeping.

He hated Aden from the very first. 'That horrible rock!' he called it.[3] There was not a blade of grass and not a drop of fresh water, for they were obliged to drink distilled sea water. Later he wrote:[4]

You can't imagine the place! Not a tree, even a withered one, not a sod of earth! Aden is the crater of an extinct volcano filled up with the sand of the sea. You see nothing but lava and sand everywhere which cannot possibly produce the slightest vegetation. It is surrounded by desert sands. Here the crater of our extinct volcano prevents the air from coming in, and we are roasted as if in a lime-kiln.

He soon grew dissatisfied with the kind of work he was given; he considered that he was being exploited by the firm; for he was the only intelligent employee in the store, and he was determined that, as soon as he had saved some money, he would move on elsewhere. However, he won the confidence of his employer so that soon everything went through his hands, and he was left in sole charge of the store when Bardey went up to Harar to investigate the conditions in the interior, to see whether he could open there a branch of his business.

Bardey, who was a coffee, hide and gum exporter, had hitherto done all his business at the quayside at Zeyla—the port for Harar —or at Aden itself; he had bought through caravans coming from the interior, not direct from those who produced the coffee, the hides and the gum. But Harar, which for centuries had been closed to outsiders, had recently been opened to European trade by its conquest by Raouf Pacha in 1874, though up to 1880 no Frenchman had ever set foot in the city. Now Bardey, with his head clerk, Pinchard, went up to Harar to discover whether it would be possible to open there a trading station where produce could be stored until sufficient quantity had been collected to make it worth while forming a caravan to bear it to the coast.

Bardey was struck by the possibilities for trade; he immediately rented a house in the principal square and made arrangements for the building of store-houses; then leaving Pinchard in charge, returned to Aden. He decided to send his one intelligent employee inland to look after the new venture until his own brother, Alfred Bardey, was ready to take up the post as manager of the branch.[5]

Rimbaud's salary was to be raised to nine shillings a day and his keep; he was to receive as well a two per cent. commission on all profits. His duties were to collect coffee-beans, hides, gum, ivory and musk from the natives and to give in exchange the European goods he had for barter, particularly cotton cloth. He left Aden in November 1880, crossed the Red Sea to Zeyla, and in the first fortnight of December, after a journey on horseback of twenty days through the deserts of Somali, arrived at Harar, cherishing warm hopes of a brilliant future in which he was soon to make a large fortune.

Harar was a city rising on a plateau, 6,000 feet above sea-level, entirely enclosed by high thick walls of rough stones cemented with mud, wide enough for sentinels to pace up and down as they kept watch on the access to the town. At first sight the town had the appearance of a heap of stones and mud standing out in relief against the surrounding green. This was because the houses were built of rough rubble and held together, not by mortar, but by mud, roofed not with tiles or thatch but again with mud. There was dried mud everywhere; the only violent contrast was the snow-white Turkish mosque, with its curious twin minarets,

Rimbaud at Harar in 1883

ISABELLE RIMBAUD IN LATER YEARS

and this could be seen from afar shining white above the mud-coloured houses.

The chief place in the city was the principal market square; it was surrounded by a high wall and one whole side was taken up by Raouf Pacha's palace, which he built when he conquered the city in 1874, but no later Governor would inhabit it. It was the only large building in the town, the only building with a second storey, and this was the house rented by Bardey for the branch of his store. It could not have been in a better position, standing, as it did, all along one side of the business square.

Rimbaud was, at the time, the only Frenchman in Harar, but the following year Alfred Bardey arrived, and Father Taurin Cahagne, a missionary; and a couple of years after that Father Jarosseau, who eventually became Bishop of Harar and only left the country when the Italians occupied it in 1935, dying some years later at an advanced age, during the war, at Djibuti. Rimbaud hoped, on arriving at Harar, as the only Frenchman, to have the monopoly of all the trades and thus to increase his possibilities of making a fortune quickly. With his usual impulsive eagerness and his customary lack of a sense of proportion, he imagined that he would be able to master all the crafts, in a short space of time, from popular treatises. He therefore wrote to his mother, requesting her to send him a collection of cheap handbooks on various crafts; on iron-forging, on thatching, glass-blowing, candle-making, brick-making and so forth.[6] It is pathetic to see these puerile efforts at self-instruction on the part of a man of twenty-six, who at school had carried all before him and then, in a fit of arrogance, had despised scholastic learning and had decided that all book knowledge was worthless. In those days there was nothing that he might not have achieved, intellectually, had he been willing to learn. Now, regretting his past waywardness, he turned, like a gullible reader of advertisements, to the most popular and most inefficient form of instruction. But he soon tired of learning to become a multiple craftsman as he tired of everything else, and gave the books away.

Soon he began to grow lonely in Harar, shut away from any one of his own nationality, with no companionship or interest outside his work. He felt as if he might as well be on a desert island with no hope of relief. There were no posts to Harar, no regular messengers even; news only came when a caravan arrived from the coast. He found that the life began to weigh heavily on him. The long evenings, particularly, were endlessly wearisome. At sundown the gates of the city were always closed and the keys brought to the Governor. This ceremony was made the more lugubrious by the baying of dogs that always accompanied the closing of the gates, for wild dogs were loosed on the ramparts at night to keep off the hyænas, panthers and lions. These lived in large numbers on the slopes surrounding Harar and sometimes forced their way into the town. It was the sick then who generally fell victims to them, for invalids, in Harar, were always put in the streets until they recovered.[7] No one was permitted to leave his house at night, except those with a special permit, and armed guards patrolled the streets to see that the law was obeyed. There was the long night somehow to be passed and for a man as restless as Rimbaud the enforced imprisonment was well nigh unendurable.

In the morning a guard used to go to the Governor to fetch the keys of the gates and when these were unlocked the bustle of the day began. The caravans which had been waiting outside, sometimes for several hours, were allowed to enter. If the guard with the keys had been too long in coming a great commotion would be heard behind the gates, which increased in volume and intensity the longer he delayed. When the gates were finally opened the stream of merchants and small traders flowed into the town. There was a hurry and a scurry and angry shouts and disputes at the entrance, for dues were levied on every object brought into the town, and these dues were never fixed and were frequently exorbitant.

As the city filled up with the outside merchants the streets began to buzz with feverish activity. The coffee-houses and drinking-shops were open. The great market-place, near Bardey's store, was crowded with merchants for the big business of the day, the selling of cattle, hides, gums, ivory, musk and coffee. The deep voices could be heard disputing and bargaining. Then, for a time, Rimbaud could forget his restlessness and his boredom, in the business of obtaining his goods at the lowest price.

But months seemed to slip by without bringing any appreciable change in his fortunes and his discontent grew. He had expected, as usual, things to go too fast and now he felt that he was wasting his youth toiling for others and not advancing his own interests. He felt this more strongly when Alfred Bardey arrived to take over the position that he himself had filled now for so many months.

I don't expect to stay here long! [he wrote to his mother,[8]] I'll soon know when I'll leave. I've not found what I expected to find and I live in the most boring manner possible with no profit to myself. As soon as I've saved sixty or eighty pounds I'll leave and I'll be very glad to do so. I hope to find something better further on. Send me news of the work being done in connection with the Panama Canal. As soon as that begins I'll go over there. I'd be glad to leave here immediately.

And four months later he wrote again to his mother who had been ill.[9]

My dear mother, I'm glad to hear that you're better and that you can rest. At your age it would indeed be miserable to be obliged to work. I, unfortunately, don't care a bit about life, and I'm used to living on fatigue. Nevertheless, if I'm forced to continue, as now, to wear myself out, living on nothing but worries, as absurd as they are violent, I greatly fear that my life will be shortened. . . . Well! Let's hope that we may enjoy a few years of real rest in this life. It's fortunate that this life is the only one, and that this is quite certain, since one couldn't imagine another life with more boredom than this one.

To add to his other worries he fell seriously ill. Syphilis was rampant in Harar and he, less careful or more unlucky than others, contracted the disease.[10]—It was difficult for him to get proper treatment in the primitive town in which he was stationed, and he was attended by a doctor in the Egyptian Army Medical Corps. It is not known whether he was ever fully cured, but as long as he thought that he was contagious he kept himself rigorously away from others, eating alone and apart from them.

At this time, in order to escape from his life of slavery, he even toyed with the idea of accompanying Father Taurin Cahagne on his missionary journeys to convert the Gallas tribes. It would have been yet another ironical chapter in the career of Arthur Rimbaud, if the poet had turned missionary as well as trader, gun-runner, slave-dealer and explorer. But he dropped the project as soon as conceived, for he was learning to plan for the future, and a missionary journey, however exciting, could not have led to financial gain.

In the meantime his disgust with life at Harar went on increasing and in September, after a quarrel with his employer, he was on the point of throwing up his position. He even tendered his resignation, but Bardey persuaded him to reconsider his decision, holding out to him promises of greater possibilities in the future. When, in December, these greater possibilities had not yet materialized, he returned to Aden, determined to throw up his appointment, and to look for more congenial work. But his employer then offered him a new post at the main store in Aden and this he temporarily accepted, for he had not sufficient capital to embark on anything on his own account. He could not even live if he were not earning a regular salary, for he had nothing to fall back on except the few hundred francs he had saved and these would soon have melted away in idleness in an expensive British garrison town like Aden.

He remained at Aden toying, in his unmethodical, eager and childish way, with various plans for improving his prospects. He tried to obtain a contract from the Société de Géographie to write articles dealing with his travels in the province of Harar. He was the first European who had ever resided in Harar; Burton had stayed there only for a short and dangerous visit, more than thirty years before, but Rimbaud had remained there for a year, living the life of the citizens. He had, however, no influential support, no one to recommend him, and the lofty Société de Géographie was not interested in an obscure employee of a coffee exporter at Aden.

Next he turned his thoughts to exploring, and vaguely planned an expedition to the Kingdom of Shoa, in the Empire of Abyssinia. He sent home for books on exploration, thinking, once more, that the subject could be mastered in a few weeks through a correspondence course. Thousands of francs he spent on books and instruments which were to help him to discover what no man had ever seen. Even at twenty-eight Rimbaud remained the child he had been twenty years before, day-dreaming and planning adventures in exotic lands in which he was to play a glorious part. The only difference was that he now possessed, in his hard-earned savings, money to spend on the toys to implement his games and on the fancy dress to make them more real. His mother, whom he entrusted with the task of ordering the books and instruments, looked with disapproval on the frittering away of good money on these unnecessary purchases. At one time, when he had been a brilliant schoolboy, she had encouraged him, and had been willing to spend extra money on his schooling; then she had urged him on towards book-learning, but in the recognized regular channels, leading eventually to well-salaried, black-coated positions. This indiscriminate buying of books for no fruitful purpose seemed to her criminal extravagance. Indeed who shall say that she was wholly wrong, since no man could have learnt what Rimbaud was trying to learn, in such an inefficient fashion? He had now reached the pathetic and touching belief that everything could be learnt from a book. As far as possible she placed difficulties in the way of buying the books and instruments, and it was only when he persuaded her that he would suffer financially through lack of them, that grudgingly, she finally agreed to their purchase.

But life in Aden cost so much that he spent almost everything he earned and finally he accepted Bardey's offer to return once more to Harar as his agent. He signed a contract for two years and, as his salary was to be increased, he hoped by the end of that time to have saved a considerable sum of money.

This time he went inland at a moment when everything was in a very disturbed condition on account of the Abyssinian war with Egypt and the Egyptian war with the Dervishes; no one could predict what the outcome would be, nor especially what was to become of Harar in the event of an Egyptian defeat.

During this stay he was able to go on a journey of exploration into the provinces round the city where no white man had ever yet penetrated. Bardey was anxious to enlarge the field of his activity, to find fresh sources of supply of gum, ivory and musk, he also wished to open further markets for French goods. He sent Rimbaud and his clerk, Sottiro, down into the province of Ogaden and they went in a far more simple manner than Rimbaud had ever dreamt in his day-dreaming of exploring.[11] They trekked down south of Harar into a country where no white man had ever penetrated, where the only signs of human life were a few round huts sparsely scattered in the bush. They remained there a fortnight studying the possibilities of the firm's expansion in that direction, then Rimbaud moved further south and south-west until he came to the River Web. On his return to Harar, he drew up a full report describing his journey and giving an account of the trading possibilities of the region. This report is interesting even to-day for it is a district that has changed little since the time of Rimbaud.

Rimbaud's article which was published in the proceedings of the Société de Géographie,[12] did not remain unnoticed. It brought him a certain amount of fame and would have brought him more had he known how to take advantage of the chance he had gained. The Société de Géographie wrote asking him for a photograph to publish in their collection of famous explorers and begged for any biographical information he cared to give them.[13] But he, however, did not even deign to reply. Had he acted with more worldly wisdom he might, eventually, have been granted a mission for exploring the unknown regions in that part of Africa, for the years from 1883 to 1890 were significant years for African exploration. It is during those years that we have the travels of Paulitschke, Robecchi-Brichetti, Borelli and many others. Arthur Rimbaud was the first in the field, though, by now, his name as an explorer is forgotten.

He remained in Harar lonely and discouraged.

Solitude is a bad thing [he wrote to his mother[14],] and I'm beginning to regret never having married and not having a family of my own. At the present moment, however, I'm obliged to wander over the face of the earth, tied as I am to a distant undertaking. And every day my taste grows less and less for the climate and the ways of living in Europe. But alas, what do these ceaseless comings and goings profit me, these adventures, these hardships amongst foreign races, these languages with which I fill my mind; what is the use of all this indescribable suffering, if I'm not one day, after a few years, to rest in a place that I more or less like, and have a family of my own, a son at least, whom I shall spend the rest of my life in training according to my own ideas, providing him with the best and most complete education which can be obtained to-day, and whom I'll see grow into a famous engineer, a man rich and powerful through science. But who knows how long I may last in these mountains here; I may lose my life amongst these people, without any news of me ever coming out again.

To while away his long hours of inactivity and to fill his solitude, he sent for further books of study; treatises on hydraulics, on mechanics, on astronomy; works dealing with the construction of railways and subterranean tunnels.[15] We can guess from the titles of the books the nature of the schemes, of the daydreams, on which his mind was feasting. 'These books will be useful to me,' he wrote home,[16] 'in a country where there is no information whatsoever. The days, and the nights especially, are very long in Harar and these books will help me to pass the time agreeably.'

It is pathetic that so much creative energy and eagerness should have overflowed and spread so widely, draining away and leaving no trace; it is sad that it could not have been canalized in one single channel so that it could have reached some destination. But Rimbaud's interest never took him the whole way, the match burned with a bright spurt and then always flickered out. Even his ambition to make money rapidly could not sustain him, the work he was obliged to do bored him unutterably, and he was never able to do day after day what bored him, in the hope of greater gain. It was this characteristic, which made him unsuccessful when others less courageous and less intelligent than he succeeded.

Things of the outside world unconnected with his own affairs, his own future, and his own family ceased now to interest him.

It was at this time that Verlaine approached him again, telling him of his plan to devote an article to him and to his writings, and begging him for further material. But Rimbaud did not trouble to answer the letter and he was not sufficiently interested to read the article when eventually it appeared. To his mother who always thought it necessary to keep him posted with the latest political news of France, he answered:[17]

If only you knew how indifferent I am to all that now. It's two years since I've looked at a paper. All these debates and arguments are now totally incomprehensible to me. Like the Muslims I know what has happened and no more.

He used to say that in his loneliness and solitude all that interested him now was news of home, and to sit refreshing his mind with the mental image of their calm and pastoral life in France, so different from the brutality of his. A change was gradually taking place in him; it was as if he now no longer was content with being an independent man, owing nothing to anyone, neither obligation, nor service, nor help. It was as if he had thoughts of coming back into the flock of human beings, after roaming alone in the desert, as if he were beginning to feel regret that he had not followed the normal human trend, regular work, marriage and the founding of a family. But the time had not yet come for him to lay down his arms and to find normal human peace.

CHAPTER II

THE GUN-RUNNER

WHILE Rimbaud was in Harar the Mahdi Rising had turned out disastrously for Egypt and had ended in the complete ruin of her rule in the Sudan. England's help was of no avail to stem the advance of the Dervishes. When the rebellion spread to the eastern Sudan the British Government decided that the outlying Egyptian garrisons in the Sudan should retire as well as those on the Somali coast and in Harar. In September 1884 Harar, which the Egyptians had held for ten years only, was evacuated with confusion and hardship for everyone. Then, on England's advice and with England's support, the son of the last Emir was made Governor of the city. This was not a wise solution of the problem of the ownership of Harar. Egyptian occupation had opened the city to European trade, to foreigners and Christians, who had settled within its walls. The new Emir, however, was as fanatical a Moslem as his father had been in the days before the conquest by Raouf Pacha; he had learnt nothing during the ten years of Egyptian occupation, but had nourished secretly his bitter hatred of all foreigners and of all Christians in particular. His dream was that the city should become once more what it had been before the coming of the Egyptians, a mysterious city closed within its high walls to all alien and infidel eyes. The European merchants in Harar grew anxious for their lives and property and most of them left. Bardey closed his branch and gave Rimbaud three months' salary in lieu of notice.

Rimbaud then returned to Aden to look for another employment, but finding nothing, he resumed his previous menial post in Bardey's main store.

He brought back with him from the interior an Abyssinian woman, probably a slave girl. Perhaps she was a Harari and not an Abyssinian—Europeans usually called all the people from the interior Abyssinians—for she is described as being a tall slim girl of so light a colour that she might have passed for a European. He rented a house, although he himself had free lodging provided at Bardey's store, and he lived with her all the time that he remained at Aden.[1] It is said that they were happy together and that he always treated her with kindness and affection. He seems to have cherished the hope of making her an intelligent companion, for he sent her to be educated at the French mission school. Bardey's maidservant, Françoise Grisard, used to go every Sunday to Rimbaud's house to keep the young woman company, and to teach her to sew; she says that the girl was so shy and retiring that she would never go out unless Rimbaud accompanied her, that he was always good to her and that he intended eventually to make her his wife.[2] Yet this did not take place, for in October 1885, when he first planned his expedition to Shoa, he gave her a sum of money and sent her back to her own people. As Bardey says, 'Elle fut repatriée convenablement.'[3] We never hear of her again and she is the only woman known to have occupied a place of some importance in Rimbaud's life. Yet he never mentioned her to anyone, in none of his letters home; on his deathbed he did not talk of her to Isabelle, his sister, when the name of Djami, his Harari servant, was always on his lips. It was certainly not this girl he planned to marry in 1891, when he turned his thoughts to matrimony and the founding of a home. Perhaps he was disappointed that she did not give him the son for whom he longed, for there were no children from the union; perhaps she was stupid and he grew weary of the effort of educating her.

At this time the difficulties of Egypt became Abyssinia's opportunity. None of the kingdoms of the interior had accepted the pretensions of Egypt, all had resented them and had feared what might be in store for them. Henceforth, with the weakness of Egypt, the two contestants for power in Abyssinia can clearly be seen; John, King of Tigré and Emperor of Ethiopia; and Menelek, King of Shoa. All the European powers struggling for positions on the Red Sea watched with interest the internal moves for power and supported one or other contestant.[4] The European competition, combined with the internal struggle for power by the two most important Kings of Ethiopia, gave rise to the very serious problem of traffic in firearms. It was not merely a question of the trifling sale of odd firearms to the Somali tribes; such trade could never have amounted to much on account of the poverty of the local sheikhs. The problem was one of the traffic of arms on a large scale with the princes of the interior, resulting in a race of armaments between the Emperor and his vassal, Menelek, King of Shoa. All the Europeans on the Red Sea coast—travellers, merchants, pedlars, swindlers—were not slow to take advantage of this state of affairs, and all of them, even distinguished explorers like Soleillet, trafficked in arms.[5] They used to buy up stocks of old rifles in France and Belgium, of the kind which the government of these countries had discarded half a century previously;

these they bought at eight or ten francs a piece and sold afterwards for forty francs. There was, naturally, to be set against
this large profit, the enormous expenses of the undertakings and
the very great dangers of the expedition. But many were still
prepared to take the risks in the expectation of great ultimate gain.
The French and the Italians sold arms chiefly to Menelek, King
of Shoa.

Rimbaud, eating out his heart at Aden with frustration and
disappointment, was seized, like his fellow countrymen, with
the gun-running fever, and saw in the arms traffic with Menelek
the means of making his fortune quickly. He decided to risk all
the money he had saved since coming to the Red Sea, on one big
venture, hoping thereby to make several thousands of pounds
out of the transaction. He was becoming increasingly conscious
of the passage of the years, and his advancing age in which he had,
as yet, achieved so little. The previous year he had commented
on his thirtieth birthday, saying:[6]

Excuse me for having given you these details of my worries, but I
see that I am about to reach the age of thirty (half my life) and I am very
tired of rolling round the world without any tangible result.

He was, in fact, to have only seven years more of life. He wanted
now to make an effort to establish his fortunes and then to return
to France for a holiday in the summer or autumn of 1886, for the
first time for seven years, and then he might even think of
marriage. Day-dreaming, like the girl in the fable with the pitcher
of milk, he was already laying out the sum he would gain, count-
ing on adding, in the ensuing three or four years, another four or
five thousand pounds to what he had already saved, and in leaving
the cursed country behind him for ever.

After a quarrel with Bardey, more violent than any before, he
resigned his position in October 1885. He did not feel that this
was a rash act since he was about to engage on so lucrative an
occupation.

I've thrown up my employment in Aden [he wrote to his mother],
after a violent row with these disgusting blackguards who imagined
that they could keep me as a beast of burden for ever. I've rendered

them many services in the past and they thought that merely to please them, I was going to stay with them *ad infinitum*. They did their utmost to keep me but I sent them to the devil, all of them, their prospects, their horrible store and their dirty town.

He did not, however, at this early stage, realize all the difficulties of the undertaking. First he had the British authorities to contend with. On many accounts they were viewing with great apprehension the growing traffic in arms, the chief reason being that they did not wish to see Menelek grow too strong. A strong Menelek meant a united Abyssinia, and a united Abyssinia would be a difficult problem for Egypt and so a source of ultimate trouble, if not of danger, to England. The British Government had been trying for a long time, without much success, to reach an agreement with France and Italy to suppress entirely the importation of arms into the Somali coast. This was not easy since France and Italy now had their own ports on the coast; these, however, were still in a very undeveloped state and large ships did not yet call there. Goods were landed at Aden and thence were transhipped to the Somali coast.

At the·end of 1884, however, an agreement was made between the British Resident at Aden and the French Consul, which stipulated that arms and ammunition would be passed by the British authorities at Aden only on production of a special permit to be granted by the French representative, and it was further stipulated that these permits were not to be too easily granted. Rimbaud would be obliged to obtain such a licence if he wished to import arms to sell to King Menelek. He also did not realize, for he had not yet done business with him, that Menelek was no longer a naïve and simple negro like those whom he met on the coast, but well accustomed by now to dealing with Europeans, aware of all their deceits and plans to make money out of him; indeed Menelek himself practised many deceits of his own and frequently got the better of the bargain. He had been buying arms from Italy and France for six years now, he was not ignorant of the imperial ambitions of the two countries and hoped, therefore, to obtain his arms very cheaply, paying for them in vague promises of future support.

Rimbaud had a mere six hundred odd pounds to invest in the undertaking. These six hundred pounds of which his brother-in-law was ashamed, are a large sum when we consider that they represent the savings of a man over a short period of six years, a man who has never earned a salary of more than three pounds a week, with an additional small percentage on profits; who, moreover, on several occasions had lived on his capital in an expensive British garrison town. It is a sum that represents a frugality and a sobriety of living rarely found amongst Europeans stationed in the tropics.

He decided to start his expedition from Tajoura, the new concession which France was claiming, although this claim was not yet recognized by Great Britain. If he started from this point and not from Obock, which was unquestionably French, he would considerably shorten the journey to Shoa.

Tajoura was a curious little Danakil village, a small straggling place consisting of low huts of the usual African type, standing on the shore of a narrow bay which extended inland for a distance of twenty miles. Nothing in the world could be imagined more dreary, writes Rochet d'Héricourt,[8] than Tajoura with its untidy huts thrown up, as it were, by the sea on the shore against the background of dark volcanic mountains rising to a considerable height.

The only trade of the town was the slave traffic and the British authorities were doing their utmost to ruin that.

Rimbaud arrived in Tajoura in November 1885 and he was to remain in that dreary spot for a year before he could even start on his expedition.

In October 1885 and in May 1886 he signed contracts of partnership with a trader called Labatut, but the terms of the partnership are far from clear.[9] It was, however, a wise move on Rimbaud's part to enter into partnership with Labatut for there were few people who knew Menelek or his entourage better than he. He was a curious fellow who had now been living for fifteen years in Ankober, the capital of Shoa, and he was the wild adventurer type calculated to appeal to Rimbaud. He was a pedlar who had drifted inland who had settled down in Shoa, marrying an Abyssinian wife and living, quite happily, the native life in an African hut with a large retinue of slaves. He was an intelligent, though not too scrupulous man, and he earned a good living in a variety of ways, selling ivory and musk and dealing in slaves and arms. He was a good business man who succeeded in getting on well both with black men and white, and it was he who was the first link between Menelek and Europe. It was sheer bad luck that made Rimbaud's combination with him turn out so disastrously.

By the end of January 1886 Rimbaud's arms were ready and he was only waiting for camel transport. Then the difficulties began which were to drag on until the month of October. First there was the matter of the necessary licence for his arms. The British authorities had recently become aware that the French Consul at Aden was being too generous in the granting of the special licences stipulated by the agreement of December 1884, and they brought pressure to bear on him to inform the Sultan of Tajoura that he was to stop all caravans with stocks of arms proceeding to the interior.[10] This order was a serious setback to Rimbaud's plans and would have meant complete ruin if it had been adhered to. It was, however, pointed out to the British authorities that the agreement had been intended to refer to the future, and that in any case, these guns had been transhipped before the agreement had been reached. Eventually after much lengthy discussion, Rimbaud obtained his licence.

The next difficulty was that of obtaining camels for transport. Tajoura was a Danakil village and the Danakils had only sufficient camels for their own private use, and always refused to hire them out to others. Even if camels could have been obtained elsewhere, they would certainly have been stolen immediately and the culprits have gone undiscovered and unpunished. The only way of obviating this was to obtain the aid of the Sultan and he always demanded very high *bakhshish* to persuade him to urge his tribesmen to provide camels, or to prevent them from stealing those obtained elsewhere.[11] All this meant endless discussions and bargaining and further delays if one did not wish to add exorbitant charges to the already heavy and mounting expenses. It took

Rimbaud months to collect the means of transport for his goods.

Then natives had to be hired to accompany the expedition as porters. There was a general hatred among the natives of all white people on the coast on account of the efforts they were making to stop the slave trade. It rarely happened that a caravan left for the interior or returned thence without being assaulted. Labatut had been attacked on his last journey down from Shoa; he had, unfortunately, in self-defence, killed one of the attackers and he was now a marked man on the route. More recently still, in April 1886, the trader Barral on his way back from Ankober had been attacked and the whole caravan exterminated. Chefneux, who had heard of the disaster when passing with his own caravan at a short distance from the scene of the massacre, hurried to the spot, but all he found were the remains of corpses half devoured by beasts and birds of prey, mutilated beyond all possible recognition. He thought, however, that he recognized amongst the mangled heaps of flesh, by a gold tooth shining in the sun, the head of Barral's young wife.[12] The massacre of the Barral expedition by the savage Danakils had, naturally, serious repercussions in Tajoura, and greatly added to the already numerous difficulties in collecting the members of the caravan.

Little by little, however, Rimbaud succeeded in preparing everything for his departure, but it was now a year since he had begun to embark on the undertaking. Fortune was, indeed, not yet to favour him. Just as they were getting ready to set off, Labatut fell seriously ill, and since he could not obtain good medical advice locally, he returned to France. There it was discovered that he was suffering from advanced cancer which no treatment could cure. He died shortly afterwards leaving nothing in writing which could clarify the terms of his partnership with Rimbaud.

Rimbaud, not wishing to start alone for a country he had not yet visited, with no one to act as intermediary between himself and Menelek, no one to protect his interests from the rapacious and dishonest Shoanese, decided to join forces with the explorer Soleillet who had also been trying to organize an expedition bearing arms to sell to King Menelek, and finding no less difficulty in obtaining transport and followers. It was to Soleillet's advantage to join up with Rimbaud's caravan which was ready to set out, just as it was to Rimbaud's interest to reach Ankober with him, for Soleillet had known Menelek now for five years and could make him do what he wished, and had, moreover, a partner in Shoa working in his interest.

But here once more fortune betrayed Rimbaud. In September 1886 Soleillet fell dead in the streets of Aden. Rimbaud was now desperate; there was no one left amongst the French traders with whom he could join forces. With Barral murdered, and Labatut and Soleillet dead, all gone in the short space of a few months, he could think of no one else. With all his money invested in the undertaking he was now too deeply involved to retreat. In desperation he decided that he would wait for no one, he would set out alone, taking on his own shoulders the full charge and the responsibility of the whole caravan. The preparations had taken a year to complete and he had gone too far to turn back.

At the beginning of October 1886 the caravan gloomily wound its way out from amongst the little round huts of Tajoura and Rimbaud, riding at its head, felt that his venture was starting under very evil omens.

CHAPTER III

## THE EXPEDITION TO ABYSSINIA

THE road from Tajoura to Ankober was, according to the accounts of travellers, one of the most terrible in the world. Four months it took Rimbaud to reach the capital of Shoa. Mile after mile—hundreds of miles—he rode without meeting the smallest shelter or the smallest stream, 'par des routes horribles rappelant l'horreur présumée des pays lunaires,' he himself described it. All they had to drink was the water they had carried from the coast and it was not of a refreshing nature. It was carried in fresh hides stripped from rank goats, smeared inside and out with old tallow and strong bark tar, these were filled from a well not too fresh to start with and were shaken during days and nights on the camel's back in the heat. This beverage was measured out drop by drop as if it had been the most expensive cocktail, yet no American shaker has ever invented a drink of so rare a flavour; it poured out a pale and sickly yellow colour, a mixture of goat's hair, rancid mutton fat and bark.

The road wound endlessly along, upwards and downwards among huge, jagged blocks of black lava, or lava the dirty colour of elephant's hide, intersected by perilous rises and descents.

They were harried by day and harried by night; hordes of savages appeared every now and then on adjacent heights and had to be fired on, and they were only kept at a distance by superior force of arms. A great part of the journey lay through the territory of the savage Danakils, of all African tribes the most to be feared. All travellers say that amongst them are found the most scowling, evil-favoured and hideous-looking savages in the universe. As theirs was a poor and barren land, the competition for food was necessarily great, and they looked with horror and anger on the appearance of any stranger in their country. The greatest claim one of their number could put forward for respect and honour was the claim of having killed a stranger who might have been a competitor for food. Murder was held as an honourable pursuit among them and no Danakil was considered sufficiently virile for marriage, or the obligations of family life, until he had at least one corpse to his credit, and could vaunt, as his most glorious ornament, the genital organs of his victim. Since each fresh assassination was rewarded by a further personal ornament, the destruction of a sleeping guest or a fighting foe contributed alike to the reputation of the brave.

The usual attitude for the Danakils in repose, says Johnston,[1] was to sit in conversation with their faces appearing just above the upper edge of their shields. This may have given rise to the rumour spread by earlier travellers of an Ethiopian people who had no heads, but whose eyes and mouths were placed in their breasts. They were, however, not always motionless. At the call of their chief, at the beating of the drums, or the clash of spear on shields—the signal that an enemy had been sighted in their territory—a fiendish whoop is heard for the gathering of the clan, and obediently each man jumps to his feet and bounds off, with the agility of a panther, to attack his foe. To the eyes of Europeans they are almost invisible for their colour is the same, dark, dirty hue as the surrounding cliffs of lava. They dart out from behind their shelter of bush and boulder, swift as lizards, bent almost double as they move, so as never to be seen silhouetted against the sky-line. They always appear suddenly, with uncanny, stealthy silence and invisibility; it is as though they rose out of the soil at your feet, taking shape from it like some spirit summoned by a magician, out of the very spot your eyes were fixed on and could have sworn was empty. They strike terror into all those who come into contact with them. Even to-day, so famous is their reputation for cruelty and savagery, the Danakils are feared amongst the Abyssinians themselves.

The nightmare road wound on until it reached Lake Assal, the salt lake which has astounded all travellers. This lake, at one time, formed part of the sea and its dead and stagnant waters stretch in a circular expanse, forming a basin of many miles diameter, round which an uninterrupted range of volcanic mountains rises sheer from the waters of the lake forming as it were a giant funnel. Through this funnel the sun has been pumping out the moisture of the water for centuries, leaving a salt deposit on the borders of the lake. The salt surrounds the greenish water with a bluish-white fringe about half a mile wide, strong enough to support the camels of a caravan. Another bluish band of about fifty feet high rises up the sides of the mountain, showing how the level of the water has fallen in the course of the centuries. It is said to be the most lugubrious landscape in Abyssinia, this dead and stagnant sea, this sea for ever a prisoner, slowly and gradually solidifying.

The caravan then left the dead lake behind it, and moved wearily forward on the road that wound over basalt and lava. The sun was now reflected not only from the dun-coloured lava cliffs but from the snow-white limestone. They passed beside the deep and mysterious cavern, at the Gunther extremity of the plain, which is believed by the simple-minded to be a shaft leading to a subterranean gallery which eventually comes out at the head of Ghubbet-Khareb at the sea six miles away. Travellers describe this spot as the last stage of the habitable world.

When this was passed there were twenty-three stages to Herer, through the most hideous country in the whole of Africa, wrote Rimbaud. From Herer it was only eight or nine days' journey to the Hawache river, the boundary of Menelek's kingdom, and here they reached comparative safety. The road now descended, by several sloping terraces, to the level valley through which the river wound. Here was no longer the arid lava-stone, the vegetation was becoming luxurious and tropical. The eye now rested with delight on waving tamarisk, on lofty trees, on the jungle undergrowth teeming with game and fowl. They could not use the river as a thoroughfare, for the Hawache was a winding, twisting stream, obstructed at every point by trees and rocks and impossible for navigation. They were obliged to cross it at several points, and there were no bridges. At that time there were only two bridges in the whole of Shoa, and these consisted merely of tree-trunks; they had been built by Menelek's order and they were, according to Rimbaud, remarkable for Abyssinia. To transport goods across the stream rude rafts had to be constructed, and the camels were towed across, buoyed up on inflated skins. All this was a lengthy undertaking, but Rimbaud was by now so well inured to delays that he scarcely noticed them. Eventually, after a journey of indescribable hardships, which had lasted more than four months, he arrived at Ankober on 6 February 1887. He had, however, not yet come to the end of his disappointments. Menelek was absent, for he had gone forth on a punitive expedition against Harar intending to seize it before the Italians made plans to take possession of it in retaliation for the massacre of Count Porro's expedition.[2] Menelek conquered the city and made a triumphal progress to Entoto, preceded by musicians playing martial music on the trumpets he had confiscated in Harar. He was followed by two Krupp cannons, each carried by twenty men, while the arms and ammunition from the arsenal in Harar were borne in their wake in a long stream of carts.[3]

Menelek was now planning to make Entoto the capital of his kingdom in place of Ankober, partly because he preferred to be as far as possible from his Emperor, and partly because he wished to be nearer Harar and the trade route to the Red Sea. He did not hurry back to Ankober to meet a mere trader and Rimbaud decided, therefore, to go to Entoto to settle his business with him. The journey from Ankober to Entoto took more than three days and Rimbaud discovered on his arrival that the king had again departed on another punitive expedition amongst his rebellious tribes and he was obliged, once more, to possess his soul in patience. In any case a few days more or less made little appreciable difference to the added total of days, weeks and months which had elapsed since he had started on his venture, eighteen months before. With discussions, negotiations and final reckonings Rimbaud was eventually to remain in Entoto until May, growing more exasperated and less able, through impatience, to safe-guard his own interests. This was unfortunate, since infinite patience and diplomacy were needed to come successfully out of any transaction with the Shoanese. Rimbaud, although gifted with dogged endurance that nothing could shake, soon reached the end of his limited stock of patience.

At last, one morning, in Entoto, as they got up, the inhabitants heard the guns that Menelek had confiscated in Harar being fired in royal salute. The king was back! It was a humorous sight to see modern Krupp cannon fire a royal salute in the midst of the branch huts in an African bush town!

Rimbaud went immediately to the *palace* officials to crave the honour of an audience with the King, for he was anxious to have his account settled and then return to Aden.

Menelek was, at this time, at the height of his physical and intellectual power. A man of about forty-five, of magnificent health and energy, he stood just over six feet high, and he was broad in comparison, with a body that looked in perfect condi-tion. He was not good-looking, for his complexion in colouring and texture was somewhat similar to an elephant's hide, and his face was, moreover, pitted with pox marks, while his black beard and moustache were too near the colour of his skin to be effective. His countenance in repose was sullen and somewhat suspicious, but it was relieved from positive plainness by a pleasant expression when he smiled, revealing a perfect set of even white teeth. His eyes were bright and intelligent, though at times their expression could be crafty. His general appearance was of undisguised and unashamed good-humoured knavery.

He received Rimbaud, dressed in his usual manner, in a black silk-embroidered cloak over a profusion of muddled, shapeless, white linen garments; with these he wore incongruously a black, wide-brimmed quaker's hat over a white silk handkerchief that tightly bound his head.

Now in his dealing with Menelek Rimbaud's real difficulties were beginning. The king was in need of arms but not in the desperate need he had been a few years before, for he had received in the last five years more than 25,000 guns of various kinds.[4] He also knew well that in the existing state of affairs between the European powers there was little likelihood of a watertight agreement being reached that would prohibit the gun traffic and that therefore he would always be able to procure arms. He did not mean now to pay for Rimbaud's arms unless obliged to do so, he was determined, in any case, to obtain them as cheaply as possible; he thought that this would be an easy matter with a new and inexperienced trader. He intended to exact a large discount on the goods on account of his promises of future friendship with France. But Rimbaud cared little about the friendly relations between his country and Shoa; he was a trader concerned only with the making of his fortune as quickly as possible so as to be able to leave behind him a country that was devouring his youth.

Menelek first ordered his officers to impound Rimbaud's goods, and then obliged him to sell them wholesale for a lump sum, not to retail them, as he had hoped, for so much a gun. He threatened, if he refused, to send the whole caravan back to the coast at Rimbaud's expense. When Rimbaud had finally, reluctantly, agreed to the wholesale purchase, Menelek conceived of the ingenious and brilliant plan of holding him responsible for

Labatut's alleged debts to him. He stated that he had advanced large sums to him for the purchase of the arms two years before, and now he wanted to charge interest on that money for the whole period. Rimbaud demanded proof of these assertions and the king said he needed two days to consult the royal archives. A few days later he summoned Rimbaud to his presence and unrolling some records, he showed him writing in Amharic which he alleged stated that Labatut owed him 3,500 thaler. He said he would deduct this sum from what he himself would owe Rimbaud, and added with a crafty smile that this was a concession, since in reality the late Labatut's goods were now his by right. He would not listen when Rimbaud produced proof of Labatut's indebtedness to himself.

It is impossible now to discover the rights of the affair, how much money Labatut had ever sunk in the expedition, and his indebtedness—if any—to Menelek. There were also other alleged creditors of Labatut in Ankober and Entoto besides King Menelek, and when these heard of the king's claims and of the likelihood of their being honoured, hosts of them sprang up on all sides. Menelek supported each of them, meaning to deduct the alleged debts from what he himself owed Rimbaud, then to pay the creditors a reduced sum, or not to pay them at all, which was more likely. All these creditors now gathered round Rimbaud, like poisonous flies impossible to dislodge. By certain of them, however, he allowed himself to be touched. He was, unfortunately for his interests, always moved at the sight of the helplessness of the childish natives whom the others exploited and bullied, and who, invariably, got the worst of any deal, whether with the foreigners or with their own people. Now he allowed himself to be moved by the claims of the widows of these unfortunate men who had perished on the terrible journey from the coast, or those who had been massacred when Labatut's caravan had been attacked on his last trip from Shoa. He also paid in full the small sums claimed by poor peasants, who alleged that they had given these to Labatut for the purchase of goods at Aden. 'These poor people were always honest and in good faith,' he said[5] 'and I allowed my heart to be touched.'

The news of his quixotic generosity, however, spread rapidly, and further alleged creditors arrived post haste in the hope of picking up an odd coin or two. This changed his softness to hardness and made him more determined than ever to leave Shoa as soon as possible.

The day of his departure, when he was already on his horse, there rose up from a ditch at the side of the road a man who said that he was a close friend of the late unfortunate Labatut and begged for a thaler for the love of the Virgin Mary. Further along, as he rode out of the town, a man sprang down from a high rocky eminence, and asked whether he had paid his brother the twelve thalers he had lent Labatut. To all these Rimbaud waved his hand, as he made away as fast as he could, crying to them that it was now too late.

Labatut's widow was not, however, so easy to dispose of. As soon as she heard of Rimbaud's arrival at Ankober, she started one of those interminable law-suits of which Abyssinians are so fond, in her endeavour to gain possession of the whole caravan, as Labatut's next of kin. After the most wearisome quarrels and discussions, in which Rimbaud sometimes had the upper hand and sometimes was defeated—these fluctuations are to the Abyssinians the fun of a law-suit—the judge gave him an order allowing him, provisionally, to seize all Labatut's property, pending the final settlement. He discovered, however, on arriving at the hut, that the seemingly prostrated widow had already hidden away in a safe place what goods and ready money there had been. All he found were some worn-out soiled undergarments which, he remarked sardonically,[6] the widow tore out of his hands and washed with tears of wifely regret. This was all that was left of Labatut's property except a few pregnant slaves, and these he declared he had no desire to remove.

Finally the judge, reversing his previous decision and deciding that Rimbaud's case was hopeless, gave judgment that he was to abandon the land and the property to the widow in settlement of her claim.

Rimbaud was completely lost and bewildered in the midst of all the claims and counter-claims in this type of law-suit with which he was unfamiliar; he did not in the least understand what was happening and there was no one to whom he could apply for advice and help. He determined to take what he could get and to leave the country as soon as possible. Menelek was, however, at the moment, very short of ready money; the royal chests were empty, and in any case coin was a rare commodity in Abyssinia and he himself was usually paid in kind. He offered Rimbaud ivory in exchange for the guns, but reduced the value of the goods sold to him, reckoning the price of the ivory too high and the arms too low so that Rimbaud refused. Finally, in order not to lose everything, he agreed on a compromise which was very advantageous to Menelek. The king was to keep the arms at a very low valuation; Labatut's debts—or at least a very large percentage of the alleged total—were to be deducted from this sum, and Rimbaud was to be given a draft for the amount left, to be paid by Ras Makonnen, the new Governor of Harar, who had a certain amount of ready money in the chests of the city. The sum was small, a far cry from the thousand pounds net profit which he had hoped to bring away with him. In his letter to the French Consul at Aden, he stated that he had come out of the transaction with a loss of 60 per cent of his capital not taking into account the twenty-one months of fatigue and suffering spent on organizing and winding up the miserable business.[7] He seems, however, to have calculated the 60 per cent of loss on the sum he had hoped to gain and not on the actual sum he had invested in the expedition, for there is little doubt that he was left with the original £600 with which he had started.[8]

There seems no doubt that Rimbaud was cheated and robbed in Shoa. On the other hand, it is clear that he acted neither with astuteness, diplomacy, nor with commercial skill in his dealings with the king or with his subjects. It is certain that he came out of the transaction worse than he need. It was partly due to the kindness of heart which he hid under his gruff, hard exterior, and softness of heart was fatal in dealing with negroes who considered it only a weakness to be turned to their own advantage. He had also the disability of his stubborn pride which had always stood in his way and was a serious obstacle in commercial dealings. He would ask for no concessions and could not bear to be under an obligation to any one; he would not even accept a good turn from those willing to help him. But he was too poor to afford the luxury of such pride and self-sufficiency. Weary of all the distasteful bargaining and disputing, he proudly admitted the full sum of Labatut's alleged commitments and accepted the obligations with arrogance, but with savage rage in his heart. He did not even succeed in enlisting the sympathies of the other Europeans in Entoto. His pride and arrogance seemed to them foolish and uncalled for, and moreover it irritated them as a tacit reflection on their own methods of business. While Menelek, on his side, lay back on the multi-coloured cushions of his divan, with a cunning smile of satisfaction, proud in the feeling that he was a great fellow, that he had once more got the better of a foreigner.

Later, on his return to Aden, Rimbaud tried to enlist the services of the French Consul on his behalf, to recover part at least of his losses, but he was gently rebuked for his pains. Gaspary acknowledged, with many protestations of sympathy and admiration, that his fellow countryman had acted in a noble and disinterested manner in assuming the liabilities of the late Labatut, in having sacrificed his own interests and rights in order to satisfy the creditors of the deceased. He admitted, with regret, that the expedition had ended disastrously for Rimbaud, but he added that he had nevertheless gathered from the accounts of other traders in Shoa that his losses might have been considerably less severe, had he been able, like other men involved in business relations with the Abyssinian kings, to adapt himself to the special contingencies of these countries and their rulers.[9]

Rimbaud arrived in Aden in a state of fatigue and dejection; he reflected bitterly on all the hardships which he had endured since he had come to the Red Sea coast, seven years before, hardships which had brought him no gain. He had spent two years of indescribable sufferings on his adventure in Shoa, on which he had built such high hopes, and now he was back again, where he had been before he started, grateful to have saved from the wreck the amount he had invested in the undertaking, for at one moment he had feared that the whole might be lost.

My hair is quite grey [he wrote to his mother,[10] and he was then only thirty-three]. It seems to me that my whole life is decaying. You have only got to imagine what one must be like after hardships such as these—crossing the sea in an open rowing boat, travelling for days on horseback without change of clothes, without food, without water. I'm terribly tired! I've no work and I'm terrified of losing the little money that I have.

He did not remain in Aden for the heat there in the summer was unendurable, but moved on to Cairo, taking the little weekly boat that plied between the ports of the Red Sea. His torn clothes, his starved mien, his ravaged face and his general appearance of weariness and bitterness did not inspire confidence and the French Consul at Massawa, where he first put in without any papers, detained him and wrote to the Consul at Aden for information concerning 'this fellow whose appearance is somewhat shady.'[11] When Gaspary had vouched for his honesty and respectability he was allowed to depart, and he proceeded to Cairo, and there he published in *Le Bosphore Egyptien*, the account of his trip to Shoa.[12]

In spite of its financial failure, Rimbaud's expedition had not been entirely vain, at least as far as France was concerned. He was able from personal experience, to prove the waste in time, hardships and money, of continuing the Obokh-Tajoura route to Shoa, and to point out the advantage of the new road which he had taken on his return, linking the coast with Harar and Entoto.[13] This journey could be done by easy stages through friendly country at less expense, since there would be no need for the amount of armed protection which was necessary to keep the savage and always hostile Danakils at bay. It was, moreover, a trip of only thirty-five days whereas the earlier one took fifty or sixty. Soon this was to be the route exclusively used by Menelek for his imports and exports, and it was to become one of predominantly French influence after the laying down of the railway.

Rimbaud's report has also a further interest in that it is a valuable contribution to the history of the Abyssinian Empire in a critical moment of its development. It is an account by a clear-sighted observer of Menelek's rise to power at the time of his

THE EXPEDITION TO ABYSSINIA

conquest of Harar, of his warlike ambitions, his relations with his Emperor and finally his attitude towards the various European powers that were struggling for supremacy on the Red Sea.[14]

In the autumn Rimbaud returned to Aden but he had no employment, no income and he was in terror of squandering the little that was left to him after his débâcle in Shoa. All his schemes for the future proved abortive but this is not to be wondered at since he pursued none of them with much energy. He first applied to the Société de Géographie for a contract to write articles dealing with Abyssinia, but the society was apparently not interested and refused on the grounds that the fee he had asked was too high. They advised him, however, to apply to the Ministère de L'Instruction Publique, which had such missions in its gift, with a view to being employed by them in future journeys of exploration, but they did not hold out to him any great hope of success since the Government, at the moment, was economizing in all directions, especially on scientific missions. They suggested, however, that he might work up his travel notes into a memoir to send it as a proof of his fitness for being entrusted with such an undertaking, promising him, in the interest of learning, to make all efforts to collect the funds for its printing.[15] Many writers would have been pleased at this chance of publishing their work free, but here Rimbaud proved that he was short-sighted and devoid of vision; he showed his usual lack of staying power. He was in low spirits, he felt that he would not work unless certain of material gains—substantial material gain— he allowed himself to be discouraged and he dropped the project. He did send articles on his Abyssinian journey to various papers, such as Le Temps and Le Figaro, but with no success, and he considered sending some to one of the local home papers, which in his youth, he had so much despised, to the Courrier des Ardennes, and he, who had never thought of the effect his writings might produce, said to his mother: 'I don't believe it can do me any harm.'[16]

He next considered the possibility of being appointed as war-correspondent to Le Temps, to report on the Italian war with Abyssinia—few could have been better qualified than he for such a post. He had been for seven years in these parts, he knew the country intimately, he spoke the native languages and dialects freely, he had been in personal contact with the Abyssinian chiefs and understood clearly the position of King Menelek between the Italians and his Emperor. He wrote to Paul Bourde, who had been at school with him, and who was a literary correspondent to the paper, hoping that he would support his claim. But Paul Bourde did not recommend him, and he was not appointed. As it happened most of the French papers sent out, as their war correspondents, ordinary reporters with no knowledge of the language and little knowledge of local conditions and local politics.

Paul Bourde who, two years before,[17] in *Le Temps*, had made a violent attack on the new school of poetry, now wrote condescendingly to Rimbaud describing the vogue his poems were having in Paris, thinking that such kind words of approbation from a celebrated Paris critic might soften the refusal of work.

You probably don't know [he wrote],[15] living as far from us as you do, that you've become for a small *cénacle* in Paris a sort of legendary figure, one of those people whose death is announced but in whose existence some faithful will persist in believing, and whose return they await with impatience. They have published in a Latin Quarter review your first attempts in prose and verse, and have even made a small volume of them. Certain youths, whom I personally consider somewhat naïve, have tried to found a system on your *Sonnet des Voyelles*. This little group calls you its master and not knowing what has become of you, earnestly hopes that you will reappear one day to drag it out of its obscurity. But I hasten to add, in order conscientiously to give you correct information, that all this is without any practical value whatsoever. Nevertheless, in the midst of much incoherence and strangeness—let me speak frankly—I was struck by the astonishing virtuosity of these first youthful attempts of yours. And so it is on account of that, and also on account of your adventures, that Mary, who has become a popular and very successful novelist, and I, we often speak of you with sympathy.

Rimbaud can have felt nothing but amazed disgust at this smug condescension from a literary ignoramus, of the breed that he most disliked and despised. He had no curiosity about the fate and the success of his writings which were appearing in Paris as

the work of 'the late Arthur Rimbaud' and out of which Verlaine alone was profiting. His literary compositions reminded
him only of feelings which he had long since forgotten and which
he did not wish to revive.

In the meantime he was idle and he remained without employment until May 1888, ten months after his return from Shoa.
Despairing, at last, of finding any other work, he turned his
thoughts once more to gun-running, in spite of his earlier disaster, as the surest and quickest way of making money. As a
result of the new arms agreement which had been signed by
England and France, the price for which rifles could be sold to
the Abyssinian kings might be considerably increased, and there
was the possibility of large profits for any man able and prepared
to risk a substantial sum of money on the venture. By the terms
of the agreement arms could be imported under special conditions
if covered by a licence. Rimbaud hoped, if he could obtain such
a licence, to be able to find men with capital willing to enter into
partnership with him, since he could no longer finance a second
expedition on his own resources alone. Under the new conditions, which seriously restricted the importation of arms, such a
licence would be a valuable piece of property.[19]

After many difficulties he finally managed to obtain from the
government a licence for importing arms into the Kingdom of
Shoa,[20] and, not having sufficient capital to utilize it himself, he
used it to go into partnership with the two most important
traffickers in arms, Tian and Savouré of Aden. As far as Savouré is
concerned Rimbaud's only connection with him was in the
contraband arms traffic, but Tian was his employer as well as
his partner.[21] He was, nominally, as was Bardey, a coffee, hide
and musk exporter and it was in this capacity that he was Rimbaud's employer. Most of his money, however, was made in the
unsavoury channels of gun-running and perhaps even of slave-
trading—for the two traffics were inseparably linked together. It
was in his capacity as gun-runner that Rimbaud was his partner.

In May 1888 Tian sent Rimbaud up to Harar to direct a trading
station which he was opening there very similar to the one which
Bardey had owned under the Egyptian occupation.

CHAPTER IV

THE COLONIST

AFTER the three terrible summers spent on the coast, Rimbaud was glad to be back again in the comparative freshness of the uplands; Harar is protected by its semi-circle of mountains on the north and north-east from the ravaging monsoon, but a valley opening towards the south-west receives a breeze that keeps the city temperate all the year round. He was glad to be back once more in a town for which he felt a certain affection, which more nearly resembled a European town than any other in Abyssinia. However uncivilized were the Shoanese they would never be able to destroy entirely its character, the Hararis themselves were too strong an influence, too good business people.

It seemed to him like a homecoming to see once more the high mud-coloured walls pierced with the five huge fortified gates, and the Turkish mosque, with its curious tacked-on minarets, shining so white above the dun-coloured houses. He was glad to walk again in the twisted streets, which, although ravined by the heavy season rains, were nevertheless veritable streets, flanked by stone houses, and not the mere mud tracks which passed for streets in Ankober and Entoto. After the usual Abyssinian bush town Harar seemed to him almost luxurious with many of the so-called amenities of civilization. There were real shops where all manner of cheap goods could be bought; there were drinking-booths and coffee stalls and there were, moreover, the clearest sign of civilized life, houses of prostitution. Even what Paulitschke calls 'die eigenartige Abendmusik', the baying of the wild dogs on the ramparts all night, struck his ear with a welcome sound, as if promising safety and an organized life.

Here in Harar there was the possibility of making a kind of home. The houses were not the mere branch huts of Tajoura or Ankober; they were built of stone, in the Arab style so that from the street nothing could be seen except a blank wall and the windows pierced high above the ground. But at the back there were courtyards, and sometimes gardens. And in these court-yards, hidden from the streets, in the rooms opening out on to them, a happy simple life was carried on, especially when evening fell and the gates of the city were closed for the night against all outsiders. Then the fires were kindled and the family gathered round to cook the evening meal, and those who were not engaged in its preparation used to sing and dance, and gossip round the fire until it was ready. Then the tables and stools were brought out into the court, the bright red wooden bowls and spoons were set ready and the family and guests would crowd round for the evening meal. There were no hotels or inns at Harar and the traveller had perforce to be the guest in some private house and he became, temporarily, a member of that family. This state of affairs was welcome to both parties, for the Hararis, who were always late to go to bed and late to rise, were glad of an excuse to prolong the evening with music, singing and dancing, and these were more enjoyable if there were an audience.

Rimbaud was glad to get back to this life which he knew so well.

For the next three years he travelled backwards and forwards from Zeyla to Harar, and later, from the new French port of Jibuti. He trekked far into the provinces of Harar and Ogaden, collecting coffee, hides, gum, ivory and musk, giving in exchange cheap European goods. This was the work for which he was employed by Tian, but he carried on other activities as well, either alone or in partnership with Savouré,[2] sometimes in partner-ship with Tian and even with Menelek's foreign engineer and adviser, the Swiss Ilg.[3] It is humorous to imagine a minister for foreign affairs dealing, at the same time, in kettles, pots and pans, but that was, in fact, what Ilg did. Rimbaud also accompanied clandestinely the caravans bearing slaves to Tajoura to be sold in Turkey or Arabia,[4] and he may even himself have procured them for sale. On account of the convention abolishing slavery, the traffic was, in spite of its dangers, a very lucrative occupation, and it is a well-known fact that almost all French nationals who, at this time, made large fortunes in Abyssinia, made them through the slave trade, either by directly taking part in it themselves, or indirectly by fostering it and not hindering it. Ilg, however, although anxious to make a fortune quickly and not, in other directions, too scrupulous, was loth to help Rimbaud in this matter. 'As for slaves,' he wrote,[5] 'please forgive me, I cannot undertake to procure them for you. I have never bought any and do not wish to begin. Even for myself I would not do it.'

But Rimbaud chiefly sold arms and ammunition. With the licence he had obtained from the French Government, he was able to get good terms from Savouré who provided the capital.[6] This was at first his most lucrative activity, especially as it had to be carried on clandestinely since the British authorities did not recognize the right of the French to supply Menelek with arms. There was, however, little danger of French nationals being hindered in the traffic since Lagarde, the French Minister at Obokh, aided and abetted them.[7] Later, however, when the international arms convention completely broke down, he had many competitors and it was less easy to obtain a good price for the antiquated guns.[8] By that time, moreover, Menelek's need for arms was less acute, for he had no rival in Abyssinia since, after the death of John, he became Negus Nagasti, and united the whole empire under his rule.

These were years of great commercial activity on the Somali coast for under the firm rule of Menelek trade could be carried on with almost complete safety. Harar was the chief business centre of the empire and remained so until Addis Ababa was built, but this was not in Rimbaud's time.

Life developed quickly under Menelek's rule, especially at Harar, for the Hararis had possessed, since time immemorial, a genius for traffic of all sorts. In the narrow, twisting streets, in the dark, mysterious booths, in the secret little hovels, whose doors were never more than ajar, the crafty little merchants plied their trade, piling up their money, slowly but surely. The natives succeeded in making money, but it was becoming increasingly difficult for the foreigner to make more than a mere pittance. Menelek held all the threads in his own hands, exempting from duty his personal goods and imposing exorbitant ones on those of his competitors. He was thoroughly alive to the necessity of keeping in touch with the various European nations if he wished to become

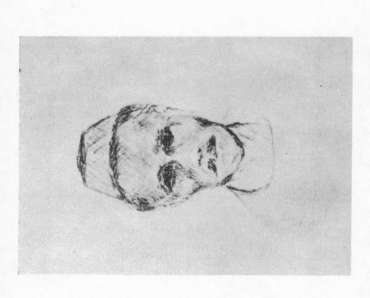

RIMBAUD ON HIS DEATH-BED
*drawings by Isabelle Rimbaud*

their equal. But he kept in touch in his own way, and for his own advantage, to make them help him, free of charge, to develop his country. To achieve this he was obliged, at first, to allow them access to his empire. He realized, however, that they would, if they were given the chance, fasten their claws into his country and devour it. As he had an excellent business head himself and as few scruples as his competitors alleged to be civilized, he finally managed to exploit the Europeans for his own ends. He succeeded in using their activities to obtain an outlet for his own trade, and having once obtained it, gradually, drew all the business of the country in his own hands, with the result that the Europeans found their profits dwindling from year to year.

All this was not very encouraging for those who settled in the empire for commercial purposes. Generally speaking he was more favourably inclined towards the French than towards the other nations and, on the whole, treated them better, so that they had the bulk of the trade. Nevertheless Rimbaud used to say that the business was not sufficient to employ all his energies.[9] Yet, besides the missionary Jarosseau, who could not compete with him, he was the only Frenchman settled in Harar, in the great business centre of the empire. The difficulty was that Menelek had power to forbid his subjects to sell except to him, and eventually, the chief commodities which Rimbaud collected for his employer —ivory, gold and musk—were unprocurable except from Menelek and the prices he asked were too high to make the transaction profitable to the Europeans.[10] And the King once confiscated all the property of a French trader called Pino because he had sold goods to the natives without his permission.[11]

Rimbaud was not making money as quickly as he had hoped. But the blame of his lack of success must not solely be attributed to circumstances. The perusal of the voluminous correspondence from his partners and clients in Abyssinia, leads[12] to the conviction that he was lacking in business sense. He never even managed to settle, once and for all, the question of Labatut's debts, and creditors were still claiming money from him, after he went back to settle at Harar. He used to pay up because he was afraid that his caravans might be attacked on the trade route. Nevertheless, it is hard to imagine Tian, Savouré or Ilg countenancing, in their own case, such claims. It was not only with the natives that he was at a disadvantage, but also with his fellow countrymen. With those with whom he was connected he lost, sometimes—as with Savouré—through not knowing when he could trust them; sometimes—as with Ilg—through being unable to make favourable conditions for himself, so that he bore the bulk of the hardships and the risks and others pocketed the largest part of the gain. As Menelek's chief adviser, Ilg was in a good position to sell profitably European produce, but he seems to have demanded a higher percentage on sales from Rimbaud than from any of the other traders.[13]

Rimbaud, in spite of the toughness of his appearance, never learned to drive a hard bargain to his own advantage. Savouré once wrote to him: 'I consider that you failed because you were not insistent enough and because you would not believe what I told you.'[14]

Moreover, in spite of the number of years he had spent among negroes, he seems, even as late as 1888, not to have known what were the most suitable goods to bring for barter and Ilg used frequently to complain of the objects he expected him to dispose of amongst the natives, religious medals, rosary beads and holy-water fonts. Ilg, as a Swiss Protestant and a materialist, was very scornful of such merchandise.[15]

I have just inspected the jumble you have sent me. One would imagine that your intention was to get the few pence I possess confiscated—that is all too common nowadays. To try to sell rosary beads, crosses, crucifix, at a time when his majesty has ordered Father Joachim to return to Harar, is more dangerous than a journey in the desert. For the present I wouldn't even dare to give them away. As for your famous beads from Ducour and Co. you would do better to use them to shoot sparrows than to try to sell them at a few miles from Harar. And it's really asking too much to try to sell writing-pads to Abyssinians who don't know how to write and who don't even know the private uses to which such commodities can be put. It is a great pity you haven't some carved mother of pearl to send me or a few hundred shoe-horns [he added sarcastically].

But whatever happened Rimbaud scraped and pinched in order to collect the capital which was finally to make him independent. This became the ruling passion of his life. His Ardennais peasant strain was coming out in him and no sum of money was too insignificant to earn or to accept, no sum too small to save. He had become a hard-headed French peasant sticking to his halfpence and taking no chances, for he had abandoned the dream of making a fortune in a rapid and sensational manner. His idea was that one scrapes and one pinches, one puts the farthings away and in the end they become pennies and later, if luck is favourable, shillings and even pounds. He was developing his mother's inability to spend ready money and Ilg used to complain to him of the state in which his caravans used to arrive in Entoto.[16] He economized in so cheese-paring a manner that he did not allow sufficient provisions for the men and the beasts on the journey and all of them used to arrive famished and too weak to move. None of his Ardennais peasant ancestors ever scraped as he scraped; no peasant ever used his body more hardly, nor lived in a more miserly or penurious manner. Winter and summer he dressed in cheap cotton; day in and day out he lived like the meanest tribesman on roughly cooked grain, drinking nothing but water. A traveller who met him at that time said that he looked like a poor devil of an Armenian or a Greek rather than a Frenchman.[17] Mgr. Jarosseau who knew him at Harar says that he lived soberly and chastely, like a Benedictine monk, and that he should, by rights, have been a Trappist.[18] The drinking-shops at Harar, where the Europeans used to foregather, never knew him, nor even the coffee-houses. Not one of his servants worked as hard as he worked; he was up the first in the morning and in bed the last at night, supervising everything himself. He tramped on foot twenty to forty kilometres a day on the rough mountain paths where not even a mule could go. He rode hundreds of miles on the uneven tracks. And when he left home he used to put a handful of rice in his pocket, this he afterwards cooked, and that was all the food he would have all day.

This extreme meanness to himself was contrasted by his generosity to others when his heart was moved. In his rebellious youth he had considered it a weakness to have been moved to pity, but now he allowed himself, at times, to perform an act of kindness without being ashamed of it. He was well known for his generosity to his own countrymen who had failed, to those poor human wrecks thrown up on these desolate and unfriendly shores, whose only desire was now to get home to die. His own suffering, his own comparative failure, had made him sympathetic to the failure of others. Many were those whom he helped out of his own pocket to return to France. 'His charity was lavish, unobtrusive and discreet,' wrote Bardey, his old employer.[19] 'It is probably one of the few things that he did without disgust and without a sneer of contempt.'

It is difficult to discover precise information of his life at Harar during his last years. He no longer lived in Raouf Pacha's palace since Ras Makonnen had taken it as his private residence. Evelyn Waugh, while travelling in Abyssinia, discovered that he had lived in a little house which was subsequently pulled down and that he had living with him a native woman. Waugh marvelled that Rimbaud, residing at Harar where all women are beautiful, should have chosen a mistress from amongst the ugliest race, the race of Tigré.[20] He spoke no more of her than he spoke of his earlier mistress nor was it this woman he thought of marrying in 1891, when he was planning to settle down permanently in Abyssinia.

He was not without friends in Harar and it is said that his house became, as it were, the club of all those who visited the city; of most Europeans in Abyssinia. It is with him they left their money on deposit, it was he who forwarded their mail and arranged for camel transport. 'We would like to give you a little memento,' wrote one of them,[21] 'to thank you for all you've done for us, but you are so peculiar that we don't know what would please you.' The French traders Chefneux, Savouré and Brémond were constantly there. Robecchi-Bricchetti, the Italian explorer, spent many nights with him, and also Count Teleki, the Hungarian traveller, on his return from his journey to the unexplored regions of West Kenya. He must, by this time, have altered, on the surface at least, since the days of his insolent and hooligan youth. Many speak of his wit and the irrepressible, biting humour of his conversation. The lad of seventeen in the Latin Quarter would have been incapable of making any but an obscene or scatological joke. Yet for Robecchi-Bricchetti he symbolized the sparkling wit of the best French conversationalists. While Ilg once wrote to him: 'With your description of Bidault you entertained us divinely, and my only regret is to be incapable of describing him as you did for I'd then be certain of popularity. Savouré tells me you've written to him. I'm delighted for his sake, but I too would like to enjoy the honour of having my spirits raised by your delightful reminiscences.'[22] While someone else wrote, 'Will you tell us your secret? I think that your pen is magic like Orpheus's lyre.'[23]

Nevertheless the old Rimbaud was not completely tamed, and when he broke loose one realized that, in spite of everything, his temperament remained as difficult and as uncertain as it had been when he was a youth of seventeen. His ungovernable temper would at times blaze up and his biting irony made him many enemies. 'What is this I hear about your being in prison?' wrote Savouré to him.[24] 'It seems that everyone now says "Rimbaud or the terror of dogs".' Not a few travellers, not a few of those who came into contact with him in the business way, kept bitter memories of the sharpness of his tongue. Many were the letters written, even to clients, in anger at white heat, regardless of the consequence of his insults.[25] It is the same merciless clarity of vision which, as a boy, had made him see through all shams, the same cold honesty which had made him so unwelcome a guest to his sophisticated hosts in the Paris of 1872, the same ruthless irony which had inspired him, as a youth of sixteen to write *Les Assis*. The intervening years have only softened the crust, they have not radically changed him. Once, when Borelli, the eminent French explorer, had been staying with him and had, perhaps unintentionally, made him feel the great gulf which separates an explorer from a mere trader, anger suddenly blazed up in Rimbaud and to humiliate his guest he tried to compel him to clean out his sleeping quarters before he departed. Jules Borelli was a hot-tempered Marseillais,

with a strong sense of personal dignity. He too lost his temper
and angry words ensued on both sides, but later he realized that
he had allowed his anger to get the better of him, and he subsequently apologized to his host for his 'unseemly words'.[26]

Five years earlier Rimbaud had written: 'And every day my
taste grows less and less for the climate and the ways of living in
Europe.'[27] Now he found that he was growing genuinely fond
of the Abyssinians, and that because he tried to see their point
of view and to be human with them, they gave him in return
devotion and gratitude. He had none of the racial arrogance
usual in white men stationed amongst the coloured races. He
could talk to all classes of people, from the highest to the lowest,
to all sorts of tribesmen, on account of his amazing facility for
languages and because he understood the natives and sympathized with them. 'I enjoy on the route quite a bit of consideration,' he wrote to his mother.[28] 'This is due to my being human
with the people. The people at Harar are neither more stupid
nor greater scoundrels than the white niggers of countries alleged
to be civilized. They are merely of another breed, that is all.
They are, if anything, less nasty, and can, in certain cases, show
gratitude and fidelity. It is only a question of being human with
them.'

Borelli tells us that by his honesty and his blunt sincerity he
even managed to gain the confidence of the Abyssinian chiefs;
this was extremely rare on the part of a European. Menelek's
nephew, Ras Makonnen, the Governor of Harar, became a close
friend of his. He was a very different man from his coarser-
grained uncle. He was small and dark with delicate, graceful
hands, and large expressive eyes; his voice was gentle and his
manner quiet and dignified. His expression was intelligent, and
it would have seemed, to judge from his appearance, that he
would have been more suitably a priest, a scholar, or a philosopher, than a soldier or a governor.

But it was to the simple poor negroes that his affection chiefly
went; those he regarded as helpless children whom he must
protect. He was renowned for his goodness towards all who
worked for him. 'These stupid negroes,' he wrote to his mother:

'expose themselves to the danger of tuberculosis and pleurisy by remaining naked under torrents of rain. It sometimes happens that I have to go home with nothing on under my *burnous* because I have dressed one or other of them on the way back.'

He used to try to improve their harsh lot, but was often mis-understood for his pains. 'One would like to improve their hard life,' he said,[30] 'but they, on their side, only try to exploit one and one has to put up with the thousand and one annoyances due to their laziness, their treachery and their stupidity.'

In Harar, as the years went by, the charity, which had always been one of his outstanding qualities, became active and practical. He was being transformed from a rebel into a public-spirited man, with ideas for the betterment of others. His own future, the making of money, were no longer sufficient for him. The tragedy was that he did not live long enough to show the full results of this change. 'I would like to do something good, something useful,' he wrote home,[31] 'What will be the outcome of it all I don't yet know.' Now he cared what others thought of him and the possession he most valued was the high reputation for integrity and reliability he enjoyed in the region. One of his business associates wrote to him, 'We thank you for the intelligence, the integrity and the devotion you have always shown in support of our interests.'[32] His employer Bardey wrote after his death,[33] 'He was the embodiment of loyalty and in-tegrity. Nothing that he ever did was contrary to honour.'

'No one at Aden can say anything bad against me,' he wrote to his mother.[34] 'On the contrary, for ten years now I have been highly considered by everyone in this country.' And once, when she wrote to him complaining of the gossip and slander to which the family had been subjected on his account, he answered,[35] 'Your news distresses me. What you tell me is extremely annoy-ing and may cause us all serious prejudice. Well! I can only hope, for your sake as well as mine, that this will all quickly blow over. As for what they say about me, my conduct here is known as elsewhere. . . . My reputation stands high in these parts, and will permit me to earn my living decently anywhere. If I've had bad times to go through in the past, I've never tried to live on anyone else nor by evil means.' Later he said again:[36] 'Believe me my conduct here is irreproachable. In all that I've done it is others who have exploited me rather than the contrary.' 'I've never done any harm to anyone,' he said in his last year at Harar,[37] 'On the contrary, I do a little good whenever I get the chance, it is indeed my only pleasure.'

A graphological study of Rimbaud's handwriting at various periods of his life—if any reliance can be placed on these deductions—claims to reveal the fact that, intellectually, the colonist was quite the equal of the former poet, and that, morally, he was vastly superior to the old Rimbaud.[38]

That was the Rimbaud whom the outside world saw. But there was, as well, the lonely, hidden Rimbaud, desperately unhappy and starved for affection and intellectual companionship. 'He was silent and contemplative,' said Jarosseau.[39] 'He often came to see me and we talked only of serious things, but he never spoke of himself. He used to read a great deal and always seemed far away from everyone.'

I'm weary and bored [he wrote home],[40] I've never known anyone as bored as I. Isn't it wretched this life that I lead, without family, without friends, without intellectual companionship, lost in the midst of these negroes, whose lot one would like to improve, and who try, for their part, only to exploit one. . . . Obliged to chatter their gibberish, to eat their filthy messes, to endure their treachery and their stupidity! But that isn't the worst. The worst thing is the fear of becoming besotted oneself, isolated as one is, and cut off from any intellectual companionship.

That is the cry that burst from him so frequently during these last years abroad, his lament at his intellectual starvation. Bardey was of the opinion that Rimbaud, in his heart, was convinced that he had made a mess of his life and that this explained his bitterness.[41] He also had the feeling that he intended, when he had saved a sufficient sum of money, to retire from business and to return to the world of letters.[42] He was said to be writing incessantly, but none of these writings were found amongst his papers. Perhaps he left them in Abyssinia, when he returned to France in 1891 expecting to stay there only until his leg was cured. Since the liberation of Abyssinia many false rumours of the discovery of papers and poems have been circulated. Perhaps they may one day be found. Then we shall know what was the core of this figure of stone walking on stone, what was the constellation that guided him when the morning star which shone for him as he emerged from Hell, had faded in the sky. The only paper concerning literature which was found amongst his belongings is a letter from a review inviting him to return to France and to put himself at the head of the new literary movement. This paper, for some reason, he preserved as if it was something important to him.[43]

Monsieur et cher poète [wrote the editor of *La France Moderne*, Laurent de Gavoty], I have read your beautiful poems. That explains how happy and proud I should be to see you head of 'l'école décadente et symboliste' and a contributor to *La France Moderne*. Please be one of us.

In the meantime the paper declared that it had discovered his whereabouts and, at last having heard that he had received its letter, *La France Moderne*, in its number of 19 February 1891, announced with a cry of triumph.[44]

This time we have got hold of him! We know where Arthur Rimbaud is, the great Rimbaud, the only true Rimbaud, the Rimbaud of *Illuminations*. We proclaim that we know the hiding-place of the missing man.

Rimbaud does not seem to have answered the paper. It must, however, be remembered that this was at the moment when he fell ill with the disease which was, the following November, to kill him. It was in February that he informed his mother of the poor state of his health and of the condition of his right leg. Perhaps he intended, later, to do something about the invitation, for he certainly did not destroy the letter.

At this time he was upheld by the thought that, one day he would be able to escape, with sufficient money saved to live as he would like. It was at this time that he was toying with the idea of taking out an annuity with his savings.

Indeed I'll not always be here [he wrote to his mother],[45] I hope one day to be able to live as I'd like, to travel over the whole world, which isn't, after all, so very big; then perhaps I'd find somewhere that would satisfy me a little.

Perhaps the poem he had once written as a youth in Paris, *Le Pauvre Songe*, then rose to his mind, for it was in keeping with his mood.

> Peut-être un soir m'attend
> Où je boirai tranquille
> En quelque vieille ville,
> Et mourrai plus content:
> Puisque je suis patient.*
>
> Si mon mal se résigne,
> Si jamais j'ai quelque or,
> Choisirai-je le Nord
> Ou les pays des vignes? . . .
> —Ah! songer est indigne,
>
> Puisque c'est pure perte!
> Et si je redeviens
> Le voyageur ancien,
> Jamais l'auberge verte
> Ne peut m'être ouverte.

He who, in the past, had despised family life now found his thoughts reverting continually to home. In his solitude at Harar he used to sit, trying to imagine what they were doing, his mother and his sister, in the only home he knew. Whenever he was left for a time without news he used to write desperately asking whether they were forgetting him.

'Write to me more often! Do not forget your son,' he begged.[47]

To his mother his heart now turned with more gentleness and affection than in the past, when she had been his oppressor, 'La Bouche d'Ombre'. He could not forget how she had answered his desperate appeal when he had returned broken from his disaster in Abyssinia, in the autumn of 1887.[48]

* Patient here = enduring.

Dear ones [he wrote],[49] I would have liked to return to France to see you, but it's absolutely impossible for me to leave this wretched Africa for a long time yet. But, dearest mother, do rest and look after yourself. Your previous fatigue is enough. Spare your health at least and rest. If I could do anything for you I wouldn't hesitate to do it. . . . My life in this country, I've said it often, but I haven't said it too often and I've nothing further to say, my life is wretched, shortened by mortal tediousness and by fatigue of every kind. But what matter! —I would like to know that you are happy and in good health. As for me I've long ago become inured to this kind of life and I'm working.

Rimbaud's sole comforter at Harar, and the only person to whom he seems to have given real affection, was Djami, the Harari boy, his body servant, his constant companion. The youth was one of the few people in his life whom he remembered and talked of with affection, the only friend of whom he spoke on his deathbed, when the thoughts of other men usually turn to those whom they have known in their early youth. It was Djami's name that was always on his lips when he finally sank into unconsciousness. There is, however, no shred of evidence to support the contention that his relations with Djami were immoral. Alfred Bardey in a letter to Paterne Berrichon,[50] states categorically that Rimbaud in Abyssinia was never suspected of sodomy, but, on the contrary, was known to associate with women. During his last year in Harar Djami, although only twenty, married and became father of a child;[51] the sight of his happiness made Rimbaud long once more for a family of his own, and it was then he made plans for returning to France to choose a wife whom he would bring back with him to Harar.

He had hoped to be able to go to Paris for the exhibition of 1889, but, at the last moment, he found that his finances would not permit so costly a journey, and he was afraid moreover, that if he remained absent for so long a time the business he had built up at Harar might melt away.

'I shall come for the next exhibition,' he wrote to his mother who was disappointed at not seeing him.[52] 'Perhaps I shall then exhibit some of the produce of this country, or even myself, for

I imagine that one must look very strange indeed after a long sojourn in a country like this.'

The following year he managed to save some money and was beginning vaguely to consider the plan of going to France for a holiday in the dim future. To his mother who asked him why he should not take advantage of the trip to get married, he answered,[53] 'As for me, alas! I've not yet either the time to get married myself or to see others getting married. It's quite impossible for me to leave my business within any definite time. When you're engaged in business in these cursed countries it's impossible to get out of it.'

But the thought of marriage was in his mind and a few months later he wrote:[54] 'May I come home and get married from your house next spring? But I couldn't possibly consent to live at home, nor to give up my business here. Do you think that I could find some one willing to come out here with me? I should like an answer to this question as soon as possible.'

In November, after he had received his mother's answer in which she begged him to come home to marry and to settle down in France, he wrote:[55]

When I spoke of marriage I always meant to make it clear that I intended to remain free to travel, to live abroad, and even to go on living in Abyssinia. I've become so unused to the climate of Europe, that I should find great difficulty in getting acclimatized to it again. And then what work should I find, how should I build up business connections? That's another question. And besides there is one thing definite that a sedentary life would be absolutely impossible to me. I'd have to find someone willing to accompany me in my wandering.

If he married it was to be clearly understood that he was to remain free to travel, to roam wherever he wished, for his passion for wandering had not yet burnt itself out. He had said the same thing a few years earlier.[56]

And don't cherish the hope that my spirit has lost its passion for wandering, for the contrary is the truth. If I'd the means of travelling, and were not tied to the one spot by work and the necessity of earning a living, you'ld not see me two months in succession in the same place. The world is so full of wonderful countries that the total lives of a thousand men wouldn't suffice to visit them all. On the other hand I'd not like to vagabond in poverty. I'd like a few thousand francs of income and to spend the year in two or three different places, occupying myself in an intelligent manner at some interesting work. I'd always find it very wretched indeed to live in the same place for ever.

## CHAPTER V

# THE EXILE'S RETURN

RIMBAUD had said in *Une Saison en Enfer*, 'Je reviendrai avec des membres de fer, la peau sombre; sur mon masque on me jugera d'une race forte. J'aurai de l'or.'

But his return was very different!

Before the following spring had set in, when he was to go home to find a wife, he was seriously ill. It started in February with a recurrent twinge in his right knee-cap, but he was not anxious, thinking it merely a rheumatic ache due to the damp of the Harar winter, which the warm spring would soon dispel. He had always heard that exercise was the best cure for rheumatism, and he submitted his leg to this violent treatment. With his habitual disregard for bodily comfort, his usual contempt for physical pain, he continued his ordinary life, his walks of twenty to forty kilometres a day over the rough paths, his long rides on horseback over the uneven mountain tracks. But the pain continued to beat, night and day, like a sledge-hammer against his knee-cap.[1]

Later he began to notice swellings above and below the joint, but these he attributed merely to varicose veins. He bandaged them tightly until a surgical stocking could be obtained, and continued his violent exercise as hitherto.

Next a fever began to consume him; he felt nausea at the sight of food; while every day his leg became more crippled and useless. Nevertheless he still continued to force himself to ride and walk.

The disease then spread to his thigh and finally to his calf as well. Every time he dismounted from his horse he thought that he would never be able to use his leg again. The circulation of the blood seemed now to be impeded and pain used to rack every nerve, from his ankle to his hip.

But business was heavy at the moment, he could not ease off work; he tried to forget the condition of his leg and the throbbing ache which left him no respite. He was losing weight rapidly and his strength was being undermined by his persistent nausea at the sight of food which made him unable to eat, and by the stubborn insomnia which tortured his nights.

After six weeks of these painful efforts to continue his normal life, he decided to remain in bed, or at least to lie up on a couch, to see whether constant rest would improve the condition of his leg. His couch was carried into the store and placed between his desk and the window; from there he could keep an eye on the work going on in the yard and on the scales where his servants were weighing the coffee-beans and the musk. It added further strain to his distraught state of mind, to be obliged to pay men to fetch and carry, while he lay motionless doing nothing, with his eyes restlessly following those who came and went.

Day by day, however, the swelling on his knee increased, until the joint became impossible to bend. The whole leg grew stiff in a week, with the thigh and the calf wasting to nothing, while the knee-cap had grown to double its normal size.

There was no doctor in Harar whom he could consult, now that the Egyptian garrison had left, and, at last, when for weeks now he had been lying up, suffering torture, unable to move and never sleeping, he decided that he would go down to the coast and then to Aden. To leave so precipitately he was obliged to wind up his business rapidly and at great loss.

Since he could not ride he caused a rude litter to be constructed, with a canvas awning and hired sixteen men to carry him the three hundred kilometres to Zeyla, a fortnight's journey. His sufferings on that march through the desert can be imagined; we have, in any case, his letters to his sister which describe it, and the rough notes on the expedition to the coast which he kept, almost from force of habit.

He left Harar on 7 April 1891. The porters were clumsy, their jolting, as they walked, was almost intolerable to him, and coming down from the high plateau was unspeakable agony. It was raining hard and those that carried him slipped continuously with their bare feet on the slime and the loose stones. The stretcher was rudely constructed, and he thought at every jerk it would break asunder. Thinking that he might be more comfortable riding, he tried to get on to a mule, with his injured leg lashed to a pole and extending out over the neck and head of the beast. But the pain soon became more than he could endure, and he returned to his stretcher once more.

On 9 April, the third day of the journey, a storm arose scattering the caravan, and his bearers carried him on ahead of the other porters and the camels with the provisions. For thirty hours he had nothing to eat and drink; for sixteen of these hours a tropical rain was falling, and he lay on his stretcher, without shelter, unable to move, in the torrential downpour. They waited thus until the whereabouts of the camels could be discovered. On the 11th, they finally got in touch with the rest; the caravan was once more complete and the weary journey continued.

After a week of this torture the bearers began to grow discouraged and weary. At the evening halt on 14 April, they flung the litter down in anger, causing the invalid severe pain; for the sake of discipline he felt obliged to fine them.

At last he reached Zeyla, almost unconscious with pain. A boat was leaving that day for Aden and he got himself carried on board.

For three days he lay on a mattress on deck, without food, and without any attention, unable to move, until finally he arrived at Aden. He was taken to the European hospital and there the British doctor said that his leg was in a very serious condition and that immediate amputation might be necessary, but he tried first to see what treatment would do. For six days the treatment was carried out, six further days of torture; Rimbaud lay with his leg bound and hoisted to the ceiling so that he could make no movement. The heat at Aden was already tropical and he could find no rest or sleep, for he had become as thin as a skeleton and his back was flayed and raw from lying so long unattended, in the same position without movement.

At last, seeing that the treatment was bringing no improvement in the condition of the leg, the doctor ordered his immediate return to France. From the very first he considered Rimbaud's case as hopeless, but he had been afraid to take the responsibility of an amputation in case of the sudden death of the patient, and had preferred to hand him on to someone else's care.[2]

Before Rimbaud left for France he had, first, to settle his affairs with Tian and to liquidate everything. He realized then about fifteen hundred pounds; these, with another couple of hundred that were outstanding, added to the eighty-odd pounds that his mother had invested in land on his behalf, seven years before, was all that he had made out of his second *Saison en Enfer*, the hell of the eleven years on the Somali coast.

When everything was wound up he said farewell to his faithful Djami and knew in his heart that he would never see him again. Djami begged to be allowed to accompany him all the way; he was prepared to abandon everything—home and family—to follow his master to the ends of the earth. 'Il rampait à mes pieds' said Rimbaud to Isabelle:[3] But he was unwilling to separate the young man from his wife and baby.[4] Then he took the boat for Marseilles, but he was so ill when he landed that they took him immediately to the hospital of the Immaculate Conception.

I'm very, very ill [he wrote to his mother],[5] I've become a skeleton on account of the disease in my right knee, which has now swelled to an enormous size, and looks like a pumpkin. It will all last a very long time, if further complications don't necessitate amputation. In any case I'll be a cripple for the rest of my life. . . . Life has become unbearable! I'm so wretched! How wretched I am! I've a draft for thirty thousand francs on the *Comptoir National d'Escompte* in Paris, but I've no one to cash the cheque for me, nor to look after my business. I've also a lot of money on me which I can't even keep an eye on. I can't get out of bed. What am I to do? What a wretched life! Can't you help me in any way?

Next he sent off a telegram which said:[6]

Today, you or Isabelle come Marseille, by express. Monday morning they are amputating my leg. Danger of death. Serious business to settle.

ARTHUR

Answer: Rimbaud, Hospital of the Immaculate Conception.

His mother was quickly stirred to action and immediately on receipt of his telegram she sent one in reply: 'Am leaving. Shall arrive tomorrow evening. Courage and patience.'[7]

After her arrival, when further treatment proved of no avail, Rimbaud's right leg was amputated.

During the latter years of his exile at Harar, Rimbaud had thought frequently about his mother and had eagerly looked forward to the time when they would once more be united. He hoped much from the intimacy of their relationship, now that he had left all his waywardness behind him, and was prepared to see that she had not been wholly wrong and cruel in her earlier behaviour towards him. His affection was, however, turned to bitterness when he discovered, as he thought, the same hard woman—older and more rigid—who had made his youth so arid. People do not alter, and Madame Rimbaud, though capable of great acts of generosity and sympathy, when she thought the occasion demanded them, was as incapable now as she had always been of showing her affection to her children and of surrounding those she loved with the warmth of her feelings. Arthur was bitterly hurt, when ten days after the operation was over, she left him alone in a state of great distress, to return home. He did not realize at the time that Isabelle was ill; the illness was not serious, but was sufficient to make his mother feel that her place was beside her daughter since there was nothing further she could do for her son; others were being paid to nurse him and it was incumbent on them to perform their service conscientiously. It was, moreover, a busy time on the farm and, with Madame Rimbaud, work and duty were never allowed to wait upon sentiment. She wrote then to Isabelle.[8]

My boxes are ready, and I mean to leave tomorrow, Tuesday. I'll not be at Roche until Thursday evening. Let no one meet me. I'd rather arrive alone. I'd meant to leave today but Arthur's tears moved me; however if I'd stayed I'd have had to stay at least a month; that's impossible! I'm trying to do everything for the best; may God's will be done. Please don't write to me any more here. Yours. V. Rimbaud.

But, after she had gone, Rimbaud was full of remorse at his annoyance with his mother, and full of anxiety for his sister. He wrote to her:[9]

What do you mean with all your tales of funerals? Don't be so frightened, and have patience; look after yourself and be brave. Alas! I'd love to see you, what can be wrong with you? What illness? All illnesses can be cured with time and care. In any case one must be resigned and not despair.

I was very angry when mother left me, as I didn't understand the reason. But now I see that it's better for her to be with you to look after you. Will you ask her to forgive me, and greet her from me. Goodbye till who knows when.

But his mother had left him behind in great distress, with nothing to occupy his mind but dark and gloomy thoughts of his broken life, with no friends to console him. But there sprang up between him, starved for affection and sympathy, and Isabelle, the little sister whom he had scarcely known, a close relationship developed and fostered from a distance. It was to her that all the last letters were addressed and it was to her always that he wrote bewailing his sad fate.

Dear sister [he wrote],[10] you've not written to me. What has happened? Your other letter frightened me, and I'd like news of you. I hope this won't mean fresh troubles for us. We have, as it is, too much on us all at once. As for me I do nothing but weep, night and day. I'm a dead man! I'm crippled for life! In a fortnight, I think I'll be well, but I'll be able to walk only on crutches. As far as an artificial leg is concerned, the doctor says that I'll have to wait a long time—six months at least. And for all that time what on earth shall I do? If I went home, the cold would drive me away in three months, or even less. I'll not move from here for six weeks, any way; I need time to practise with my crutches; I'll not be home until the end of July, and I'll have to leave at the end of September.

I don't at all know what to do! All these worries are driving me mad. I don't sleep a wink at night. Life is nothing but wretched distress, distress without end. Why indeed are we alive?

The following day he tried to walk with his crutches, but his leg had been cut off so high up that he found it extremely difficult to keep his balance. His remaining leg had, moreover, become weak with inaction and it seemed to him, at times, as if he felt twinges in it similar to those he had felt in the other leg, at Harar. He brooded over this, thinking that it too had become attacked by the mysterious disease. Terror than gripped his heart, especially in the long watches of his wakeful nights, when he used, in memory, to go over all the stages of his illness, and remember that the trouble in his right leg had started with twinges of pain followed by insomnia.

He used to spend nights and days devising ways and means of getting about quickly and easily; this necessity was a torture to him, for his body, in spite of its mutilation, was as active and as restless as ever. He would have liked to do this and that, to go here and there, but everything was impossible for him, because he could move only with extreme difficulty. He could not even dress himself without the most horrible contortions, since he could not stand up unaided. By now he had learnt to move on his crutches, provided he kept to level ground, but he could not yet go upstairs or down, and if the ground were too rough and uneven, his crutch would cut into his armpit and the pain in his shoulder soon become unbearable.

If anyone in the same condition in which I found myself [he wrote to Isabelle],[11] came to me for advice, I should say to him, never allow yourself to be amputated. If death comes otherwise it will be preferable than life without a limb. Better to endure the tortures of hell for a year than to allow oneself to be amputated. Here is the fine result! Here is what happens! You're seated, and then you want to get up. You hop a few steps with your crutches, and then you are forced to sit down again. Your hands can hold nothing, you can't, as you walk, take your eye off your only foot and the tips of your crutches. Your head and shoulders are bent forward, your back is bowed like a hunchback's. You're terrified at the sight of people, for fear they should knock you over and break your second stump. People only grin at the sight of you hopping about like that. When you sit down your hands twitch and your expression is idiotic. Despair then seizes hold of you. You remain seated, paralysed, weeping and waiting for night to come; night that will bring the same endless insomnia and, eventually, a morrow more gloomy than the previous day, etc., etc. A fine new instalment to-morrow.

He used to reflect bitterly on how active and energetic he had been only five months before. Gone were his days of wandering, his rides over the mountains, through the deserts, his journeys over rivers and seas. All that lay before him now was the existence of a wretched cripple.

What tediousness, what fatigue, what misery, as I think of all my journeys, and how active I was only five months ago. Where are the trips through the mountains, the rides, the walks, the deserts, the rivers and the seas? Now all I have is the life of a legless cripple. For I am beginning to realize that crutches, wooden leg, artificial leg, are all eyewash, and that with all those one can only drag oneself around unable to do anything. And I who had just planned to come home to France this summer, to get married. Farewell, marriage! Farewell, family! Farewell, future! My life is over! I'm nothing more than a dead tree-trunk![12]

## CHAPTER VI

## THE UNRETURNING SPRING

RIMBAUD remained in hospital in Marseilles until the end of July, then he returned to the family house at Roche; like a wounded animal seeking shelter and a place to hide. It was twelve years since he had set off, in the autumn of 1879, with his brand-new suit of clothes and his fresh hopes, to endeavour to come to terms with life, to make his peace with it and to build for the future. But life had not accepted his submission and had thrown him back home, broken in body and in spirit. He had planned to return with money in his pockets and to take his place, once more, in the world of intellect and literature. He came back, however, to escape from life and he made no attempt to renew his relations with his early friends, not even with Delahaye, nor to meet those rising poets who had begged him to come to Paris; none of them knew of his return until he was dead. From hospital in Marseilles he wrote to Isabelle, saying, 'In France, except for you, I've no friends, no acquaintances, no one.'[1]

Isabelle, however, received him with love and rejoicing. During his absence she had grown from a girl to a woman, for she had been barely nineteen when he had left for the last time. During these twelve years she had thought much about this adventurous brother of hers, whom she scarcely knew, for, as long as she could remember, he had always been away from home, returning only in the winter. In these twelve uneventful years, which should have been the happiest of her life, living in close proximity with a dour and silent mother, who scarcely allowed anyone to cross the threshold of her house, during these long years, the letters from her distant brother on the Somali coast had been her only breath of adventure and romance. In imagination she had followed him across the world, she had shared in spirit in his adventures and had grieved with him in his disappointments.[2] Now the man whom she had idolized in her mind without truly knowing him, was returning home and in need of her care and her tenderness, and she gave him all the passionate affection of her thwarted heart and all the maternal instinct which had never yet found an outlet. In this she reached, for the first time self-expression and independence from her mother, and in this her Rimbaud pride and despotism found vent. 'Je m'étais attachée à lui telle qu'une petite poussière d'argent qu'un artiste divin aurait coulée dans le moule d'une colossale statue d'or.'[3]

She prepared for his reception the finest room in the house, decking it with flowers, and her heart leaped with joy when, on his return, stopping with amazement on the threshold of the room before he entered, he cried: 'Why! it is Versailles here!' No room had ever yet been garnished with flowers for his reception.

At home there was now only Isabelle and her mother. Frederick was making his life entirely away from the family. He was a coarse fellow who thought only of drinking with the peasants, and he was bored with his bigoted mother and his prim spinsterish sister. Curiously enough, Madame Rimbaud herself, who, in the past, had had very precise ideas of what the wife and children of an officer should be, was herself reverting to her peasant ancestor type. All she thought of now was the accumulating of her savings and the profitable working of the farm at Roche. In this she wore herself out, and her daughter as well; in this she poured all the thwarted ambition she had once placed in her children who had all failed her; into this one passion went all the generous feelings which, in spite of what her detractors say, she had once devoted to them. And into this went all the Rimbaud obstinacy and inflexibility. In the little village in the north of France, she was submitting herself and her daughter to very much the same treatment that her son had meted out to himself on the Somali coast. For almost twelve years now the two women had worked the farm alone with the help of one man. In 1879, the previous tenant had refused to renew his lease as the conditions offered by Madame Rimbaud had been too severe.

Love of money seemed to be, as far as outsiders could tell, the ruling passion of Madame Rimbaud's life, and there seemed little room in her heart for any other emotion. Her apparent coldness deeply hurt her son when he came home ill and in need of sympathy and love. During the six years of his vagabondage, he had always returned for rest and recuperation from his hard-ships; he had always thought of his family as being there to receive him with open arms, and at Harar he had looked forward to his home-coming with longing and eagerness. Now his mother's hardness and lack of warmth and sympathy broke something in him, and those who saw him at Roche, during these last months, were struck by his growing resentment against her. Doctor Beaudier, who was Rimbaud's medical adviser, said that the one vivid recollection he had of Arthur's last visit home was the indifference he showed towards his mother, it was as if he endured physical discomfort in her presence. One day, when he was attending him, his mother peeped round the door, and immediately his face grew hard and set; he spoke roughly to her and told her to be off.[4]

On the other hand his affection and tenderness for his sister grew in intensity with each passing day. His appreciation for all she did increased and particularly his complete dependence on her, while this dependence of his especially endeared him to her. It was she alone who looked after him and she devoted to the task much time stolen from the work of the farm. She went with him wherever he wished to go; she helped him upstairs and down, removed the obstacles from his path on which his remaining foot might stumble; she accompanied him on his slow and laborious walks through the country. It was she who always set his room to rights and kept it bright with flowers; jealously she refused to allow anyone else to care for him but herself.

As soon as he reached home he settled himself into his new quarters as if for a long stay. His few coarse Oriental mats were laid on the ground, his coloured hangings on the walls, and round the room were placed all the knick-knacks which he had collected during his wanderings and which were very precious to him. He tried to make his room look, as far as possible, like his house at Harar.

He used to talk to Isabelle frequently of his life in Abyssinia and of his longing to return there; now that fate had removed him from that hell he began to regret it and to endow it with all the virtues. He knew that, even in his crippled condition, he would always be able to obtain work of a sort there, for he had many friends who thought highly of him and who were willing to employ him.

'I hope to be able to return where I was,' he said earlier, [5] 'for I have friends there of ten years' standing, who will have pity on me. With them I shall always be able to find work and live as best I can.'

Isabelle never tired of hearing him describe the life he had led in a country which was hard for her to visualize. Sometimes he joked and turned it all to fun, pointing out the humour of everything, mimicking those with whom he had been thrown into contact, and then there was something irresistible in his ironical and acid wit. But at other times nothing could rouse him to cheerfulness and he only sat in gloomy silence, with his head sunk in his hands, refusing to say a word.

Suddenly, sometimes, his restlessness would seize hold of him and he would call to Isabelle to come out with him, and whatever she was doing she left aside to accompany him. On Sundays, when the pony was not busy with the work of the farm, she used to drive him round the countryside in the old rickety trap. He liked particularly to be taken where crowds used to gather on holidays and Sundays; he used to stop the trap and sit watching, with solemn wondering eyes, the antics of the people, and marvel at all the changes that had taken place in country life during his twelve years of absence abroad.

Although he was maimed he had not abandoned his project of matrimony and of returning with a wife to Abyssinia, but his hopes were now less ambitious. He was afraid to risk rebuff from a bourgeois family and he intended now to choose a poor and honest girl from an orphanage, or else to marry a Christian Abyssinian.

In spite of rest and quiet his health did not improve at home. It was thought, at first, that the insomnia and the fever, the continuous pain, were merely due to the fatigue of the long journey from Marseilles in his enfeebled condition. But the insomnia persisted and the continuous pain did not abate. He began soon to notice that the stump of the severed leg seemed to be increasing in size, while an intolerable ache was beginning to be felt in his right armpit, and his right arm, at times, seemed to be deprived of feeling. When Beaudier came to attend him, Rimbaud would look up at him, with cold, piercing eyes, from which all colour seemed to have faded, trying to read what might be hidden from him. Yet he kept on repeating that whatever happened he would undergo no further operation, that he was determined to keep all his remaining limbs.

The pain was, however, on the increase and allowed him no respite. Then the doctor ordered for him a soporific, to be taken at night, so that he could snatch some sleep. But Arthur preferred to the doctor's prescription a tea made from the poppy seeds which Isabelle used to gather in the garden. When he had drunk a cup of this beverage he used to reach a state of half dreaming in which his faculties seemed to loosen and all his reserves seemed to break down. Then he felt, what he never experienced otherwise, a desire for confidences, a longing to open his heart. When he was in this condition, he used to close the shutters and doors of his room, even in broad daylight, light lamps and candles, and in that close, mysterious atmosphere, while he gently turned a little barrel-organ or plucked an Abyssinian harp, he used to relate the story of his life, tell of his dreams of the past and of his secret hopes for the future. His slow, sad voice then seemed to take on beautiful modulations and the language in which he spoke was very different from his everyday speech, full of Oriental turns of phrase and Oriental images. At such moments he was living in a wakeful dream and returning to the visions of his childhood, to all that he had buried deep in himself for twenty years and which now burst through the hard crust in a burning stream. Yet once, when Beaudier spoke to him of his poetry and literature, he made a gesture of disgust and answered coldly: 'Il s'agit bien de tout cela. Merde pour la poésie.' Yet at this very time, in 1891, Rimbaud's fame was at its height in the literary circles in Paris, but none of those who acclaimed him as the greatest poet of the nineteenth century, knew that, scarcely three hours' distance away, the poet they revered was ending his life in a kind of dream.

Sometimes, in the warm weather, when night had fallen, the village people used to come and stand beneath the window to hear the harp being gently played and the rise and fall of Rimbaud's incanting voice. They thought that he had gone mad, out east, and that the music was being played to soothe his nerves. Later in the night, he would fall asleep and Isabelle would sit beside his bed watching over his slumber, in case he should awaken and need her care. Then, at dawn, she would creep away and he, faintly stirring in his sleep, would feel the chill of her departure, and call to her, only half awake, and she would return, happy to serve him still.

With repeated use of the poppy tea, however, the state of hallucination became permanent. One night, suddenly awaking and forgetting, momentarily, that he was now a cripple, he jumped out of bed to pursue something that he imagined was in the room, and he fell heavily to the ground. His sister, hearing the noise of his fall, rushed in to his aid and found him lying helpless and dazed on the floor. She helped him to bed; luckily his fall had done him no injury, but it brought him back to reality out of his protracted dream. He wondered, then, what he might have revealed of his inner self when under the influence of the poppy tea, and he refused to touch it again. Henceforth he would have no more opiates and his sufferings grew in intensity with the passing days.

He tried, however, all manner of remedies, both quack and scientific: internal and external; massage and exercise. The internal remedies only affected his digestion, the external ones did nothing whatsoever, and the massage only irritated his nerve centres and increased his agony.

Gradually he lost, almost entirely, the use of his right arm, without at the same time, ceasing to suffer pain in it. He then became more dependent than ever on his sister. She used to cut up his food for him, bit by bit, and feed him, as if he were a child, holding the cup or the spoon to his lips. His appetite, however, had almost entirely vanished. His insomnia grew more obstinate and almost every night Isabelle used to sit with him and play to him on the piano, to pass the long weary hours, until the pale light of dawn crept in under the lowered blinds. Her music could never be anything but sad, it seemed to weep with her inward and unshed tears. Only when morning came could Arthur ever sleep; then she would steal away, and stand outside with her ear glued to the door, waiting for him to wake again, ready to fulfil his smallest wishes.

In proportion as his health grew worse his spirits fell. He used to have fits of anger and sudden tears, followed by moods of repentance and sentimentality. He was haunted chiefly by the terror of becoming completely paralysed, for what could he then do? Now he was willing to submit to anything; months or years of barbarous tortures, all that he would willingly have endured with joy, if he could only keep the use of his arms and his remaining leg.

But as the weeks slipped by he became more morose and irritable. Roche, which has always been called *terre des loups*, inspired in him a feeling of growing horror. He could no longer use his crutches and driving in the old trap, devoid of rubber tyres or springs, on the rough country roads, was agony. He gave up going out entirely and only sat under the chestnut-tree in the court and talked of the past, while tears flowed down his emaciated cheeks. Isabelle would try to comfort him, but she knew well that life would never smile on him again, and she used to look with a distress, which she could scarcely disguise, at his cheeks which, each morning, seemed to her to have sunk further than the previous night, at the hollows under his eyes which had become deeper and blacker.

Even nature was unfriendly that year and all the elements seemed leagued against him. Roche is in the north of France, near the borders of Belgium and there was rain and fog all that summer. Even when the sun, so ardently longed for, did occasionally show its face, it was only with the palest of smiles. It was always bitterly cold and they rarely ventured out without being met by storms and rain. On 10 August a terrible storm blew up one night, followed by frost, and it stripped bare the trees as if autumn had already come. The crops lay rotting in the fields, or else were burnt up by the early frost. Rimbaud, who had always loved heat and the sun, suffered intolerably from the inclement weather, from the cold to which he had grown unaccustomed. His one idea was to escape from Roche, to return as soon as possible to Harar. He thought that if he could even reach Marseïlles, the gate of the East, his health would surely improve, for there he would at least find sun and heat. Then, when he had grown somewhat stronger, he would embark for Aden. His mother, whose common sense and experience of life told her how desperately ill he was, tried to discourage this plan. Since die he must, why not die in his own home amongst his own people? She opposed the move with all her habitual violence, but his own obstinacy won the day and he was supported by Isabelle who had promised to accompany him.

On 23 August 1891, exactly one month after his home-coming, he set out for Marseilles, his last journey, and this journey had in it the hardships of his travels in Abyssinia and his expedition to Shoa in 1887.

The journey started badly. In his anxiety that nothing should make him miss the train, he had been up and dressed at three o'clock in the morning, and had insisted on being driven to the station, only three kilometres distant, to catch the train which did not leave until half-past six. On the way to the station, however, the pony, annoyed at having been disturbed in the middle of the night, stood still in the road and refused to budge. There was no whip in the trap to beat him into activity, and Rimbaud took off his leather belt to belabour the animal, and eventually got him to move. But when they finally reached the station, they found that the train had left two minutes before. What was he to do? The jolting of the trap was exceedingly painful to him and he thought of waiting in the station the six hours until the next train was due; but the cold morning fog and the unheated condition of the waiting-room made him shiver and he decided to go home.

By half-past nine he was growing impatient again; it was a couple of hours too soon, but he would insist on setting out for fear of being late again, and would not wait to have a meal before he departed. Just as he was leaving, however, his exaltation fell and it was as if the knowledge suddenly came to him that he would never see his home again. As he looked around him the tears came into his eyes and in a moment of weakness he cried; 'Oh! Lord! Shall I not find a stone on which to rest my head, nor a dwelling wherein to die? I would rather not leave. I would like to see all my friends around me and to distribute to them all that I possess.'[6]

He held his mother and sister clasped in his arms as he wept. The despair of his words moved Isabelle and she said to him; 'Do stay then! We'll look after you well and never leave you! Do stay!'

But his moment of faltering was past, and hearing the step of the farm servant coming to carry him to the trap, he pulled himself together and said: 'No! I must try to get well!'

This time they were obliged to wait two hours in the station before the train arrived. Here, in spite of his weariness and his pain, the old witty Rimbaud of Harar appeared in flashes, and he amused his sister with caustic descriptions of their rustic fellow travellers and of the tiny formal garden—the pride of the station-master—which consisted of a couple of daisy plants standing round a scrappy dahlia, the whole thing surrounded by a ring of sand.

Then they heard the whistle of the coming train; it stopped and Rimbaud was hoisted into the carriage by a porter. The jolting of the badly constructed local train was excruciating torture to him. In no position could he find rest; every inch of his body was aching. He was holding on to the stump of his leg in agony and repeating as a refrain, as if he did not realize what he was saying: 'What terrible pain! What terrible pain!'

At Amagne they were obliged to change and there was twenty minutes to wait. The next train, the Paris express, was very crowded, and in spite of Isabelle's care it was impossible to get a carriage to themselves or to spare him suffering. By this time, however, he was so worn out with fatigue that he was able to get brief snatches of sleep. His eyes seemed to remain half open, even as he slept. Illness had hollowed out his face and fever had put two red patches on his cheek-bones. He looked to his sister very ill indeed.

All the way to Paris people crowded into the train; happy people, playing children, newly married couples, Sunday crowds. Occasionally Rimbaud opened his eyes and gazed about him in a dazed, bewildered way, as if wondering where he was, then closed them once more in weariness.

Towns and villages slipped by the carriage window; rivers, gardens, fields with yellow standing corn. Everywhere could be seen the carefree spirit of an August Continental Sunday. In the stations, along the country roads, in the little towns, in the cafés, they saw people dressed in their holiday clothes, and everywhere, except in Isabelle's heart, there was gaiety and laughter. On the river, as they approached Paris, they saw the canoes, the little sailing-boats with their bright sails reflected in the water; and from the windows of the houses, they heard, as the train slowed down, snatches of music and dance tunes. And Rimbaud, who might have looked out on this scene of gaiety with interest and curiosity, lay in the stifling atmosphere of the train, in his corner seat, gazing with half-open eyes at the wooden partition opposite.

It was half-past six when they reached Paris, the sun had by then disappeared, and the sky had clouded over. They had, before they started, planned to spend the night in Paris so that the invalid could rest thoroughly, but the rain began to fall as they left the Gare de l'Est; then Rimbaud said that nothing would induce him to break his journey and he ordered the cabby to drive them to the Gare de Lyon. The streets were almost empty that Sunday evening, for the crowds had gone home and there were no shops to disgorge their hordes of working people. The pavements glistened in the wet and the rain in the gutters made melancholy music. The shops were all shut; it was dismal!

At the Gare de Lyon they were obliged to wait until eleven o'clock for the express to Marseilles. Isabelle thought that her brother might be able to sleep, or at least to rest, in what in those days corresponded to the modern *Wagon-lit*, the *Lit-Coupé*. He took a soporific before he settled down for the night, but sleep would not come. Suffering, both mental and physical; weakness, fatigue and fasting—he had taken no food since the very early morning—all this brought on a fever over which the narcotic had no effect. For the whole of that night, as the express carried them to Marseilles, Isabelle was the silent spectator of the most distressing scene of anguish that she had ever imagined in her uneventful life. Arthur, as if unconscious of her presence, in agonized despair, compared this journey with the one he had made, only a month before, in the opposite direction, his present weakness with his comparative strength then. A month ago he still cherished the hope of cure, now in the depths of his heart he knew that there could be none. Isabelle did not think of trying to sleep herself; she knelt, hunched up in the narrow space between the wall of the carriage and the seat, in order to be as near as possible to her suffering brother, to hold her arms about him, and to bring him what comfort and support she could from her physical presence.

In the morning, when they came to Lyons and saw the rising sun glinting on the golden stars of the bridge over the Rhône, making them seem real stars, Rimbaud, worn out with emotion and suffering, fell into a doze, more like coma than real sleep, and was oblivious, for some hours, of the horror of reality.

As the day crept on the southern heat grew more intense; they could scarcely breathe in the cushioned carriage; it was like a padded cell in an infernal prison from which no escape was possible. They passed through Avignon, Nîmes, Arles and through the lonely stretches of the Camargue. Then came Marseilles!

It was evening when they arrived and Rimbaud was carried immediately to the hospital of the Immaculate Conception, which he was not to leave alive.

Here begins the last phase in the desperate fight between Death and the man still longing to live, to live in spite of everything.

## CHAPTER VII

## LE VAINCU

THE doctors at the hospital at Marseilles diagnosed Rimbaud's disease as carcinoma, but some critics have wondered whether it might not rather be the tertiary stage of the syphilis he contracted at Harar. Diagnosis in those days was more imperfect than now and Rimbaud himself would, probably, not connect the tumour which had recently appeared on his knee, with the earlier disease which he had thought cured and which, ten years before, had presented quite different symptoms. However, according to modern medical opinion, there is nothing in the progress of the disease, as described by Isabelle in her letters to her mother,[1] to preclude its having been, in fact, carcinoma; on the contrary, judging from the symptoms, this appears to be the most reasonable diagnosis.

To Isabelle, who asked for their opinion, they answered: 'He's very ill indeed, poor fellow, and is fast slipping away. It's only a question of weeks, or months at best, unless some unforeseen complication intervenes—which eventuality may occur at any moment—and that would end everything more quickly. As for recovery, that cannot even be considered, for there is no hope of that.' The eldest of them, a white-haired old man, added that since she had come so far with her brother, she should remain until the end. 'To leave him now would only be cruel.'

That was the doctors' verdict, as communicated to Isabelle, but to Rimbaud himself, in an effort to raise his sinking spirits, they promised cure, and endeavoured each day, to make him believe that he was indeed better. Isabelle, hearing their cheerful words, was bewildered, scarcely knowing when to believe them for they seemed as convinced and sincere when speaking to her brother as when speaking to herself. Rimbaud, who had always wished to face the truth squarely, with fierce and savage joy, without being deluded in anything, was now being deceived at the ultimate crisis of his life, concerning his own death. Yet, with hope, his condition seemed, for a time, to improve. His colour became more natural, his appetite somewhat returned and he was more peaceful in his mind.

His mother, up in the north, at Roche, sent no words of affection and sympathy to her child who was dying so far away from her. It is alleged that she was continuing against him her policy of silent resentment, but this is only conjecture. Nevertheless it is difficult to understand her behaviour at this time, but her character was no more comprehensible or simple than that of her son. She wrote once, but then so briefly—merely asking for news of the patient—that Isabelle thought that she must be ill. She did not even answer the long letter which her daughter sent giving her the doctors' verdict. Then Isabelle wrote once more, this time in great distress:

My dear mother [she wrote],[2] I beg and implore you to answer me, or to get someone to write me even a note on your behalf. I'm almost out of my mind with the anxiety in which I live. What have I done that you should be so cruel to me? Are you ill, or something, that you don't answer? If so you had better tell me and I'll come right back to look after you, although Arthur begs me not to leave him until he dies. What has happened to you? Oh! If I could only go at once to you! But without knowing exactly whether you're ill or not, I can't leave my unfortunate brother, who swears, if I leave him, to strangle himself or to commit suicide somehow.

Her mother then sent a short note, excusing her delay in replying on the score of all the work that had to be done on the farm, of the endless difficulties she was having with the labourers and the harvesters. To this Isabelle sent, in answer, wise and pedestrian advice concerning the work of the farm, with suggestions on the most economical manner of marketing the stock, the crops and the dairy produce. Who can say whether this is the kind of letter that the mother wished to receive in answer to her laconic note with its unbelievable excuse? Her detractors have always accused her of being heartless and of being occupied solely with material and petty preoccupations when her son was dying. Perhaps, on the contrary, it was the daughter who was insensitive to treat seriously the incredible excuse, as if her mother had expected it to be believed; perhaps her letter to her mother, who had never asked for gentleness or affection, was only crude, stupid and unfeeling. Perhaps Madame Rimbaud would now have liked the warmth and sympathy she did not know how to ask for. Who can know what deep and agonized suffering this reserved and bitter woman now hid under these seemingly material preoccupations? To go on from day to day with the work in hand; to drug oneself with work so as to forget all else; to work until one dropped; that had been the only philosophy this hard peasant woman had ever known. She had never relaxed before her children, never shown them that she loved them and was proud of them; her letters to her daughter[3] have no terms of endearment, no affectionate messages; they begin baldly, 'my daughter' and end simply, 'your mother'. She had never shown her sons and daughters that she was capable of human weakness. Expansiveness is a characteristic not easily acquired and she could not now suddenly reveal her feelings at a time when she was afraid that they might sweep her away to a total loss of self-control. It was probably more than she could have borne, to sit by, with hands folded idly in her lap, and watch Arthur die, the finest of all her flock, in whose future her early dreams had been centred, and in whom latterly, she had begun again to hope. Nine years after his death she wrote to Isabelle, forgetting all the worry and anxiety he had caused her for so many years:[4]

My poor Arthur, who never asked me for anything, and who, by his work, by his intelligence and by his good conduct had amassed a fortune, and amassed it very honourably, never cheated anyone; on the contrary they made him lose a great deal of money, they still owe him, and the poor child was very charitable, which is well known.

It is not true, as critics allege, that she had always hated him and that she did not forget her grudge even as he lay dying. When he was in Abyssinia she was always anxious for him, and, in 1889, when she had had no news of him for a long time—his letters had not reached her, nor hers him—she wrote to his employer César Tian to ask for news of him.[5] Another time, when she had not heard from him, because he was on his expedition to Abyssinia, she wrote in great distress.[6]

Arthur my son. Your silence has lasted a long time, and why this silence? Happy those who have no children, or who, having them do not love them or are indifferent to what happens to them.

His letters this time had been held up for eight months. Finally, in March 1891, when she had received his letter informing her of his state of health, she sent him an answer full of anxious advice on what to do with his injured leg, advice she had got from her doctor, and she enclosed a pot of ointment.[5] It is also obvious from her letters to Isabelle that, although she always refused to speak of him to those who were not members of the family, he was constantly in her thoughts so that, eight years after his death, she could write:

I was still kneeling in church saying my prayers, when someone came and sat near to me, someone that I had not noticed. Then suddenly I saw in front of my eyes a crutch like those poor Arthur used to have. I turned my head and was astounded for it was my poor Arthur himself. Same height, same age, same face, white complexion, no beard but a little moustache, and one leg missing; and this young man was gazing at me with extraordinary sympathy and gentleness.

I could not, in spite of all my efforts, keep back my tears, tears of sorrow doubtless, but there was as well something that I could not explain. I knew it was my beloved son who was beside me. And all through Mass I thought to myself: Is my poor Arthur indeed looking for me? I am ready. I am only warning you, my daughter, for when I shall no longer be there.[7]

Rimbaud's calmness of mind did not, however, continue indefinitely. He clung tenaciously to life, deceived by the fair words of the doctors. Yet he did not realize that, even if he lived, he would remain completely paralysed. Sometimes, when he found that he could not move his limbs, he began to doubt the doctor's words; he thought that they were lying to him, or that they were ignorant and did not understand his case. But his most serious preoccupations were anxiety and care for the future, and what was to become of him if he did not get back the use of his right arm. Then he would fall into the deepest depression and refuse to speak to anyone.

Every morning, when she came to the hospital, Isabelle thought that she perceived a faint change for the worse, that paralysis, particularly, was more pronounced. Every day he seemed to lose weight, and his eyes, with their immense black circles, seemed to sink right back into his head. Every day now, when he awoke, he found his limbs so stiffened that he was unable to make a movement until he had loosened them from the immobility of the night.

One morning, Isabelle, arriving early, before he had yet wakened, stood for some moments, looking down on him as he slept, with his eyes half open in his livid face, breathing in short, panting breaths, and asked herself how anyone could go on living and yet look so near to death.

His right arm was now completely useless and paralysis was beginning to gain his left; a slight nervous twitch was perceptible in his leg, and his left eye was never more than half open. In no position could his racked body find ease or rest.

Then a new and agonizing treatment was tried, which seems a senseless torture for an unfortunate man who could, in any case, not recover. Yet the treatment served to fill the day and to fan his waning hope. Each morning an electric apparatus was brought into his ward and the operator set to work on his right arm for a quarter of an hour. During the treatment his hand made certain nervous, spasmodic movements, galvanized automatically, into activity by the electricity, but when the current was switched off it fell back again into helpless immobility. All he then felt was violent pain in the arm and hand, but no more capacity for movement. This performance was repeated several times during the day on both arms and the operator declared that he was satisfied with the progress of the patient. Rimbaud would now have accepted, for all hours of the day, any treatment—however painful—anything that would have given him back the use of his arm and have arrested the paralysis. He still dreamed of re-covering sufficiently to enable him to go to Aden or Obokh, for there, he was convinced, he would get well. It was Isabelle's presence at Marseilles that prevented him from making immediate arrangements to leave, for he did not believe that she would be willing to accompany him to the Red Sea coast and he felt now that he could no longer live without her.

One day his new artificial leg arrived, the beautiful mechanic-ally jointed leg, ordered several months earlier, the leg that was to make walking and riding almost as easy as they had been to him when he had two legs of flesh and blood. But now, when the leg finally arrived, he could not even try it on, and at this he suddenly broke down. 'It's all over now!' he cried to his sister who was with him. 'It's really all over now, and I know that I shall die!'

Although his suffering increased each day, he still clung des-perately to life and longed for it more passionately than ever. He forgot all the hardships which he had endured—indeed these seemed part of his life and so desirable—he forgot how much he had always professed to hate human existence. He used to look out of the window at the clear beautiful Marseillais sky, lovelier than ever in the autumn, a sky with scarcely ever a cloud, and with a radiant sun shining in it. Then, in imagination, he saw the Mediterranean which was so near to him, with all the ships ready to sail to distant lands, but no ship waiting for him.

'I shall go underground to the dark,' he said to Isabelle, 'while you will still walk in the sunlight.'

Nevertheless, when the doctor came for the afternoon visit, he listened to his encouraging words with eagerness and feverish hope.

But the disease did not stay in its progress. It seemed now as if paralysis were gaining his internal organs as well as his limbs. Then, one day, the doctor perceived, to his dismay, a large external growth developing in the groin of his amputated thigh. When he saw this he shook his head gravely, for he knew that the end was not far off.

Isabelle was with her brother all day and far into the evening too, as long as the hospital authorities allowed her to remain beside him. It was she washed him and fed him, it was she straightened his bed. The evening, when the candles were lit, was the best time of the day for him; he was then comparatively free from pain and she used to sit and talk to him, or allow him to talk, in the flickering light, until the sister in charge turned her out at nine o'clock. Every evening he tried to detain her as long as possible, with endless unnecessary questions, as she stood at the door ready to depart, to keep her one moment longer, to shorten by so much the dreary stretches of the interminable night. Every night, as he said good-bye to her, it was as if he were never to see her again, as if she might not find him alive when she returned in the morning.

For Isabelle, in spite of her grief at her imminent loss, the time at the hospital at Marseilles seems to have been a peaceful, almost happy time, and her letters home do not reveal excess of suffering. She was able to notice and to appreciate the good terms in which she stood with the nuns at the hospital, due chiefly to the gravity of Arthur's state. She was able to relate little things that they said to her, little kindnesses that had been shown to her; she was still able to enjoy her little egoism, her little vanities.

It was here one must come [she wrote to her mother],[8] to see and to feel oneself really respected, and honour shown to one as one deserves. What a difference between the polished manners here and the boorishness of young people at Roche.

She could tell her mother, with pride, of a friend she had made, a Spanish woman who, with her husband, was staying at Marseilles to look after an uncle who was a patient at the hospital. They were rich people, she boasted, and the husband had the Legion of Honour. She had time and thought for casual friendships. She told her mother of a happy afternoon she had spent with a letter from home, in expressions that ring hollow, affected and insincere. 'I kissed it and bathed it with my tears,' she wrote.[9] 'Exiled as I am here with my poor invalid, it's a long time since I've spent so happy an afternoon as I spent with my dear letter.'

It was as if the act of devoting herself entirely to someone for the first time in her life, being needed and wanted by someone, gave her complete happiness, a feeling of entire fulfilment and also a sense of importance. Hers had been, hitherto, emotionally and otherwise, a stunted and restricted life. Now suddenly she found herself freed from her mother's despotism, with leisure and with friends; she was now somebody of account with authority and responsibility, to whose opinions others deferred, and she was enabled for the first time to express her individuality. Her letters to her mother show no signs of that overwhelming agony at the thought of her loss, which stuns and dazes others, nor yet the intolerable regret that some would have felt on Rimbaud's behalf, at the thought of his life so soon coming to a close; regret for his own sake not for hers who might miss him; regret for all the years to come which might have been his to enjoy, in which even to suffer, in which he might have found himself and have reached complete fulfilment. Her brother's death, as it happened, would affect her own life very little, she had known him for so short a time. Now she would always be able to treasure the memory of those last months in which she had devoted herself utterly to him, in which he had clung to her and needed her; in *Mon Frère Arthur*, she wrote:[10]

Je connais ce délire qu'on nomme le dévouement, et pardessus tout j'ai senti l'ineffable allégresse d'aimer absolument un être de mon sang, de l'aimer dans la joie, dans l'épreuve, dans le malheur, m'élançant d'esprit et de cœur vers lui; de l'aimer dans la souffrance et la maladie, en ne le quittant plus, de l'aimer dans l'agonie et dans la mort, en l'assistant sans faiblir.

These lines were written by a person who has experienced unnatural joy rather than deep suffering; they were written by a vain and proud, egoistical and somewhat insensitive woman.

She had, however, not yet accomplished her great and proud mission, her brother was not yet in the condition in which she wished to hand him into the keeping of the Almighty. So far all her attempts to turn his thoughts to religion had been in vain. In spite of all she would like us to believe, he remained, until the last days, violently anticlerical and opposed to Catholicism. Doctor Beaudier, who attended him at Roche, heard him make various remarks about religion that left no doubt as to the opinions which he held. And an old peasant told Goffin that Rimbaud used to swear like a trooper and make fun of him because he still continued to attend Mass on Sundays.[11]

Now Isabelle, as she sat with Arthur in the evenings, let her conversation fall, as frequently as possible, on the tremendous mystery of Mass, on Communion, on Confession and the forgiveness of sins. She used to describe to him the beautiful services of High Mass and Benediction which she attended on Sundays and feast days in the convent chapel attached to the hospital. It was a long time, she said, since she had been to Mass so beautifully sung, and there was something divine in the appearance of the little altar- and choir-boys in their sky-blue cassocks, their snow-white surplices, while the purity of their voices made her think of a choir of angels.

Little by little she wore down his resistance and she was able to write to her mother on 28 October, less than a fortnight before his death, that all was now well and that her brother was converted.

My dear mother, God be blessed a thousand times! [she wrote].[12] I experienced on Sunday the greatest happiness I could ever have had in this world. It is no longer a miserable damned soul who is dying beside me; it is a martyr and a saint; one of the Chosen.

Isabelle Rimbaud's work was now complete and she was handing into God's keeping, with true Rimbaud pride and arrogance, not a sinner but a repentant Catholic in a state of grace, a martyr and a saint; and God was indebted to her alone for this gift. What more could the Almighty ask of her?

Much has been written about this death-bed conversion of Rimbaud. Some, like Claudel, accept it as the full explanation of *Les Illuminations*, as the epilogue of *Une Saison en Enfer*, some refuse to admit its existence at all. Nevertheless, whatever may be our personal view of the spiritual value of death-bed conversions, there can be little doubt that Rimbaud was so converted. The letter which Isabelle wrote to her mother, immediately after the event, rings too true. In this she has given too exact a picture of Rimbaud's mind for it to have been invented; she did not, at this time, know his work, and had not read *Illuminations*. It is very different from the later effusions published in *Rimbaud Catholique*.[13]

There had always been in Rimbaud a thirst for religion and a longing for the certainty of belief. The struggle expressed in *Une Saison en Enfer* had been partly between his reason and his desire for faith, and he had given the victory to his reason; he had clung to the topmost rung of the ladder of common sense, he had kept 'la liberté dans le salut'. Nevertheless without religious faith he had remained for the rest of his life a maimed figure, deprived of a vital organ. It does not come as a surprise that he should have returned, at the end, to the comfort of belief.

Several times, during the week which preceded his conversion, Isabelle begged the priest to visit Arthur, but he always found such weariness and disgust in the patient that he did not dare to speak to him of Confession and of death. Finally, one Saturday, Isabelle requested all the nuns to send up a prayer, after their own confession, for a good death for her brother. The following morning, after High Mass, the priest returned to Rimbaud and found him more calm and resigned. He asked whether he would like him to hear his confession and Arthur agreed. Then, when the priest had heard the confession, he gave Rimbaud absolution and left the ward. Outside he met Isabelle, who was waiting, anxiously, for him, and he said to her in a voice of deep emotion, 'What did you tell me, my child? Your brother has faith. He believes. Indeed I have rarely met a faith of the quality of his.'

I kissed the ground! [wrote Isabelle ecstatically to her mother, expressing her feelings rather than absolute truth].[14] Weeping and laughing at once. Oh! Lord! What joy! What joy! Even in death! Even through death! What can death and life, and the whole universe, and all the happiness of the world do to me now, since his soul is saved? Lord soften his agony! Help him to bear his cross! Have pity on him, still more pity! You who are so good, so good! Thank you, my Lord, thank you!

When Isabelle went in again to her brother, she found him singularly moved, but he was not weeping, although he was sadder than she had ever seen him before. All hope of life on earth had now left him. He looked at her as he had never looked at her, and said: You are of the same flesh and blood as I and you do believe, don't you? Tell me you do believe!' And Isabelle answered: 'Yes! I believe. Those wiser than I have believed and still believe. And moreover I'm certain now. For I have proof.'

Then Rimbaud answered with exceeding bitterness: 'Oh! yes they say that they believe; they pretend to be converted, but it's only so that people should read their books!'

Was he perhaps thinking of Verlaine's short-lived conversion and of his poems in *Sagesse*?

He still looked at her intently, then he kissed her and said: 'Perhaps we may have the same souls since we have the same flesh and blood. And so you truly believe?'

And Isabelle answered once more: Yes! I believe. One must believe.' Then Arthur sighed, and there was in him, at that moment, infinite sadness, for he knew that he was now going to yield. His hunger and thirst for spiritual food must now be assuaged, at the end, even though perhaps it was not real food, only an opiate. His body was kept free from pain with morphia, why should not the intolerable agony of his soul have its own soporific? He was now sacrificing the last shreds of his pride; he was finally laying down his arms. Rimbaud's conversion seems to have had some of the quality of the *Pari* of Pascal, his famous wager. If there is one hundredth chance of God's existence being true, we must believe, for that is only reason, 'Si vous gagnez, vous gagnez tout; si vous perdez, vous ne perdez rien.'[15] We lose nothing by belief, but by incredulity we may lose eternity.

His conversion was perhaps the final humiliation of his pride, the ultimate chastisement of the man who had dared to think himself the equal of God. Through all his failures and sufferings he might have cried to God, asking if this were chastisement and God might have answered, 'Not yet!' There was no final chastisement for Rimbaud until he had sacrificed everything, until he had yielded all.

When Isabelle answered him again: 'Yes! I believe. One must believe,' he said wearily, 'Then the room must be prepared and set to rights. The priest is returning with the Sacraments. You'll see what it will be like. They will bring candles and fine lace. White cloths must be put everywhere. Am I then so ill?'

After that he blasphemed and swore no more, but prayed continuously.

In *Une Saison en Enfer* he had written: 'Si Dieu m'accordait le calme céleste, aérien, la prière,—comme les anciens saints—Les Saints des forts.'[16] In those days he had added, 'Farce continuelle!' but now he possessed this peace and this strength. Now, as he was about to leave the world, he stilled the voice that had always cried to him that he must, at all costs, keep his personal liberty.

With the laying down of his arms the hard outside shell broke, the Abyssinian mask and armour burst asunder, allowing the imprisoned poet to escape; the poet who had seemed to shrivel up and die, but who had only slept for nearly twenty years, until the light from beyond this world, the light that seems to fall on those who stand on the threshold of the grave, touched his eyes and he awoke. Now he looked once more on all the visions that had been his at the time of *Les Illuminations*, and allowed himself to enjoy them again. Then he had written, at the moment of vision, 'Tourné du côte l'ombre, je vous vois, mes filles, mes reines!'[17] These came to him once more. He ended his last days in what those around him thought was a dream. As Isabelle Rimbaud sat beside him and saw his life gently ebbing to its close he told her what he was seeing and described his visions in language he had seemed to have forgotten. He had shown no trace of it in his letters from Abyssinia, nor in the baldness of his account of his expedition to King Menelek. Now the imagination of his boyhood seemed to have returned to him and the words with which to render his experience. 'Sometimes he became a *voyant*,' says Isabelle[18] 'a prophet. Without losing consciousness he had the most marvellous visions. He saw columns of amethyst, angels in marble and wood; countries of indescribable beauty, and he used to paint these sensations, expressions of curious and penetrating charm.'

A few weeks after his death she was startled to find in *Illuminations*—which she had not yet read—the same visions and dreams but she says that those of his death-bed had greater depth and tenderness. We can only regret that, amongst all the other things that she wrote, as she sat beside her dying brother, she did not keep a record of his words, which she declared enchanted her, if it were not that they pierced her heart. We might then know something of the thoughts which occupied his mind during the last lonely years in Abyssinia, when Father Jarosseau, the Bishop of Harar, regarded him as a saintly character and said that he was always reading and writing.

One evening, as he lay murmuring in a low voice, describing what he was seeing, one of the sisters said to Isabelle: 'Do you think that he has lost consciousness again?' But he overheard her words, a blush flooded his face, and he became suddenly silent. And when the sister had left the room, he said to Isabelle: 'They think me mad! But you don't think me mad, do you?'

Sometimes he asked the doctors whether they too could see what he was seeing, and he then described his visions. As he spoke his eyes became more lovely and expressive than they had ever been before. His face had now assumed great spiritual beauty, something of the beauty it had possessed at the time of his visionary period, all the toughness of the Abyssinian had fallen away from him. The drawings which Isabelle made of him on his death-bed,[19] reveal a face of indescribable sadness, a face made incorporeal and spiritual by suffering.

He was, by now, taking almost no food; all his limbs were paralysed and lay motionless beside his trunk, like dead branches still hanging to a tree, itself not yet quite dead. His face had the chiselled immobility of marble, and in that face—indeed in all that body—the eyes alone still seemed to live.

Just at the end the Abyssinian awoke for a short space. He talked with longing of Harar, and of his anxiety for those who were dependent on him and whom he had grown to love. There was, that autumn, a disastrous famine in the province of Harar, with fifty or sixty people dying every day in the town of hunger. Hyenas climbed over the ramparts into the city, day and night, attracted by the stench of putrefying corpses which no one seemed to have time or thought to bury. Robecchi-Bricchetti describes the harrowing scenes he witnessed,[20] and Rimbaud's clerk Sottiro wrote to him that Ras Makonnen had been obliged to execute many of the Gallas convicted of eating their own children, their own brothers and sisters.[21] Rimbaud loved these natives and understood them. His anxiety was now that they should come to no harm. He knew that they were only children, even the oldest of them, wayward children needing his loving care and attention. They too thought of him with affection. Savouré in a letter to Rimbaud wrote:[22] 'Ras Makonnen speaks to us incessantly of you, saying that you are the most honest of men and that you have often proved to him that you are his true friend.'

And after Rimbaud's death Ras Makonnen himself wrote to Isabelle:[23] 'I am ill of the death of your brother and it seems to me that my soul has left me.'

As he lay dying, Rimbaud thought also of his fellow country-men on the Somali coast and in Abyssinia, who were struggling just as he had struggled, and when he realized how seriously ill he was, he sent part of his capital without any conditions, to friends away there, business men in a small way, who were in difficulties.[24]

In his delirium, or in the long nights when he could not sleep, he used to talk to Isabelle of Harar, and it seemed then to him as if he were there with her and that she was part of his life and accompanied him on all his journeys.

We are at Harar [she wrote to her mother],[15] and we are always leaving for Aden. We must find camels and organize the caravan. It seems to him then that he walks easily with his new artificial leg. We go for rides together on mules with beautiful harnesses. Then we must work! Quick! Quick! They are waiting for us and we must pack our bags and leave. What will they say if we do not arrive on the appointed day? No one will trust his word again. No one will have faith in him again.

He talked to Isabelle at great length of Djami, Djami his one friend, his only friend. Sometimes he confused together the two people whom he best loved, his sister and his servant, and he used then to call her Djami. One of his last thoughts was for the Harari boy, and he begged that he might be sent three thousand francs out of his estate. With loving care he asked that Djami be told, as the last order and injunction of his master who had loved him dearly, to make good and wise use of this money; to invest it perhaps in some honest and prudent enterprise from which he might obtain reasonable interest, but that the money was not to be a pretext for idleness and intemperance.[26] But Djami never received this legacy; in the Rimbaud case at the *Symbolist* exhibition in Paris, in July 1936, was shown a receipt signed by the French Bishop of Harar, Taurin Cahagne, and the heirs of young Djami. Djami must have died almost as soon as his master, dying perhaps in the famine of 1891, or killed in some savage raid.

On 9 November 1891, Rimbaud, while only semi-conscious, dictated to his sister a letter for a steamship company, in which he said: 'I am entirely paralysed and so I wish to embark early. Please let me know at what time I should be carried on board.'[27]

In *Une Saison en Enfer* he had written: 'Et à l'aurore, armé d'une ardente patience, nous entrerons aux splendides villes.' The following day he died, less than three weeks after his thirty-seventh birthday. Isabelle alone was at his side, for his mother had remained in the north.

When all was over Isabelle Rimbaud travelled back to the Ardennes with the mortal remains of the brother whose soul she had entrusted to God. As soon as the body arrived in Charleville,

Madame Rimbaud went to the parish priest at nine o'clock in the morning, on the day on which she wished the burial to take place, and ordered a funeral *de première classe* for ten o'clock that morning. Father Gillet pointed out to her how difficult it would be to make all the arrangements in so short a time; he added that he had been Arthur's religious instructor at school, and that he would like to collect some of his contemporaries and some of his own colleagues to attend the funeral. Madame Rimbaud would not, however, hear of altering her plans. 'Do not insist, Father!' she answered sharply. 'My mind is quite made up!'[28]

Even now, in death, she kept her old grudge against her son's friends, against his teachers, against literary men, against all those who, in her opinion, had led him astray and had caused his failure.

At ten o'clock that morning a magnificent funeral was held, with all the trappings that accompany a funeral *de première classe*. Rich black hangings, embroidered with the deceased's initials and spangled with silver tears, draped the church door and a full peal of bells was rung. There were five principal singers, accompanied by a choir of eight, the altar was a blaze of lights and several priests officiated. When the service was over, the imposing coffin, which had cost eight pounds, was borne, through the streets of Charleville, in the richly draped hearse, with plumes waving from the horses' heads, followed by a stately procession; the priests in their vestments, the choirboys in their surplices and cassocks, and twenty orphans each holding a lighted candle. Behind all this splendour, that slowly wended its way to the cemetery, there walked two solitary black-veiled figures. Madame Rimbaud and her daughter Isabelle.[29] There were no speeches at the graveside of the man who, at that very moment, was being acclaimed in Paris as the greatest poet of his age; there were present none of those who had known and who had been his companions in his early youth; not even Verlaine, with whom he had spent the most vital and passionate years of his life, was there to bid him farewell. Rimbaud was as solitary in his committal to earth as he had been through his life.

Nine years after the death of her son, Madame Rimbaud had his body exhumed and that of her daughter Vitalie, now dead more than twenty years, and reburied them in a permanent plot on which she raised a white marble monument in the worst bourgeois taste, to pay honour to the family pride. She alone was present at the exhumation; Arthur's coffin was still intact, but Vitalie's had rotted away and the mother, without a qualm, collected, herself, the bones of her daughter in a clean white sheet, until another coffin could be brought. This strange, un-accountable woman in a letter related the scene realistically to Isabelle who had dearly loved her sister whose death had left her lonely and without companionship at home. The mother described the condition of the body; the hair still soft and fair as it had been in life, but little else was left of the body. 'The flesh was completely rotten but there was still some ribs and bones holding together.'[30]

In 1901, when the tenth anniversary of Arthur's death was celebrated in his native town by the unveiling of the Rimbaud Monument in the Square de la Gare, Madame Rimbaud had not yet forgiven literature for the part it had played in her son's ruin, and she refused to be present at the ceremony. It is even said that she never once went to look at the statue, although the apartment which she occupied during the last years of her life was scarcely sixty yards away from the square. Yet she was pleased to see Alfred Bardey, her son's employer, when he came to Charleville for the unveiling of the monument and welcomed him warmly.[31] It was against literature and literary men that she nourished so bitter a hatred.

It is not only Arthur's literature that she hates [wrote Isabelle],[32] but every literary and scientific work which could not be put into the hands of a child of fifteen of mediocre intelligence. Although I have left Arthur's works lying about I doubt if she has ever read them. It is just as well that she should be ignorant of them for, given their style and their inspiration, she would dislike them intensely. She is totally uninterested in any question concerning them and even unaware of them, keeping firmly to the unalterable decision which she reached formerly.

She had the same obstinate inflexibility of character as her son, she was as incapable as he of yielding or of making concessions and she never gave way on what was to her a question of principle. Nothing that anyone might say or think—no question of tenderness, affection or pity—would make her deviate from the path she had thought fit to choose.

# CONCLUSION

It is now seventy years since Rimbaud died physically at Marseilles, and considerably more than eighty since he died to poetry —which is more significant.

In 1936 France celebrated the fiftieth anniversary of the Symbolist Movement and, at the same time, the fiftieth anniversary of the publication of *Illuminations* in *La Vogue*. In that half century Rimbaud's work did not cease to grow in significance and importance. Few poets in the world to-day are the object of more passionate study and interest—not even Baudelaire. There is no movement, in whatever country it may be, which does not claim to owe its origins to him, though he himself would have disclaimed sympathy with most of their views. Literary youth, all the world over, finds in Rimbaud to-day, the expression of its impatience with the past, with tradition; its disgust with accepted standards, and with what so-called civilization has made of the world in which we live; the same desire to destroy everything. Rimbaud had cried:[1]

> Qu'est-ce pour nous, mon cœur, que les nappes de sang
> Et de braise, et mille meurtres, et les longs cris
> De rage, sanglots de tout enfer renversant
> Tout ordre; et l'Aquilon encor sur les débris;
> Et toute vengeance?—Rien!—Mais si, toute encore,
> Nous la voulons! Industriels, princes, sénats;
> Périssez! puissance, justice, histoire: à bas!
> Ça nous est dû. Le Sang! le sang! la flamme d'or!

Rimbaud's writings are often difficult of understanding and interpretation, and they are thus a rich source for those in search of texts to support their doctrine. In Rimbaud—as in the Bible— confirmation of almost every theory can be found, and his work has been submitted to the same treatment as the Bible: small excerpts have been taken from it and these have been made the text of literary sermons and commentaries which sometimes require a vivid imagination in order to follow them.

Rimbaud has been seen by his various detractors and admirers as respectively: a scoundrel and a martyr; a *voyou* and a *voyant*; a waster and, finally, a saint who was called away from this world because France was not worthy of his presence.[2] Yet no single one of these descriptions adequately fits him, and Etiemble, in his doctoral thesis, *Le Mythe de Rimbaud*, published in 1952, has devoted more than twenty years of patient and exhaustive research to the destruction of each separate theory.

When Rimbaud's life is fairly viewed as a whole, little that is bad or vicious can be imputed to him. In his Paris and London days, according to conventional standards, he was dissolute and immoral; but these were standards which he did not accept. 'Oui! j'ai les yeux fermés a votre lumière' he said in *Une Saison en Enfer*,[3] 'mais je puis être sauvé.' He was depraved because he wished to be so, because it was part of his philosophy. When he came to believe that this had been an error, no hermit in the desert could have surpassed the austerity of his living. As for the immorality of his homosexuality, which many consider his most heinous crime, the only relationship of this nature which he is known to have had, was the one which occurred when he was seventeen and came under the influence of a man ten years older than himself, who was weak, self-indulgent and vicious, and who was known to have practised homosexuality before he ever met Rimbaud. Rimbaud was, at that time, an unhappy adolescent, over-developed intellectually and under-developed physically, and he was left with a sense of guilt and frustration. In any case modern psychology should, by now, have produced a saner outlook on the question, especially in connection with a youth of that age. For a short time he tried to sponge on his friends, but the attempt was only half-hearted, clumsy and short-lived. During his latter years he was renowned, on the Somali coast, for his scrupulous honesty and his great charity. His honour and his good name meant much to him. His letter home proved this, and, on his death-bed, in his delirium, his subconscious anxiety was that he might not scrupulously and punctually perform the tasks that had been entrusted to him and which he had undertaken. On the other hand, the theory of Rimbaud saint and martyr cannot be entertained. In the period when he imagined that he had become the equal of God, he was willing to pay the necessary price for this honour, in great personal suffering; yet it was not as a martyr he intended to suffer, but as a God. During the rest of his life, there was austerity and asceticism; there was charity, kindliness and generosity towards those of whom he had charge, and whose lot he pitied; but there was no real saintliness. His letters home—the sole record we have of his life on the Somali coast and in Abyssinia—are proof of this. He may have been, beneath the Abyssinian mask and armour, a religious and philosophical thinker—perhaps even still a poet—but he was certainly not a saint in his life.

Rimbaud's career is a tragic example of ultimate waste. Perhaps his work would never have arisen without this waste; perhaps that is the price which we have to pay for it. The mysteries and methods of genius cannot be reckoned and maybe the meteor-like quality of Rimbaud's art was its essence, its only possibility of birth. He seems to have been an unfortunate man whose breath was fire which burned up everything which came into contact with him and everything turned to ashes in his hand. He had potentialities for many things, but everything disappointed him in the end. Scholastic triumphs seemed to promise a distinguished intellectual career for him, but these proved tasteless and he cast them from him. His poetic talent would have placed him in the first rank of the literary men of his day; but he bit into that fruit and, finding the canker in its heart, threw it away. He tried to live from day to day, without planning for the morrow, awaiting events, but this proved a disillusionment like everything else.

His last endeavour, a life of violent action—exploration and commerce—was his final failure. There was in him the fatality of failure. He was a grandiose failure and remained to the end 'le grand maudit'. He remained in Hell all his life. In occult philosophy the word 'enfer' means 'le monde inférieur', the ante-room to the celestial regions, 'le lieu des épreuves', and it follows thus that this world is 'l'enfer'.[4] This world was indeed hell for Rimbaud, in which he was exiled from the heaven of which he dreamed, which he had once experienced, and which made it impossible for him to settle down happily anywhere on earth. It can but be hoped that life was in reality only the ante-room to a world where everything was made good to him.

Rimbaud was primarily an adventurer. His first adventure had been in books; next he had escaped on his gypsy wanderings, his first material adventures. The greatest had been exploration of the heavenly regions, and henceforth everything proved tasteless to him; henceforth this world was too small a place to satisfy him. He said to his sister.[5]

I should like to wander over the face of the whole world, which is not so very big after all, then perhaps I'd find a place that would please me a little.

He expresses this nostalgia symbolically in *Mémoire*—perhaps the loveliest and most perfect of his poems:[1]

Jouet de cet œil d'eau morne, je n'y puis prendre
ô canot immobile! oh! bras trop courts! ni l'une
ni l'autre fleur: ni la jaune qui m'importune,
là; ni la bleue, amie à l'eau couleur de cendre.

Ah! la poudre des saules qu'une aile secoue!
Les roses des roseaux dès longtemps dévorées!
Mon canot, toujours fixe; et sa chaîne tirée
Au fond de cet œil d'eau sans bords—à quelle boue?

His failure must not be attributed solely to ill-luck, to 'le guignon'. Baudelaire had shown that man's chief cause for suffering came from his own weakness, from his inability to follow what he knew was highest. Rimbaud brought many of his reverses on himself by being incapable of adapting himself to life, and most particularly by his great pride. He preferred, in the spiritual as well as in the material realm, to pocket loss rather than to make concessions or bow to circumstances. From his earliest youth he had been unable to endure any criticism, or any kind of rebuke, and he often saw them where they were not intended. This pride led him to imagine that he was the equal of God and thus exempt from the ordinary obligations which bound lesser mortals, exempt from ordinary payment. Baudelaire had paid for each of his pleasures, each of his joys, all his weakness, with burning tears of repentance and suffering; he had paid willingly seeing the justice of the payment. He was ready to put himself in the wrong; he knew well that he was a miserable sinner, and his pride consisted in recognizing this willingly, and in obliging others to admit that they too were sinners. 'Hypocrite lecteur, mon semblable, mon frère.' Rimbaud was incapable of true humility, of seeing himself in a lowly position. He could never beg for pity, for forgiveness or for mercy. Verily he saw himself a sinner—a sinner damned—but damned gloriously, conquered by the fire of the Almighty's wrath and vengeance, who had been obliged to use his full strength against him, and, as he burned, he sneered at the God who was destroying him. Yet, in the end, it was through this very pride and arrogance that he was finally chastised, when he laid down his arms and yielded completely.

He had a further weakness, the curse of instability. He could do nothing thoroughly, go to the bottom of nothing and he mastered nothing in the end. He always wanted to advance too fast and he could never wait to lay the foundations solidly; the palace had to rise instantaneously, as if by magic. Indeed in everything he relied more on the power of magic charms than on his own efforts. As soon as he had conceived a thing, it had forthwith to reach completion; he saw the end but never the means of reaching it, and he was never to learn moderation and patience. 'La science est trop lente,' he said in *Une Saison en Enfer*,[7] 'que la prière galope!' His swiftness and impatience ripened his gifts too quickly and they became atrophied, like windfalls from a tree. Psychologists might find the explanation for this in his self-mutilation, in his stifling of his natural means of expression. It is interesting to speculate what he might have become had he been able to allow his magnificent talents to burgeon slowly and, in their right season, come to full fruition. We do not know what he might have become had he been able, like Baudelaire, to accept humiliations and misunderstanding. Baudelaire said, 'Mes humiliations ont été des grâces de Dieu.'[8] Rimbaud's pride and arrogance were too great and he was never able to learn anything from his failures. He lacked that quality which is one of the vital ingredients of great genius—humility and simplicity.

Psychologists might consider that his impatience was, to a certain extent, a sign of arrested development, and in this he remained a child to the end of his days. Whenever a thing took his interest or his fancy, he imagined that this was the one thing, above all others, which he had always wanted, the one thing which would make everything else clear, the one thing which would make up to him for his previous disappointments. He pursued it for a time with all the passionate energy of his nature, but dropped it again as swiftly, when his interest flagged. How often did he write home from the Somali coast: 'I've not found what I expected to find! I'll not remain long here!' How many plans he toyed with and began, how few he ever brought to full fruition! 'Ah! tarir toutes les urnes!' he cried in *La Comédie de la Soif*.[9] And he attempted to drink from all the vessels at once lest the savour of one of them be lost to him. But so great was his desire to drink, so quickly did he gulp down the draught, that it only choked him and he tasted nothing.

He was never able to accept outside restraint and he was never to learn to discipline himself; right to the end his character remained in a state of undirected revolt. He revolted against everything. Against social conditions, against accepted religion, against art, and against the whole conditions of life. This fanatical desire for freedom, a further outcome of his pride, was morbid in its extreme manifestations. He could bear no man's hand on his shoulder and he preferred to destroy himself. The tragedy was that he learned—but only when it was too late—that freedom is no birthright, that it is on the contrary a commodity which, like everything else in this ill-constructed world, must be paid for, and that the price is high in personal servitude and bitter humiliation. There is no freedom to be fully ourselves unless we have first bought it with submission and many painful concessions, unless we have wearily struggled up to the higher peaks where alone there is air to breathe. Too late Rimbaud decided to purchase freedom and the price was by then far higher than it would have been earlier. Then, during the best years of his maturity, when he might have enjoyed a certain measure of liberty, feverishly—as he did all things—he was buying it at the highest price of the most painful servitude and bitter suffering.

At the time of his tragic struggle which is expressed in *Une Saison en Enfer* he was longing for a religion in which to lose himself entirely, but he would not pay the price of any alienation of his personal liberty. He preferred to stifle the longing of his heart and this he—pathetically—considered a victory. Dostoeffsky in *The Possessed* painted a character who killed himself in order to prove his complete independence before God.[10] Rimbaud's action is similar, only his was a spiritual and not a physical suicide.

Since the shock which stunned him, when he was a boy, Rimbaud remained incapable of accepting life as he found it; its conditions he considered intolerable and he hated it because it was not what he had thought it was, and what he thought that it should be. He would not, indeed could not, accept ordinary human nature, the weaknesses of others and their petty meannesses. He had no tolerance or pity and saw nothing pathetic in their failure to live up to any ideal, they only aroused his disgust. The only people for whom he felt any gentleness and sympathy, were primitive negroes who lived almost the irreflective and patient life of dumb beasts of burden. He had none of Baudelaire's understanding of simple human conditions and, except occasionally, at the very end of his life, none of his genuine tenderness for the driftwood of existence. Of Pascal's 'grandeurs et misères de l'homme' he saw only the 'misères'. He could not endure the trivial happiness with which those around him seemed satisfied, and he turned away from all those things which made life beautiful or sweet for others; peace, love and simple toil. He destroyed all these things in himself, regretting them when it was too late, leaving himself nothing with which to build. His life never became enriched from his experience; experience only left behind scarred and burnt-up patches.

He had thought at first that he could make his own conditions, alter everything himself, find 'la vraie vie'. But when this failed he would not accept what he would have called 'dope', anything which would make life sit less heavily on his shoulders— art and dreams—he threw all these away since they were not ultimate reality, since they were not absolute perfection. 'Il faut toujours être ivre!' said Baudelaire,[11] 'tout est là: c'est l'unique question. Pour ne pas sentir l'horrible fardeau du Temps qui brise vos épaules et vous penche vers la terre, il faut vous enivrer sans cesse. Mais de quoi? De vin, de poésie ou de vertu, à votre guise. Mais enivrez-vous.' Rimbaud was incapable of this and the world hurt him intolerably—he kept, to the end, this adolescent faculty of perpetual hurt. Finally he was left with no anæsthetic to make bearable the 'painful operation of living'. He never discovered a working principle and he never came to terms with life. All he ever attained was a kind of bitter resignation which was not a Byronic pose. Once, writing home concerning his future plans, he said:[12] 'Well! the most likely thing is that one will go where one doesn't in the least want to go, that one will do what one doesn't in the least want to do, and that one will live and die quite differently from what one would have wished, without any hope of later compensation.'

The only partial compensation he seemed to find, in his last years at Harar, was in the small amount of good he succeeded in doing to the natives of whom he had charge. He had, however, no illusions on the nature of that good, or the return it might bring him; he knew well that it was only the sort of kindness one might show to dumb animals, that they would never understand it or appreciate it.

Rimbaud was a man more naturally gifted with artistic possibilities than any poet in French literature, but when he discovered that it did not bring him the ideal for which he thirsted he could have none of it. Just as he would not accept the humble position of ordinary Christian, in the same way he could not accept the position of mere poet. He made then, what seems to have been a tragic mistake, the greatest of his many mistakes, that of abandoning literature. The time of his greatest poetic creation was the only period of his life when he was more or less happy, his only time of joy and fulfilment. With his habitual violence and lack of consideration for himself, he cut out what was his greatest asset, his one human 'raison d'être' and he remained in hell for ever afterwards. 'Un homme qui veut se mutiler est bien damné, n'est-ce pas?' he asked in *Une Saison en Enfer.*[13] Verily he damned himself by mutilation. And the tragedy was that, in the end, he came to realize that he had wasted himself and his life. It was the same treatment, on the spiritual plane, as that to which he subjected his body, on the physical plane, at Harar, when, refusing to see the gravity of his condition, he bound his diseased leg tightly and tortured himself with violent exercise. He killed his talent through obstinacy.

The continued abandonment of poetry may not have been entirely voluntary. Perhaps he could never have written again; perhaps when poetry ceased to be the image of absolute truth, he had nothing further to say. He could never write by formula, and, when the faith was gone, perhaps there was not left in him the substance to make a poet. Perhaps the gods were in this kinder than we know; this may have been the one kindness that Fate showed him, to make it impossible for him to produce less than his best, to make him cease at the peak of his achievement.

In that high achievement Rimbaud has enlarged the scope of poetry. When he rose on the horizon of poetry in 1871, the Parnassian ideal of logic and reason was still at its height and even Baudelaire was not fully appreciated. French poetry, was, on the whole, little more than pictorial or else the arrangements of intellectual ideas in noble language. Baudelaire had increased the suggestive power of poetry and had given it back spiritual content; but Baudelaire in so doing had kept to logic, to grammar and syntax; his words mean what they say and they convey a definite and easily comprehensible meaning. Rimbaud increased the evocative power of poetry, independently of the sense it conveyed; words with him are no longer intended to bear their dictionary meaning; they are no longer to express a logical content, or to describe; they are a form of magic charm, they are intended to evoke a state of mind and soul. The essence of poetry does not consist in the words, or in the images—however beautiful these might be—poetry is the very sensation itself, and this sensation is to be allowed to find it own best expression, just as the lava stream burns out its own bed. Rimbaud left out all the unnecessary words, all the connecting links, leaving only the essential vision itself, and this vision is not always easily seen by others. Inspiration had come to him first in a boiling torrent but he had sifted out what was the essence of his vision, casting away what was not absolutely necessary, all the explanatory relative clauses. In endeavouring to reach the unknown, Rimbaud did in fact give poetry an evocative power that has been equalled by few other poets.

Rimbaud's poetry has proved—even if this was not his aim—how much rich material there is for art in the subconscious mind, in the half-remembered sensations of childhood, in these sensations which have been registered without our realizing their full meaning. This has opened up a rich field to literature and it can be claimed that Rimbaud started—in France at all events—the literature of the subconscious depths of human nature. The Symbolist Movement, in its desire to probe the unconscious, to reach beyond earthly life, owes much to him, albeit their efforts more nearly resemble those of the writers of the German Romantic Movement, who consciously, and without Rimbaud's economy of method, sought to express the unconscious—the unconscious rather than the subconscious. Rimbaud would, however, have sympathized with few of the ideals of the Symbolist Movement. It is true that many of these ideals owed much to him, but, on the other hand, they owed more to the *Spleen* and *ennui* of Baudelaire than to his fierce revolt. Rimbaud had never been smothered under the heavy blanket of *ennui* as Baudelaire was. 'Je suis celui qui souffre et qui s'est révolté' he cried, even as a boy.[14] It is fierce revolt and disgust he felt, but never lassitude. When, in his letters from Harar, he wrote of his 'ennui' the word must not be taken as having the same meaning as when Baudelaire uses it. Baudelaire felt himself slowly dissolve in weary boredom as he contemplated the same old things, 'le spectacle ennuyeux de l'immortel péché,' and Verlaine wept, 'il pleure dans mon cœur'; Rimbaud lifted up his hands with horror and disgust, and struck at all around him, leaving broken fragments at his feet. He walked through life on the shattered remains of dreams and ideals which he had destroyed.

In poetry Rimbaud dug many new roads, and cleared large sections of the bush, and when he fell by the wayside, others were able to continue along the new road towards the unknown, beyond the horizon, 'où l'autre s'est affaissé.' Without Rimbaud it is doubtful whether there would ever have been the Surrealist School of Art. André Breton says that it is through *Illuminations* that we have acquired the power of coming into communication with our deepest selves and that from Rimbaud we have learnt that poetry must lead somewhere.[15] The Surrealists consider poetry as being the concrete shape which the writer has succeeded in giving the irrational thought which floats through his mind in the form of vague images of which he is often unaware, but which, with a certain mental discipline, can be brought to light. André Breton's definition of Surrealism owes much to Rimbaud's conception of poetry.

Surrealism is the psychic automatism by means of which the artist intends to express either verbally, or in writing, or in any other way, the real working of his thought. It is dictated by his thought with complete absence of any control of his vision, and without any æsthetic or moral preoccupation. Surrealism is based on the belief in a superior reality of certain forms of association which have been hitherto neglected, in the omnipotence of dreams, and in the free and disinterested play of thought.[16]

The Surrealists' artistic programme has many similarities with Rimbaud's theory of poetry. It aims at discovery of the precise relations existing between metaphysics and poetry, to remove all moral ban from literature and art. Poetry, like the poet, must be beyond good and evil. And finally it seeks to bring about a fuller acknowledgment of the supreme poetic quality of ballads and anonymous literature. A great many of his later verse poems were written on the model of simple and naïve folk-songs. It was as if Rimbaud felt that the soul of a people wrote itself

unconsciously in its folk-literature, that this was a form of
unconscious folk-symbolism.

Rimbaud is, however, for us to-day, more than merely a poet
who is important in the history of poetry, important because he
symbolizes his own time, or because he opened the gates of
another kingdom to us. He is significant also in his right, because
the collected edition of his writings is the bedside book of many
who do not concern themselves with the history of literature or
the craft of poetry. These read him for the direct message he has
for them.

Rimbaud's work may not have, perhaps, the depth of the work
of Baudelaire; it does not reveal the same adult experience and
reflection on the eternal problems which trouble the souls of
men. Through Baudelaire we reach a fuller conscious knowledge
of ourselves, of human nature and of the problem of human
weakness faced with right and wrong. Rimbaud felt acutely,
had violent intuitions, violent enthusiasms, but he rarely gave
himself the time to reflect deeply. But it must be remembered
that he was probably no more than twenty when he ceased to
write and that by then he had not had time to know himself or
others fully. Most of what he knew he had obtained through his
reading. He was inspired with brilliant conceptions, he was seized
with wild enthusiasms and like the slum child on its first visit
to the country, he rushed from flower to flower, smelling each
one in turn, then dropping each bloom to wither on the ground
while he flew on to the next—the most beautiful of it all seemed—
at the far end of the meadow.

There is with Rimbaud the paradoxical situation that he who
in his writings was, in spite of what some critics claim, an unbeliever—a mystical unbeliever—he who at the end of *Une
Saison en Enfer* refused belief for himself, should have led others
back to the faith. Many—Daniel-Rops, Rivière and Claudel—
found in him the fullest expression of their need of God and their
final belief. His action was, in the words of Isabelle Rimbaud, 'de
pousser des âmes d'élite vers Dieu.' Claudel says that after
reading *Illuminations* and *Une Saison en Enfer* he experienced
'l'impression vivante et presque physique du surnaturel.'[17] And

again he writes, 'C'est Arthur Rimbaud qui m'a instruit et construit. Je lui dois tout. Il n'était pas de ce monde.' In his experience of God Rimbaud reached, without orthodox beliefs, the stage which mystics seek to attain, where there is no longer possibility for belief or disbelief, for doubt or for reflection, but only pure sensation, ecstasy and union with the Almighty.

Many to-day find much in Rimbaud that harmonizes with their own views. He had their hatred of what civilization has become, their dislike of hypocrisy and smugness. For Rimbaud Monsieur Prudhomme* was born at the same time as Christ. He poured contempt on what the world calls progress and of which it is so inordinately proud.

La race inférieure a tout couvert—le peuple, comme on dit, la raison, la nation et la science. Oh! la science! On a tout repris. Pour le corps et pour l'âme—le viatique,—on a la médecine et la philosophie,—les remèdes de bonnes femmes et chansons arrangées. Et les divertissements des princes et les jeux qu'ils interdisaient! Géographie, mécanique, chimie! La science, la nouvelle noblesse! Le progrès. Le monde marche! Pourquoi ne tournerait-il pas?[19]

He felt nothing but disgust for the modern form of democracy which had arisen from the honest beliefs of the revolution.[20] Like so many to-day he would have liked to set it all at a bargain sale, give it all away, if anyone would take it.[21]

In *Illuminations* is found expressed, as nowhere else—except perhaps in the poems of Saint John of the Cross—man's eternal longing for spiritual satisfaction and beauty. *Une Saison en Enfer* is the hell of doubt which is always with us, the age-long struggle between the angel and the beast, and few writers have expressed in so poignant and moving a manner, the bitterness of the cry that bursts from us; while in *Le Bateau Ivre*, we find all the nostalgic longing of human nature, its aspirations and its passionate desire to escape from outworn values and to sail towards new hopes. *Le Bateau Ivre* is freighted with the suffering of a stricken world, with its infinite weariness with all that surrounds it; it carries on board the world's ardent longing for escape to the open

* M. Prudhomme is a character in Henri Monnier's novel and play, a canting man given to uttering grandiloquent platitudes.

sea from the stifling stench of the port, there to wash itself clean from all that has soiled and defiled it and to find a newer and cleaner self. The ship speeds along, far out to sea, sailing as it were between two skies, two infinities, drawn upwards by the beam of light; but may it not, like Rimbaud's craft, come hurtling down again, may it not prove like his 'un bateau frêle comme un papillon de mai,' a fragile paper boat which a sad child launches on a cruel sea only to be swallowed up by its devouring waves.

> Mais, vrai, j'ai trop pleuré. Les aubes sont navrantes,
> Toute lune est atroce et tout soleil amer,
> L'âcre amour m'a gonflé de torpeurs enivrantes.
> O que ma quille éclate! Oh que j'aille à la mer!

## THE END

446

# IZAMBARD'S PARODY OF RIMBAUD'S POEM,

## *Cœur Supplicié, La Muse des Méphitiques*

VIENS sur mon cœur, Muse des Méphitiques,
Et roucoulons comme deux amoureux
Pour bafouer toutes les esthétiques.
Viens dans mes bras, Muse des Méphitiques
Je te ferai des petits rachitiques,
Froids au toucher, verdâtres et goitreux.
Viens dans mes bras, Muse des Méphitiques.
Et folâtrons comme deux amoureux.

Viens! tu verras le bourgeois qui s'offusque
Se cramponner d'horreur à son comptoir,
Comme à son roc s'agglutine un mollusque.
Viens! tu verras le bourgeois qui s'offusque
Et son œil torve, au fond d'un vase étrusque
San main crispée aggripant l'éteignoir.
Et tu verras le bourgeois qui s'offusque,
Se cramponner d'horreur à son comptoir.

Voici venir l'ère des pourritures,
Où les lépreux sortent des lazarets.
O fleurs du Laid, rutilantes, ordures,
Voici venir l'ère des pourritures.
Nous, fourrageant dans les monts d'épluchures,
Psalmodiant l'hosannah des gorets!
Voici venir l'ère des pourritures
Où les lépreux sortent des lazarets.

Published by Izambard in *La Revue Européenne*, Octobre 1928.

## Ces Passions

CES passions qu'eux seuls nomment encore amours
Sont des amours aussi, tendres et furieuses.
Avec des particularités curieuses
Que n'ont pas les amours, certes! de tous les jours.

Même plus qu'elles et mieux qu'elles héroïques,
Elles se parent de splendeurs d'âme et de sang,
Telles qu'au prix d'elles les amours dans le rang
Ne sont que Ris et Jeux ou besoins érotiques,

Que vains proverbes, ou riens d'enfants trop gâtés.
—'Ah! les pauvres amours banales, animales,
Normales! Gros goûts lourds ou frugales fringales,
Sans compter la sottise et des fécondités!'

Peuvent dire ceux-là que sacre le haut Rite,
Ayant conquis la plénitude du plaisir,
Et l'insatiabilité de leur désir
Bénissant la fidélité de leur mérite.

La plénitude! Ils l'ont superlativement:
Baisers repus, gorgés, mains, privilégiées
Dans la richesse des caresses repayées,
Et ce divin final anéantissement!

Comme ce sont les forts et les forts, l'habitude
De la force les rend invaincus au déduit.
Plantureux, savoureux, débordant le déduit!
Je le crois bien qu'ils l'ont, la pleine plénitude!

Et pour combler leurs vœux chacun d'eux tour à tour
Fait l'action suprême, a la parfaite extase.
—Tantôt la coupe ou la bouche, et tantôt le vase,—
Pâmé comme la nuit, fervent comme le jour.

Leurs beaux ébats sont grands et gais. Pas de crises:
Vapeurs, nerfs. Non, des jeux courageux, puis d'heureux
Bras las autour du cou, pour de moins langoureux
Qu'étroits sommeils à deux, tout coupés de reprises.

Dormez, les amoureux! tandis qu'autour de vous
Le monde inattentif aux choses délicates
Bruit ou gît en somnolences scélérates,
Sans même (il est si bête!) être de vous jaloux.

Et ces réveils francs, clairs, riants, vers l'aventure
De fiers damnés d'un plus magnifique sabbat?
Et salut, témoins purs de l'âme en ce combat
Pour l'affranchissement de la lourde nature!

*(Parallèlement)*

## ON THE TRAIL OF RIMBAUD

ALL the early biographers say that when Rimbaud left London in July 1874 he went to take up a post in a school in Scotland. Houin and Bourguignon, his friends, write* that he left London to stay in Scotland. Professor Carré got the same information from Delahaye, while Mme. Méléra, who was a friend of Isabelle Rimbaud, wrote† that Arthur, having seen his mother and sister off at Victoria, with new clothes on his back and money in his pockets went to take up a post in Scotland where he remained a year. The errors in this statement are easy to refute. First Rimbaud did not see his mother and sister off at Victoria since he left before them. Secondly he did not remain a year in Scotland since he was back in Charleville for Christmas. It is hard to find a reason to explain Rimbaud's early start if it was to Scotland that he went—we know from Vitalie's *Journal* that he left the house at 4.30 a.m. In July 1874 there was no train for Scotland as early as that. It is true he only left the house at that hour. After 6 in the morning there were several trains for Scotland. The most probable were the two fast trains, the 6.25 from Euston arriving in Glasgow at 5 o'clock in the afternoon and at Edinburgh at 6.15; the 10 o'clock from King's Cross, the best of the day, arriving at 7 o'clock in the evening at Edinburgh and at Glasgow at 9.5. Rimbaud might have preferred the first train if he wished to arrive in Scotland early in the afternoon. But why leave at 4.30, since it was only ten minutes' walk from his lodgings to Euston?

All the schools in Glasgow and Edinburgh and in their vicinity were approached in an endeavour to discover any trace of Rimbaud, but in vain. It is true that if he had accepted a post *au pair* his name would not appear on a list of teachers. An advertisement was published in the principal daily papers of Scotland inquiring

* *Revue d'Ardenne et d'Argonne*, Sept.–Oct. 1897.   † *Rimbaud*, p. 124.

whether there was anyone who remembered a young French teacher called Rimbaud in Scotland in 1874, but the advertisement remained without an answer.

Next researches were made in the direction of the address in Reading given by Rimbaud in the rough draft of the advertisement which was supposed to have been written before he and Verlaine separated. In those days provincial directories were not published every year and in the British Museum only the directories for 1869 and 1877 were found. The year 1877 gave the name of the occupier of 175 King's Road, Reading, as a certain Camille Le Clair, B.A. But his name did not appear as the occupier in 1869. It seemed fitting that this Camille Le Clair—probably a Frenchman—should be connected with Rimbaud, but it would appear that this connection must have been in 1872 or 1873 if the advertisement was in fact corrected by Verlaine. Investigations at the Town Hall in Reading showed that 165 King's Road, Reading, was occupied by a Mr. William Hall in 1872 and 1873 and that Camille Le Clair had only gone there as tenant in 1874 and had remained there until 1880. It was possible that Mr. Hall had sublet part of the house to M. Le Clair and so it was necessary to discover who was M. Le Clair. At the public library in Reading a guide of the city showed an advertisement which indicated that he had been a teacher of French at the Kendrick School in 1877, but further investigation proved that this school was not founded until that date. Researches into the registers of the British Museum proved that he had applied for a reader's ticket in September 1885, signing his name Camille William Henry Le Clair. The anglicization of his Christian names suggested that he might have taken out British naturalization papers. Investigation into the archives of the Home Office proved, however, that this was not the case. Although he seems to have settled definitely in England he kept his French nationality. Research into university records showed that he was a graduate of no British university and so the B.A. which he attached to his name probably only referred to his French *baccalauréat*.

Finally researches in the local Reading papers led to his discovery. From the month of December 1872 Camille Le Clair was

APPENDIX III

advertising in the *Reading Mercury*, offering to give lessons in French language and literature.

French Language.
Monsieur Camille Le Clair,

Professor of the French language and literature, attends schools and families in Reading and its neighbourhood. Private lessons given and classes held at his Residence. Terms on application at M.C. Le Clair's residence.

8 Russell Terrace, Reading.

This proved that in December 1872 he had not yet gone to live at King's Road. The same advertisement appeared every week in January 1873, but with a new address, this time 31 Russell Square. At the end of the month the advertisement suddenly ceased appearing. It is not known what happened to M. Le Clair —perhaps he took up a resident post.

In August 1873 the advertisement began to appear again and he asked for his correspondence to be addressed care of a bookseller. This advertisement continued to appear until the end of September. Then there was nothing until December. This is beyond the date of the break between Verlaine and Rimbaud and Verlaine was now in prison. Search was, however, continued as Camille Le Clair seemed a more likely friend for Rimbaud to have had than the respectable British-sounding William Hall. In December, Le Clair advertised that he was going to start new French classes.

French Language
Monsieur Camille Le Clair.
Graduate of the University of France
Professor of the
French Language and Literature

Has much pleasure in announcing that in consequence of his increased engagements in Reading and the Neighbourhood, he has now made Reading his permanent residence. Private lessons given. Candidates prepared for the various Appointments. Classes held at Monsieur Le

Clair's residence, where terms and particulars can be obtained on application.

37 Waylen Street, Reading

In the January advertisement he added that he was a teacher of French at the school of the Rev. Stephen Hawtrey, Saint Mark's School, Windsor, and at the school of the Rev. F. Rutley, The Queen's School, Basingstoke.

The advertisement continued to appear until July 1874, becoming more and more important. He advertised also courses of commercial French, and classes for ladies. All advertisements gave the same address, 37 Waylen Street, Reading. At last on 25 July 1874, he advertised a change of address and said that he was going to settle definitely at Montpellier House, 165 King's Road, Reading. After that the following advertisement appeared each week.

Monsieur Camille Le Clair (Graduate of the University of France), Professor of the French Language and Literature, attends Schools and Families. Private lessons given. Morning and evening classes held at his residence. Montpellier House, 165 King's Road, Reading. Removed from Waylen Street.

Later he added another advertisement.

French classes for Ladies. Mons. Camille Le Clair begs to announce that in addition to the Graduate Classes held at his residence, he has formed a Finishing School for Advanced Pupils, which will commence on 18 January. Particulars can be obtained at Mons. Le Clair's residence, Montpellier House, 165 King's Road, Reading.

Having now discovered the exact date of Camille Le Clair's arrival at King's Road, Reading, one of two possibilities had to be accepted. Either that William Hall was the person with whom Rimbaud had dealings or else that he had drafted the advertisement after his break with Verlaine, after July 1873. The second possibility seemed more likely and the main daily papers were investigated after July 1874, after the arrival of Camille Le Clair at King's Road. Finally the advertisement was discovered in *The Times* for 9 November 1874.

It has been impossible to discover how and where Camille Le Clair and Rimbaud met, or at what moment Rimbaud went to Reading. But it is significant that Camille Le Clair's advertisement was appearing in the *Reading Mercury* in July 1874 when Rimbaud was on the look-out for a post. Montpellier House, where Le Clair was about to settle, is a fine three-storied house in a good locality of Reading. It is unlikely that he would be able to occupy it entirely for residential purposes. It is possible that he intended to make of it a kind of French Institute, since he was proposing to hold there classes in French, and that he would need the help of other teachers to deal with all the work he was advertising. It is possible that he engaged Rimbaud at an agency in London, at the time he was advertising in the *Reading Mercury*.

It may have been to Reading that Rimbaud departed early in the morning on 31 July 1874. Perhaps he was obliged to leave so early because he ought to have gone the previous day—we know that his departure was delayed. To be in Reading before 9 o'clock he would have had to take the 6 o'clock train from Paddington or the 6.23 from King's Cross. The first reached Reading at 6.55 and the second at 7.45. The Paddington train would have been the more likely one to take, and if he had gone on foot from Argylle Square to Paddington it would not have been too early to start at 4.30.

# BIBLIOGRAPHY

## A

The fullest—and only complete—edition of Rimbaud's writings is the one edited by Jules Mouquet and Rolland de Renéville for the *Bibliothèque de la Pléiade* in 1946. It includes everything that can be needed for the study of Rimbaud—an account of all the known manuscripts at the time—further ones have come to light since then—all the family documents, and all the known correspondence from and to Rimbaud. It does not contain *Lettre du Baron de Petdechèvre*, which Mouquet discovered in 1949 and attributes to him. It is published in Rimbaud: *Oeuvres*, edited for the *Classiques Garnier*, by Suzanne Bernard. This is the best annotated edition available.

## B

There are many works—and the number increases each year—dealing wholly, or partly, with Rimbaud and his works. The chief of these are given in the list below.

Bouillane de Lacoste (H.): *Rimbaud et le Problème des Illuminations*, 1949.
Breton (A.): *Flagrant Délit*, 1949.
Briet (S.): *Rimbaud Notre Prochain*, 1956.
Carré (J. M.): *La Vie Aventureuse de Rimbaud*, 1926; *La Vie de Rimbaud*, 1939.
Chadwick (C.): *Études sur Rimbaud*, 1960.
Chisholm (A.): *The Art of Rimbaud*, 1930.
Clarke (M.): *Rimbaud and Quinet*, 1946.
Clauzel (R.): *Une Saison en Enfer*, 1931.
Coulon (M.): *Le Problème de Rimbaud*, 1923; *Au Cœur de Verlaine et de Rimbaud*, 1927; *La Vie de Rimbaud et de son Oeuvre*, 1929.
Daniel-Rops: *Rimbaud*, 1926.
De Graaf (D. A.): *Arthur Rimbaud et la Durée de son Activité Littéraire*, 1948.

Delahaye (E.): *Verlaine*, 1919; *Rimbaud*, 1923; *Souvenirs Familiers*, 1925.

Delattre (J.): *Le Déséquilibre Mental d'Arthur Rimbaud*, 1928.

Dhôtel (A.): *L'Oeuvre Logique de Rimbaud*, 1933.

Edmond-Magny (C.): *Rimbaud*, 1949.

Etiemble & Gauclère: *Rimbaud*, 1936.

Etiemble: *Le Mythe de Rimbaud*, Vol. I, 1952, Vol. II, 1954.

Fondane (B.): *Rimbaud le Voyou*, 1933.

Fontainas (A.): *Verlaine and Rimbaud*, 1931.

Fontaine (A.): *Le Génie de Rimbaud*, 1934; *Verlaine Homme de Lettres*, 1937.

Fowlie (W.): *Rimbaud*, 1946; *Illuminations*, 1953.

Gengoux (J.): *La Symbolique de Rimbaud*, 1947; *La Pensée Poétique de Rimbaud*, 1950.

Godchot (Col.): *La Voyance de Rimbaud*, 1934; *Rimbaud ne varietur I*, 1936; *L'Agonie du Poète*, 1937; *Rimbaud ne varietur II*, 1938.

Goffin (R.): *Rimbaud Vivant*, 1937.

Hackett (C. A.): *Le Lyrisme de Rimbaud*, 1938; *Rimbaud l'Enfant*, 1948; *Rimbaud*, 1957

Hare (H.): *Sketch for a Portrait of Rimbaud*, 1938.

Izambard (G.): *Rimbaud à Douai et à Charleville*, 1927.

Jacquemin-Parlier (E.): *Jean-Nicolas-Arthur Rimbaud*, 1929.

Lepelletier (E.): *Verlaine*, 1907.

Méléra (M. Y.): *Rimbaud*, 1930; *Ébauches*, 1938; *Résonances autour de Rimbaud*, 1946.

Moore (G.): *Impressions and Opinions*, 1891.

Morrissette (B.): *The Great Rimbaud Forgeries*, 1956.

Mouquet (J.): *Rimbaud raconté par Verlaine*, 1931.

Noulet (E.): *Le Premier Visage de Rimbaud*, 1953.

Paterne Berrichon: *La Vie de Jean-Arthur Rimbaud*, 1897; *Arthur Rimbaud, le Poète*, 1912.

Petitfils (P.): *L'Oeuvre et le Visage d'Arthur Rimbaud*, 1949.

Porché (F.): *Verlaine tel qu'il fut*, 1933.

Renéville (R. de): *Rimbaud le Voyant*, revised edition, 1947.

Rickword (E.): *Rimbaud*, 1924.

Rimbaud (I.): *Reliques*, 1922.

Rivière (J.): *Rimbaud*, 1930.

Ruchon (F.): *Jean-Arthur Rimbaud*, 1929.

Silvain (R.): *Rimbaud le Précurseur*, 1945.

Starkie (E.): *Rimbaud in Abyssinia*, 1937; *Arthur Rimbaud*, 1938, revised edition, 1947; *Rimbaud en Abyssinie*, 1938; *Le Coin de Table* by Fantin-Latour (*The French Mind*), 1951, *Rimbaud 1854–1954*, 1954.

Vaillant (J. P.): *Rimbaud tel qu'il fut*, 1930.

Verlaine (Ex-Madame): *Mémoires de ma Vie*, 1935.

Wilson (E.): *Axel's Castle*, 1931.

## C

Here are listed some of the chief articles dealing with Rimbaud or his writings, which have appeared in reviews. Only those which throw some special light on the poet are given here, and those not used by their authors in subsequent works.

*Archivum Linguisticum*. F. Scarfe: *A Stylistic Interpretation of Rimbaud*, Vol. III, Fasc. II.

*Bateau Ivre, Le*: A. Adam: *Parade*, Sept. 1950; *Phrases*, Mar. 1951; *Génie*, June 1957.

*Bulletin des Amis de Rimbaud*: *Rimbaud et la Caravane*, No. 2, 1931; *Le Témoignage du Médecin de Rimbaud*, No. 3, 1933. Marmelstein, *Rimbaud Soldat*, No. 6, 1937.

*Durham University Journal*: Meyerstein: *The Latinity of Rimbaud's Bateau Ivre*, Mar. 1940.

*France et Asie*: Guy-Luc: *Rimbaud à Java*, June–July 1946.

*Mandrake III*: Meyerstein: *Baudelaire and les Illuminations*, 1946.

*Ma Revue*: *Les Droits d'Auteur de Rimbaud*, No. 45, 1933. *Le Procès de Rimbaud*, No. 48, 1934; *La Dernière Maladie de Rimbaud*, No. 56, 1935; *La Rencontre de Verlaine et de Rimbaud*, No. 67, 1936.

*Mercure de France, Le*. Béraud: *Les Sources d'Inspiration du Bateau Ivre*, 17 Jan. 1922; Marmelstein: *Rimbaud à Stuttgart et aux Indes Néerlandaises*, 15 Jan. 1922; Coulon: *Les Vraies Lettres de Rimbaud arabo-éthiopien*, 15 May, 1935; Izambard: *Les Sources du Bateau Ivre*, 15 Aug. 1935; Bouillane de Lacoste: *L'Evolution Psychologique de Rimbaud d'après son Ecriture*, 1 Nov. 1936; *Verlaine Editeur de Rimbaud*, 15 June 1937. Starkie: *Sur les Traces de Rimbaud*, 1 May 1947. Guiraud: *L'Évolution Statistique du Style de Rimbaud et les Illuminations*, Oct. 1954.

*Nouvelle Revue Française*, Thibaudet: *Mallarmé et Rimbaud*, 1 Feb. 1922.

*Revue d'Ardenne et d'Argonne*, Houin & Bourguignon: *La vie de Rimbaud*, Nov.–Dec. 1896; Jan.–Feb. 1897; May–June, 1899; Jan.–Feb. 1901; July 1901.

*Revue de France.* Prévost: *Sur les Traces de Rimbaud,* 1 Nov. 1929; Carré: *Rimbaud en Éthiopie,* 1 June 1935.

*Revue de Littérature Comparée.* V. P. Underwood: *Rimbaud et l'Angleterre,* Jan. 1955.

*Revue des Sciences Humaines.* Adam: *L'Énigme des Illuminations,* Oct.–Dec. 1950; De Graaf: *Les Illuminations et la Date Exacte de leur Composition,* Oct.–Dec. 1950. *Deux Lettres d'Ernest Delahaye,* Oct.–Dec. 1951; Hackett: *Rimbaud et Balzac,* April–June 1955.

*Revue Hebdomadaire.* Acremont: *En Abyssinie sur les Traces de Rimbaud,* 27 Aug. 1932.

*Revue de la Jeunesse.* Claudel: *Ma Conversion,* 10 Oct. 1913.

*Lingue Straniere,* De Graaf: *L'Auteur Véritable de Crimen Amoris,* July–Aug. 1957.

# NOTES

## PART ONE

### CHAPTER I

## THE PARENTS

1. The information concerning the Rimbaud family has been obtained chiefly from Godchot: *Arthur Rimbaud ne varietur.*
2. Godchot, op. cit., p. 41.
3. Ibid., p. 12.
4. Ibid., p. 24.
5. From the rough draft of a letter from Isabelle Rimbaud to Houin, communicated by H. Matarasso.
6. Godchot, op. cit., p. 60.
7. *Rimbaud le Poète*, p. 18.
8. Quinet, *Merlin l'Enchanteur*, Vol. I, p. 10.
9. Delahaye, *Rimbaud*, I. 17.

### CHAPTER II

## THE EARLY YEARS

1. *Les Poètes de Sept Ans (Oeuvres Complètes* p. 77).
2. Ibid., p. 3.
3. Ibid., p. 4.
4. *Souvenirs Familiers*, p. 38.
5. *Les Poètes de Sept Ans (Oeuvres Complètes*, p. 77).
6. Ibid.
7. *Souvenirs Familiers*, p. 39.
8. *Les Poètes de Sept Ans (Oeuvres Complètes*, p. 77).
9. Paterne Berrichon: *Arthur Rimbaud le Poète*, p. 31.
10. *Les Poètes de Sept Ans (Oeuvres Complètes*), p. 78.
11. Houdin & Bourguignon, *Revue d'Ardenne et d'Argonne*, Nov.–Dec. 1896.
12. Vide Godchot, op. cit., p. 87.

13. Delahaye: *Rimbaud*, p. 87.

14. Godchot, op. cit., p. 88.

15. Delahaye died in 1930 and Labarrière during the late war.

16. Labarrière in conversation with the present author.

17. Delahaye, *Souvenirs Familiers*, p. 46.

18. Labarrière in conversation with the present author.

19. *Les Poètes de Sept Ans* (*Oeuvres Complètes*, p. 77).

20. Delahaye, *Souvenirs Familiers*, p. 35.

21. Vide Godchot, op. cit., p. 88. In 1869, when he was not fifteen, the school entered him for the *Concours Académique* in which he won first prize in Latin Verse and a third prize in Greek translation. That same year he won all the first prizes in his own form at school.

22. Vide *Mercure de France* (1 April, 1930).

23. Vide *Vers de Collège* (*Oeuvres Complètes*, p. 11).

<h3 style="text-align:center">CHAPTER III</h3>

<h2 style="text-align:center">LES LAURIERS SONT COUPÉS</h2>

1. *Rimbaud à Douai et à Charleville*, p. 15.

2. Op. cit., p. 20.

3. Delahaye, *Rimbaud*, p. 87.

4. Letter 4 May 1870 (*Oeuvres Complètes*, p. 527).

5. This is one of the three poems published by Rimbaud himself. The other two are, *Comédie en Trois Baisers*, in *La Charge*, 13 August 1870; and *Les Corbeaux*, published in *La Renaissance Littéraire et Artistique* on 14 September 1870. A fourth poem, *Petits Pauvres*, was printed in *The Gentleman's Magazine* in January 1878, over the signature Arthur Rimbaud. This poem is *Les Effarés*, written on 20 September 1870, and which was alleged to have been printed for the first time in *Les Poètes Maudits* in 1884. The poem published in England lacks lines 7–12, and has some variants, the most striking being *dos* for *culs* in the first verse—probably to suit English prudery. (Vide letter by E. H. W. Meyerstein, *The Times Literary Supplement*, 11 April 1935. It is not known who published the poem in England, unless it was Verlaine who was in England at the end of 1877, and who, already in 1878, was considering publishing Rimbaud's poems. (Vide letter to Charles de Sivry 27 Oct. 1878). If so he had forgotten this by 1884 for he does not mention it when publishing *Les Poètes Maudits*. After 1884, during Rimbaud's lifetime, he often made extensive publication of his work without consulting him.

6. *Sensation* (*Oeuvres Complètes*, p. 41).

7. *Credo in Unam* has an extra passage of 36 lines.

8. Letter 24 May 1870 (*Oeuvres Complètes*, p. 239).

460

9. Soleil et Chair (*Oeuvres Complètes*, p. 46).

10. *Ophélie* (Ibid., p. 10).

11. He won a second prize for Recitation and a fourth prize for History and Geography. It is stated that he would have been more highly placed for this second subject had his teacher and examiner, Father Willeme, not disapproved of the views which he held; he professed admiration for all those who had destroyed law and order. He won first prize in Religious Knowledge, Discours Latin, Discours Français, Latin Verse, Latin Translation, Greek Translation and over and above, a *Prix d'Excellence*.

12. Izambard, op. cit., p. 29.

CHAPTER IV

## FIRST FLIGHT

1. Letter 25 August 1870 (*Oeuvres Complètes*, p. 241).

2. This poem was formerly thought to have been written in September 1870, but Weil discovered its publication in *La Charge*, in August 1870. (Vide Fontaine, *Le Génie de Rimbaud*, p. 118, note 1).

3. Delahaye, *Rimbaud*, p. 25.

4. Letter 5 September 1870 (*Oeuvres Complètes*, p. 244).

5. Vide *Bulletin du Bibliophile*, 1945, Rimbaud à Douai.

6. Izambard, op. cit., p. 77.

7. Letter 24 September 1870 (*Oeuvres Complètes*, p. 522).

8. Letter 8 October 1870 (*Oeuvres Complètes*, p. 248).

9. *Ma Bohème* (*Oeuvres Complètes*, p. 69).

10. *Rêvé pour l'Hiver* (*Oeuvres Complètes*, p. 65).

11. Letter 2 November 1870 (*Oeuvres Complètes*, p. 248).

CHAPTER V

## COEUR SUPPLICIÉ

1. Delahaye, *Souvenirs Familiers*, p. 57.

2. Ibid., p. 58.

3. Ibid., p. 73.

4. Jellinek, *The Paris Commune of 1871*, p. 91.

5. Delahaye, op. cit., p. 108.

6. Lepelletier, *Verlaine*, p. 253.

7. Vide letter to Démeny, 17 April 1871 (*Oeuvres Complètes*, p. 149).

8. *Adieu* (*Oeuvres Complètes*, p. 228).

9. Jellinek, op. cit., p. 93.

10. Ibid.
11. Jellinek, op. cit., pp. 93–9.
12. Letter to Démeny, 17 April 1871 (*Oeuvres Complètes*, p. 249).
13. *Rimbaud*, p. 13.
14. Vide Godchot, op. cit., p. 167.
15. Letter to Démeny, 15 May 1871 (*Oeuvres Complètes*, p. 253).
16. Letter 10 June 1871 (Ibid., p. 258).
17. Vide *La Revue Européenne*, Oct. 1928. Carré, in publishing the letter in *Lettres de la Vie Littéraire*, has made the error in transcribing, ' Ça ne veut rien dire!'
18. Izambard's poem is published in Appendix I.
19. Letter published in *La Revue Européenne*, Oct. 1928.

CHAPTER VI

LE VOYOU

1. Godchot, op. cit., p. 170.
2. Letter to Démeny, 17 April 1871 (*Oeuvres Complètes*, p. 249).
3. Delahaye, *Rimbaud*, p. 31.
4. Vide Fontaine, *Le Génie de Rimbaud*, p. 21.
5. Delahaye's notes in the Doucet Collection.
6. *Les Sœurs de Charité* (*Oeuvres Complètes*, p. 85).
7. *Souvenirs*, published in *Lettres de la Vie Littéraire* by Rimbaud, p. 154.
8. *Mes Petites Amoureuses* (*Oeuvres Complètes*, p. 74).
9. *Les Sœurs de Charité* (*Oeuvres Complètes*, p. 86).
10. *Mauvais Sang* (*Une Saison en Enfer*) (*Oeuvres Complètes*, p. 209).
11. *Les Premières Communions* (*Oeuvres Complètes*, p. 88).
12. Delahaye, *Souvenirs Familiers*, p. 136.
13. It was published by Aragon and Breton in 1924. *Un Cœur sous une Soutane ou Intimités d'un Séminariste.*
14. We do not, in any case, know the precise dates of the composition of the poems. Rimbaud usually dated them with the date on which he copied them, not with that of composition.

CHAPTER VII

LE VOYANT

1. *Oeuvres Posthumes.* The lines occur in the rough draft of a poem intended to form part of the second version of *Les Fleurs du Mal.*
2. Letter to Izambard, 13 May 1871 (*Oeuvres Complètes*, p. 251).

3. Delahaye, *Souvenirs Familiers*, pp. 144–9.

4. Rolland de Renéville, *Rimbaud le Voyant*, p. 46. 'La littérature de la Grèce ancienne le fit accéder à la métaphysique de l'Orient. Platon le conduisit aux mystères orphiques que l'Orient transmit à la Grèce. C'est dans cette somme qu'il convient de chercher la conception de la personnalité proposée par le poète.'

5. *Les Sources Occultes du Romantisme.*

6. Godchot, op. cit., pp. 255–6.

## CHAPTER VIII

# THE CABALA

1. Franck, *Histoire de la Kabbale*, pp. 338–90.

2. Lévi, *Histoire de la Magie.*

3. Franck, op. cit., p. 178.

4. Ibid., p. 252.

5. *Du Ciel et de ses Merveilles et de l'Enfer.*

6. Fabre d'Olivet, *L'Histoire du Genre Humain*, Vol. I, p. 26.

7. Lévi, *Les Clefs des Grands Mystères*, Preface III.

8. Lévi, *L'Histoire de la Magie*, p. 8.

9. Ibid., p. 61.

10. Ibid., p. 76.

11. Lévi, *Les Clefs des Grands Mystères*, p. 32.

12. Ibid., p. 265.

13. Lévi, *Histoire de la Magie*, p. 36.

14. Letter to Démeny. (*Oeuvres Complètes*, p. 253).

15. Lévi, *Les Clefs des Grands Mystères*, p. 79.

16. Lévi, *Dogmes et Rituels de la Haute Magie*, p. 79.

17. Lévi, *Histoire de la Magie*, p. 542.

18. Ibid., p. 92.

19. Ibid., p. 544.

20. Ibid., pp. 551–2.

21. Ibid., p. 581.

22. Lévi, *Les Clefs des Grands Mystères*, p. 16.

23. Lévi, *Histoire de la Magie*, p. 90.

24. Ibid., p. 559.

25. Ibid., p. 348.

26. *L'Emancipation de la Femme*, p. 57.

CHAPTER IX

## BAUDELAIRE

1. Letter to Démeny, 15 May 1871. (*Oeuvres Complètes*, p. 251).
2. Notes (*Oeuvres Posthumes*, p. 17).
3. *Le Génie Enfant* (*Les Paradis Artificiels*).
4. *L'Homme Dieu* (Ibid.).
5. Ibid.
6. *Morale* (*Les Paradis Artificiels*).
7. Baudelaire, *Le Voyage* (*Les Fleurs du Mal*).

CHAPTER X

## THE AESTHETIC DOCTRINE

1. Jowett's translation quoted by Read in *Surrealism*, pp. 31-2.
2. Letter to Démeny, 15 May 1871 (*Oeuvres Complètes*, p. 251).
3. Ibid.
4. Vide also Ballanche, *Orphée*, p. 283.
5. Ibid., p. 283.
6. Vide Lévi, *Les Clefs des Grands Mystères*, p. 16.
7. Letter to Démeny, (*Oeuvres Complètes*, p. 251).
8. Letter to Izambard (Ibid., p. 251).
9. Vide Ballanche, *Essai sur les Institutions Sociales*, p. 331.
10. Letter to Démeny (*Oeuvres Complètes*, p. 251).
11. *Adieu* (*Une Saison en Enfer*) also Lévi, *Histoire de la Magie*, p. 76.
12. Letter to Démeny, 15 May 1871 (op. cit.).
13. Ibid.
14. Vide Ballanche, *Essai sur les Institutions Sociales*, p. 97.
15. Vide Ballanche, *Essai de Palingénésie Sociale*, p. 172.
16. Vide Ballanche, *Orphée*, p. 283, and also Lévi, *Histoire de la Magie*, p. 552.
17. Lévi, Ibid., p. 82.
18. Ibid., p. 542.
19. Vide Lévi, *L'Emancipation de la Femme*, p. 57, and also *Histoire de la Magie*, p. 348.
20. Vide Ballanche, *Essai de Palingénésie Sociale*, p. 172.
21. *L'Alchimie du Verbe* (*Une Saison en Enfer*) (*Oeuvres Complètes*, p. 219).
22. Vide Ballanche, *Orphée*, p. 240.
23. Letter to Démeny, 15 May 1871 (op. cit., p. 251).
24. Challemel-Lacour, *Un Boudhiste Contemporain en Allemagne*.
25. Delahaye, *Souvenirs Familiers*, p. 62.

## CHAPTER XI

# LE BATEAU IVRE

1. Godchot, op. cit., p. 223.
2. Vide letter 15 August 1871 (*Oeuvres Complètes*, p. 262).
3. Coulon, *Au Cœur de Rimbaud et de Verlaine*, p. 133.
4. Letter to Démeny, 28 August 1871 (*Oeuvres Complètes*, p. 262).
5. Delahaye, *Rimbaud*, p. 41.
6. Letter from Verlaine to Rimbaud, September 1871 (*Oeuvres Complètes*, p. 265).
7. Letter September 1871 (*Oeuvres Complètes*, p. 265).
8. *Oeuvres Complètes*, p. 78.
9. *Lettre du Baron de Petdechèvre*, (*Classiques Garnier*, p. 138).

# PART TWO

## CHAPTER I

# THE VERLAINES

1. Ex-Madame Verlaine, *Mémoires de ma Vie*.
2. Ibid., p. 59.
3. Ibid., p. 180.
4. *Les Hommes d'Aujourd'hui* (*Oeuvres Complètes*, Vol. VII).
5. Verlaine, *Notes Nouvelles sur Rimbaud* (*La Plume*, Oct. 1895).
6. Ex-Madame Verlaine, op. cit., p. 184.
7. Ibid., p. 185.
8. Paterne Berrichon, *La Vie de Rimbaud*, p. 154.
9. Ibid., p. 140.
10. Delahaye, unpublished ms. on Rimbaud and Verlaine in Doucet Collection.
11. Ibid.
12. Verlaine, *Le Poète et la Muse* (*Jadis et Naguère*).

## CHAPTER II

# PARIS

1. Vide Verlaine's letter to Blémont, 27 Oct. 1875.
2. Vide *Le Manuscrit-Autographe*, March–April 1928.
3. Delahaye, *Rimbaud*, p. 44.

4. Now at the Louvre Museum in Paris.

5. The writers who figure in the picture are: Valade, Blémont, Aicard, d'Hervilly, Pelletan, Verlaine and Rimbaud.

6. Vide Starkie: *Le Coin de Table by A. Fantin-Latour* (*The French Mind*, pp. 318–26).

7. Letter to Démeny, 15 May 1871 (op. cit., p. 25).

8. Lepelletier, *Verlaine*, p. 261.

9. Letter 20 October 1871, published in *L'Almanach des Lettres Françaises et Etrangères*, Jan.–Mar. 1929

10. The recipient of this letter was to be, in 1872, the editor of *La Renaissance Littéraire et Artistique*, which published, on 14 Sept. 1872, Rimbaud's poem, *Les Corbeaux*.

11. After the 'gamin' in *Les Misérables* by Victor Hugo.

12. Letter June 1872 (op. cit., p. 269).

13. *Comédie de la Soif III* (*Oeuvres Complètes*, p. 127).

14. Unpublished ms. by Delahaye in the Doucet Collection.

CHAPTER III

# ALCHEMY AND MAGIC

1. *Histoire de la Magie*, p. 528.

2. *Alchimie du Verbe* (*Une Saison en Enfer*) (*Oeuvres Complètes*, p. 222).

3. *Matinée d'Ivresse* (*Illuminations*) (*Oeuvres Complètes*, p. 176).

4. L'Abbé Lenglet du Fresnoy, *Histoire de la Philosophie Hermétique*. The Hague, 1742.

5. *Les Fables Egyptiennes et Grecques*.

6. *Alchimie du Verbe* (*Une Saison en Enfer*) (*Oeuvres Complètes*, p. 219).

7. *La Nouvelle Revue Française*, 1 Oct. 1934.

8. The alphabet had already been printed in *Le Mercure de France*, 1 Nov. 1904, without any deductions.

9. *Voyelles*, (*Oeuvres Complètes*, p. 105).

10. *Illuminations* (*Oeuvres Complètes*, p. 178).

11. *Larme*, (*Oeuvres Complètes*, p. 125).

12. *Illuminations* (*Oeuvres Complètes*, p. 186).

13. *Being Beauteous* (*Illuminations*) (*Oeuvres Complètes*, p. 173).

14. *La Science des Esprits*, p. 13.

15. *Illuminations* (*Oeuvres Complètes*, p. 175).

16. Miss Margaret Clark, in her booklet, *Rimbaud and Quinet*, has tried to prove that Rimbaud was greatly influenced by Quinet, and borrowed much from him. I am not entirely convinced by her arguments, and feel that the parallels are accidental, and that they could be found in any writers of the period.

Rimbaud and Quinet were very different in mind and imagination, and the small excerpts she has made from both authors have a totally different significance in the contexts. An exception should, it seems to me, be made for *Merlin l'Enchanteur*. It seems certain that Rimbaud must have read it and borrowed from it.

17. *Enfance (Illuminations) (Oeuvres Complètes*, p. 175).

18. *Nuit de l'Enfer (Une Saison en Enfer)* (Ibid., p. 215).

19. *Merlin l'Enchanteur*, Vol. I.

20. *Adieu (Une Saison en Enfer) (Oeuvres Complètes*, p. 229).

21. *Mes Prisons*, Chapter VI.

22. Letter Nov. 1873, published by Mouquet in *Rimbaud raconté par Verlaine*, p. 107.

23. Published by Bouillane de Lacoste in *Rimbaud et le Problème des Illuminations*, p. 107.

24. Published in *Revue des Sciences Humaines*.

25. *The Symbolist Movement in Literature*, p. 76.

26. The poem is quoted in the first version since this is nearer to Rimbaud than the first version.

CHAPTER IV

## L'EPOUX INFERNAL ET LA VIERGE FOLLE

1. *Oeuvres Complètes*, p. 116.

2. Op. cit., p. 148.

3. *Oeuvres Complètes*, p. 162. It is quoted in the English as it is used for psychological rather than literary purposes.

4. Many critics and translators interpret 'chien' literally, and see here an example of the poet's daring symbolism. I prefer to take the word in the sense in which it was sometimes used in the nineteenth century, 'chien' meaning a 'little duck' or a 'little darling'.

5. *Délires I (Une Saison en Enfer) (Oeuvres Complètes*, p. 215).

6. *Enfance (Illuminations)* (Ibid., p. 168).

7. Vide *Le Mercure de France*, Nov. 1936.

8. Porché: *Verlaine tel qu'il fut*, p. 416. He quotes the following from a doctor: 'Les contestations qui ont pu être faites quant aux déformations de *la virgula viri* ou de *l'antrum amoris*, n'ont aujourd'hui aucune valeur probante du point de vue médico-légal.'

9. *Verlaine et Rimbaud*.

10. Published in *Parallèlement*.

11. *Le Poète et la Muse (Jadis et Naguère)*.

12. *Le Bon Disciple*, published in Mouquet op. cit., p. 21.

13. *Verlaine et Rimbaud*.

14. Poem printed in Appendix II.
15. Vide *Le Mercure de France*, Feb. 1927.
16. Ex-Madame Verlaine, op. cit., p. 211.
17. I tried to get hold of this correspondence in another quarter. I imagined that copies might have been made by the lawyer and preserved with the rest of the papers of the proceedings. The law reports of the case cannot, however, be consulted until 1974. It occurred to me that copies might still exist in the papers in the lawyer's office, but I discovered that the son of the lawyer, himself a lawyer, Guyot-Syonest, had destroyed all the papers in the office on his retirement.
18. Ex-Madame Verlaine, op. cit., p. 185.
19. Porché, op. cit., p. 183.
20. Ex-Madame Verlaine, op. cit., p. 184.
21. Ibid., p. 195.
22. Ibid.
23. Quoted in Mathilde Verlaine's demand for a separation. Vide *Le Mercure de France*, Feb. 1927.
24. *Rimbaud raconté par Verlaine*, pp. 19–21.
25. Letter from Verlaine to Rimbaud, May 1872. (*Oeuvres Complètes*, p. 268).

CHAPTER V

## LA CHASSE SPIRITUELLE

1. *Les Poètes Maudits.*
2. Vide Breton, *Flagrant Délit* and Morrissette, *The Great Rimbaud Forgeries.*
3. *Mémoire* (*Oeuvres Complètes*, p. 121).
4. *Chanson de la plus haute Tour* (*Oeuvres Complètes*, p. 131).
5. *Age d'Or* (*Oeuvres Complètes*, p. 133).
6. *Larme* (Ibid., p. 219). It is quoted in the version given by Rimbaud in *Une Saison en Enfer.*
7. *Oeuvres Complètes*, p. 125.
8. Lévi, *Dogmes et Rituels de la Haute Magie*, Vol. I, p. 261.
9. Goffin, *Rimbaud Vivant.*
10. Quinet: *Merlin l'Enchanteur*, Vol. II, p. 294.
11. Letter April 1872. It is quoted in French since no translation could render its characteristic flavour.
12. Letter June 1872.
13. It is true that 'œuvre', in the alchemical sense, is usually masculine, for the final stage of 'le grand œuvre'. Some alchemists, however, use the feminine to indicate all branches of alchemy, not merely the final stage.
14. Michelet, *Histoire de France*, Vol. II, p. 138.

15. There are no grounds for giving the poem the title *Bonheur* as Paterne Berrichon does.

16. Meyrac, *Traditions, Coûtumes, Légendes et Contes des Ardennes.*

17. Letter to Izambard, 25 Aug. 1870 (*Oeuvres Complètes*, p. 243).

18. *Oeuvres Complètes*, p. 125.

19. Ibid., p. 126.

20. Ibid., p. 134.

21. Ibid., p. 135.

22. Ibid., p. 125.

23. Ibid., 140.

24. Ibid., p. 132.

25. *Introduction à l'Histoire Universelle*, p. 253.

26. Ibid., p. 83.

## ILLUMINATIONS

1. Letter from de Sivry to le Cardonnel published in *Oeuvres Complètes,* p. 695.

2. *Le Mercure de France*, 16 April 1914.

3. *Arthur Rimbaud et la Durée de son Activité Littéraire*, p. 68.

4. Bouillane de Lacoste, Introduction to his edition of *Illuminations*, 1949.

5. *Études sur Rimbaud.*

6. Letter to Delahaye, 1 May 1875, published in *Oeuvres Complètes*, p. 692.

7. Lucien Graux MS. now in the Bibliothèque Nationale in Paris.

8. Introduction to his edition of *Illuminations.*

9. Verse: *Bannières de Mai, Mémoire, Jeune Ménage, Fêtes de la Faim,* Prose: *Fairy, Génie, Jeunesse* and *Solde.*

10. Vide letter from Verlaine to Vanier 3 Feb. 1888.

11. *Rimbaud*, p. 108.

12. Letter to Lepelletier 1872, n.d. but probably Sept. or Oct.

13. *Rimbaud l'Artiste et l'Etre Moral*, p. 147.

14. Letter to Pierquin, 21 Sept. 1896 (*Oeuvres Complètes*, p. 590).

15. Vide *Le Mercure de France*, Aug. 1956.

16. Delamain in *La Graphologie*, April 1950, as quoted by Chadwick, op. cit., p. 83.

17. *Oeuvres Complètes*, p. 186.

18. De Graaf, op. cit., Adam, *Revue des Sciences Humaines*, Oct.–Dec. 1950; *Le Bateau Ivre*, Sept. 1950, Mar. 1951, June 1957.

19. Op. cit., p. 121.

20. *Oeuvres Poétiques Complètes*, p. 956.

21. *Oeuvres Complètes*, p. 108.

22. *Rimbaud*, pp. 37 and 41.

23. Ibid., p. 48.

24. *Oeuvres Complètes*, p. 169.
25. *Phrases (Illuminations)* (Ibid., p. 177).
26. *Enfance* (Ibid.) (Ibid., p. 168).
27. *Veillées II* (Ibid., p. 185).
28. *Oeuvres Complètes*, p. 188.
29. Unpublished letter to Paterne Berrichon in the Doucet Collection.
30. *Premières Communions* (*Oeuvres Complètes*, p. 192).
31. *Génie (Illuminations)* (*Oeuvres Complètes*, p. 197).
32. *Oeuvres Complètes*, p. 184).
33. *Phrases (Illuminations)* (Ibid., p. 178).
34. Godchot, *La Voyance de Rimbaud.*
35. *Oeuvres Posthumes*, Vol. II, p. 362.
36. *Oeuvres Complètes*, p. 175.

<br>

CHAPTER VII

# METROPOLIS

1. Letter June 1872.
2. Verlaine: *Mes Prisons*, III.
3. Ex-Madame Verlaine, op. cit., p. 210.
4. *Birds in the Night* (*Romances sans Paroles*).
5. *Le Mercure de France*, Feb. 1927. '100 chef de l'articulet de Mme Verlaine, produit le 2 Oct. 1872 pour sa demande en séparation.'
6. Ex-Madame Verlaine, op. cit.
7. *Le Mercure de France*, Aug. 1956. De Graaf, *Autour du Dossier de Bruxelles.*
8. *Verlaine Dessinateur.*
9. Letter Sept. 1872.
10. Letter to Lepelletier, Nov. 1872.
11. Letter from Verlaine to Lepelletier, 8 Nov. 1872.
12. Letter Nov. 1872.
13. Letter 1 Oct. 1872.
14. Letter to Lepelletier, 24 Nov. 1872.
15. Letter to Blémont, 1 Oct. 1872.
16. *Life & Letters of Oliver Madox-Brown*, p. 48.
17. Delahaye: *Verlaine*, p. 161.
18. Letter from Verlaine to Lepelletier, 14 Nov. 1872.
19. Paterne Berrichon, *Rimbaud le Poète*, pp. 211-17.
20. Verlaine letter to Lepelletier, 23 Nov. 1872.
21. *Romances sans Paroles*, III.
22. *Oeuvres Complètes*, p. 108.
23. Letter Jan. 1873.

24. Letter 1873.
25. Letter to Lepelletier, Oct. 1872.
26. *Revue de Paris*, 15 Oct. 1872.
27. Letter to Lepelletier, Nov. 1872.
28. *Délires* (*Une Saison en Enfer*) (*Oeuvres Complètes*, p. 216).
29. *Villes* (*Illuminations*) (Ibid., p. 183).
30. *Rimbaud le Poète*, p. 31.
31. *Mon Cœur mis à nu.*
32. *Mauvais Sang* (*Une Saison en Enfer*) (*Oeuvres Complètes*, p. 210).
33. *Départ* (*Illuminations*) (Ibid., p. 175).

CHAPTER VIII

## PARADISE LOST

1. *Rimbaud le Poète*, p. 230.
2. Vide Starkie: Arthur Rimbaud, 1938 edition, p. 226.
3. Published by *Le Mercure de France*, 1938.
4. *Rimbaud le Poète*, p. 229.
5. Eliphas Lévi, *Dogmes et Rituels de la Haute Magie*, Vol. II, p. 24.
6. Eliphas Lévi, *Les Clefs des Grands Mystères*, p. 261.
7. Eliphas Lévi, *Histoire de la Magie*, p. 189.
8. Eliphas Lévi, *Dogmes et Rituels de la Haute Magie*, Vol. I, p. 34.
9. *Alchimie du Verbe* (*Une Saison en Enfer*) (*Oeuvres Complètes*, p. 221).
10. Lévi, *Histoire de la Magie*, p. 47.
11. Lévi, *Dogmes et Rituels de la Haute Magie*, Vol. II, p. 181.
12. Letter to Delahaye, May 1872.
13. *Ébauches*, p. 36.
14. Op. cit., p. 36.
15. Lévi: *Histoire de la Magie*, p. 266.
16. Letter to Delahaye, May 1872.
17. Paterne Berrichon: *Vie de Jean-Arthur Rimbaud*, p. 230.

CHAPTER IX

## THE BRUSSELS DRAMA

1. *Vagabonds* (*Oeuvres Complètes*, p. 182.)
2. Yerta-Méléra: *Rimbaud*, p. 108.
3. *Rimbaud le Précurseur*, p. 113.
4. Meyrac, op. cit.

5. *Vagabonds* (*Illuminations*) (*Oeuvres Complètes*, p. 182).
6. Letter, 4 July 1873.
7. Vide *Mercure de France* (1 Nov. 1936). The graphological study of Rimbaud's handwriting.
8. Letter, 6 July 1873. Published by Dullaert in *Nord* (Brussels) Nov. 1930.
9. *Romances sans Paroles.*
10. Printed by Mouquet in *Rimbaud raconté par Verlaine*, p. 140.
11. Goffin: *Sur les Traces de Rimbaud* (*Le Rouge et le Noir*, 2 May 1934).
12. All the documents are published by Mouquet, op. cit., pp. 149–63.
13. *La vie de Jean-Arthur Rimbaud*, p. 93.
14. *L'Eclair* (*Une Saison en Enfer*) (*Oeuvres Complètes*, p. 277).
15. Paterne Berrichon, *Rimbaud le Poète*, p. 279.

## CHAPTER X

## UNE SAISON EN ENFER

1. *Rimbaud*, pp. 45–6.
2. *Mauvais Sang* (*Une Saison en Enfer*) (*Oeuvres Complètes*, p. 208).
3. Ham's descendants were thought to be the negro race.
4. *Mauvais Sang* (*Une Saison en Enfer*) (*Oeuvres Complètes*, p. 208).
5. *L'Eclair* (*Une Saison en Enfer*) (*Oeuvres Complètes*, p. 227).
6. *Mauvais Sang* (*Une Saison en Enfer*) (*Oeuvres Complètes*, p. 211).
7. *Matin* (*Une Saison en Enfer*) (*Oeuvres Complètes*, p. 228).
8. Ibid.
9. Delahaye, *Rimbaud*, pp. 177–79.
10. *Mauvais Sang.* Until further notice all quotations are taken from this chapter.
11. Michelet, *La Renaissance.*
12. *Nuit de l'Enfer.* Until further notice all quotations are taken from this chapter.
13. This question has been fully treated earlier.
14. *L'Epoux Infernal* (*Une Saison en Enfer*) (*Oeuvres Complètes*, p. 218).
15. This matter has been more fully treated in an earlier chapter.
16. *Alchimie du Verbe* (*Une Saison en Enfer*) (*Oeuvres Complètes*, p. 221).
17. Ibid., p. 223.
18. *L'Impossible* (*Une Saison en Enfer*) (*Oeuvres Complètes*, p. 225).
19. *L'Éclair* (*Une Saison en Enfer*) (*Oeuvres Complètes*, p. 227).
20. *Matin* (*Une Saison en Enfer*) (*Oeuvres Complètes*, p. 228).
21. *La Bible de l'Humanité* (*Conclusion*).
22. *Introduction à l'Histoire Universelle*, p. 42.
23. *Histoire de France* (*Introduction*), 1868 edition.

24. *Le Renaissance*, p. 400.

25. *La Bible de l'Humanité*, p. 485.

26. *Adieu* (*Une Saison en Enfer*) (*Oeuvres Complètes*, p. 228.)

27. Delahaye says that it was the winter 1871–72, but he must be mistaken for Rimbaud had not yet begun to write prose poems until 1872. He certainly had not written them a year before 1871–72. The fact that *Christ's First Miracle* was to belong to the series is further proof that it must have been early in 1873 that Rimbaud had the conversation with him, for this poem is on the reverse side of the rough draft of *Nuit de l'Enfer*, written after April 1873.

28. *Rimbaud*, p. 45.

29. *Mercure de France*, 1 Aug. 1956.

30. *Jean-Arthur Rimbaud*, p. 104.

31. Paterne Berrichon: *La Vie de Jean-Arthur Rimbaud*, pp. 244–5.

32. In 1901 M. Losseau discovered, in the attics of a printing firm in Brussels, a bundle of hundreds of copies of *Une Saison en Enfer*, the whole edition—except for the author's copies—which Rimbaud had never claimed or distributed—or paid for. Vide Carré's article in *Lettres de la Vie Littéraire d'Arthur Rimbaud*, p. 221.

33. *Paradis Artificiels* (Conard), p. 179.


CHAPTER XI

SOLDE

1. Vide Starkie: *Arthur Rimbaud*, 1938, p. 226.

2. Op. cit., p. 172.

3. *Ouvriers* (*Illuminations*) (*Oeuvres Complètes*, p. 178).

4. Unpublished letters, communicated by M. H. Matarasso.

5. Vide Appendix III for details of how this was discovered.

6. *Revue de Littérature Comparée*, January 1955, *Rimbaud et l'Angleterre*.

7. *Ville* (*Illuminations*) (*Oeuvres Complètes*, p. 180).

8. *Metropolitain* (Ibid.) (Ibid., p. 189).

9. *Démocratie* (Ibid) (Ibid., p. 196).

10. *Parade* (Ibid (Ibid., p. 171).

11. *Introduction to La Science Nouvelle* by Vico, p. 40.

12. *Déluge* (*Illuminations*) (*Oeuvres Complètes*, p. 167).

13. *Le Voyage* (*Les Fleurs du Mal*).

14. *Soir Historique* (*Illuminations*) (*Oeuvres Complètes*, p. 193).

15. *Vies II* (Ibid.) (Ibid., p. 174).

16. Ibid.

17. *Solde* (Ibid.) (Ibid., p. 200).

18. *Merlin l'Enchanteur*, Vol. I, p. 174.

19. *Vertige (Oeuvres Complètes*, p. 123). The poem is not dated and it is generally believed that no poems in verse were written after Aug. 1872. But the spirit seems to harmonize with the state of mind in this period, and so it is quoted here.
20. Vide Appendix III.

## CHAPTER XII

## L'HOMME AUX SEMELLES DE VENT

1. Introduction to 1869 edition.
2. Notes in the Doucet Collection.
3. *Malheureux tous les Dons (Sagesse).*
4. Letter from Rimbaud to Delahaye, 5 Mar. 1875. (*Oeuvres Complètes*, p. 290).
5. Delahaye: *Rimbaud*, p. 60.
6. *Ébauches*, p. 209.
7. Ibid., p. 119.
8. Letter 17 Aug. from Nouveau to Verlaine (Unpublished, Doucet Collection).
9. Letter from Delahaye to Verlaine (Unpublished, Doucet Collection).
10. Ibid.
11. Letter 14 Oct. 1875 (*Oeuvres Complètes*, p. 292).
12. Vide Coulon: *Au Cœur de Verlaine et de Rimbaud*, pp. 45-83.
13. Vide letter to Delahaye, 14 Oct. 1875 (*Oeuvres Complètes*, p. 292).
14. Letter from Delahaye to Verlaine (Unpublished, Doucet Collection).
15. Published in *Oeuvres Complètes*, p. 294.
16. Houin et Bourguignon, *Revue d'Ardenne et d'Argonne*, Sept.-Oct. 1897.
17. Letter to Delahaye, 14 Oct. 1875 (*Oeuvres Complètes*, p. 292).
18. Letter from Verlaine to Delahaye, 27 Nov. 1875.
19. Houin et Bourguignon, op. cit.
20. *Rimbaud et la Musique (La Grive*, 20 Oct. 1954).
21. *Rimbaud*, p. 63.
22. Letter from Delahaye to Paterne Berrichon, unpublished, communicated by M. H. Matarasso.
23. *Adieu (Une Saison en Enfer) (Oeuvres Complètes*, p. 228).
24. Delahaye: Notes in Doucet Collection.
25. *Mercure de France*, 15 July 1922. Marmelstein: *Rimbaud à Stuttgart et aux Indes Néerlandaises.*
26. *Revue des Sciences Humaines*, Oct.-Dec. 1951. De Graaf: *Deux Lettres d'Ernest Delahaye à Ernest Millot.*
27. Vide Starkie: *Sur les Traces de Rimbaud (Mercure de France*, 1 May 1947).
28. Letter from the Registrar to the present author, 11 October 1960.

29. Delahaye: *les Illuminations*, p. 16, note 2.
30. *Ébauches*, p. 207.
31. Vide Starkie: *Sur les Traces de Rimbaud*.
32. Letter Aug. 1877 (Doucet Collection, Unpublished).
33. Letter from Delahaye to Verlaine (Doucet Collection, Unpublished).
34. Drawing (Doucet Collection, Unpublished).
35. Delahaye, notes in Doucet Collection.
36. Vide letter home, 17 Nov. 1878 (*Oeuvres Complètes*, p. 296).
37. Letter from Christian Ayoub, 2 April 1950.
38. Letter home, Dec. 1878 (*Oeuvres Complètes*, p. 299).
39. Vide Starkie: *Rimbaud in Abyssinia*, p. 3.
40. *Première Fugue de Rimbaud en Arabie* (*Lettres de la Vie Littéraire*, p. 237).
41. Letter 15 Feb. 1879 (*Oeuvres Complètes*, p. 300).
42. Letter from Austin St. B. Harrison to the present author, 5 May 1950.
43. Houin & Bourguignon, *Revue d'Ardenne et d'Argonne*, May–June 1899.
44. Unpublished (Doucet Collection).
45. Delahaye: *Rimbaud*, p. 72 note 1.


PART III

CHAPTER I

THE COFFEE EXPORTER

1. Starkie, op. cit., p. 12.
2. Letter 23 May 1880 (*Oeuvres Complètes*, p. 303).
3. Letter 25 Aug. 1880 (*Oeuvres Complètes*, p. 306).
4. Letter 28 Sept. 1885 (*Oeuvres Complètes*, p. 394).
5. Unpublished letter from Bardey to Paterne Berrichon, communicated by M. Matarasso. It has generally been said that Rimbaud remained head of the branch until Harar was evacuated by the Egyptians, but, in fact, he was head, only until 1881.
6. Letter 2 Nov. 1880 (*Oeuvres Complètes*, p. 309).
7. Paulitschke: *Harar*.
8. Letter 15 Feb. 1881 (*Oeuvres Complètes*, p. 318).
9. Letter 25 May 1881 (*Oeuvres Complètes*, p. 324).
10. Letter from A. Bardey to Paterne Berrichon, 16 July 1897, communicated by M. Matarasso.
11. Vide Starkie: *Rimbaud in Abyssinia*, pp. 24–6.
12. February 1884.
13. Quoted by Paterne Berrichon in *La Vie de Rimbaud*, p. 160.
14. Letter 6 May 1883 (*Oeuvres Complètes*, p. 358).

15. Letters 19 and 20 Mar. 1883. (*Oeuvres Complètes*, pp. 356–7).
16. Letter 19 Mar. 1883 (*Oeuvres Complètes*, p. 356).
17. Letter 6 May 1883 (Ibid., p. 359).

## CHAPTER II

## THE GUN RUNNER

1. Letter from A. Bardey to Paterne Berrichon, 7 July 1897. (Communicated by M. Matarasso).
2. Letter published by Paterne Berrichon in *La Vie de Rimbaud*, p. 158, note.
3. Letter from A. Bardey to Paterne Berrichon, 16 July 1879, communicated by M. Matarasso.
4. Vide Starkie: *Rimbaud in Abyssinia*.
5. For a full account of the traffic in arms, vide Starkie, op. cit.
6. Letter 5 May 1884 (*Oeuvres Complètes*, p. 379).
7. Letter 22 Oct. 1885 (Ibid., p. 596).
8. *Voyages sur les Rives de la Mer Rouge*, Vol. I, p. 36.
9. Vide Starkie: *Rimbaud en Abyssinie*. Also *Oeuvres Complètes*, p. 396, for the first contract.
10. Starkie: op. cit., pp. 77–80.
11. Fauriot: *Voyage au Golfe de Tajoura*, p. 23.
12. Borelli: *Journal*, p. 51.

## CHAPTER III

## THE EXPEDITION TO ABYSSINIA

1. Johnston: *Travels in Southern Abyssinia*, p. 265.
2. Vide Starkie: *Rimbaud in Abyssinia*, pp. 87–90.
3. Rimbaud's report is published in *Oeuvres Complètes*, p. 416.
4. Vide Starkie, op. cit., p. 91.
5. Letter to Gaspary, 9 Nov. 1887. (*Oeuvres Complètes*, p. 447).
6. Ibid.
7. Letter to Gaspary, 30 July 1887 (*Oeuvres Complètes*, p. 416).
8. Letter quoted by Paterne Berrichon in *La Vie de Rimbaud*, p. 188.
9. Letter 8 Nov. 1887 (*Oeuvres Complètes*, p. 446).
10. Letter 23 Aug. 1887 (Ibid., p. 429).
11. Letter 5 Aug. 1887 (*Oeuvres Complètes*, p. 417).
12. On 25 and 27 Aug. 1887.

13. Vide Starkie: *Rimbaud en Abyssinie*, pp. 97–9.

14. Ibid., pp. 101–3.

15. Letter 4 Oct. 1887 (*Oeuvres Complètes*, p. 437).

16. Letter 15 Dec. 1885 (Ibid., p. 455).

17. Letter Aug. 1885 (Published by Moréas in *Les Premières Armes du Symbolisme*).

18. Quoted by Paterne Berrichon in *La Vie de Rimbaud*, p. 203.

19. Vide Starkie, op. cit., pp. 106–20.

20. Ibid., pp. 108–12.

21. Letter 15 May 1888 (*Ouevres Complètes*, p. 465).

## CHAPTER IV

## THE COLONIST

1. *Harar*, p. 269.

2. The correspondence from Savouré to Rimbaud, now published in *Oeuvres Complètes*, pp. 821–23, shows that Rimbaud was doing extensive business with him at this time.

3. For Ilg's career in Abyssinia, vide Starkie. *Rimbaud en Abyssinie*.

4. Vide Starkie, *Rimbaud in Abyssinia*.

5. Letter from Ilg to Rimbaud, 23 Aug. 1890, (*Oeuvres Complètes*, p. 491).

6. Letter from Savouré to Rimbaud, 27 Jan. 1888. (*Oeuvres Complètes*, p. 461).

7. Letter from Savouré to Rimbaud, 26 April 1888 (ibid., p. 464).

8. Starkie, *Rimbaud en Abyssinie*, pp. 119–20.

9. Letter 4 Aug. 1888 (*Oeuvres Complètes*, p. 471).

10. Letter from Ilg to Rimbaud, 30 Jan. 1891 (ibid., p. 492).

11. Letter from Ilg to Rimbaud, 21 Aug. 1889, unpublished, communicated by M. Matarasso.

12. Unpublished, communicated by M. Matarasso.

13. Letter from Ilg to Rimbaud, 3 Feb. 1889 (*Oeuvres Complètes*, p. 475).

14. Letter from Savouré to Rimbaud, 26 April 1888 (*Oeuvres Complètes*, p. 464).

15. Letter from Ilg to Rimbaud, 16 Sept. 1889 (*Oeuvres Complètes*, p 482).

16. Ibid., 8 Oct. 1889 (ibid., p. 483).

17. M. Yerta-Méléra, *Résonnances autour de Rimbaud*, p. 154.

18. D'Acremont, *Sur les Traces de Rimbaud* (*La Revue Hebdomadaire*, 27 Aug. 1932.

19. Letter quoted by Paterne Berrichon in *La Vie de Rimbaud*, p. 182.

20. *Some Remote People*.

21 *Ébauches*, p. 17.

22. Letter from Ilg to Rimbaud, 16 June 1889 (*Oeuvres Complètes*, p. 481).

23. *Ébauches*, p. 171.

24. Letter 11 April 1889 (*Oeuvres Complètes*, p. 479).

25. Letter quoted by Paterne Berrichon, op. cit., p. 215.

26. Ibid., p. 215 Ibid., p. 213.

27. Letter 6 May 1883 (*Oeuvres Complètes*, p. 358).

28. Letter 25 Feb. 1890 (*Oeuvres Complètes*, p. 487).

29. Letter quoted by M. Yerta-Méléra, in *Ébauches*, p. 169.

30. Letter 25 Feb. 1890 (*Oeuvres Complètes*, p. 487).

31. Letter 10 Nov. 1888 (ibid., p. 472).

32. *Ébauches*, p. 171.

33. Unpublished, communicated by M. Matarasso.

34. Letter 10 Nov. 1890 (*Oeuvres Complètes*, p. 491).

35. Letter 7 Oct. 1884 (ibid., p. 385).

36. Letter 10 Nov. 1888 (ibid., p. 473).

37. Letter 27 Feb. 1890 (ibid., p. 488).

38. *L'Évolution Psychologique de Rimbaud d'après son Écriture* (*Mercure de France*, 27 Aug. 1932).

39. *En Abyssinie sur les Traces de Rimbaud* (*La Revue Hebdomadaire*, 27 Aug. 1932).

40. Letter 4 Aug. 1888 (*Oeuvres Complètes*, p. 472).

41. Unpublished letter, 9 Dec. 1897 to Paterne Berrichon, communicated by M. Matarasso.

42. Unpublished letter, 16 July 1897, to Paterne Berrichon, communicated by M. Matarasso.

43. Letter 17 July 1890, (*Oeuvres Complètes*, p. 490).

44. *Le Bateau Ivre*, Sept. 1954.

45. Letter from Isabelle Rimbaud to Paterne Berrichon (*Oeuvres Complètes*, p. 582).

46. *Comédie de la Soif* (*Oeuvres Complètes*, 428).

47. Letter 10 Nov. 1888 (*Oeuvres Complètes*, p. 472).

48. Vide letters 24 and 25 Aug. 1887 (ibid., pp. 430–32).

49. Letter 10 Nov. 1888 (ibid., p. 472).

50. Letter to Paterne Berrichon, 7 July 1897, unpublished, communicated by M. Matarasso.

51. Isabelle Rimbaud's notes, unpublished, communicated by M. Matarasso.

52. Letter 18 May 1889 (*Oeuvres Complètes*, p. 479).

53. Letter 21 April 1890 (ibid., p. 489).

54. Letter 10 Aug. 1890 (ibid., p. 491).

55. Letter 10 Nov. 1890 (ibid., p. 491).

56. Letter 15 Jan. 1885 (ibid., p. 338).

CHAPTER V

## THE EXILE'S RETURN

1. Letter 20 Feb. 1890 (*Oeuvres Complètes*, p. 493).
2. Letter from Tian to Isabelle Rimbaud, unpublished, communicated by M. Matarasso.
3. Letter 30 April 1891 (*Oeuvres Complètes*, p. 497).
4. Isabelle Rimbaud's unpublished notes, communicated by M. Matarasso.
5. Letter 23 May 1891 (*Oeuvres Complètes*, p. 500).
6. Telegram 22 May 1891 (ibid., p. 500).
7. Telegram 22 May 1891 (ibid.).
8. Letter 8 June 1891 (ibid., p. 524).
9. Letter 17 June 1891 (*Oeuvres Complètes*, p. 501).
10. Letter 23 June 1891 (ibid., p. 502).
11. Letter 15 July 1891 (ibid., p. 512).
12. Letter 10 July 1891 (ibid., p. 509).

CHAPTER VI

## THE UNRETURNING SPRING

1. Letter 24 June 1891 (*Oeuvres Complètes*, p. 503).
2. Isabelle Rimbaud: *Mon Frère Arthur* (*Reliques*, p. 13).
3. Ibid., p. 13. Ibid., p. 94.
4. Goffin: *Sur les Traces de Rimbaud* (*Rimbaud Vivant*, p. 47).
5. Letter 24 June 1891 (*Oeuvres Complètes*, p. 503).
6. We have only Isabelle's word for this scene. Vide *Le Dernier Voyage de Rimbaud* (*Reliques*, p. 113).

CHAPTER VII

## LE VAINCU

1. Letter 22 Sept, 1891 (*Oeuvres Complètes*, p. 553).
2. Letter 2 Oct. 1891 (ibid., p. 553).
3. Letters (ibid., pp. 527 et seq.).
4. Letter 1 June 1890 (ibid., p. 531).
5. Letter published in *Le Bateau Ivre*, Sept. 1954.
6. Letter from his mother, 1887 (*Oeuvres Complètes*, p. 415).
7. Letter 9 June 1899 (ibid., p. 527).

NOTES

8. Letter 5 Oct. 1891 (ibid., p. 556).
9. Ibid.
10. *Reliques*, p. 90.
11. Letter 28 Oct. 1891 (*Oeuvres Complètes*, p. 561).
12. Some critics, witness Goffin, allege that this letter was written later by Paterne Berrichon; while Fondane says that he will not believe in its authenticity unless he sees the postmark; that Isabelle herself might have written it later. There seems, however, no adequate grounds for adopting so sceptical an attitude. The letter reads as if it was contemporaneous with the events described later; there are facts that she would not have thought of adding later. It is not easy to fake atmosphere. The letter is in the Doucet Collection and an examination of the writing reveals that it is the hand that Isabelle wrote at this time, not in her later hand, which is hard to distinguish from that of her brother.
13. Letter 28 Oct. 1891 (*Oeuvres Complètes*, p. 561).
14. Ibid.
15. *Les Pensées* (Section III).
16. *Mauvais Sang* (*Une Saison en Enfer*) (*Oeuvres Complètes*, p. 211).
17. *Phrases* (*Illuminations*) (*Oeuvres Complètes*, p. 128).
18. *Ébauches*, p. 181.
19. Shown in the Rimbaud case at the Symbolist exhibition in Paris, July 1936.
20. *Nell, Harer*, p. 124.
21. Letter 10 July 1891 (*Oeuvres Complètes*, p. 511).
22. Unpublished letter communicated by M. Matarasso.
23. Isabelle's unpublished notes, communicated by M. Matarasso.
24. The rough draft of a letter from Isabelle to an unknown correspondent —probably Paterne Berrichon—unpublished, communicated by M. Matarasso.
25. Letter 28 Oct. 1891 (*Oeuvres Complètes*, p. 563).
26. Letter from Isabelle to the French Consul at Aden, 19 Feb. 1892 (*Oeuvres Complètes*, p. 568).
27. *Oeuvres Complètes*, p. 517.
28. Pierquin: *Souvenirs* (published in *Lettres de la Vie Littéraire*, p. 149).
29. This account is based on the bill for the funeral, unpublished, communicated by M. Matarasso. All the items are listed separately, e.g., Twenty orphans, with candles, 2 francs each, was charged 87 francs. The candles on the altar cost 75 francs; and for the clergy 30 francs. The peal of bells was charged 25 francs, the hangings on the church door, 82 francs, etc.
30. Letter from Madame Rimbaud to Isabelle, 24 May 1900 (*Oeuvres Complètes*, p. 532).
31. Letter of thanks from A. Bardey to Madame Rimbaud, unpublished, by M. Matarasso.
32. Letter from Isabelle Rimbaud to Paterne Berrichon, unpublished, communicated by M. Matarasso.

## CONCLUSION

1. *Vertige* (*Oeuvres Complètes*, p. 123).
2. This is Paterne Berrichon's view, *La Vie de Rimbaud*, p. 254.
3. *Mauvais Sang* (*Une Saison en Enfer*) (*Oeuvres Complètes*, p. 209).
4. Vide Ballanche: *Orphée*, p. 28.
5. Letter from Isabelle Rimbaud to Paterne Berrichon, 2 Aug. 1896 (*Oeuvres Complètes*, p. 562).
6. *Mémoire* (*Oeuvres Complètes*, p. 122).
7. *L'Éclair* (*Une Saison en Enfer*) (ibid., p. 227).
8. *Mon Cœur mis à nu.* CXV.
9. *Comédie de la Soif* (*Oeuvres Complètes*, p. 127).
10. Vide Daniel-Rops, *Rimbaud*, p. 154.
11. *Enivrez-vous* (*Spleen de Paris*).
12. Letter 15 Jan. 1885 (*Oeuvres Complètes*, p. 390).
13. *Nuit de l'Enfer* (*Une Saison en Enfer*) (*Oeuvres Complètes*, p. 212).
14. *L'Homme Juste* (*Oeuvres Complètes*, p. 93).
15. *Les Pas Perdus.*
16. *Premier Manifeste du Surréalisme*, p. 46.
17. *Ma Conversion.*
18. Letter to Paterne Berrichon, unpublished, in the Doucet Collection.
19. *Mauvais Sang* (*Une Saison en Enfer*) (*Oeuvres Complètes*, p. 207).
20. Vide *Démocratie* (*Illuminations*) (*Oeuvres Complètes*, p. 196).
21. Vide *Solde* (*Illuminations*) (*Oeuvres Complètes*, p. 200).

# INDEX

# INDEX TO RIMBAUD'S WORKS
## QUOTED IN THE TEXT

# New Directions Paperbooks